THE BRITISH ARMED NATION
1793–1815

THE BRITISH ARMED NATION

1793–1815

J. E. COOKSON

CLARENDON PRESS · OXFORD

1997

Oxford University Press, Great Clarendon Street, Oxford OX2 6DP

Oxford New York

Athens Auckland Bangkok Bogota Bombay
Buenos Aires Calcutta Cape Town Dar es Salaam
Delhi Florence Hong Kong Istanbul Karachi
Kuala Lumpur Madras Madrid Melbourne
Mexico City Nairobi Paris Singapore
Taipei Tokyo Toronto

and associated companies in
Berlin Ibadan

Oxford is a trade mark of Oxford University Press

Published in the United States
by Oxford University Press Inc., New York

British Library Cataloguing in Publication Data
Data available

Library of Congress Cataloging-in-Publication Data
Cookson, J. E.
The British armed nation, 1793–1815 / J. E. Cookson.
p. cm.
Includes bibliographical references.
1. Great Britain—History, Military—19th century. 2. Great
Britain—History, Military—18th century. I. Title.
DA68.C66 1997
941.07′3—dc20 96-44824
ISBN 0-19-820658-5

1 3 5 7 9 10 8 6 4 2

Typeset by Graphicraft Typesetters Ltd., Hong Kong
Printed in Great Britain
on acid-free paper by
Bookcraft Ltd., Midsomer-Norton,
Nr. Bath, Somerset

Preface

OVER twenty years have elapsed since I began work on the 'war and society' history of Britain during the Napoleonic period. Despite notable contributions by Clive Emsley, Linda Colley, and others, it continues to be a relatively neglected subject, a state of affairs which this book can only hope to repair in a small way. Three major concerns have claimed my attention. The first was to do justice to the Scottish and Irish dimensions of the topic, beginning with the fact of Scotland and Ireland's very significant military contribution. The second was to emphasize the distinction between 'loyalism'—the British counter-revolution—and what I have called national defence patriotism. I have long come to the conclusion that the two drew significantly different social responses and that it is patently unsatisfactory to conflate them to the degree historians have accepted. At the very least, national defence far surpassed anti-revolutionism as an organized, nationalized, and popular movement. A third concern, linked to the others, was to treat the demands of war as a topic in itself. The Revolutionary and Napoleonic Wars imposed a situation on Britain where it became necessary to organize national defence based on mass participation and, generally, to find and deploy military manpower equal to the state's requirements. Much more has been written about the ideological mobilizations of the period than about the strategic, military, and political constraints within which government and society were acting. In the last analysis, war and society history cannot get away from the fact that the events and situations that occur in war create a powerful dynamic of their own.

Much more than is in this book could still be said about the British armed nation. I am very aware of large omissions. Britain's financial mobilization was an aspect that would have forced me into technicalities I was not confident of understanding, and I gladly leave this ground to experts like Patrick O'Brien. Navalists will object that the navy receives only passing mention. My excuse is that the navy does not seem to have impinged on politics, government, and society to nearly the same extent as the land forces, perhaps mainly because of the physical remoteness of seamen in comparison with soldiers and auxiliaries. While Scotland and Ireland are given due attention, Wales is ignored. My defence is that at the level of government England and Wales existed as one, and I could find no evidence that the Welsh themselves came out of the war with a heightened sense of their identity. Doubtless, if I had had space and time to devote to local and regional responses to national defence and the war, differences would have emerged between Wales and other parts of England. On this last point I remain convinced that national defence is an excellent subject for deepening our knowledge of social structure and social relations in late Hanoverian Britain.

Most of the archival work for this book was done while I was on study leave from the University of Canterbury in 1990–1. I gratefully acknowledge the support and assistance the University has given me at all stages of the project. In Britain and Ireland I spent much time at the Public Record Office, British Library, Scottish Record Office, National Library of Scotland, National Library of Ireland, and State Paper Office (Ireland), and I particularly wish to place on record the good service I received from those institutions. The bibliography will reveal many debts of the same kind incurred at numerous record offices, archives, and libraries. I hope they can regard *The British Armed Nation* as a form of repayment. The British Council in New Zealand kindly supported the cost of research overseas with a grant. As the graduate of a Scottish university, I was also privileged to receive a Carnegie award for the Scottish leg of my travels. I thank the Duke of Buccleuch for permission to consult the family papers in the Scottish Record Office.

Many individuals, too numerous to name, helped me to research and write this book. I give them my thanks. The Dean of St Patrick's Cathedral, Dublin, Ronald J. Marino, Dr Conrad Swan, Garter Principal of Arms, Marion Stewart of the Dumfries Archives Centre, Dr Austin Gee, and Dr I. J. Catanach answered particular inquiries. Professor David McIntyre of the History Department at Canterbury kindly read a draft of the complete manuscript. Joanna Innes (Somerville College, Oxford), Professor Frank O'Gorman (University of Manchester), Dr Jeremy Black (University of Durham), Professor Patrick O'Farrell (University of New South Wales), and Dr Rory Muir read chapters and gave me the benefit of their comments and criticism. Pamela, my wife, with her companionship and love, once again made possible what would otherwise have been impossible.

J.E.C.

Contents

List of Maps   ix
Abbreviations   x

Introduction   1
1. The Addition of Mass   16
2. The French Encirclement   38
3. The Rise and Fall of the Volunteers   66
4. The Manpower Ceiling   95
5. Scotland's Fame   126
6. Ireland's Fate   153
7. The Problem of Order   182
8. Armed Nationalism   209
9. The Legacy of the Armed Nation   246

Bibliography   264
Index   281

List of Maps

1. The Volunteers and Home Defence in 1804   43
2. The Defence of Ireland   51

Abbreviations

Add. MSS	Additional Manuscripts, British Library
BL	British Library
Brit. J. Sociology	*British Journal of Sociology*
Bull. Inst. Hist. Res.	*Bulletin of the Institute of Historical Research*
CJ	*Journal of the House of Commons*
CSO	Chief Secretary's Office (Ireland) Papers
DNB	*Dictionary of National Biography*
Econ. Hist. Rev.	*Economic History Review*
Eng. Hist. Rev.	*English Historical Review*
Essex Rev.	*Essex Review*
EUL	University of Edinburgh Library
Hist. J.	*Historical Journal*
Hist. Research	*Historical Research*
Hist. Today	*History Today*
Hist. Workshop J.	*History Workshop Journal*
HMC	Historical Manuscripts Commission
HO	Home Office Papers, Public Record Office
Irish Hist. Studies	*Irish Historical Studies*
J. Brit. Studies	*Journal of British Studies*
J. Mod. Hist.	*Journal of Modern History*
J. Soc. for Army Hist. Res.	*Journal of the Society for Army Historical Research*
J. of Soc. Hist.	*Journal of Social History*
NCSTC	*Nineteenth Century Short Title Catalogue*
NLI	National Library of Ireland
NLS	National Library of Scotland
PD	*Parliamentary Debates*
PH	Cobbett's *Parliamentary History*
PRO	Public Record Office
RO	Record Office
Scot. Hist. Rev.	*Scottish Historical Review*
SP	*House of Commons Sessional Papers 1801–1900*
SPOI	State Paper Office, Ireland
SRO	Scottish Record Office
Trans. Royal Hist. Soc.	*Transactions of the Royal Historical Society*
WO	War Office Papers, Public Record Office

Introduction

THIS book should be a safe bet. War, in recent years, has assumed a central place in the history of the Hanoverian state and society, almost as if historians had set out to prove the wisdom of Asa Briggs's remark, made long ago, that 'the way into the nineteenth century led across the battlefield as well as through the cotton mill and the iron foundry'.[1] Through war eighteenth-century Britain became an imperial state and established its credentials as a great power, beginning a career, it has been suggested, which is deeply fascinating to the generation that has experienced Britain's decline. The power Britain wielded internationally, however, has not distracted from, indeed it has attracted eighteenth-century historians to internal developments, and in particular to state-making and nation-making. The first has been summarized by John Brewer as the emergence of a 'fiscal-military state' in which the central government was powerfully organized to extract the resources needed for war and the defence of British interests all over the world. Linda Colley has provided a social setting for the fiscal-military state in describing the Protestant and Francophobic consciousness of British society and how it was 'forged', mainly under conditions of recurrent war with France, into an immensely powerful sense of national identity capable of turning political, class, or any other differences into irrelevancies. Colley's work helped to make understandable the relative ease with which the eighteenth-century 'growth of government' was accomplished, the pride in national achievement that successful war excited. Brewer concentrated on the institutional sources of state power in an age of warfare; Colley on the moral sources.[2]

These two are the reigning overviews of eighteenth-century 'war and British society' history. Though Brewer's study ended somewhat strangely in 1783, leaving out of contention the climactic period of the 'Second Hundred Years War'— the mighty struggle against revolutionary and Napoleonic France—it did not seem a difficult task to trace the further outline of the fiscal-military state, as, in fact, soon was done.[3] Nor does the idea of the British 'armed nation', on first appearances, sit uncomfortably with either Brewer's or Colley's work. Indeed, it would

---

[1] A. Briggs, *The Age of Improvement* (London, 1959), 129.

[2] J. Brewer, *The Sinews of War: War, Money and the English State 1688–1783* (London, 1989); L. Colley, *Britons: Forging the Nation 1707–1837* (New Haven, 1992). Brewer and Colley returned to the subject in essays contributed to L. Stone (ed.), *An Imperial State at War* (London, 1994).

[3] P. Harling and P. Mandler, 'From "Fiscal-Military" State to Laissez-Faire State, 1760–1850', *J. Brit. Studies*, 32 (1993), 44–70.

seem to be an excellent way of fusing the developments they dealt with; the armed nation, of course, can easily stand as the epitome of an increasingly nationalistic British society while, in terms of the manpower and other resources it mobilized, it also marked a quantitative leap for the warfare state that Brewer described. To study the British armed nation invites us to depict the wars of the French revolution as the 'wars of the nations' in which Britain, along with the other states of Europe, responded to the growth of French military power by adopting French methods, especially the methods of national defence in 1793–4—mass mobilization, the rhetoric of the 'nation in danger', strong government to the point of war totalitarianism. The very phrase, 'armed nation', provided a contemporary link with the Jacobin republic. As early as February 1794, when the French armed nation was beginning to show its strength, one of Pitt's correspondents wanted volunteers but wondered whether 'the "rising in a mass" or becoming an "armed nation" at short notice [was] congenial with the spirit of Englishmen'.[4] After 1796, as the country faced up to the possibility of a full-scale French attack without benefit of allies, the 'national character' (considered as unvolatile and circumspect!) and the population's inexperience of war were lesser problems. Henry Dundas and William Windham, as the two ministers most directly concerned with military affairs, agreed that becoming an 'armed nation' was necessary for national survival, much as France had been saved a few years before.[5]

Pitt's correspondent, however, had a point. His views hardly suggest a warfare state able to command from its society the resources it required. If anything, he represents the weakness of the state in relation to society; and this, remember, on a matter as vital as national defence. The service expected of civilians will have to be appropriate, not to the threat to which the country is exposed, but to the 'national character' and to 'a people wedded to peace on whose territories a foe has not appeared for many centuries'. Early modern historians have beaten along this path often enough in contemplation of the complex interaction of centre and localities, which, in spite of the intricacies, made up working political systems throughout *ancien régime* Europe. There is a bagful of terms they use to describe this limited centralism—mosaic states, multiple monarchies, composite states, corporate states. Of course, taken too far, an emphasis on the independence or semi-independence of local and provincial rulers can degenerate into 'pointillism', the minute examination of peripheral power structures and their politics totally obscuring the fact that on some important matters they marched roughly in step under the command of central authority. On the other hand, state-building as a historical process can exert a fatal fascination, diverting the historian into recording what is

---

[4] C. Buchanan to Pitt, 21 Feb. 1794, Chatham MSS, PRO30/8/117, fos. 26–7.
[5] Dundas to Windham, 10 Apr. 1798, Melville MSS, SRO GD51/1/912/2.

made to appear as the inexorable progress of bureaucratic centralism against its opposition. The association of war with the 'growth of government' is a particularly enticing combination. European war, from the fifteenth century at least, was pitiless in the demands it made on governments, steadily increasing in scale, cost, and technical complexity, steadily therefore, some would say, forging a link with domestic reform. Here might be found the great engine of political modernization relentlessly driving on the state's control of society.[6]

Brewer and Colley's overviews, both founded on the impact of war, preserve such a strong sense of direction—even 'a whiggish tone'—that they make it seem the only way forward for Britain was towards the centralized state and the nationalistic society.[7] Brewer concentrates attention on central institutions, including parliament: the armed forces expanded, so did the civil bureaucracy and the financial resources it could muster, and parliament provided the means by which the political classes were satisfied that they had ultimate control of the levers of power. The localities and regions were largely left to govern themselves without interference from the centre; 'the domestic effects of the fiscal-military state' were restricted 'and the bureaucracy's growth limited to those circumstances necessary for its successful operation'.[8] War, not domestic concerns, provided the dynamic for state development, necessarily establishing the primacy of centre over locality. If this was so, a particular lacuna of Brewer's argument is how home defence, specifically the organization of the militia after 1757, affected local self-government. Another is how much army and naval recruitment depended on local offers and cooperation. In his account the British warfare state is simply not presented as an *ancien régime* in which the central government's relationship with local rulers was constantly being negotiated.

Colley, for her part, is impressed by the way British society increasingly cohered around the monarchy, national triumph in war, and the notion of British 'freedom'. Other loyalties besides national loyalties are not denied, as they could not be, but the mode of argument adopted, thematic but also broadly chronological, conveys a sense of strengthening nationalism derived from a kind of accumulating fund of images, events, and experiences. Colley's Britain by the early nineteenth century is a society which not only has a heightened sense of its identity against other societies but also contains major national issues within this concept of Britishness. The key chapter may be allowed to be that on the huge anti-invasion

---

[6] Three influential formulations of this idea have been M. Roberts, *The Military Revolution 1560–1660* (Belfast, 1956); J. H. Plumb, *The Growth of Political Stability in England 1675–1725* (London, 1967); C. Tilly, 'Reflections on the History of European State-Making', in Tilly (ed.), *The Formation of National States in Western Europe* (Princeton, 1975).

[7] This was E. P. Thompson's complaint of Colley. See his review of *Britons* in *Dissent*, 40 (1993), 377–82.   [8] Brewer, *Sinews of War*, p. xix.

mobilizations of the Napoleonic Wars, where it is insisted that the tens of thousands of ordinary folk enrolled for home defence represented the depth and intensity which nationalistic feelings had assumed in British society. This was the culminating episode in the development of a national culture of patriotism which hereafter was to provide an unusually powerful consensual element in the polity. Though much play is made of the social cohesion resulting from industrialization and urbanization, the fact that something very similar happened in other less well-integrated or 'developed' societies, France 1793-4, Spain 1808-13, Germany 1813-14, when they were threatened, attacked, or occupied by foreign armies is nowhere critically considered. Nor is importance given to how national service related to the different interests and concerns in the social structure, though this could provide valuable clues as to whether patriotism really was an agent of change. In Colley's account perceptions of a British nation came to envelop society; whereas social particularisms and political conflicts may have shaped and controlled these more than she imagines.

Much of the argument of this book, therefore, works towards a reassessment of the rather neat linear developments that Brewer and Colley describe. Outright revision of their conclusions has not yet been attempted; but a number of historians, without themselves addressing the subject, have been extremely suggestive as to where a start might be made. First of all, on the question of central–local relations, Joanna Innes reminds us that state-building most typically proceeded with an untidy sequence of advances and retreats of central power, the different movements perhaps occurring together or with varying force or as largely unprogrammatic and circumstantial. The Anglo-Scottish state of the seventeenth century, for example, oversaw its domestic policies in the localities more vigorously than happened in the eighteenth century, this later 'disengagement' being one result of the central government's fiscal-military priorities.[9] It is now well accepted that local authorities became ever more active as the eighteenth century went on in launching public enterprises of various kinds. Paul Langford, on this account, gives us a very different-looking British polity from Brewer's. His Hanoverian society has a broad-based propertied class much involved in local affairs as office-holders, professional advisers, subscribers to public charities, and partisans in often fierce local conflicts which had little to do with national issues. Much of parliament's time was taken up with local business as rival groups jostled for advantage or as local bodies sought to define their powers and establish their authority.[10] In the last decades of the eighteenth century, important initiatives were taken by local magistrates in the areas of prison-building, penal reform, and

[9] Innes, 'The Domestic Face of the Military-Fiscal State: Government and Society in Eighteenth-Century Britain', in Stone (ed.), *Imperial State at War*, 96–127.
[10] P. Langford, *Public Life and the Propertied Englishman 1689–1798* (Oxford, 1991).

provision for the poor which stimulated and largely directed parliament's interest in these matters.[11] But such initiatives were only part of a general invigoration of local government and local development, even more obvious in the towns. Town-making in the late eighteenth and early nineteenth century was a response to the uncertain relationship of towns to other authorities in the counties, to the status concerns of urban élites against 'county families', to the expanding economic interests of towns, and to the social and environmental problems that accompanied urban growth and industrialization. Quite small towns, 'the Banburys', as they have been called, could display self-awareness in endeavouring to hold off patrons or to control the effects of changes occurring outside them—for example, the growth of rural disorder.[12] All this local activity sets strong limits to any idea of the state redressing central–local relations significantly in its favour. A veritable thickening of local government was going on that only added to the amount of patronage and authority out of the state's reach and to the consequence of the little empires which were the beneficiaries.

Yet it was the character of the British warfare state of the eighteenth century to require ever larger mobilizations of manpower and money, and therefore to press ever more firmly on society. Between the war of 1689–97 and the American War the number in the armed forces doubled, if the militia is included; each successive war over the same period almost exactly doubled the national debt. As scarcely needs to be stated, the Revolutionary and Napoleonic Wars were of an altogether different order of magnitude. Counting militia and volunteers, the size of the armed forces reached about three times the highest total achieved during the American War, and the debt also was trebled; government expenditure per annum averaged £16,000,000 in 1786–90 and £97,000,000 in 1811–15.[13] In the absence of any extensive bureaucracy, the state loaded most of the war administration on to local

---

[11] Langford, 403–5; D. Eastwood, '"Amplifying the Province of the Legislature": The Flow of Information and the English State in the Early Nineteenth Century', *Hist. Research*, 62 (1989), 281–3. Eastwood's book *Governing Rural England: Tradition and Transformation in Local Government 1780–1840* (Oxford, 1994) insists on the continuation of local self-government and its effectiveness and adaptability.

[12] R. J. Morris, 'The Middle Class and British Towns and Cities of the Industrial Revolution, 1780–1870', in D. Fraser and A. Sutcliffe (eds.), *The Pursuit of Urban History* (London, 1983), 286–306; P. J. Corfield, 'Small Towns, Large Implications: Social and Cultural Roles of Small Towns in Eighteenth-Century England and Wales', in A. Maczak and C. Smout (eds.), *Gründung und Bedeutung Kleinerer Städte im nördlichen Europa der frühen Neuzeit* (Wiesbaden, 1991), 85–101; F. O'Gorman, *Voters, Patrons and Parties: The Unreformed Electorate of Hanoverian England 1734–1832* (Oxford, 1989), 259–85.

[13] Brewer, *Sinews of War*, 30 (for figures up to and including the American War); B. R. Mitchell, *Abstract of British Historical Statistics* (Cambridge, 1962), 401–3; E. J. Evans, *The Forging of the Modern State: Early Industrial Britain 1783–1870* (London, 1983), 390; P. Mackesy, *The War for America 1775–83* (London, 1964), 524–5 (his figures do not include perhaps 100,000 seamen, marines, volunteers, and troops on the Irish establishment); C. Emsley, *British Society and the French Wars 1793–1815* (London, 1979), 133.

governments. That this entailed a 'growth of government' at the local level is not generally recognized, it usually being assumed that already existing authorities accepted the additional responsibility, though not without plenty of complaint. There was, however, an expansion of local government, both in terms of new organization and of an increased number of officials. Most obvious was the system set up to assess and collect the income tax, in which the local gentry administering the tax were chosen by their fellows. The number of magistrates prepared to act, a more significant figure than the number holding commissions, rose appreciably during the war, accentuating a trend of the late eighteenth century.[14] A much more complex development occurred around the county lieutenancies, which had always administered the militia acts but who now took on supervision of the volunteers and the organization of their county's part in national defence. In Scotland lord lieutenants were first appointed in 1794, before a militia existed or seemed likely, perhaps an indication of the real value attached to them which was their ability to activate local leaders and form a broad alliance of the county élite.[15] Certainly, at times during the war the counties were genuinely defence communities, with the lord lieutenant acting through 'general meetings' of the deputy-lieutenants, who became permanently active and numerous, or through the deputies and their clerks in the subdivisions down to the parish level. Volunteers and later local militia were new forms of public enterprise in the localities, often having permanent staffs and in the large towns usually closely related to corporate authority. Volunteer corps, in fact, could be similarly organized to voluntary societies which were the main public charities and which proliferated from the late eighteenth century.[16]

Of course, the income tax, national defence, and military service might be taken as further examples of the centralism the warfare state engendered, since each was set up by and linked to central authority. If national defence began with the proclamation of May 1792 against radical activity, it began with the crown initiating policy and summoning local rulers to act. But it was also usual for these interactions to remain very fluid, the state striving to balance its requirements with the need to pay sufficient respect for local interests and the localities responding much as suited them. Pitt in 1794 used the good offices of Lord Radnor to try out the

[14] A. Hope-Jones, *The Income Tax in the Napoleonic Wars* (Cambridge, 1939); Langford, *Public Life*, 405–6; N. Landau, *The Justice of the Peace 1679–1760* (Berkeley, 1984), 395.
[15] H. Dundas to the king, 6 Mar. 1794, *Later Correspondence of George III*, ed. A. Aspinall (5 vols., Cambridge, 1962–70), ii. 183; Dundas to the Scottish lord lieutenants, 14 May 1794, HO102/11, fos. 26–34.
[16] J. E. Cookson, 'The English Volunteer Movement of the French Wars 1793–1815: Some Contexts', *Hist. J.* 32 (1989), 867–91; R. J. Morris, 'Voluntary Societies and British Urban Elites 1780–1850: An Analysis', ibid. 26 (1983), 95–118. Bristol can serve as an example of these points. See *Rules and Regulations to be Observed by the Bristol Volunteer Association* (Bristol, 1797); J. Brown, *The Rise, Progress and Military Improvement of the Bristol Volunteers* (Bristol, 1798).

government's proposals for volunteers and additional militia on the Berkshire grand jury. There could even be a reverse flow of measures, as when the home secretary circulated to the counties a Rutland plan for forming volunteer cavalry and a Dorsetshire plan for 'driving the country'.[17] On two occasions, both at critical stages of the war, the amount of non-compliance from below actually forced the abandonment of policy—over the provisional cavalry, instituted in 1796 and given up in 1798, and the Additional Force, which also lasted only two years from its inception in 1804.

The other more permanent auxiliary forces showed the same delicate balance between local interests and the requirements of the crown. Volunteer localism—especially the refusal to form corps of an appropriate tactical size—was condemned from the outset of the volunteer system for standing in the way of its efficiency. When the volunteers were superseded by the local militia, that force too in the closing stages of the Napoleonic War would not oblige the government by leaving their counties to take up garrison duties. Nor was the 'old' militia, permanently embodied and incorporated into the regular garrison of the country for the duration of the war, the instrument of state that the army was. The militia colonels regarded their regiments as patronage fiefs, immensely valuable to them as county magnates and public men, so that important changes in the militia laws had to be negotiated with them and even the practice of regular drafts into the army was carefully done to protect their interests. Above all, we need to keep in mind the scale of these less than centric military establishments that the war produced—up to 129 regiments of 'regular' militia, 199 regiments of local militia in 1810, over 2,000 volunteer corps at the peak of the volunteer mobilization in 1804.[18] There is little trace here of the advance of central authority that distinguishes Brewer's fiscal-military state; rather, military growth of this kind looks more like an extension of an *ancien régime*.

Colley would say that the institutionalized localism present in militia or volunteers was overwhelmed by the idea of national defence, just as class differences were and political conflict. National defence patriotism was one reflection of the relative cohesiveness of British society alongside Continental societies, a cohesiveness underrated as long as the historiography emphasized such subjects as

---

[17] R. Dozier, *For King, Constitution and Country: The English Loyalists and the French Revolution* (Lexington, Ky., 1983), 141–2; 'Plan for forming volunteer cavalry agreed to by general meeting of Rutland', 22 Mar. 1794, HO102/11, fos. 42–3; J. Cramner-Byng, 'Essex Prepares for Invasion', *Essex Rev.* 60 (1951), 187.

[18] These totals include Irish units. For militia and local militia see the returns printed in *CJ* lxv (1810), 605–6, lxix (1813–14), 546–8. For volunteers in Britain see P. Haythornthwaite, 'The Volunteer Force 1803–4', *J. Soc. for Army Hist. Res.* 64 (1986), 193–204. There were 800–900 corps of Irish yeomanry (volunteers) in 1804. Memo by Sir E. Littlehales, 1 June 1804, Hardwicke MSS, BL Add. MS 45037, fos. 113–19.

Introduction

party struggles within the ruling élite, popular disorder, crime, and class formation. Colley pointed out that in Britain, particularly in contrast to Napoleon's
France, state-promoted patriotism was secondary to the patriotism promoted by
private interests, including public-spirited individuals and commercializers. Lesser
public bodies, like municipalities and voluntary societies, undoubtedly were also
important, commencing with the great campaign against popular radicalism of
1792–3.[19] However, if patriotism was mainly derived out of society itself, we have
more reason to expect it to be a variegated thing. A feature of the 'war society' of
1793–1815 was the strength and continuity of public opposition to the war; and
discernible there were the beginnings of the different patriotisms later prominent in the nineteenth century—radical patriotism which associated war with
non-democratic government, evangelical patriotism which associated it with the
moral decay of societies, and liberal patriotism which associated it with the inadequacies of the international system. Each, too, made its own response to national
defence in the crises Napoleon inflicted on Britain between 1798 and 1805; radicals
equated military service with political rights, evangelicals worried about national
guilt and divine judgement, and liberals drew a careful distinction between the
'war whoop' and 'defensive war'. A further concession Colley has to make is that
among the staunchest supporters of the war there were mixed feelings about
arming the populace from fear thay they might turn on those who armed them.
The fact that the volunteers were always under suspicion and eventually replaced
by a local militia suggests that this was an issue fought out at the highest level of
government.[20]

Neither should impressive national mobilizations at critical times in a climate of
patriotic incitement blind us to the realities of a hierarchical society such as Britain
was. The amount of anti-invasion rhetoric directed at the volunteer rank and file
has often raised speculation that no one took their loyalty, or the loyalty of the
common people generally, for granted; but the point must remain inconclusive
because it is impossible to tell whether or not the propaganda accurately depicted
popular feelings.[21] A better place to start is with the culture and lives of the working population, much studied for the eighteenth and early nineteenth centuries yet
something Colley ignores. One feature of large sections of the labour force was the

[19] For Colley on the national defence mobilization see her *Britons*, ch. 7; 'The Apotheosis of George
III: Loyalty, Royalty and the British Nation 1760–1820', *Past and Present*, 102 (1984), 94–129; 'Whose
Nation? Class and National Consciousness in Britain 1750–1830', ibid. 113 (1986), 97–117.

[20] Cookson, 'Volunteer Movement', 869–71, 883–4. My book *The Friends of Peace: Anti-War Liberalism in England 1793–1815* (Cambridge, 1982) focuses on liberal patriotism. At present evangelical
patriotism is perhaps best approached through J. H. Pratt (ed.), *The Thought of the Evangelical Leaders:
Notes on the Discussions of the Eclectic Society, London, 1798–1814* (Edinburgh, 1978).

[21] S. Cottrell, 'The Devil on Two Sticks: Franco-phobia in 1803', in R. Samuel (ed.), *Patriotism:
The Making and Unmaking of British National Identity* (3 vols., London, 1989), i. 259–73.

constant search for work and, therefore, their mobility, which the muster rolls of volunteer corps, in the few cases so far considered, abundantly confirm and other evidence indicates.[22] When volunteering is related to the improvised existence of the poor, it becomes altogether more self-interested than is suggested by Colley's impressionistic account. Volunteer commanders testify to the importance their men placed on the pay and other material benefits of service. Exemption from the militia, granted to volunteers in 1799, was an obviously valuable privilege which produced an ebb and flow of men according to the militia ballots. The amount of dispute within volunteer corps also requires explanation. The lower orders entertained a deep, indeed an obsessive, fear of being inveigled into the army, which made them suspicious about any form of military service and liable to resist any heavy-handed exertion of military authority. The 'slavery' into which soldiers were believed to cast themselves inevitably set up a contrast with 'British freedom'. When the issue of the treatment due volunteers from their officers arose, the libertarian, and even egalitarian, tendencies of popular protest were never far from the surface, sometimes strengthened in the face of officers whose status put them outside the established social leadership and whose authority was thus seen to be assumed. Whatever rules of conduct were drawn up and recommended to the men, volunteer corps were mainly governed by the code of behaviour regulating relations between the 'lower sort' and their betters, which came down to the one being saved from servility, in the form of 'military subordination', and the other from the reduction of social distances.[23]

A look at volunteering, in short, seems to be the best way of understanding the patriotism of the poor. That patriotism is shown to have been opportunistic, interested, and conditional, a subject rich in connotation and context underneath the blanket of Francophobic ardour Colley is inclined to throw around it.[24] This does not mean that Britain could never have fought a war of national resistance; for an instinctive self-defence against military attack resides in most communities, and in this case it would have been stiffened by a considerable degree of organization and perhaps by propaganda that emphasized, above all, how personal survival was connected to national survival. The main departure from Colley's argument has to be over the question of whether the great wartime mobilizations were a formative experience for British society. If popular patriotism was essentially atavistic and

---

[22] See below, 233–4.

[23] J. E. Cookson, 'The Rise and Fall of the Sutton Volunteers 1803–4', *Hist. Research*, 64 (1991), 46–53. In 1803–4 Charles Yorke, the home secretary, was almost overwhelmed by 'an inconceivable number of appeals and statements of imagined serious grievances, most of them proceeding from disputes upon trifling points of military etiquette or some other frivolous matters'. N. Jekyll to G. Rose, 26 Feb. 1804, Chatham MSS, PRO30/8/241, fo. 194.

[24] I am this cautious because Colley, *Britons*, 300–8 says sensible things about the different motivations that operated.

largely formed within a framework of popular culture and life experience, we are entitled to remain sceptical.

The social context of war patriotism sooner or later will return us to the towns. Colley valuably identified the prominence of the middle classes in patriotic activity. Furthermore, volunteering has been shown to be significant for urban society, perhaps not to the extent of urban dominance of the movement but certainly in the way it was so well attuned to the interests and concerns of urban rulers and élites.[25] As already stated, the war coincided with a period of rising urban consciousness and self-government, especially in the larger municipalities where élites backed by impressive personal wealth and their own propertied constituencies could deal with county rulers on equal terms. Patriotic celebration, patriotic propaganda, patriotic service, commercialized patriotism (as yet unstudied), all were on the largest scale and most actively carried on in the towns. Urban volunteer corps, organized like the voluntary societies which dominated philanthropic endeavour in the towns, mobilized élites and brought elements of the urban populace under their influence. Volunteers, too, were invariably used to contribute military glamour to patriotic spectacle, and the patriotic crowd of the war years became the most powerful physical expression of the town as community. It can be contended that national defence patriotism was the pre-eminent town-making force of a period when the status concerns of the middle classes and problems of urban growth and order gave town-making greater importance and urgency than ever before. Through patriotism urban leaders promoted the consequence of themselves and their towns, developed identities for them, found a source of cohesion for their populations, and reinforced their own, sometimes too limited, authority. The patriotism of the towns appears to be another case of patriotism needing to be interpreted against social particularisms, not in the sense of transcending them so much as providing another mode for their expression. Infused into the new civic culture, it incorporated both middle-class sensitivities and urban localism.

Finally, both Brewer and Colley eschewed a 'three kingdoms analysis' of their subject, even though from the time of the Seven Years War the state began to draw heavily on Scotland and Ireland for military manpower and the two societies responded as much as England did—perhaps more, if the number of Scots and Irish seeking imperial careers is any indication—to Britain's new imperial role.[26] Brewer's concern was with the 'English' state, and, set on that course, he allowed himself to deal with the financial 'sinews of war' as thoroughly as he neglected the 'more Celtic' topic of military recruitment. Ireland actually poses special problems for his thesis, for the crisis of the American War, by creating an independent

[25] Colley, 'Whose Nation?', 109–15; Cookson, 'Volunteer Movement', 872–7.

[26] However, Brewer in Stone (ed.), 65–8, does discuss the problematic relationship between the metropolitan power and the subordinate territories.

militia in the form of Charlemont's volunteers, led to a constitutional settlement which gave the Irish parliament much increased legislative authority and thus the British state a more composite structure than it possessed before. The military exigencies of the state had earlier persuaded Lord North's government to promote Catholic relief in order to reconcile further the Scottish Jacobite clans. In England itself home defence organized around county militias and volunteers in the large towns came to depend significantly on local rulers.[27] In short, Brewer's portrayal of a British warfare state successfully organizing its resource base and politically secure has another side, with the Irish case being particularly instructive. From 1778 the strains and pressures of 'world war' forced the centre into greater dependence on and greater dealing with the localities, but especially with very powerful Scottish and Irish particularisms, the latter of which was able to extract enormous concessions.

As Colley explains, the Scots in the eighteenth and nineteenth centuries readily identified themselves with *British* imperial achievements and the national destiny constructed around these.[28] However, she does not consider the Britishness of Irish nationalisms, leaving out of account, of course, the separatist republicanism of Wolfe Tone and the United Irish movement. Even Catholic nationalism remained essentially loyalist well into the early nineteenth century, uninterested in any French alliance and concentrating on getting representation and other civil rights from the British state. Protestant nationalism in Ireland was a colonial nationalism *par excellence* in that any Hibernian identity it cultivated was overlaid by an ultimate reliance on British power and therefore a total determination to keep the British connection—as the pathetic protest against the Union showed. Dublin, interestingly, was ahead of Edinburgh and London in erecting a Nelson monument as early as 1809.[29] The monument was one indication of the deepening Britishness of Ascendancy feeling as the Protestant minority reflected on continued peasant unrest and what might have been in 1798 and on the continued demand of the Catholic élite for emancipation and full political participation.

Enough has been said to show that war offers promising insights into England's relationship with Scotland and Ireland in the late eighteenth and early nineteenth century. Henry Dundas, the uncrowned king of Scotland as its political manager in the 1780s and 1790s, avidly exploited the Highlands as a military resource and, in the same cause, completed the state's reconciliation with the Jacobite chiefs.

---

[27] R. B. McDowell, *Ireland in the Age of Imperialism and Revolution 1760–1801* (Oxford, 1991), 254–88; K. P. Ferguson, 'The Volunteer Movement and the Government 1778–93', *Irish Sword*, 13 (1979), 208–16; R. K. Donovan, 'The Military Origins of the Roman Catholic Relief Programme of 1778', *Hist. J.* 28 (1985), 79–102; I. F. W. Beckett, *The Amateur Military Tradition 1558–1945* (Manchester, 1991), 68–70. [28] Colley, *Britons*, 117–32.
[29] *Nelson's Pillar: a Description of the Pillar with a List of Subscribers . . .* (Dublin, 1846), NLI MS 20845.

But this was not a clear-cut case of internal colonization because Scottish participation in the empire and Britain's wars, with the Highland soldier the symbolic
figure, became the main building materials for a Scottish national identity that
fitted comfortably within the Anglo-Scottish Union. Ireland's links with England
were profoundly affected by war in the same period, first because it conferred
semi-independence in 1782 and, secondly, because it eventually made such semi-
independence untenable once Pitt and Dundas were convinced that the security
and military exploitation of Ireland required them to treat with Catholic Ireland
against the intransigent opposition of Ireland's Protestant rulers. The Union of
1801 left Catholic Ireland unpacified, though without Ireland's military contribution being affected, a powerful riposte (insufficiently noticed by historians) to emancipationist argument. With Catholic nationalism unsuppressible and its alliance
with peasant discontent always something to be feared, the state moved towards
the Britannicization of the Irish garrison and the military occupation of Ireland.
J. C. D. Clark has wondered whether the relations of England with the other kingdoms might be 'defined most clearly by the history of public policy'.[30] For a quarter
of a century public policy was dominated by the concerns of war, which included
the provision of national defence and the reinforcement of internal order in every
part of the British Isles.

The armed nation particularly impinges on the history of the three kingdoms;
for Scottish and Irish self-defence was organized for the first time and then these
auxiliaries, in common with their English comrades, increasingly accepted service
outside their separate territories. By the end of the war the embodied militias were
truly a British Isles defence force and even coming to be deployed in garrisons
overseas, since some units went to the Continent in the last months. Earlier, at
the time of the invasion crisis in 1803, Scottish and English volunteers had been
committed to service anywhere in Britain if the French ever came. These home
forces, therefore, were British but also very consciously Scottish, Irish, and English,
particularly, we can imagine, militia regiments which, starting in 1811, were moved
both ways across the Irish Sea.[31] Scotland's contribution to its own defence, and to
the wider nation's, bolstered the myth of Scottish martialness. Ireland's mobilization could not have the same effect because Protestant and Catholic Ireland shared
different military traditions—the latter, indeed, looking to Catholic Europe—and
different national histories. This was a defeat for the civic humanist ideas that still
lay behind civilian military service.[32] Pitt and Dundas imposed a militia that would
not exclude Catholics on the Dublin government in 1793 in the hope of building

---

[30] Clark, 'English History's Forgotten Context: Scotland, Ireland, Wales', *Hist. J.* 32 (1989), 228.
[31] Cf. Colley, *Britons*, 314.
[32] As expounded in J. Robertson, *The Scottish Enlightenment and the Militia Issue* (Edinburgh, 1985).

Catholic loyalty and a 'union of property' against the revolutionary threat of the United Irishmen and the French. They ended up with a militia force that was too Catholic ever to be trusted by Protestants and with yeomanry or volunteers who acted as a kind of Protestant paramilitary. Dundas in 1793 also sought a militia for Scotland and the next year proceeded to establish the county lieutenancies that had been lacking to underpin its organization. When a Scottish militia was finally formed in 1797, it was accompanied by a volunteer movement whose patriotic feeling was sufficient recommendation for Dundas. The armed nation was born of the same strategic necessity in the three kingdoms and was fashioned by the same ideal of a gentry-led patriotic body of citizens who, representing the communal order, would offer no threat to it. But the outcome of the Napoleonic mass mobilization was so particular to Scotland and Ireland that we can readily cite national defence as a further example of how the English integration of the British Isles produced only a limited assimilation.

This book, then, meditates on the pressures the armed nation imposed on an *ancien régime*, a hierarchical society, and a three-kingdoms state. The armed nation is primarily conceived as a military rather than as an ideological mobilization, not because it is held that situations predominate over ideas but because in this case, in the complex interaction between the two, the nationalism inherent in the armed nation has received by far the most attention. 'Britishness' and 'patriotism' during the Napoleonic period are better understood in themselves than their setting in war, state, and society—not to say national defence, where these three contexts happen to come together best.[33] Chapter 1 therefore considers the genesis of the British armed nation of the 1790s in the light of the eighteenth-century military expansion and attitudes to civilian defence, the latter deeply affected by the American and French revolutions. The crucial change is seen not to have occurred with the loyalist reaction beginning in 1792 but with Britain's likely military isolation and strategic encirclement after 1796. This strategic situation lasted virtually to the end of the war in 1814. A vital dimension of the subject, it is explored in detail in Chapter 2, together with the development of a system of home defence based on civilian service, the interchange of forces between Britain and Ireland, and, in Ireland, a military infrastructure intended to meet internal as well as external threats.

---

[33] The main works, apart from Colley's book, are: Colley, 'Radical Patriotism in Eighteenth-Century England', in R. Samuel (ed.), *Patriotism: The Making and Unmaking of British National Identity*, i. 169–87; Colley, 'Britishness and Otherness: An Argument', *J. Brit. Studies*, 31 (1992), 309–29; S. Cottrell, 'English Views of France and the French 1789–1815', D.Phil. thesis (Oxford, 1990); H. Cunningham, 'The Language of Patriotism 1750–1914', *Hist. Workshop J.* 12 (1981), 8–33; D. Eastwood, 'Patriotism and the English State in the 1790s', in M. Philp (ed.), *The French Revolution and Popular Politics* (Cambridge, 1991), 146–68.

   The European tradition of militia did not look towards conscription or some form of universal service since its focus was on defence without jeopardizing social and political privilege. Britain's strategic circumstances, however, pulled the country towards an armed populace, as was first powerfully evident in Scotland in 1797 when a mass volunteer movement was a response to weak British naval defences in the North Sea. The following year the same happened with respect to England on the appearance of the 'Army of England' on France's Channel coast. Chapter 3 investigates the tension set up between a huge volunteer force and governments which successively sought a militarily more effective and politically more reliable alternative. Castlereagh's local militia of 1808 is seen to represent the triumph of the militia model, which provided for firmer county and army control, over Windham's model of an 'armed peasantry' and Pitt's of a nation-in-arms. The addition of mass to war had the further effect of establishing national manpower as a matter of concern to the state. Yet the state's recruitment of military manpower continued to be tightly constrained by pre-bureaucratic localism, social privilege, economic interest, and popular anti-militarism. As Chapter 4 shows, the compulsion upheld by the militia ballot caused relatively little public disorder since local rulers, private individuals, and the state conspired to mitigate its effects. Meanwhile the army went on struggling for men, never able to break decisively into the social catchment that sustained the volunteers. Both militia and regulars as forces on permanent service filled their ranks from the social types traditionally attracted into the army, setting up the paradox of the nation's military achievements winning increasing admiration from the wider society while soldiering continued to be despised.

   In Scotland the paradox was less apparent, for there there was proud evocation of a Scottish military tradition and military participation on a scale exceeding England's. Chapter 5 offers a composite explanation of the success of military recruitment in Scotland, including the popularity of volunteering, before going on to consider the impact of military service on Scotland's national identity. Pitt and Dundas's promotion of Highland service looks much like their promotion of Catholic service in Ireland, and, in further pursuit of a three-kingdoms analysis, Chapter 6 has as its main theme the very different response Pittite 'military politics' generated on the other side of the Irish Sea. Catholic military service, particularly in the Irish militia, did much to provoke Protestant self-defence and nationalism, and after Pitt the British government moved away from the idea that Ireland could be made secure by a policy of Catholic conciliation and inclusion. The raising of Irish home forces raised the question of who it was safe to arm in an acute form, part of the immensely divisive effect the war had on Irish society. Chapter 7 deals more widely with the state's problem in a revolutionary age of control over the armed power it was forced to create. In England the volunteers remained the most doubtful proposition, with the local militia providing an answer. In Ireland a solution to the Irish militia was eventually found in the militia interchange of 1811 which from then on significantly Britannicized the Irish garrison. Since the early nineteenth-century state continued to take the threat of revolution seriously, it is also important to consider the extent to which the great war mobilization left a legacy of expanded police resources.

The last two chapters are most concerned with whether the Napoleonic armed nation was a formative episode in the history of the British state and society. National defence patriotism is, first of all, separated from loyalism; loyalism, though it was not state-promoted to nearly the same degree, bearing more resemblance to revolutionary and Napoleonic nation-building in France in that it was immediately concerned to legitimize a political order. The 'king and country' patriotism that developed from 1797 was a broad appeal for national unity, calling for the suspension of party differences, emphasizing universal service, strongly identifying with a monarchy above politics and with community at the local level. The greatest impact was in the towns, where patriotism can be conceived as a ruling device linked to urban display and the paternalism of urban élites. If national defence helped to strengthen urban civic cultures and promoted wider participation in public affairs, it made a contribution to the weakening of aristocratic power. On the other hand, there is little connection between the armed populace called into existence during the war and the great popular mobilizations organized around parliamentary reform and Catholic emancipation afterwards. Probably the British state was affected most profoundly because there was a change towards mass warfare that could not be undone and because national defence enhanced the trend in government towards increasing local enterprise but with localities tied more closely to the centre by national information and publicity networks and by parliamentary and executive support. We must, too, acknowledge in the end the extent to which domestic policy interlocked with national security. It is possible to argue that cheap and limited government in the early nineteenth century was only made possible by the unusually strong strategic position, backed by an unusually stable international order, that Britain achieved out of the greatest conflict it had ever fought.

I

The Addition of Mass

THE armed nation entered history in France in the great crisis of *patrie* and revolution of 1793–4. Earlier in the revolution the citizenship of the soldier had been declared, incorporating him into the revolutionary society in contrast to the marginality that had been his lot under the *ancien régime*. Then, with France stricken with internal rebellions and under attack from the powers of Europe on several frontiers, it was the turn of civilian citizens to be incorporated into war. The conscriptions of 1793, particularly the famous *levée en masse* of August, not only signified the 'addition of mass' to war but made the nation the moral entity that required such service and sacrifice. Military service thus shifted from being a career to being a public duty informed and inspired, in the case of France, by a quite sophisticated national ideology. So the 'cabinet wars' of the eighteenth century passed away, to be succeeded by the 'wars of the nations'; for Britain and other states followed suit as they themselves came under unprecedented military threat from the very monster they had helped to create. Military nationalism in Britain was epitomized by the volunteers, in Spain by the *guerrilleros*, in Prussia (and Austria) by the *Landwehr*. New possibilities in the scale and intensity of war were revealed in the revolutionary and Napoleonic era, with each state characteristically making its own response to the changes, both during the war and subsequently.[1]

The sheer magnitude of these changes has tended to dissuade historians from paying attention to possible eighteenth-century antecedents of the armed nation. André Corvisier, for example, who ended his survey of European armies and their societies at the French revolution, held that France and Great Britain were among the least militarized societies in the eighteenth century, but he failed to connect this idea with the fact that they also happened to be states which organized the largest and longest sustained military mobilizations after 1789.[2] One response has been to claim that a 'growth of militarism' was occurring in the later eighteenth century, embracing increasing respect for the professionalism, progressiveness, and achievements of armies and the idea of raising a truly national force from a

---

[1] Three useful surveys are J. Gooch, *Armies in Europe* (London, 1980); G. Best, *War and Society in Revolutionary Europe 1770–1870* (London, 1982); J. Black, *European Warfare 1660–1815* (London, 1994).

[2] A. Corvisier, *Armies and Societies in Europe 1494–1789* (Bloomington, Ind., 1979), ch. 6.

patriotic citizenry. The evidence adduced in support of this argument relates mainly to France, where after the Seven Years War military reform came to be associated with national regeneration in influential circles. On the other hand, reform in France ignored auxiliary forces like the militia and remained narrowly focused on the professional army, which may make it right to dismiss the Comte de Guibert and other 'prophets' of the armed nation as theorists without a public.[3] Moreover, the Prussian military model, dominant in Europe after Frederick the Great's achievements, emphasized the importance of training, discipline, and professional competence, the cardinal features of 'regular' armies prepared for a highly formalized system of warfare which had no place for civilians.

If European military development for most of the eighteenth century centred on the permanent armies of states, we should prefer perhaps a purely 'catastrophic' explanation of the armed nation to the effect that warfare in the revolutionary age inflicted immense national crises on most states which forced them suddenly to change in the opposite direction towards the arming of their populations. Britain's case, however, seems to go against such a clear-cut conclusion, though that case points, in some repects, more strongly to British exceptionality than to general European experience. The key military difference between Britain and other powers hardly needs to be spelt out. They were predominantly land powers whose armed expansion concentrated on the army, where Britain was predominantly a sea power able to operate on the Continent at any time during the eighteenth century with only relatively small armies. Britain, furthermore, was increasingly an imperial state with most of her possessions overseas and therefore with a sizeable proportion of her army always overseas. In wartime the army could be dispersed over a wide area, part for home defence, part for operations in Europe, and part for wherever in the empire they were needed. From the time of the Seven Years War (1756–63) home auxiliaries were crucial to Britain's strategic position because in helping to secure the national base they liberated scarce regular troops for service elsewhere. Military change in eighteenth-century Britain contributed strongly to what has been called the country's 'amateur military tradition'. The English militia, established in 1757, was expanded and much improved during the American War, which also saw the appearance of volunteer units. Meanwhile fencibles (unlike the militia, a wholly enlisted force) provided for the defence of Scotland in every war from 1756.[4] It can be said that the leading feature of the military organization behind the British imperial state was not so much the regular army and its expansion as the non-regular forces it increasingly depended on—at home those already

[3] M. S. Anderson, *War and Society in Europe of the Old Regime 1618–1789* (London, 1988), 167–80, 196–204.
[4] Beckett, *Amateur Military Tradition*, 62–70; A. Whetstone, *Scottish County Government in the 18th and 19th Centuries* (Edinburgh, 1981), 96.

mentioned, outside Britain the 'private' army of the East India Company, the provincial corps of the American colonies, and in Ireland the volunteers, later succeeded by the militia of 1793. For these reasons Britain's military destiny before the advent of the armed nation was already shaped to the extent that military participation outside the professional army was on a large scale, well established, and taken seriously by the state.

But the importance of local forces to the state also made the state highly sensitive to the political outcomes of military change. Such forces were invariably linked to powerful social élites with whom the crown had to negotiate in other respects and they therefore, potentially at least, weakened the ability of the centre to direct the localities or the various territorial governments. Many of the crown's worst fears of local military revolt materialized with the Irish volunteers at the time of the American War; they provided an opposition that was unassailable as long as the crown lacked the military means to overawe them, and the consequence was the crown's humiliating concession of a large measure of political autonomy to Ireland. The memory of this episode scarred Britain's rulers for a long time. It was to forestall a revival of volunteers that the Irish militia was established in 1793, but even that substitute force was always suspect and its continued existence far from wholly secure.

Debate over the Irish militia went on only because there was an opposite view that the militia was a valuable way of building Catholic loyalty to the state and would ultimately serve to strengthen the Anglo-Irish relationship. Military service in eighteenth-century Britain was consistently seen as an antidote to particularisms and other divisive influences within the state, beginning with the issue of militia reform after 1745 which in promoting the formation of a more truly indigenous armed force than the regular army was did much to spell the end of dynastic instability. Catholic relief was supported by powerful elements in Lord North's government in 1778 with a view to promoting army recruitment in the Scottish Highlands and among Irish Catholics.[5] Thus commenced a long relationship between Catholic emancipation and military affairs in which relief was hailed as the means of enticing Catholics into the service of the crown and Catholic service was held to entitle Catholics to relief. Henry Dundas, who was prominent in 1778, should be acknowledged as the leading exponent of the state's interest in extending its military resources while also using recruitment and service to extend its political authority over territories whose closer incorporation was difficult. Scotland, his domain, and the Highlands, particularly, showed how military exploitation could build a loyalty to the crown and reconcile local élites to the far-off authority of

---

[5] E. H. Gould, 'To Strengthen the King's Hands: Dynastic Legitimacy, Militia Reform and Ideas of National Unity in England 1745–1760', *Hist. J.* 34 (1991), 329–48; Donovan, 'Military Origins', 79–102.

London where once there had been suspicion, if not open rebellion. Dundas, too, was almost certainly touched by the ideas of leaders of the Scottish Enlightenment, like Adam Ferguson and Alexander Carlyle, who wanted a Scottish militia based on a trained population in order to recover a sense of Scottish nationhood.[6] Dundas it was, anyway, who helped Pitt to force an Irish militia on a reluctant Irish government in 1793 and who looked towards universal training and service as the crisis of national defence took hold from 1796. He saw the armed nation as invigorating the loyalties of the hierarchical society; an armed population would be less rather than more susceptible to revolutionary designs in that all men would be brought into the service of the crown under the proper authorities and the 'natural' leaders of society, in which circumstances accustomed allegiances would have their full effect in a patriotic union.

Proof of what an armed nation was capable was found not only in the French example. The idea that the state should look to its own subjects for its best defence had a long pedigree in European thought, and in Hanoverian Britain its authority was strongly felt in the arguments over the institution of militias in England and Scotland; the necessary separation of the militia from the army continued to be defended well into the nineteenth century. Yet it mattered that popular militias were also demonstrably effective because the professionalization of war advanced rapidly in the eighteenth century as armies became huge permanent organizations making unprecedented technological and administrative demands. The virtually continuous conflict between 'free' but vulnerable Britain and powerful 'despotic' France gave special point to British interest in the resistance of peoples to foreign attack. Switzerland's long history of independence was, not surprisingly, the standard reference to the sources within a society to provide for its own defence.[7] Corsica's struggles in the 1760s and 1770s against Genoa and France made Paoli, the Corsican leader, into a British hero. But it was the war in America that produced the deepest effect, as Edmund Burke's warnings that he did not know how a whole people could be coerced were only too well fulfilled in the event. The generals on the ground found that while Washington denied them a decisive battle neither could they disperse into the country to establish pacified areas which could also be expected to reduce their supply problems. Cornwallis in his southern campaign of 1780–1 was opposed by only small numbers of regulars from Washington's Continental Army, so that he was the particular victim of the militias which kept threatening his communications, appropriating supplies, and terrorizing loyalists. He, significantly, was to outline a plan of civilian mobilization for the government in 1796, including specific reference to his American experiences.

---

[6] Robertson, *Scottish Enlightenment*.
[7] A good example is found in HMC, *Laing MSS* (2 vols., London, 1914–25), ii. 598–601.

No doctrine of a people's war came out of the American revolution, though it did add to European writing on *la petite guerre*, the raids and ambuscades carried out by light or irregular troops in support of the main body. Clausewitz identified the 'phenomenon' of 'people's war' but located its origins definitely in the revolutionary-Napoleonic period.[8] Nevertheless, the British army's failure in America was an extraordinary event, and much pondered—which had Frederick the Great complaining that 'the people who come back from America imagine they know all there is to know about war'.[9] The American War, for European military, presented unusual features of heavy civilian participation and predominantly irregular warfare, but not so unusual that they stood altogether outside European military practice. Charles Lee, the American general and advocate of a people's war against the British, admired Switzerland as 'those bless'd regions of manly democracy' and himself had soldiered for some years in eastern Europe where military operations often took the form of small war and he had seen with his own eyes how effective it could be. In western Europe, it is worth adding, the militia principle, the right of central governments to impose military service on subjects in aid of the state, was well established. Faced with the French 'armed horde', the leader of the European counter-revolution, the Habsburg emperor, responded immediately (January 1794) by asking the diet to approve a general arming of the German people.[10] In these contexts the *levée en masse* of 1793 appears as a development of, rather than a discontinuity in, European warfare. And this in turn helps to explain how the armed nation, the idea as well as the phrase, was so quickly received by the British.

If there was much in Britain's military and political experience that preluded the armed nation, was British society itself becoming more militaristic as a result of Britain becoming a successful imperial state and European power? Corvisier said definitely not, England, along with Holland, being in the van of a west European withdrawal from military values and preoccupations.[11] He, in effect, repeated the perception commonly held in the late eighteenth century—the rise and progress of a 'commercial spirit' that made the population unaccustomed to bearing arms and inexperienced at war. Those who propound a 'growth of militarism' in Europe pre-dating the revolutionary and Napoleonic period readily admit that England provided a less than favourable environment. While there was admiration for the Prussian military model, military reform excited little interest, even among the military; the British army continued to lack a permanent staff and schools for the formal

---

[8] W. Laqueur, *Guerrilla: A Historical and Critical Study* (London, 1977), 100–7; Laqueur (ed.), *The Guerrilla Reader: A Historical Anthology* (London, 1978), 31–6, citing Clausewitz.

[9] P. Paret, *Yorck and the Era of Prussian Reform 1807–15* (Princeton, 1966), 43; Best, *War and Society in Revolutionary Europe*, 54–5.

[10] J. Shy, *A People Numerous and Armed: Reflections on the Military Struggle for American Independence* (Princeton, 1976), 135–62. For Francis II see J.-P. Bertaud, *The Army of the French Revolution* (Princeton, 1988), 239 n. 2.   [11] Corvisier, *Armies and Societies in Europe*, 12–17.

training of cavalry and infantry officers, the two most obvious signs of military professionalism. Casualness and ineptitude showed in the neglect of the rank and file. In no sense was the self-consciousness of soldiers fostered by the segregation the widespread building of barracks would have enforced or by the medals, pensions, and elaborate military funerals that conferred honour and distinction in France. Nothing was done to improve pay and pensions until 1792, on the very eve of war; meanwhile material conditions for the soldier worsened as the government cut back on expenditure and civilian wages advanced appreciably ahead of his. Recruitment was noticeably slower in the 1780s than it had been in the 1770s; it took until 1789 to rebuild the line regiments after the American War. The adjutant-general represented that the crisis would continue until 'the comparative situation of the soldier is restored, such as it was 30 or 40 years ago'.[12]

Yet soldiers had an increasing physical presence in British society and there were increasing fears about home defence. Britain raised larger wartime armies than ever before during the eighteenth century (over 150,000 men in the latter stages of the American War),[13] and the home garrison on these occasions more than quintupled to guard against invasion. The creation of an effective national militia after 1757 further added to the amount of military activity taking place in British society. Kept alive in peacetime mainly by the colonels' concern to protect a source of patronage, the militia added greatly to the pageantry of local occasions and to the county season. Thus it can be placed in the contexts of the gentry's renewed interest in local affairs and the increasing splendour of civic ceremonial, including victory celebrations, in the second half of the eighteenth century.[14] Public interest in the military was amply demonstrated in the summer of 1778 when crowds flocked to the camps of militia and regulars formed in southern England. During the invasion scare of the next year, a number of places raised volunteer corps; up to seventeen in Sussex and twenty-four in Devon, for example.[15]

[12] Sir William Fawcett, memo on recruiting, 10 Aug. 1787, Chatham MSS, PRO30/8/242, fos. 5–6; J. A. Houlding, *Fit For Service: The Training of the British Army 1715–95* (Oxford, 1981), 129; G. A. Steppler, 'The British Army on the Eve of War', in A. Guy (ed.), *The Road to Waterloo: The British Army and the Struggle Against Revolutionary and Napoleonic France 1793–1815* (London, 1990), 4–15. See Anderson, *War and Society*, 175 for indications of the changing status of the soldier in France.

[13] Mackesy, *War For America*, 524–5.

[14] Colley, *Britons*, 225–6; Langford, *Public Life*, 405; P. Borsay, ' "All the World's a Stage": Urban Ritual and Ceremony 1660–1800', in P. Clark (ed.), *The Transformation of English Provincial Towns* (London, 1984), 228–58. Some examples of the militia's adornment of local occasions are in C. A. Markham, *History of the Northamptonshire and Rutland Militia* (London, 1924), 11, 12; E. Thoyts, *The Royal Berkshire Militia* (Reading, 1897), 100; R. Postgate, *That Devil Wilkes* (London, 1930), 25 and n.

[15] A. T. Patterson, *The Other Armada: The Franco-Spanish Attempt to Invade Britain in 1779* (Manchester, 1960), 127–8; *York Courant*, 7 July 1778; *Creswell and Burbage's Nottingham Journal*, 8 Aug. 1778; Earl of Bessborough (ed.), *Georgiana: Extracts from the Correspondence of Georgiana, Duchess of Devonshire* (London, 1955), 35–41. For volunteers in 1779 see Beckett, *Amateur Military Tradition*, 69–70. Patterson, 120, says there were 7,500 volunteers by the end of 1779.

There is still room for doubt that these events and activities did anything much to close the gap between civilian society and the army. Certainly the army had become a 'familiar' and 'accepted' institution, free of the old constitutional suspicions surrounding a permanent force and recognized, though less so than the navy, as an instrument of national power and greatness.[16] But the attractiveness of military service and military values remained severely limited. Most of the army's recruiting problems came back to a deeply felt aversion to soldiering among the popular classes, who saw it as a sort of living death in that a man exchanged freedom for military servitude and in other ways cancelled all ties with his previous existence. The gentry, for their part, were among the least militarized élites in Europe, to some extent affected by the opportunities of civilian society in Britain but also deflected away from the army because of the lesser amount of military patronage available and the army's generally lower social importance. Their disinclination for military service, even in the auxiliaries, was and would continue to be often remarked. Many county meetings in 1779 preferred volunteers to additional militia companies, evidence of how unpopular militia service outside the county was. But when Shelburne's government proposed further volunteers in 1782, the response was poor on all sides, from towns as well as counties.[17]

The British armed nation, then, did not arise out of a society that was highly militarized either in terms of the social esteem given to military men or actual military participation by the élite; George III set this tone by firmly presenting himself as a civilian king, and perhaps by keeping his heir out of the army. If the theatre be any guide to the public standing of the soldier, he appeared infrequently in the repertory and lacked definite characterization; even during the 1790s he was merely a patriotic mouthpiece and had no significance in his own right.[18] The truth is that George III's instincts were right. In eighteenth-century Britain the sphere of national service encompassed much more besides the armed forces, whatever repeated war did to highlight the achievements of generals and admirals and build a cult of heroism around them. There was equally a cult of commerce, which upheld commerce as the basis of British power and which, in some hands, compared kings and conquerors unfavourably with manufacturers, engineers, and inventors.[19] The marked expansion of philanthropic activity from the middle of the century was recognized as another source of national greatness, the charity of British society helping to produce social union and its piety divine approbation. Finally, Britain's

---

[16] See e.g., B. Allen, 'Rule Britannia? History Painting in 18th Century Britain', *Hist. Today*, 45/6 (June 1995), 12–18.

[17] Beckett, *Amateur Military Tradition*, 69–70. Langford, *Public Life*, 296–301 on difficulties of filling militia commissions.

[18] I take this much from an unpublished research essay: R. Wilkie, 'The Set Scene: English Theatre and Public Opinion 1789–1799', BA Hons. (Canterbury, 1986).

[19] Cookson, *Friends of Peace*, 77.

public culture included a bid to outdo French taste and excellence in the arts, exemplified by projects like the *Encyclopaedia Britannica* (1768–71) and occasions like the Shakespeare jubilee of 1764 and the Handel commemorations of the 1780s. Such a multifarious concern for national power and achievement did not deny the military conspicuousness, but it did represent a respect for civil endeavour that was never overborne by the martial triumphs of the British imperial state.[20]

The paradox of this unmilitarized society was that its sense of identity in the eighteenth century was largely shaped by rivalry and conflict with France. Britain's Francophobia has been well studied,[21] though it is worth emphasizing the disparities of power and the vulnerability that were perceived at the time. France's populousness made her 'internal resources' many times greater than Britain's and her monarchy therefore capable of nursing hegemonic ambitions in Europe while aggressively seeking trade and empire overseas. France remained a serious maritime rival up to the time of the Napoleonic War of 1803–14 in the only two areas that mattered—the Caribbean and the Indian Ocean. Whatever Britain's commercial wealth and thus state power, this trading system was as vulnerable to attack as it was extensive and operated with a delicate web of credit which broken at one point might rapidly unravel.[22] Nor can the effect of quite serious invasion preparations during each war be discounted. If invasion for the French remained a chancy operation, the British realized only too well that the mere threat created nervousness in the markets and weakened imperial defences by detaining forces at home. At a more emotional level, British society responded to France with a Protestant nationalism that invoked old, pre-eighteenth-century fears of Catholic universal monarchy and the distinction to be made between a free and Protestant people and those subjected to tyranny and priestcraft. The 'national character' fixed on the French extended the comparison. French vanity, fickleness, and superficiality were contrasted with British genuineness, moral sense, and courage, stereotyping the Frenchman as monkey.[23]

[20] Much of this paragraph makes use of chs. 2 and 4 of Colley, *Britons*. For cultural nationalism see G. Newman, *The Rise of English Nationalism: A Cultural History 1740–1830* (London, 1987).

[21] M. Duffy, '"The Noisie, Empty, Fluttring French": English Images of the French 1689–1815', *Hist. Today*, 32/9 (Sept. 1982), 21–6; Duffy, *The Englishman and the Foreigner* (Cambridge, 1986); J. Black, *Natural and Necessary Enemies: Anglo-French Relations in the 18th Century* (London, 1986).

[22] Napoleon revived France's Caribbean interests by sending an army to Haiti in 1802, though with the outbreak of war Martinique and the other French possessions were quickly seized. Until the French occupation of Egypt was ended in 1801, France offered a strategic threat to the British position in India. The sea route to India was not fully secure until the Cape was recaptured in 1806 and the Seychelles in 1810. For contemporary anxiety about the impact of war on the commercial system see [W. Roscoe], *Thoughts on the Causes of the Present Failures* (London, 1793); [J. Currie], *A Letter Commercial and Political Addressed to the Rt. Hon. William Pitt by Jasper Wilson* (Liverpool, 1793).

[23] Duffy, 'French', 24. Newman, *Rise of English Nationalism*, 123–33, says British national character was defined in terms of 'sincerity', by which was meant 'innocence, honesty, originality, frankness and moral independence'.

The onset of the French revolution, as is well known, took the Francophobia of British society to new heights. In a reworking of the old Anglo-French antithesis, the loyalism of the 1790s upheld a stable, prosperous, God-fearing society against the lawlessness, egalitarianism, tyranny, and irreligion seen to distinguish revolutionary France. This attack on the revolution gained particular ferocity from the connections perceived between the regime in Paris and parliamentary reform radicals, along with some religious Dissenters, these two groups providing ideal conditions for nationalistic politics of enemies at home in league with enemies abroad. The loyalist reaction, conventionally dated from the royal proclamation of May 1792 against seditious publications, was on a scale and of an intensity to justify calling it the greatest attempt yet seen in Britain to make public opinion. The enormous volume of printed propaganda included cheap tracts specially written for and distributed among the poorer classes. The Established Church, undoubtedly the single most powerful opinion-forming agency in the country, went into action through the pulpit and the social influence of the clergy. Hundreds of loyalist associations sprang up in late 1792 and early 1793, a few engaging in vigilante action against radicals but all making some public testimony of their allegiance to the king and respect for the existing constitutional order. In many respects the loyalist movement can count as a classic expression of modern nationalism; it employed the rhetoric of national unity and the nation in danger, was aggressive towards outsiders, was strongly politicized, and united public authority and public opinion. How far it was genuinely popular in winning support among the lower orders is open to question, but it certainly established a consensus of propertied opinion hostile to France and to constitutional change at home.[24]

An important question, though, is whether political nationalism of this intensity led on to mass military participation. National defence patriotism, volunteering in particular, has usually been presented as a continuation of loyalism, mainly on the authority of an article by J. R. Western on the volunteers of the 1790s. Western's argument was that the volunteer corps that started to appear in 1794 marked a further development of the 'party of order' created by loyalist activity over the previous eighteen months, and he was able to point to a number of instances where loyalist associations were converted into armed volunteers under the same leadership. Later work has emphasized the loyalist language contained in the inaugural declarations of volunteer corps and the plethora of county meetings in the spring of 1794 that again mobilized propertied opinion, this time in support of

---

[24] D. Ginter 'The Loyalist Association Movement of 1792–3 and British Public Opinion', *Hist. J.* 9 (1966), 179–90; Dozier, *King, Constitution and Country*; H. T. Dickinson, 'Popular Loyalism in Britain in the 1790s', in E. Hellmuth (ed.), *The Transformation of Political Culture: England and Germany in the Late Eighteenth Century* (London, 1990), 503–33; M. Philp, 'Vulgar Conservatism 1792–3', *Eng. Hist. Rev.* 110 (1995), 42–69.

volunteering. David Eastwood's has been the most original contribution. He saw the language of war patriotism as mainly shaped by loyalist ideas and rhetoric. He further maintained that the state dealt with the problems of radicalism and national defence in basically the same way, depending on voluntary endeavour organized by local notables to provide it with broad public support. The difference between volunteer corps and loyalist associations was that the state found the former much more valuable—practically useful for police and national defence, more permanent, and able to appeal to a wider social constituency.[25]

There were obvious continuities between loyalism and volunteering which can be accepted at the outset. It should come as no surprise that local notables often passed from one to the other; for they dominated the public life of their communities and it was unthinkable for them to countenance any armed activity outside their control. The invitation to arm, moreover, came from the government in a circular to the lord lieutenants in March 1794. Such a proposal was sufficient legitimation, much as royal proclamations, charges to grand juries, and other official or semi-official expressions had made the harassment of radicals into a public duty. A greater puzzle is the predominance of loyalist language whenever volunteers defined their purpose, equally characteristic of corps formed in 1797 or 1798 as of those formed in 1794. The Royston Armed Association in 1798 required members to declare:

Our firm attachment to His Majesty King George the Third and to the constitution of this country as by law established which we will use our utmost endeavours to transmit inviolate to posterity. That considering French principles as absurd and French practices detestable we view with surprise and abhorrence any attempts to disseminate the one or to follow the example of the other and that we will resist both to the utmost of our power whether they be insidiously recommended to our imitation by treacherous friends or forcibly obtruded on us by an invading enemy.[26]

About the same time Birmingham's chief magistrate, the high bailiff, was congratulating the town's volunteers for coming forward to defend the constitution against the 'visionary phantoms of modern Illuminati'.[27] Although all volunteers also vowed to defend the country against French invasion, at first they were most able to imagine themselves checking disorder in their own communities in the event of the army taking the field. Conspiratorial notions were deeply embedded in

[25] Western, 'The Volunteer Movement as an Anti-Revolutionary Force', *Eng. Hist. Rev.* 71 (1956), 603–14; Dozier, *King, Constitution and Country*, esp. 138–71; Dickinson, 'Popular Loyalism', 522–4; Eastwood, 'Patriotism', 146–68.

[26] H. Wortham to W. Wilshere, 20 June 1798, Hertford RO, Hitchen Volunteers MSS, Box 2.

[27] C. J. Hart, *The History of the 1st Volunteer Battalion of the Royal Warwickshire Regiment and its Predecessors* (Birmingham, 1906), 37–8. See also Brown, *Bristol Volunteers*, 33–6; J. R. S. Whiting, 'The Frampton Volunteers', *J. Soc. for Army Hist. Res.* 48 (1970), 25–6.

loyalist politics—an alliance of French and English Jacobins was taken as proved—so that a combined attack by invasion and insurrection was a firm expectation. Volunteers explained themselves in the dominant political language of the time. This is simply to say that the propertied consensus built around loyalism in 1792–3 eroded only gradually and that volunteering was under the control of the propertied classes. During the 1790s volunteering was plebeianized in only some areas. In towns especially, it was usually the carefully supervised and selective arming of small property-owners; the yeomanry corps raised by the counties, their ranks generally filled by farmers or farmers' sons, were all that could be desired. Even more to the point, these volunteers were commanded or patronized by local rulers and notables who had been the key element loyalism had sought to enlist and amongst whom its influence was greatest.

Loyalism, however, did not produce mass volunteering; nor was it anything like the whole context in which the corps of 1794 emerged. Too often the events of 1792–3 and the subsequent volunteer movement culminating in the vast mobilization of 1803–5 are cited as ample cause and effect without regard for particular evidence.[28] The difference between loyalism and national defence patriotism as it developed from 1798 may be left to another chapter. A second problem, never properly recognized, is that volunteering over the three years 1794–6 was on a much smaller scale than the loyalism of 1792–3, with about 160 corps, including yeomanry cavalry, raised in England and Wales; there may have been up to 2,000 loyalist associations.[29] Most of the offers to raise corps in 1794—a time of loyalist alarm—came from places on or near the exposed coasts stretching from Cornwall to Kent and from Yorkshire to Scotland, which hardly suggests a preoccupation with the enemy at home. On the outbreak of war the government accepted volunteer companies to strengthen the defences of seaports; and the lieutenancies were circularized for the same purpose in March 1794 after a royal message to parliament had warned of impending invasion.[30] The fact is that the great majority of the communities which armed during the first years of the war did so out of fear of foreign attack, especially raiding by privateers which had caused concern during the American War. Even so, by 1796 there were still under 10,000 volunteer

[28] e.g. Dickinson, 'Popular Loyalism', 524; Dozier, *King, Constitution and Country*, 138.

[29] H. T. Dickinson, 'Popular Conservatism and Militant Loyalism 1789–1815', in Dickinson (ed.), *Britain and the French Revolution 1789–1815* (Basingstoke, 1989), 115. Dozier, *King, Constitution and Country*, 154, finds 48 yeomanry cavalry and 119 infantry corps formed by Mar. 1795, a total of 167. But not less than 30 of these, perhaps 40, were Scottish. 'State of the . . . Volunteers', 1 July 1796, Chatham MSS, PRO30/8/244, fos. 109–10 gives 161 corps in England and Wales.

[30] 'Proposal of the late Dover Association to renew their engagement of 1783', 19 Dec. 1792 in H. F. B. Wheeler and A. M. Broadley, *Napoleon and the Invasion of England* (2 vols., London, 1908), ii. 341–3; Stringer to Pitt, 11 Feb. 1793, Chatham MSS, PRO30/8/245, fo. 94; Dundas to Lord Amherst, Feb. 1793, HO50/2, fos. 32–5; 'Extract of a Plan [for volunteer companies in Kent and Sussex]', 11 May 1793, HO42/25, fo. 438; 'General Orders for the Security of the Country', 14 Mar. 1794, *PD* xxxi. 89.

infantry in the whole of England. The mottos the corps sometimes chose may be one way of distinguishing the different concerns of different places; Rye in 1794 decided on 'Pro Rege et Grege' ('For King and Country') where Leeds emblazoned on its colours 'Pro Rege et Lege' ('For King and Constitution').[31] Volunteering as an anti-revolutionary movement was most apparent in the industrial districts of the East Midlands, Lancashire, and Yorkshire, the latter in particular; in precisely those communities where public order was precariously maintained and where loyalists confronted powerful radical minorities. But such corps made up less than one quarter of the total volunteer strength.[32]

Neither can the numerous yeomanry corps that sprang into existence after 1794 be regarded as the military arm of the loyalist associations. Whatever reputation as a law and order force the yeomanry acquired, they originated more with the county élites than with the townsmen who usually organized the popular loyalism of the localities. Most corps came out of the county meetings held in April–May 1794 to consider the government's recommendations on home defence, which included a request for cavalry of this description. The military subscriptions launched by these meetings were certainly not the loyalist subscriptions they have often been made out to be. Coastal counties spent lavishly on improving their coastal defences. Elsewhere part of the proceeds often went on an increase in the militia establishment and therefore served the purposes of county magnates who used the militia as a valuable source of local influence. If more money went on raising yeomanry, that too can be regarded as an investment bringing similar returns.[33] As with the volunteer infantry, the county yeomanries were government-initiated, created primarily to fit in with the government's anti-invasion plans. Yeomanry were particularly needed in 1794 to release the small number of regular cavalry remaining in the country for field service in the event of a French attack, a situation that continued because the army wanted the defence to be highly mobile against an enemy who would bring few horses and who also might attempt several simultaneous landings. About a third of the yeomanry strength raised in the first two years belonged to the West Riding, the Midlands counties, and the west around Gloucester, areas where a heavy cavalry presence was always maintained. Even so, there were substantially more (40 per cent) in the coastal counties from Somerset to Kent and from Suffolk

---

[31] L. A. Vidler, *The Story of the Rye Volunteers* (Rye, 1954), 3; E. Hargrave, 'The Early Leeds Volunteers', *Thoresby Soc. Publications*, 28 (1923–7), 270.

[32] For lists of corps see 'Offers to raise corps . . . transmitted to Lord Amherst', Chatham MSS, PRO30/8/244, fos. 205–8; 'State of the volunteers', 1 July 1796, ibid., fos. 211–12. Even in 1796 the government had no complete record of volunteer strength; but for an estimate based on the 1796 return see W. Merry to J. P. Smith, 6 Aug. 1796, ibid., fo. 213. I. F. W. Beckett, 'The Amateur Military Tradition', *War and Society*, 4 (1986), 3, says half the corps formed in 1793–4 were for coastal defence.

[33] Dozier, *King, Constitution and Country*, 149–50; Cookson, 'Volunteer Movement', 876. Cf. Dickinson, 'Popular Loyalism', 523–4.

to Yorkshire; and these corps were soon to be incorporated in the army's counter-invasion strategy, specifically in connection with plans 'to drive the country'.[34]

One in three infantry volunteers by 1796 belonged to a Scottish corps.[35] Scotland, admittedly in the absence of a militia, also raised nine fencible battalions in 1793 and a further sixteen the following year, together with fencible cavalry. Nine Scottish battalions had been added to the line by 1795. With little more than one-tenth of the population of the United Kingdom, Scotland possibly contributed over one-fifth of the nation's military manpower at this stage of the war, if all kinds of military force are included. This is worth dwelling on because Scotland's heavy war commitment (and, to a lesser extent, Ireland's as well) points up the continued unpopularity of military service in England, and, indeed, the army's marginality in English society. If it is true that half, at least, of the British army became Scottish–Irish in 1793–4, we can appreciate how Pitt's government exercised itself over the problem of drawing more effectively on English resources. At first it was enough to turn to Scotland and Ireland whenever English recruitment proved disappointing. But, by 1796, the point at which the huge recruiting effort of the previous years petered out (while, coincidentally, France's victory over the First Coalition made it urgent to reinforce home defence), the government found drastic compulsory measures, directed wholly or mainly at England, the only way it could meet its manpower requirements.

Pitt's government met parliament in October 1796 with three proposals; a Quota Act by which counties were required to raise a specific number of recruits for the army (and navy); a provisional cavalry laid as a compulsory levy on payers of the horse tax; and a supplementary militia.[36] Together they signalled a decision by ministers to operate, if necessary, a 'command economy' for military manpower. As each was a balloted levy, they were also designed to make England contribute more in proportion to her means. The supplementary militia was particularly significant because it was on a scale to treble the size of the English militia and thus approached the principle of universal training to which Dundas had been converted; if the government required it, 60,000 men might be trained and armed during the following spring and summer. Here can be found the first practical measure taken to create a British armed nation. That it was a step initiated by government before anything like mass arming had taken place invites us to examine carefully the rapid progress of the idea in official and military circles during the crisis of 1796. Popular loyalism thus recedes further into the background.

---

[34] Yeomanry corps (with the strength given in troops) are listed in 'State of the . . . volunteers', 1 July 1796, Chatham MSS, PRO30/8/244, fo. 211.

[35] I calculate so from Merry's estimate of total volunteer numbers (see n. 32) and from the number of Scottish and English corps (47 and 161, including 46 and 100 infantry units).

[36] *PD* xxxii. 1208–13.

A paper by Lord Cornwallis, of American fame, in August 1796 is probably the closest we can get to the immediate origins of the British armed nation and the mass mobilization which was its key feature. Throughout 1795 the French were busy consolidating their victories in the Low Countries and Germany; but the British the next year had good reason to fear that they would have the enemy's undivided attention, especially as the Austrian will to fight on showed signs of wavering. Dundas predicted 'universal peace' on the Continent, war with Spain as well as France, and an invasion attempt.[37] Cornwallis, sitting in the Cabinet as master-general of the ordnance, properly regarded himself as the Cabinet's military adviser, and there can be little doubt that his paper followed another that had come from the army itself drawn up by Sir David Dundas, the Duke of York's quartermaster-general. However, Cornwallis's memorandum was not so much a rebuttal of General Dundas's views as an extension of them into areas he had left uncertain; gracefully titled though it was as 'additional hints', it embodied what might be called Cornwallis's 'American' ideas of war, which valued civilian participation in defence, as opposed to 'Prussian' ideas which rested the nation's fate on the regular army.[38] Whether Cornwallis acted on his own initiative or at the Cabinet's behest is impossible to say; but his advice made a particular impression on Henry Dundas, who shed any inhibitions he may have had about an armed populace and began to plan both the supplementary militia and a Scottish militia around the principle of universal training. Dundas told the Duke of Montrose in November 1796:

I am in no ways afraid of the general bugbear of arming too many people. I am much more afraid of their inertness & want of military feeling the moment the pressure of danger is past. By the system I have proposed every man the moment he feels himself a man would at the same time be taught to a certain degree the use of arms for his defence and would be impressed with the principle that in case of emergency he would be called upon to use those arms.[39]

General Dundas's defence plan concentrated on identifying the likely points of French attack, the distribution of force in Great Britain, and the tactical response to be made in the event of an enemy landing. He looked to a reserve of 'steady troops', who would move quickly to head off the enemy force, 'to bear the brunt of the business'. Depots and magazines prepared in advance in strategic places would add to the army's mobility while the 'driving' of the country by the cavalry

---

[37] Dundas to Cornwallis, 19 Aug. 1796, C. Ross (ed.), *Correspondence of the 1st Marquis Cornwallis* (3 vols., London, 1859), ii. 308–9.

[38] General Dundas, 'Considerations on the Invasion of Great Britain 1796', WO30/65; Cornwallis, 'Additional Hints in the Event of an Actual or Expected Invasion', 28 Aug. 1796, WO30/58 (no. 17).

[39] Dundas to Duke of [Montrose], 15 Nov. 1796, Melville MSS, SRO GD51/1/876/2. Montrose is satisfactorily identified from Dundas to the lord advocate, 7 Mar. [1797], in H. W. Meikle, *Scotland and the French Revolution* (repr. London, 1969), 278.

would starve the enemy of supplies. 'Civil arrangements', said Dundas, awaited a detailed plan but chiefly concerned police (the responsibility of the yeomanry and volunteers) and the 'management' of London so that the army could draw on its immense resources 'in men, horses, carriages and in every particular'. Most of this made civilians incidental to national defence. Cornwallis, in contrast, saw them as an integral, if not decisive, factor in any such contest once their patriotism was translated into service, especially military service. His 'hints' amounted to a scheme of national mobilization which had its inspiration, he admitted, in the examples set by America and France. The cardinal point was that every able-bodied man aged 16 to 60 was to accept an obligation to bear arms in defence of the country. Where General Dundas hoped to bring the regular regiments up to strength (from being 18,800 short of their establishment), Cornwallis wanted this and also 'two full ballots' of 'additional militia' (each raising about 30,000 men), with a third or fourth if the situation demanded it. In addition, yeomanry and volunteer corps were to increase their numbers, and the 'multitude' outside the army and auxiliaries could be employed as irregulars, attacking small parties of the enemy, interfering with his communications, and pre-empting supplies. Parochial surveys were to be made with a view to organizing evacuation and the removal or destruction of everything useful to the enemy. For these and other purposes the civil power at every level was to be reinforced by 'committees of the most zealous and determined men that can be found—as has actually been practised with success in America and France'. Here for the first time in Europe the alliance between the counter-revolutionary state and the armed nation began clearly to emerge.

The force of French example is understandable after the great victories achieved by the French nation-in-arms. The American influence is less obvious. That war had been fought under very different conditions than were found in Europe, affecting both the scale and nature of the warfare. Such lightly populated country made it impossible to maintain armies of any great size and the protection of supply lines provoked a 'war of posts' which always dominated over major actions in view of the vastness of the theatre of operations. As a war of raids rather than battles, it served to strengthen interest in light infantry, but because Britain's military command fragmented with the dissolution of the office of commander-in-chief after 1783, there were no formal post-mortems to encourage this or any other changes.[40] Generals, like Cornwallis, merely carried their experience of militias and people's war in their heads.

But did this amount to an 'American' doctrine of war in conflict with a 'Prussian' doctrine of war? It is not difficult to imagine how 'Prussian' influence might

[40] D. French, *The British Way in Warfare 1688–2000* (London, 1990), 62–87; P. Mackesy, 'What the British Army Learned', in R. Hoffman and P. J. Albert (eds.), *Arms and Independence: The Military Character of the American Revolution* (Charlottesville, Va., 1984), 191–215.

have been paramount in the army. The Duke of York, General Dundas, and Sir William Fawcett, the adjutant-general, the trio at the Horse Guards commanding the army for most of the 1790s, were all predominantly 'Prussian' by education and experience in the service. Dundas was the author of the army's drill book, which was an English version of the Prussian manual and which is said to show its bias by the short treatment given light infantry tactics.[41] However, as has been argued above, it is easy to exaggerate the European military's disdain for irregulars and 'small war'. At any rate, in 1796 York and Dundas urged the tactical import-ance of light infantry in the hedged and wooded English countryside, welcomed the provisional cavalry as providing 'a considerable body of irregular troops', and hoped that the British would display the same 'enthusiasm' as the French had 'when attacked at home'.[42] But if there was no profound disagreement there was a tension between the different views. To a man those with American experience seem to have made it a source of professional pride against the dominant 'Prussians'. Cornwallis, attending the Prussian manœuvres in 1785, pronounced them 'ridicu-lous'. General Simcoe deplored the 'fashion' that decried the 'American education' and, with Cornwallis, railed against the 'system of David Dundas' variously called 'German', 'mechanical', and 'erroneous'—and proved so in practice by the French.[43] Besides Cornwallis and Simcoe, the 'Americans' included Sir William Howe and Sir Charles Grey. Significantly, Howe and Grey were given the important com-mands of the eastern and southern districts at the beginning of the crisis in 1796, where each excelled in showing how civilians and the civilian auxiliaries could be incorporated into the country's defence.[44] None of these generals had fought the French revolutionary armies on the Continent in the campaigns of 1793–4. Theirs was an 'American way in warfare' which the government was opportunely able to draw on when Britain was forced on to the defensive in 1796–8.

[41] Mackesy, 'What the British Army Learned', 204–6 for Dundas's drill book. The Duke of York, as a young man, went to Prussia for his military education. Fawcett, fluent in German, translated Marshal Saxe's *Memoirs* and the Prussian regulations, and negotiated the hire of German mercenaries at the beginning of the American War.
[42] Dundas, 'Considerations . . . 1796', WO30/65; York to Pitt, 18 Oct. 1796, Chatham MSS, PRO30/8/106, fos. 67–8.
[43] Cornwallis to Lt.-Col. Ross, 5 Oct. 1785, *Cornwallis Corresp.* ii. 204–5; Mackesy, 'What the British Army Learned', 192, 194, 210 212.
[44] Duke of York to Grey, 4 Aug. 1796, Grey to York, 28, 30 Oct., 14, 18, 19 Nov. 1796, 10 Mar. 1797, Univ. of Durham Library, 1st Earl Grey MSS 826, 912, 916, 921, 933, 940–1, 1323; Grey, 'Suggestions for driving the cattle and drawing forth the strength of the county of Kent', WO1/407/573–608; Cranmer-Byng, 'Essex Prepares For Invasion', 188–92. Dundas informed Lord Grenville in Jan. 1798: 'Sir Charles Grey has sent me a most admirable statement of what has been settled in his district, in concert with the Lord Lieutenant and his Deputies.' Grenville, *HMC, Dropmore MSS* (10 vols., London, 1894–1927), iv. 48. However, the Duke of Richmond, lord lieutenant of Sussex, and Lord Sheffield were highly critical of Grey's plans. Richmond to Lord Hobart, 26 July 1801, Sheffield to Hobart, 2 Aug. 1801, Hobart MSS, Buckingham RO, D/MH/War/G5, 8.

Probably the 'Americans' were most important for shaping practical measures in the crisis. On the other hand, there can be little doubt that the 'Prussians' at the head of the army accepted the necessity of reconstructing the system of home defence faced with the facts of an entirely new strategic situation. One dangerous development was the likely defection of Austria from the war, which would have left Britain to face the might of France alone. In the event Austria did not make peace at Campo Formio until 1797 after another campaign; but the consequences of the final wreck of the great coalition of 1792–3 were already being felt as naval preparations began to be observed on France's western coast. The outbreak of war with Spain in October 1796 placed further heavy demands on the navy while raising the prospect of the combined fleets heading northwards against an inferior defence. All this was bad enough. Much worse was French possession of the Dutch fleet and Dutch ports which gave the enemy the outstanding strategic advantage of being able to threaten the east coast of England, Scotland, and northern Ireland. The Channel had always been a bastion of Britain's defence as it made it difficult for a fleet to pass along a north–south line; throughout the eighteenth century the greatest threat had been to England's south coast and Ireland's south and west coasts because France and Spain, the country's traditional enemies, had an easy northward passage for their navies. Now, with the enemy able to deploy a formidable amount of naval power north as well as south of the Channel, all the outer coasts of the British archipelago were exposed to attack. General Dundas, in his paper on the country's increased vulnerability, noted long stretches of coast where a landing was possible and numerous seaports whose shipping and stores could attract large-scale raids. In this situation one of the navy's priorities became the destruction of the Dutch fleet or any other potential naval threat in the North Sea, as the hapless Danes were to discover in 1801 and again in 1807.

The army's other task was to calculate the force available to defend the long periphery. These figures made lamentable reading indeed. Soon after taking office as commander-in-chief in 1795, the Duke of York consulted the generals in the various districts to arrive at a total of 127,900 troops needed for the defence of Great Britain (Scotland, 13,000). General Dundas in 1796 asked for 16,000 cavalry and 100,000 infantry, and reported the actual numbers as standing at 14,700 and 52,900. By February 1797 the army, including militia and fencibles, had made no progress at all in recruitment, being still nearly complete in cavalry (14,675) but with no more than half the infantry (50,545). The Horse Guards could not guarantee to concentrate more than 25,000 men against an invasion in southern England, fencibles and militia included. The north, from Lincolnshire to Northumberland, difficult for the reserve to reach, had under 9,000 on station. Scotland was even worse off, scarcely defensible at all, despite concern that the capture of Edinburgh could open a route for the enemy into the north of Ireland; there were probably not 2,000 regulars in the whole country. On the general situation the Horse Guards grimly reported: 'it is evident we are too weak in all the material points & that no great or sufficient regular force could be collected before an enemy who lands in great force had done irreparable mischief'.[45]

It is interesting that this was a phase of the war when the politicians largely left it to the military to shape the system of home defence, Henry Dundas was to become a much more assertive secretary for war in this respect, and he was to be followed by Windham and Castlereagh who carried out radical reconstructions. In 1794 even the less than satisfactory Lord Amherst, called back into service as commander-in-chief on the outbreak of war, excelled himself by proposing the volunteer scheme that the government soon afterwards adopted.[46] The supplementary militia of 1797 stemmed directly from Cornwallis's suggestion of a 'double ballot' to reinforce, without delay, militia numbers. Moreover, the home defence organization that began to emerge in the counties from 1797 conformed closely to Cornwallis's ideas about making detailed surveys of local resources and enrolling civilians to help with non-military tasks, with committees ready to take charge at all levels as soon as invasion occurred. The Quota Act of 1796, unsuccessful though it was, originated with Robert Anstruther, General Dundas's deputy.[47] No direct evidence exists, but it is highly likely that the provisional cavalry was also conceived by the army; for, from the military's point of view, this was preferable to the yeomanry in that it could be made to serve outside the county and thus was fully available to act in conjunction with the army.[48]

Henry Dundas saw all this legislation through parliament late in 1796. Dundas, like the generals, must have a prominent place in the making of the British armed nation. He was Britain's Carnot, effectively war minister for the whole of the Revolutionary War and the main organizer of national defence, out of which, as with France, came a much increased military capability. By the end of his time in office, Dundas's efforts left the strategically encircled national base sufficiently secure for Britain to launch long-distance and relatively powerful offensives, a

---

[45] Duke of York's memorandum, 24 Feb. 1795, WO1/617/239–42; Dundas, 'Considerations . . . 1796', WO30/65; 'Present General Distribution of the Army', 5 Feb. 1797, WO30/58 (no. 19).

[46] Amherst to Dundas, 13 Feb. 1794, HO42/28, fo. 269.

[47] Portland required the coastal counties to set about organizing the 'driving of the country' in Nov. 1796. Cramner-Byng, 'Essex Prepares For Invasion', 187. Committees appear in the defence plan in General Dundas's 'Memorandum on the Defence of England', 20 Feb. 1797, WO30/65. J. R. Western, *The English Militia in the Eighteenth Century* (London, 1965), 221 for the Quota Act.

[48] Dundas explained the roles of the cavalry thus: 'The regular cavalry should be reserved for regular attack upon the enemy. The yeomanry cavalry should have their chief attention directed to preserve the internal quiet of the country. The provisional cavalry should be employed in driving the cattle, and such other business of a Hussar nature as may occur in each district.' Grenville, *Dropmore MSS*, iv. 47–8.

change signalled by the dispatch of a British army to Egypt in 1801. Egypt was followed by expeditions to north Germany in 1805, to Sweden and Spain in 1808, and, most famously, to Portugal in 1809. This strategic freedom was Dundas's greatest, though rarely appreciated, achievement. He understood these wider implications of national defence from the time it began to engage most of his attention in 1796: 'if satisfaction is not given on that point, it will be in vain to look for either approbation or support in the conduct of any operations abroad'.[49] Cornwallis's advice of a trained population and national mobilization in the event of danger must have been immediately attractive. The 'Proposals for Rendering the Body of the People Instrumental in the General Defence', written by Dundas early in 1798, comprised a comprehensive plan for civilian-based defence which was not greatly altered during the rest of the war. As for compulsory service, he never gave up the principle though prepared to accept volunteers if they provided the necessary numbers. 'Every boy', he wrote in retirement in 1808, 'should from his infancy be taught to feel that it is not more requisite that he should be instructed in the arts of a weaver, a taylor or a shoemaker than that he should learn the portion of skill necessary to enable him to take a useful part in the defence of his country.'[50]

'General training' and an armed populace, though, do not square easily with Britain's counter-revolution. Dundas's anti-Jacobinism, in private as well as public, had been as intense as any minister's. He shared to the full classical conservative notions of social disorder, in which a 'designing few' prey on and manipulate for their own nefarious purposes popular discontents. He may even be said to have shared a 'Scottish' apprehension of the radical threat, Scotland's crisis of order during the revolutionary decade perhaps exceeding England's so great was the population mobility and urban growth and consequent perceptions of social breakdown. A point Dundas hammered again and again was the need to inculcate a 'military spirit' among the people; which reminds us that one of the central themes of eighteenth-century thought was the tension set up in a 'free', commercial society between individuals pursuing their interests and the needs of the state; 'opulence' against 'defence', in Adam Smith's words. Dundas believed that 'apathy' about national defence was where Britain's real vulnerability lay; if military service were required of or volunteered by a large part of the population, not only would patriotic feelings be released and given a powerful focus, but the propertied classes would necessarily be called into a more active role of social leadership and public duty. The yeomanry cavalry raised since 1794 stated the ideal in this respect, forming as it did 'a connexion between the gentlemen of rank and the yeomanry in

[49] Dundas to Lord Grenville, 2 Oct. 1796, Grenville, *Dropmore MSS*, iii. 257.
[50] Lord Melville to Lord Castlereagh, 9 Apr. 1808, Melville MSS, NLS MS 3835, fos. 58–61. For Dundas's plan of national defence in 1798 see his circular letter to the lord lieutenants, 6 Apr. 1798, Essex RO, D/DHa/01/10.

England and the persons of rank and substantial farmers in Scotland'. Such a force, 'not infected with the poison of large towns', Dundas could imagine outlasting the war to become part of society's permanent defences against sedition and disorder.[51] But urban volunteers were used to project the same 'fraternity' between the classes; and in Scotland, at least, it came to be said that volunteering, more than anything else, had put down radicalism.[52] Military service could be held to strengthen social relations just as Dundas knew it strengthened political relations within the state. It brought men together out of patriotism and loyalty to the crown under the leadership and authority of their superiors in a happy blend of comradeship and hierarchy, public spirit and paternalism.

It is interesting to speculate whether Dundas may have reflected on the military patriotism of his own country. Scotland's contribution to Britain's military manpower in the early years of the war has already been mentioned; whether in regulars or volunteers, the Scottish 'military spirit' put England's to shame. Much of the recruitment had been Highlands-based, using the good offices of magnates like the Duke of Argyll, the Duke of Gordon, and the Countess of Sutherland; it was a continuation of the policy the British state had regularly followed since the Seven Years War—binding the chiefs and the clans to its service as part of the process of incorporating a territory largely outside its authority. Dundas felt deeply attracted to the Highlands; he spent most of his holidays at Dunira, near Loch Earn, in the Perthshire hills. Perhaps he found here the kind of society he most admired; a cohesive hierarchy, a society free of and impregnable to radical subversion where traditional loyalties continued to be taken seriously. Scotland as a whole displayed a commitment to the war which was to persuade Dundas to press even more heavily on her resources by raising a Scottish militia in 1797. His connections and knowledge of the country might well have formed his expectations of what a public-spirited population could achieve; extensive volunteering to relieve the army for important service; a once frighteningly formidable radicalism on the wane; zeal and activity on the part of local rulers whatever the poverty of the landowning class and burgh governments in comparison with England. Scotland virtually counted as an armed nation by 1796; perhaps one in eight males of 'military age' were serving in some military capacity.[53]

Dundas appears not to have been ceded full responsibility for home defence

---

[51] Dundas to the Duke of Buccleuch, 10 June 1797, Melville MSS, SRO GD51/1/887/1.

[52] See below 243.

[53] Probably 31,500 (7,000 volunteers, 17,500 fencibles, 7,000 regulars) were recruited into new corps. But Scots would also have found their way into existing regiments where they were already numerous. Suppose a total of 40,000 men. Webster's census of Scotland in 1755 makes it possible to estimate the size of the military population at 20 per cent of the total (= 320,000), if 'military age' is taken to be 18–45 in conformity with the militia law of the period. See M. W. Flinn, *Scottish Population History* (Cambridge, 1977), 256–9 for the age structure of the 18th-cent. population.

until as late as 1798. When he was made the secretary for war in July 1794, at the time of the accession of the Portland Whigs to Pitt's government, the home office continued to deal with the militia, volunteers, and county lieutenancies while his office handled 'foreign military arrangements and correspondence'; most of the business involved organizing expeditionary forces in concert with the admiralty. Even in 1796 he was wary of taking the initiative on home defence, though he had definite views, felt the need for action, and, with the home secretary in the Lords, could expect to manage any measures through parliament.[54] This means that the subject was more open than some to ministerial discussion, particularly from Pitt and Grenville who, with Dundas, formed the triumvirate that during the 1790s ran the war.[55] The likely course of events was that Dundas represented the urgency of the matter to Pitt and that he and the prime minister, keeping Grenville informed, took the military's proposals and thrashed them into shape for parliament. Portland, the home secretary, presumably remained as indolent and obliging as ever.

Pitt's own views on an armed populace thus swim into notice. There appears to be only one memorandum of his concerning national mobilization, and that relates to a later period when he transparently bullied Addington's government into legislating for a *levée en masse* during the crisis of 1803. This is an instructive episode because Dundas accused Pitt of ignoring practicalities and Pitt himself seemed to imagine that the larger the armed host the better—London alone, he said, could furnish 200,000 men. The expense was dismissed 'as a very inconsiderable object when compared with the inestimable benefits resulting from it', and those who worried about arming the people were reminded that every subject possessed the right to bear arms.[56] Obviously Pitt in 1803 was little bothered by the usual cautions issued against a 'general array'. More so than Dundas, he was carried away by the idea of national defence producing patriotism of invincible moral and physical force, essentially a modern conception of war in which war was fundamentally the opposed wills of the belligerent societies.[57] That these were the fantasies of Pitt, the volunteer colonel of 1803, is unlikely. As prime minister in 1796, he was party to measures intended to raise 60,000 infantry (the supplementary militia) and 20,000 cavalry (the provisional cavalry) by ballot, easily the largest requisition of military manpower the British state had ever made and about which

---

[54] Dundas to Pitt, 10 Feb. 1798, Chatham MSS, PRO30/8/157, fos. 236–45; Pitt to Lord Grenville, 5, 7 July 1794, Grenville, *Dropmore MSS*, ii. 595–7; Dundas to Grenville, 2 Oct. 1796, 12 Feb. 1798, ibid. iii. 257, iv. 79.

[55] The best study of the triumvirate is M. Duffy, 'Pitt, Grenville and the Control of British Foreign Policy in the 1790s', in J. Black (ed.), *Knights Errant and True Englishmen* (Edinburgh, 1989), 151–77. Pitt communicated the decisions in favour of a provisional cavalry and supplementary militia to the Duke of York, which as prime minister he could do and Dundas could not without embarrassment.

[56] Pitt, 'Further Considerations on the Plan for a General Enrolment and Array of the People', 2 July 1803, Sidmouth MSS, Devon RO, 152M/C1803/OM15.   [57] *PH* xxxvi. 1644.

there must have been many reservations on account of previous popular protest over the militia. In 1798 Pitt confined Portland to the routine correspondence of the home office and gave Dundas full responsibility for organizing home defence.[58] Together they proceeded to preside over the formation of a volunteer mass exceeding 100,000 men and planned the involvement of many more civilians in unarmed service as labourers and drivers for the army and civil authority.

The politicians, therefore, in particular Pitt and Dundas, made ample response to the concerns of the generals, who knew from knowledge and experience what possibilities civilian mobilization contained and who found it the only answer to Britain's strategic encirclement after the French had possession of the Low Countries. One could also say the generals were acting according to the logic of Britain's situation in the eighteenth century which required auxiliary forces to cover defence of the national base if Britain were to count as a serious military power whether in Europe or further abroad. The military necessities of the case need to be emphasized because too often the military context in which Pitt's government in the 1790s was operating is ignored, and so, therefore, the relationship between defence and Pittite politics. Pitt and Dundas acted as if national defence would evoke a genuinely popular response; they saw civilian military service, even compulsory service, as a source of national unity as well as being a condition for national survival. Their engagement with radicalism was fought much more tentatively; and we know that they had every reason for being less confident about popular loyalism than about national defence patriotism, particularly after the revival of the radical societies and hunger riots of 1795. The armed nation thus became an important part of the politics of order, for Pitt and Dundas at least. Others among their followers were not so sure, increasingly unsure as the volunteer mass proved to be incorrigibly civilianized and inefficient, more like a popular movement than an army. Since an armed population could not be dispensed with, there commenced a search for appropriate controls which focused on the militia model where military authority resided with the gentry and counties. This traditional, conservative solution was far removed from Pitt's nationalism, which was more like the nationalism of the French revolution—militaristic, invoking numbers and 'spirit', preaching national unity, impatient about practicalities. In the end, conservative ideas about armed service prevailed. But Pitt, and also Dundas, the ministers of the loyalist reaction, provide another warning that the relationship between loyalism and national defence patriotism was not as simple as has been made out.

[58] Cornwallis to General Ross, 19 Feb. 1798, *Cornwallis Corresp.* ii. 330.

2
The French Encirclement

BRITAIN'S strategic interest in the Low Countries is one of the forgotten chapters of the long Anglo-French conflict commencing in 1793. Something invariably mentioned in connection with the decision to intervene in the war against revolutionary France, its importance as a 'cause' of war has done little to secure its importance during the war itself. Yet easily the most important constant in the strategic situation from the defeat of the First Coalition until the Dutch revolt at the end of 1813 was the enemy's control of the coast north of the Channel. The generals understood immediately what it portended. As early as January 1795 Lord Adam Gordon wrote from his Scottish command, that 'since the French have got possession of Holland, [Britain] seems to me full as vulnerable as Ireland'.[1] With possession of the Scheldt and the Zuider Zee, the French and their Dutch clients enjoyed safe naval havens and easy access to the North Sea by which they could threaten the whole of England's east coast, including the Thames estuary, Scotland, and northern and western Ireland.[2] Occasionally this danger was magnified by the hostility of the Baltic powers, as happened with the League of Armed Neutrality in 1801 and the Franco-Russian *rapprochement* of 1807. The expedition against Copenhagen in 1807 has to be appreciated as an action not only to keep the naval balance in Britain's favour but also to reduce a potential threat to Ireland.[3] Attack from northern Europe was an attack on the most exposed parts of the British Isles because throughout the eighteenth century the country was prepared for invasion along the southern coasts, the easiest striking point for French and Spanish fleets. All the great naval bases were in the south, and the navy was to find itself greatly stretched in throwing a defensive screen around the entire periphery.

In the Duke of York's words, Britain and France occupied 'a relative position unknown in any former contest'.[4] Britain's vulnerability because of strategic

---

[1] Lord Adam Gordon to Lord Amherst, 30 Jan. 1795, Chatham MSS, PRO30/8/139, fos. 59-60. See also Lord Fitzwilliam to the Duke of Portland, 29 Jan. 1795, Fitzwilliam MSS, Sheffield Central Library, F5/30.

[2] General Dundas, 'Considerations on the Invasion of Great Britain 1796', WO30/65, begins by making this point.

[3] Canning to the Duke of Richmond, 16 Aug. 1807, Richmond MSS, NLI MS 59/149. Sir Edward Littlehales, the military secretary at Dublin, said of the expedition: 'It will, in my opinion, contribute more to the defence of Ireland than any measure that could possibly have been undertaken.' Littlehales to B. Wyatt, 5 Sept. 1807, SPOI CSO OP225/14/32.

[4] York to Lord Hobart, 25 Aug. 1803, Melville MSS, SRO GD51/1/982/1.

encirclement made the Low Countries the most logical area for offensive operations, and, in fact, all the periods of Continental alliance were distinguished by
British intervention in this part of Europe. In 1799 the Second Coalition led
to an Anglo-Russian landing in Holland. The army sent to north-west Germany
in 1805 was intended to divert Prussian attention westwards towards the libera-
tion of the Dutch. While the Walcheren expedition of 1809 was badly timed in
terms of the Austrian alliance, it became an attempt to reduce naval bases which
threatened to establish French naval power in northern Europe and particularly
threatened the eastern and northern sectors of the British defensive circle. Finally,
when the long-awaited Dutch revolt occurred late in 1813, the few troops available
were rushed to Holland to hold on to the advantage suddenly gained.[5] The secretary for war wrote at this time: 'Our great object is Antwerp. We cannot make a
secure peace if that place be left in the hands of France. When I tell you . . . that Lord
Castlereagh is authorized to state that we will not give up any *one of our conquests*
unless Antwerp be so disposed of as not to be under the influence of France, you
may consider it almost as our *sine qua non* as far as peace with us is concerned.'[6]
Britain's decision in 1815 to oppose Napoleon in Belgium thus fittingly ended the
Anglo-French conflict exactly where it had begun in 1793, in the area that was
most vital to the territorial security of Britain itself. And the money forgone as an
indemnity for the war of 1815 and put instead into the Dutch barrier fortresses,
equally stated that Britain's European defences began on the farther shore of the
North Sea.

For most of the war, then, the French possessed advantages of attack against the
British national base which had previously been denied them. For one thing, with
bases on the North Sea, they could operate on much shorter lines against many
parts of the British archipelago, which had considerable effect on the strength of
the strike force they could deploy. The Dutch fleet, poised on the very threshold of
Essex, the Tyne, and Edinburgh, was always cause for concern during the 1790s.
During the Napoleonic War attention was transferred to the Scheldt, where Antwerp, Flushing, and several other towns made up a huge naval complex, strenuously
developed and expanded in the years after Trafalgar for the purpose of rebuilding
French sea-power. The largest sea-borne force Britain ever assembled—an army of
40,000 men—was thrown against these dockyards and arsenals in the Walcheren
expedition of 1809.[7] The other great advantage conferred on the French by their

---

[5] C. D. Hall, *British Strategy in the Napoleonic War 1803–15* (Manchester, 1992), 83–4, understands
the British preoccupation with the Low Countries.

[6] Lord Bathurst to Wellington, 31 Dec. 1813, Duke of Wellington (ed.), *Supplementary Despatches,
Correspondence and Memoranda of the Duke of Wellington* (15 vols., London, 1858–72), viii. 450–2.

[7] See R. Glover, 'The French Fleet: Britain's Problem, and Madison's Opportunity', *J. Mod. Hist.*
39 (1967), 233–52; G. C. Bond, *The Grand Expedition: The British Invasion of Holland in 1809* (Athens,
Ga., 1979).

conquest of the Netherlands followed from the first; there was now no part of the British defensive circle that they could not attack as an invading, not merely as a raiding, force. Fleet-carried armies might be moved to the point of attack with roughly equal facility, whether from southward bases against the southern and western quarters of that circle or from northward bases against the eastern and northern quarters. Such a situation both compelled the British to hold their very long perimeter in strength and gave the French a wide choice of diversionary attack in order to conceal their main thrust. The threat against Essex became as real as the threat against Kent. In 1797 the army began serious planning for the defence of Scotland as fears mounted of an invasion from Holland.[8] General Dundas's main task in the previous year had been to assess possible landing places along the entire length of the British and Irish coasts, the surest sign of all that the French had managed to outflank the country's established eighteenth-century defences.[9]

Instead of fleet landings, however, the classic French invasion plan of the period became the concentrated attack across the Channel using an armada of small craft. This sort of invasion was prepared in 1798, 1801, and, most notably, in 1803–5 when Napoleon assembled up to 2,300 vessels and 100,000 troops for the enterprise.[10] It was a strategy to take advantage of the long, thinly held defence lines of the British by attacking on a narrow front with overwhelming force, the famous column against line battle plan on a much larger scale. Both sides regarded London as the great prize to be defended or captured, so that the French were basically right in planning to enter the defensive circle at a point where they could achieve the strongest concentration and where London was nearest. Since the capital was only seventy miles or a few days' march from the Kent and Sussex coast and since there were no fortifications to delay the enemy, the problem for the British was to create a defence in this small area strong enough to buy precious time in which to rush in reinforcements but not so strong as to let diversionary or secondary attacks succeed elsewhere, especially that feared against Essex.

The French interest in a cross-Channel operation, therefore, was one particular way of exploiting their strategic encirclement of the British Isles, not an alternative policy deriving from the view that the British perimeter was attackable at one point only. Napoleon in 1803 contemplated putting troops into Ireland using the Brest

---

[8] Colonel Alexander Dirom's report of 1797 is quoted from extensively in Dirom, 'Memoir of the Military State of North Britain in 1803', NLS MS 1754.

[9] 'Considerations . . . 1796', WO30/65; 'Memorandum with regard to the Defence of Ireland', Feb. 1797, HO50/6/147–56. General Dundas later brought this information together in a single paper. See his 'Memorandum relative to the principal Bays and Harbours [in] Britain and Ireland where an Enemy might possibly make Descent', 22 Jan. 1801, WO1/407/413–27.

[10] The invasion flotilla at its maximum strength in Aug. 1805 is detailed in R. Glover, *Britain at Bay: Defence against Bonaparte 1803–1814* (London, 1973), 177–9. A good general account of Napoleon's plans is F. McLynn, *Invasion: From the Armada to Hitler 1588–1945* (London, 1987), 97–112.

fleet, which would combine with a movement from the Texel against Scotland or Ireland.[11] Even so, he was highly successful in drawing the main British force into the small south-east corner of the island, which presumably fitted in with a scenario of a short, decisive campaign culminating in a dictated peace. In the most serious invasion crisis of the Revolutionary War, in 1801, about one-sixth of the army and militia was stationed in Kent and Sussex; in 1804–5 over a third was. Nor did this proportion fall away quickly after Trafalgar; as late as 1809–11 it remained between a quarter and a third, and probably continued at this level until Napoleon began stripping his western garrisons for the attack on Russia.[12] While we cannot doubt that the flotillas and harbour works in the Channel ports were immediately designed for the purpose of effecting an invasion of England, after 1805 they, along with the naval concentrations in the Schedlt and Texel, became an important means whereby Britain was forced to hold back troops for home defence, leaving Napoleon a freer hand elsewhere in Europe.[13] How many troops is difficult to say; but it is worth noting that the size of the home garrison ranged from 65,000 to 110,000 during most of the Revolutionary War (1796–1801) and was still held at 95,000 at the end of 1810 and 80,000 at the end of 1811.[14]

The problem of holding an immensely long periphery was the strategic imperative that produced the mass arming of civilians after 1796. Though an invader could count on having a local superiority at the outset—at Bantry Bay in December 1796 it would have been six or seven to one, in Kent in August 1805 perhaps three to one[15]—the main task of the defence was to reduce this as quickly as possible. The army, in Britain at least—Ireland is a separate case requiring separate consideration—regarded the civilian auxiliaries as primarily a counter-invasion

---

[11] McLynn, *Invasion*, 102.

[12] Kent and Sussex comprised the southern district until 1805, when they were separated into two districts. The distribution of the home garrison in the years mentioned may be found in WO30/65, no. 28 (1801); SRO GD364/1/1148/11, 1158/5 (1804–5); ibid. 1184/4 (1809); WO1/644, 9–16 (1810); *CJ* lxvi. 555–7 (Mar. 1811).

[13] As Napoleon outlined to his Minister of Marine in 1810. See Glover, *Britain at Bay*, 182–3.

[14] These totals are for regulars, fencibles, and militia, but not volunteers or local militia. They also are for Great Britain excluding the Channel Islands. For the 1796–1801 figures see 'State of the Home Force in Great Britain and Ireland from 1796 to 1801', Jan. 1801, WO1/407/445–55. For returns of Nov. 1810 and 1811 see Liverpool MSS, BL Add. MSS 38361, fos. 22–3, 38378, fos. 182–3.

[15] M. Elliott, *Partners in Revolution: The United Irishmen and France* (New Haven, 1989), 111, 121, mentions that the whole force around the Cork and Bandon area amounted to no more than 4,000 regulars and half a battalion of yeomanry. General Dalrymple believed he needed to leave 2,000 troops in garrison at Cork, which would have made the defence at Bantry Bay outnumbered by seven to one. Hoche commanded a force of 14,450. Glover, *Britain at Bay*, 87–8 for 1805, 'from the uncertainty of where the enemy may direct his effort, our force must be much divided, and . . . at the instant he effects his landing, he for a time is in the advantageous situation of a collected army acting against one whose line is broken in upon, and who is assembling from cantonments', General Dundas, 'Memorandum of Circumstances to be determined and acted upon previous to and at the moment of Invasion', Feb. 1801, Hope of Lufness MSS, SRO GD364/1/1134.

force which provided the means of enveloping the enemy as he tried to advance from his landing place. In 1798 General Dundas imagined that the field army in Kent would have increased from 14,000 to 50,000–60,000, half of them auxiliaries, by the time the French reached the line of the Medway. He described the yeomanry and volunteers as 'irregulars', which suggests that they would have assembled on the enemy's flanks and made small-scale, opportunist attacks on his outposts and lines of communication while the army engaged him on his front.[16] The movement of all available men, regulars and irregulars, towards the 'seat of war' remained the basic counter-invasion strategy to which the army adhered, the aim, of course, being to pen the invader in his bridgehead, or, failing that, to confine him to the line of advance most favourable to the defence. Volunteers, over 100,000 strong by the end of 1798, did have the strength to make envelopment work. This was why the government created incentives to wean them from local service and for them to train as regular infantry. This, too, was why the army ever deplored the small corps as 'unmanageable'. Ideally, the volunteers would have fitted easily into the army's organization and plan of operations and provided the district commands, which formed the loosely articulated structure of national defence the situation demanded, with the means of immediate reinforcement.

The concentration of the Grand Army on the Channel coast opposite Kent and Sussex in 1803 made it urgent not only to form a mass levy of some kind but also to formulate a plan for moving the huge numbers into the south-east in the event of invasion. The logistics of such an operation were daunting, to say the least. The movement had to be as rapid as possible, pointing to some way of transporting the troops, and its sheer scale surely would have made it the largest bureaucratic operation the state had ever attempted. Britain's 'cordon system of defence', the strategy of meeting the enemy by 'holding him as in a net', provided sound military reasons for discounting what spontaneous, uncoordinated guerrilla warfare could achieve, but Napoleon's threat lifted the emphasis on planning and organized defence to an altogether different level. Admittedly, on the outbreak of war in 1803, the old volunteer corps having been dispersed, the Duke of York had to look to independent companies the lieutenancies might raise, which could be fed into the war zone as 'irregulars' to attack outposts and small detachments.[17] However, once a mass volunteer force was initiated, the army began intensive work on 'a methodized and continued plan' to effect the great convergence on London. Corps were to be divided into 'marching' and 'stationary' companies, the latter staying behind to police their areas. Waggons to convey the men were arranged and fitted with removable seating. Further, each corps was brigaded under the command of regular officers

---

[16] Dundas, 'General Defence of the Southern District', Feb. 1798, WO30/65 (no. 7).
[17] York to Lord Hobart, 30 June 1803, Circular to generals commanding districts, 1 July 1803, WO1/625/333–6, 337–53.

MAP 1   The Volunteers and Home Defence in 1804. The Horse Guards' plan for the movement of volunteers

Source: Hope of Lufness MSS, SRO GD364/1/1149

and was meant to move with its brigade in order to facilitate its insertion into the defence line. The routes of the brigades were worked out to avoid congestion and carefully timed. Ten 'rendezvous' were appointed for the brigades in the vicinity of London before relays of 'post carriages' carried them the rest of the way. According to the army's calculations the arrangements could provide 38,000 volunteers for the defence of the eastern district in eleven days, 48,000 for the southern in five days, and 113,000 for London in twenty days from as far away as Wales and Scotland. Two hundred thousand men were therefore involved. Had it ever come off, such a movement would have been one of the marvels of pre-railway warfare.[18]

Some criticism of the 'cordon system' of defence emerged in 1804 when Lord Mulgrave, a minister who had been a serving general, sent Pitt a scheme for reducing the number of troops in south-east England in order to create an offensive force. Mulgrave recommended two large concentrations in Kent and Essex in the vicinity of the capital and linked by a convenient crossing-place on the Thames. He believed that the enemy's own preparations would reveal where he intended to attack, and that troops could be moved to the coast from this central area in ample time to contest the invasion. Pitt was approached because of 'the delicacy of even hinting such a change of arrangement to the Duke of York or Sir David Dundas'.[19] The consensus over counter-invasion strategy indeed owed much to the authority conceded these two in such matters and their long occupation of high military office, taking in most of the war. But Mulgrave's suggestions were also at odds with an all-pervading fear within the military and political leadership of what might ensue if the French, once landed, eluded or broke free of the British net. General Dundas, in offering advice and plans, made much of the moral advantage the defenders would possess if they increasingly outmatched the French in reinforcements and resources, attacked constantly, and always had safe country behind them. On the other hand, he warned of the enemy's well-earned reputation for mobility and aggressive manœuvre.[20] If the French turned the defence to gain the initiative, they could relieve their supply problem in the country's interior and had a much better chance of defeating their opposition in detail. The wider repercussions multiplied in the imagination, from a collapse of credit and trade to popular

[18] Alexander Hope, the deputy-quartermaster-general, did most of this planning. His papers on 'the movement of volunteers towards London' are found in Hope of Lufness MSS, SRO GD364/1/1149. See also the papers at WO1/628/431–6. The development of defence plans concerning the volunteers can be followed in Duke of York to Charles Yorke, 12 Nov. 1803, Chatham MSS, PRO30/8/244, fos. 124–7; circular to generals commanding districts, 27 Mar. 1804, WO30/76; York to Lord Camden, 25 May 1804, WO1/628/1–11; circular to generals of districts, 11 Aug. 1804, WO1/629/59–64.

[19] Mulgrave to Pitt, 9 July 1804, and untitled paper, Chatham MSS, PRO30/8/162, fos. 86–93.

[20] 'General Defence of the Southern District', Feb. 1798, WO30/65 (no. 7); 'Information and instructions for commanding generals and others', Feb. 1801, WO1/407/457–87.

insurrection. Contemplating these horrors, Lord Melville returned to 'the only rational plan', which was to meet the invader on or as near to the beaches as possible with 'torrents of armed men'.[21]

Melville was responding in particular to the increasing interest of the military in fortification as a way of having a second line of defence in case the enemy broke through the coastal cordon. He was obviously afraid that 'in depth' defence would lend itself to withdrawal from the coast with all the incumbent dangers of a deeply penetrating French invasion. Much of this new thinking came out of Ireland. After the rebellion and invasion in 1798, the British reconciled themselves to the fact that in Ireland they lacked sufficient force both to hold the coast and maintain civil order, and began planning a 'system of internal fortification' on which defence and counter-attack could be based however large the loss of territorial control. Cornwallis, who was lord lieutenant of Ireland 1798–1801, was particularly associated with these views. When commanding the eastern district during the invasion scare of 1801—'I tell you that in Essex, Suffolk and Norfolk I could not assemble a greater force than 2,600 militia bayonets and three regiments of dragoons'—he seems to have drawn a close parallel between Ireland's situation and Britain's and recommended fortresses in Kent and Essex to command the approaches to London.[22] But while this idea was taken up by the Duke of York in 1803,[23] there is nothing to suggest that the 'cordon system' was being discarded. An 'entrenched camp' at Chelmsford and extension of the 'lines' at Chatham were the only major works completed away from the coast. Much more effort continued to be expended on the seaward defences. Not only were the sea fencibles and the navy's armada of small craft for shallow water defence revived and expanded, but along the now constantly threatened southern and eastern coasts the previously vulnerable 'open' batteries were replaced by the famous and formidable barrier of Martello towers.[24]

If the chief strategic concern was to defend the perimeter to prevent the enemy

---

[21] Melville to Alexander Hope, 8 Oct. 1803, Hope of Lufness MSS, SRO GD364/1/1136/9.

[22] Cornwallis to Alexander Hope, 15 Aug. 1801, to the Duke of York, 6 Sept. 1801, ibid. 1131/1, 1083/2.   [23] York to Lord Hobart, 25 Aug. 1803, Melville MSS, SRO GD51/1/982/1.

[24] Glover, *Britain at Bay*, 103–24, gives an account of coastal and other fortifications, though he makes no mention of the Chelmsford camp, and indeed sometimes wrongly assumes that works surveyed were also commenced and completed. Glover further claims that the strengthened coastal defences were impregnable, which explains why Napoleon turned his attention to acquiring naval supremacy over Britain. The British did not regard them as impregnable, if their troop dispositions are any indication. As already noted, the reduction of the garrison in the south-east in support of the forces in southern Europe did not take place until 1811 at a time when Napoleon was commencing his moves against Russia. An excellent technical description of British fortifications in the Napoleonic period is A. Saunders, *Fortress Britain: Artillery Fortification in the British Isles and Ireland* (Liphhook, Hants, 1989), 130–45. See also N. Longmate, *Island Fortress: The Defence of Great Britain 1603–1945* (London, 1991), 274–83.

from acquiring a base area within the country, the army also appreciated the tactical advantages of falling on him at the moment of landing. Britain's generals had several generations of experience behind them when it came to the conduct of amphibious operations, and if they needed any reminder of the difficulties involved they had only to recall the Egyptian landing of 1801 when Abercromby's army deploying on the water's edge had to endure artillery fire and infantry volleys from an enemy ensconced on a high sand dune ridge.[25] The towers, each with the firepower of at least one hundred infantry,[26] were built to create havoc on the beaches out of the disorganization which inevitably attended the first stages of an invasion. With or without artillery, said the Duke of York, two thousand men rushing on the boats in 'a contest of valour', not military skill, were worth six thousand later on. 'Even the appearance of a distant though ill-armed multitude is of use', added Sir David Dundas.[27] Once the enemy was established ashore the tactical plan emphasized the importance of continual attack night and day to impose delay and keep him confined to the smallest area possible. Fortunately the defence was assisted by the 'enclosed and intricate country' of the south-eastern counties, which made it difficult for an invader to break away from a single line of march; but it was still felt necessary to have large numbers of civilian 'pioneers' ready to destroy or block roads in case there was movement to a flank or an attempt to broaden the front. The envelopment of the enemy force was also designed to exacerbate his supply problems. Cavalry and infantry constantly pressing against his flanks and rear would greatly impede his requisitioning efforts, rendered increasingly desperate if in the area he occupied horses and draught animals had previously been removed and all other supplies destroyed.[28]

So much of this was a thoughtful response to the new mode of warfare the revolutionary armies were seen to have developed and pursued with great success. The French had fought wars of manœuvre, not attrition, engaging in a search for battle, avoiding sieges where they could, and placing little importance on the mere occupation of territory. Typically, they won by gaining and holding the strategic initiative and by outmarching their opposition to achieve tactical surprise. Once engaged they were also urgent in attack, aggressiveness which the British were

---

[25] 'Thoughts of Sir George Murray upon Internal Defence', Hope of Lufness MSS, SRO GD364/ 1/1139/10. A description of the Aboukir landing by an officer who was present is found in *Annual Register*, xlv. 948–50.   [26] Glover, *Britain at Bay*, 118–19.

[27] York to Lord Hobart, 25 Aug. 1803, Melville MSS, SRO GD51/1/982/1; General Dundas, 'Volunteer Corps', 30 Aug. 1803, WO30/65.

[28] The army's plan of operations, drawn up by General Dundas, is described in 'Considerations on the Invasion of Great Britain 1796', WO30/65; 'Instructions from the Duke of York to the Generals Commanding Districts, [Feb. 1797], Kilmainham MSS, NLI MS 1004; 'General Defence of the Southern District', Feb. 1798, WO30/65 (no. 7); 'Information and Instructions for Commanding Generals', Feb. 1801, WO1/407/457–87.

wont to believe stemmed from the vanity and pride of the national character. In invading Britain the French were more than ever likely to want a short, decisive campaign because the Royal Navy could be expected to sever their lines of communication back to France and there was danger in having an army locked up in Britain if the Continental war resumed. As we have seen, on landing they would enjoy local superiority, but they would lose the initiative if they could not advance to replenish their resources and open a broader front. Any strategic advantage they might possess depended on their mobility; otherwise the weight of British resources was against them. The scenario of successful defence that General Dundas painted was that of an invading force cut off from France by the navy and increasingly hemmed in by the army and civilian auxiliaries until the moment arrived when the dispirited remnant could be safely attacked. Thus French mobility was to be defeated by British numbers; French *élan*, too, by an equally characteristic British perseverance.[29]

However, the most remarkable feature of British defence plans was the reliance placed on civilian co-operation and participation. It is not too much to say that the government intended to defeat the invader by mobilizing society itself against him. At the earliest stage of preparation the old schemes for 'driving the country' were revived,[30] but in February 1798 Henry Dundas shut himself away in his villa at Wimbledon to produce his 'Proposals for Rendering the People Instrumental in the General Defence'. Later embodied in legislation, the 'Proposals' looked to the civilian population to perform a variety of tasks separate from armed service, whether 'pioneers' to break up roads, waggon owners and 'drivers' to assist with evacuation and the movement of the army, or millers and bakers to contribute to the commissariat's supply. To take account of available manpower and other resources parishes were required to make returns to their lieutenancies.[31] Elaborate and comprehensive as these plans were, they represent as well as the mass volunteer movement does, or the great French mobilization of 1793–4, a significant shift

[29] There are some interesting remarks on the differences between British and French troops in Alexander Hope, 'Military Memoir for the Defence of the Eastern District', Nov. 1797, 41–3, Hope of Lufness MSS, SRO GD364/1/1083/1.

[30] The Duke of York sent Sir Charles Grey in the southern district the 'sketch of an arrangement' for driving Kent and Sussex, presumably derived from the American War, the day after Grey took up his command. York to Grey, 4 Aug. 1796, Univ. of Durham Library, 1st Earl Grey MS 826. Portland circularized the coastal counties on this subject on 5 Nov. 1796, and then asked for returns of 'dead and live stock' the following February. It was, however, left to the lieutenancies to devise practical measures. Cranmer-Byng, 'Essex Prepares For Invasion', 132, 187.

[31] For Dundas's 'Proposals' see *Annual Register*, xl, Chronicle, 183–9. The first Defence of the Realm Act (38 Geo. III, c. 27) was passed in March 1798, another in June 1803 (43 Geo. III, c. 55), and another in July 1803 (43 Geo. III, c. 96). Dundas was much influenced by Sir Charles Grey's plans for the southern district. See Ch. 1, n. 44 and Dundas to Grey, 19 Feb. 1798, Univ. of Durham Library, 1st Earl Grey MS 1323.

away from eighteenth-century 'limited' war in which, outside actual fighting zones, the civilian's role was marginal.

The extensiveness of the counter-invasion mobilization, as planned, is revealed by the so-called 'military' censuses of 1798, 1801, and 1803. At the apogee of the volunteer movement in 1803–5, it was not unusual for particular localities to be training 20 per cent or more of their men. But when enrolments under the Defence Acts are counted as well, the figures suggest something like a total mobilization in the most threatened areas. There certainly were country parishes where every able-bodied man offered his services; Debden in Essex, for example, with just over 200 men, undertook to provide 80 'pioneers' under a 'captain', 67 armed volunteers, 2 guides, 26 responsible for evacuation, and 36 to accompany 21 of the parish's carts and waggons.[32] But the number of offers over whole counties was also impressive; in 1798 Renfrewshire indicated that it would mobilize 40 per cent of its manpower, and Essex must have come close to 50 per cent.[33] Too much, of course, can be made of offers of service, which were easy to give and more difficult to enforce. The important point is that the government embarked on such a registration scheme for the purpose of organizing resistance under the auspices of established authority and in the expectation of receiving ample public co-operation. The 1790s, while Britain was developing a system of civilian-based defence, produced few examples of a 'people's war' against the French. Later, during the Napoleonic period, such conflicts took the form mainly of localized, extemporized guerrilla operations arising out of the defeat and withdrawal of the regular army and the breakdown of government in the face of enemy occupation. Britain, in other words, prepared to resist invasion in ways which were generally absent in the Continental warfare of the period. No other country organized its defence so elaborately, and none was so committed to the employment of the civilian mass, which, moreover, was to act with rather than in default of the army.

Admittedly, much of this is explained by Britain's peculiar circumstances; lacking a large army, Britain was necessarily more dependent than most on civilian auxiliaries. Yet it is also true that the mobilization of the civilian population for

---

[32] Debden returns, 14 Oct. 1803, Essex RO, D/P 242/17; list of persons resident taken in accordance with the Census Act, ibid. 242/18/3. Another example is Threckingham in Lincolnshire, all there, except servants, offering their services in 1798. See memorandum book of John Cragg, Lincoln RO, 2 Cragg 1/13. Drax was praised in its county's newspaper (*York Courant*, 14 Nov. 1803) for the same reason. At Airth, Stirlingshire, 89 out of 254 men aged 17–55 were volunteers. 'General arming— list for Airth parish', 2 Sept. 1803, Airth MSS, NLS MS 10896, fos. 10–16.

[33] Renfrewshire return, Tods, Murray and Jamieson Collection, SRO GD237/192/3. A 'statistical map' of Essex (Essex RO, L/R 1/3) notes a total of 23,536 offers of service. The very complete list of Buckinghamshire's 'posse comitatus' in 1798 suggests that the service class (males aged 15–60) made up 45 per cent of the total male population. I. F. W. Beckett, *The Buckinghamshire Posse Comitatus 1798* (Buckingham, 1985). If the same was true of Essex, the county's 'mobilization rate' was 47 per cent. Colley, *Britons*, 289–300 is interesting on the response to the Defence Acts.

home defence was more easily done than elsewhere, both because the society was remarkably cohesive, lacking the deeply embedded, institutionalized, often ethnic, particularisms typical of the Continental monarchies, and because public authority had the further advantage of having a firm consensual basis from parliament down to grand juries and local trusts, commissions, and charities. John Brewer has traced the development of the eighteenth-century British state mainly in terms of the growth of central authority under the pressures of war. Home defence, however, especially home defence which required massive civilian participation, was one area of the warfare state—another was military recruitment—where bureaucratic methods and bureaucratic effort counted for relatively little. True, there were national plans drawn up and, in the case of the Defence Acts, these were translated into acts of parliament; but in the final analysis, as indeed with most other forms of public enterprise, virtually everything depended on local interest and co-operation, if not local initiative. The organization of home defence during the French Wars endorses Paul Langford's view of eighteenth-century government, rather than Brewer's. In Langford's England local propertied élites, often quite broad-based, controlled an expanding area of public authority in which national policy and central regulation were, if present at all, deployed to support their interests and concerns.[34] While the security and armed power of the state were properly regarded as the business of the central government, localism could still prevail over declared national requirements, as the abject failure of the provisional cavalry in 1797 showed. The volunteers, too, remained impervious to attempts to make them into the efficient national defence force that the crown and the army wanted.

Henry Dundas, a centralist who clearly knew his limitations, counted his establishment of the Scottish lieutenancies in 1794 as possibly his most important achievement. Setting up local magnates to represent the crown in their counties and investing them with patronage opportunities was, to his mind, a 'permanent' reinforcement of government.[35] The lord lieutenants themselves were of less account than the organization that developed under them—deputy lieutenants, assisted by their own clerks, in the county subdivisions, and 'general' meetings of the gentry and magistracy. These 'general' meetings, which commenced in April–May 1794 when the government asked for county subscriptions, gave the lieutenancies a highly representative character, bringing together the leading men of the county who, in turn, were dealing with parish gentry and officials. At critical times they met frequently, advice given the Duke of Gordon, one of the new Scottish lieutenants.

---

[34] Langford, *Public Life*, esp. chs. 3–4.
[35] Dundas to Alexander Dirom, 7 Aug. 1797, Melville MSS, SRO GD51/1/888/2. See also Dundas to the Duke of Gordon, 14 May 1794, Gordon MSS, SRO GD44/47/14 for his views concerning the importance of the lieutenancy for defence and civil order.

Cambridgeshire, for example, held at least six 'general' meetings in the period July to October 1803.[36] The success of the lieutenancies in winning the support and co-operation of local élites was reflected in the county defence organization at its point of fullest development in 1803, when 'lieutenants' in subdivisions, 'inspectors' in hundreds, and 'superintendents' in parishes were appointed to form a hierarchy of command under the lord lieutenant.[37] The substitution of local militia for volunteers after 1808 completed the conversion of counties into defence communities, for the volunteer corps had largely evaded control by the lieutenancies.[38]

Yet, in the main, home defence exemplified the close union of local and central rulers which helped to make the British state exceptionally cohesive alongside the 'absolutist' monarchies and even Napoleon's bureaucratic regime. In this relative view a generally efficient communication was maintained more or less everywhere between the local organizers of defence and the central secretariats.[39] Such an extensive and workable system was built fundamentally on the widespread participation in public life that Langford has identified and which had done much to promulgate the idea of 'public service', itself further advanced by the anti-invasion mobilizations.[40] Parliamentary government and the press also made vital contributions to the strength of Britain's public culture. For the purposes of home defence, legislation and instruction were all that was needed by way of central exertion to assemble coalitions of local interests under the leadership of local grandees. No *intendants* or *représentants en mission* were sent out; even the enormous demands of the mass army which would materialize in the event of invasion were to be met as far as possible by voluntary offer and legal transaction. It is worth repeating that the defence of Britain involved an extraordinarily large and complex mobilization of the civilian population, the very preparation of which says a great deal about the

---

[36] R. Dundas, lord advocate to Duke of Gordon, 6 May 1798, ibid. 47/35. The *Cambridge Chronicle* reported meetings of the lieutenancy on 16 and 27 July, 3 Aug., 24 Sept., 8 and 22 Oct. Often the general meeting appointed a committee to meet more frequently to discharge business. Two articles based on lieutenancy minute books are J. W. Lee, 'Devon on Guard, 1759–1815', *Trans. Devonshire Assoc.* 40 (1908), 226–37 and Cranmer-Byng, 'Essex Prepares For Invasion'.

[37] This organization was set out in the Defence Act of 1803. In Scotland the lieutenancy meetings used their authority to the extent of demanding patriotic subscriptions from individuals according to the valuation of their properties under the cess or land tax. See *Edinburgh Evening Courant*, 17 Apr. (Ayr), 28 Apr. (Lanark), 1 May (Dumfries), 5 May (Argyll, Forfar), 10 May (Dunbarton, Stirling), 12 May (Linlithgow), 15 May (Inverness), 7 June (Selkirk), 10 July (Banff), 17 July (Elgin), 19 July (Renfrew), 28 July 1794 (Kincardine).   [38] Cookson, 'Volunteer Movement', 876–9.

[39] One failure was Orkney's reluctance to raise the militia in 1797–8. Lord Dundas to Portland, 4 Dec. 1797, HO102/15, fo. 250; Dundas to Duke of Gordon, 10 Apr. 1798, Gordon MSS, SRO GD44/47/27. Colley, *Britons*, 296–7, provides examples of non-compliance at the parish level.

[40] Langford, *Public Life*, ch. 4. See also K. Wilson, 'Urban Culture and Political Activism in Hanoverian England: The Example of Voluntary Hospitals', in Hellmuth, *Transformation of Political Culture*, 165–84.

MAP 2   The Defence of Ireland. Places mentioned in the text of Chapter 2

level of political and social integration that had been achieved. How well that organization would have stood up to the rigours of actual invasion is impossible to say, but the intention always was to avoid the methods of the *chouans* that represented the classic response of civil populations to armed attack. Castlereagh's local militia repudiated the idea of an 'armed peasantry', around which Windham's Training Act was framed, as much as it did the old volunteer system. Meanwhile, on the other side of the Irish Sea, the army was more an occupying force than an extension of the armed nation; war there, warned the future Duke of Wellington, 'will be for us one in an enemy's country'.[41]

Ireland deserves considerable attention because its defence was very differently organized with an expensive military infrastructure of barracks, depots, and fortifications planned and developed, particularly during the Napoleonic War. This proliferation of local military strongholds partly resulted from a conviction, after the experience of 1798, that invasion would trigger another insurrection; but it also recognized the fact that the country's interior was easily accessible from most parts of the coast, Ireland being well-roaded with a topography that posed few problems for an invading army. How Ireland could best be defended was an exceptionally difficult proposition which taxed many minds. No one on the British side doubted that the loss of Ireland would mean, at the very least, a serious weakening of British naval and military power in other parts of the world as forces were withdrawn for the protection of the national base. The view that Ireland was more likely to be attacked than Britain was entirely plausible, even ignoring the disturbed state of Irish society. The defenders had an impossibly long perimeter to guard, with numerous ports and harbours along the southern, western, and northern coasts, and Dublin itself not immune from attack by a sudden, unexpected thrust through St George's Channel.

The enemy, moreover, had the choice of several eligible routes. The passage from Brest to the south-west corner of Ireland was short and direct; it was branded on the consciousness of British generals and admirals that in December 1796 the French had 16,000 troops off Bantry Bay within three days.[42] Any fleet from the French bases at Brest and L'Orient, or further south from Spain, once at sea, could sail a straight course to Ireland's southern coast while the Royal Navy would have to beat a dog-leg around the Scillies.[43] A third route greatly diminished the chances of naval interception; by heading west out into the Atlantic and then north an invading force could surprise either the western or northern coasts. The

---

[41] [Sir Arthur Wellesley], Memorandum, 13 Dec. [1807], WO1/612/219–52.

[42] Thomas Pelham, Memorandum on the defence of Ireland, Feb. 1797, WO30/66/347–68; Cornwallis to Portland, 1 Nov. 1800, WO1/771/505–9.

[43] Lord Carhampton, commander-in-chief Ireland, drew a sketch to illustrate this point in a paper of Mar. 1795, Pelham MSS, BL Add. MS 33118, fos. 257–67.

Franco-Spanish alliances of 1796–1801 and 1804–6 were particularly threatening to Ireland because the combined fleets coming from the south or west possessed the sailing advantage and were strong enough to challenge the Royal Navy's local superiority. The worst situation of all occurred if the Baltic powers were also hostile, for they could sail an easy course to northern Ireland where Britain could offer only minimal naval protection. As General Dundas observed in 1801, the effect of the Armed Neutrality was to make 'every one point of the circuit of the two islands exposed'.[44] The threat, too, from the north was why the seizure of the Danish fleet at Copenhagen in 1807 was hailed by the government: 'our left flank', exalted Lord Hawkesbury, 'is now set compleatly at liberty'.[45]

Where an attack was most likely to fall was a topic for endless discussion among Ireland's military leadership. Having disregarded the south-west until the Bantry Bay scare,[46] the generals proceeded to concentrate on that area as the weakest point in the perimeter where Cork, especially, was the first great prize; at the close of the Revolutionary War, Colonel Alexander Hope was still ready to recommend that two-fifths of the regular force should be stationed west of a line running from Limerick to Cork.[47] Yet at the beginning of the Napoleonic War Dublin rapidly became the focus of concern. The British government soon knew of Napoleon's interest in Ireland as a way of supporting the main Channel operation by diversionary attacks elsewhere, and Emmet's rebellion in July 1803 helped to convince them that the French would be most tempted to try a *coup de main* against Dublin, where the national leadership of the insurrectionary movement was concentrated. The fortification of Dublin's coast and the heavy reinforcement of the Dublin garrison followed.[48] Hardly were the Martello towers in place than perception of the threat to Ireland changed again, this time in the light of the post-Trafalgar ascendancy of the Royal Navy and the increasingly unsettled state of western Ireland. Sir Arthur Wellesley, who, as chief secretary at Dublin and general waiting for a command, produced two important papers on the defence of Ireland at the end of 1807, believed a landing on the west coast to be the most likely, Galway

[44] General Dundas, 'Memorandum relative to the principal Bays and Harbours', 22 Jan. 1801, WO1/407/413–27.

[45] Hawkesbury to the Duke of Richmond, 16 Sept. 1807, Richmond MSS, NLI MS 70/1338.

[46] Pelham, the chief secretary, admitted as much. See his paper on the defence of Ireland, Feb. 1797, WO30/66/352.

[47] Hope, 'Report upon the Military State of Ireland', Nov. 1801, Murray MSS, NLS Adv. 46. 1. 6, fo. 28. David Dundas, Abercromby, and Hope in their reports all paid most attention to the south-west. Cornwallis, significantly, warned of the danger of neglecting the rest of the west coast as far north as Lough Swilly. Cornwallis to Lord Chatham, 7 Apr. 1803, Hope of Lufness MSS, SRO GD364/1/1138/2.

[48] Some beginnings of the process can be traced in Wickham to Lord Cathcart, 29 Dec. 1803, Hardwicke MSS, BL Add. MS 35775, fos. 66–7 and Admiral J. H. Whitshed to Wickham, 12 Jan. 1804, SPOI CSO VIIIA/1/13.

Bay in particular. He knew that an approach from the west by the enemy reduced the chances of naval interception, but he also believed that the French would drive straight for Dublin to forestall British reinforcements from across the Irish Sea, counting on popular uprisings to disperse the main defensive force. Galway Bay, and the Shannon for that matter, were close to disturbed districts where insurgents could be assembled and armed, as well as being a relatively short distance from the capital over the central plain. The Irish government responded to Wellesley's assessment by extending the programme of fortification still further; to reduce the now major threat from the west, huge fortresses, each capable of holding up to 6,000 men, were asked for at Galway and Kilbeggan.[49]

Wellesley stated the object of a French invasion to be 'revolution', the overthrow of British rule in Ireland and the 'establishment of a new government', presumably under the protection of a French army. It was always considered impossible for the French to maintain themselves in Ireland unless British power there was completely destroyed. This strategic goal of total victory, however, would have to be accomplished by a force of no more than 20,000 men, which by general agreement was the largest a fleet could carry without transports being involved to increase the risk of British naval attack.[50] Moreover, the invading army would be able to bring little except its arms and munitions, and was certain to be denied access to its home base for reinforcements and supplies by the navy. Meanwhile the defenders could freely ship in troops and *matériel* from Britain, using the short sea passage across the Irish Sea. But as the British generals realized only too well, these enormous advantages amounted to much less if insurrection broke out on the arrival of the French. They took it for granted that the enemy would come prepared to foment rebellion and that the population was highly susceptible to such appeals, if not already organized. In Ireland counter-invasion planning was always based on the assumption that a mass rising would occur, but also on the probability that it would be prevented if the invader was defeated quickly and given no time to establish a territorial base. In Britain the enemy was to be stopped at the coast for the defenders to bring their superior numbers into play; in Ireland he was to be held there and expelled as soon as possible because the numbers were potentially his. Perhaps Wellesley knew the better what he could

---

[49] Duke of Richmond to Lord Hawkesbury, 11 Jan. 1808, Liverpool MSS, Add. MS 38242, fos. 162–9. Wellesley's reports are at WO1/612/219–99.

[50] Hope in his report of Nov. 1801 pointed out that the Bantry Bay expeditionary force of not more than 17,000 men was carried in forty large ships, but were 'deficient in provisions and without horses'. 'When Sir Ralph Abercromby embarked with the first part of the expedition for Holland in '99 his army consisted of nearly 12,000 men who were embarked with a requisite proportion of horses and stores. . . . The fleet amounted in all to nearly 200 sail of which not less than 150 were employed in transport.' Murray MSS, NLS Adv. 46. 1. 6, fo. 20.

accomplish in Spain by having reflected on what a small French army assisted by a 'people's war' might accomplish in Ireland.

The army in Ireland, then, like the French army in Spain, was always trying to find the right balance of its counter-invasion and counter-insurgency roles. If to defeat an invasion quickly was also to diminish the chances of insurrection, the problem still was to achieve a concentration of sufficient strength soon enough but without dangerously depleting the local garrisons. What made matters worse was that only the elements of a field force usually existed because the generals were invariably under pressure to disperse the troops into small posts for the more effective policing of the country. Abercromby's efforts in 1798 to reassemble the battalions for the purpose of restoring the army's efficiency aroused the ire of the Irish establishment and were surely one of the reasons for his forced resignation after only a few months as commander-in-chief.[51] Cornwallis in 1799 divided his army between a 'moveable force' to take the field and a 'stationary force' to control the civil population. With little more than a third of his troops in the former, the dissipation of the army's strength into occupation of the country is obvious. Cornwallis's field force of 18,993 rank and file was considerably larger than the one his predecessors could have deployed, but still fell short of giving the British in Ireland a decisive numerical superiority if a full-scale invasion occurred; Colonel Hope, for one, believed 50,000 men were needed.[52] Thus, however successfully the army concentrated against the invader, there was a good chance that it would have to fight on fairly equal terms. Contrary to the situation in Britain, it might also have to operate surrounded by a civilian population more disposed to assist the enemy than the reverse. In Ireland the organization of home defence under the civil power did not proceed much beyond the formation of volunteer corps, or yeomanry as they were called. Though their numbers reached 50,000 in 1801 and over 70,000 subsequently, no plans were made to incorporate them in the field army in the event of invasion as happened in Britain. Instead, their main task was

---

[51] John Hope to Alexander Hope, 20 Mar. 1798, Hope of Lufness MSS, SRO GD364/1/1090. Alexander Hope to Dundas, 3 Apr. 1798, Melville MSS, NLI MS 54A/132.

[52] Castlereagh agreed. Castlereagh to Wickham, 26 Aug. [1803], Wickham MSS, Hampshire RO, 38M49/1/6/34. Cornwallis's 'moveable' and 'stationary' force is listed in 'Sketch of the forces proposed to be first moved in the event of an enemy's landing', 25 Mar. 1799, Chatham MSS, PRO30/8/323, fos. 61–2. For a distribution in 1800 see Morrison MSS, NLI MS 5006/48. Hope in the first years of the war doubted whether more than 8,000 men could have been 'brought upon one point'. He wanted half of Ireland's military force, including the yeomanry, to remain in garrison in the event of invasion, and the other half to form the field army. See his report, Murray MSS, NLS Adv. 46. 1. 6, fos. 2, 27–8. In 1798 Abercromby believed that it would take a week to assemble 10,000 men to oppose the French at Bantry Bay or the lower Shannon, and this force could be increased to no more than 15,000–16,000. Abercromby, 'Outline of the Defence of Ireland', 28 Apr. 1798, Melville MSS, NLI MS 54A/135. There were similar calculations in 1803. See Wickham to Castlereagh, 14 Aug. 1803, Wickham MSS, Hampshire RO, 38M49/1/7/17.

to be the patrol of their districts, especially to prevent insurgent bands from forming and joining the French. Much of their usefulness as an anti-invasion force was
limited, anyway, because about half were raised in Ulster, remote from the more
threatened southern and western coasts.[53]

Ireland's vulnerability to foreign attack, therefore, does not need to be emphasized by historians; it kept the generals constantly on edge, at least until the latter
stages of the Napoleonic War when the threat to Great Britain also eased as the
French became embroiled in Spain and later eastern Europe. Military reports,
significantly, gave increasing attention to 'interior defence' on the supposition that
the enemy had landed in force and occupied considerable territory. Colonel Hope
in 1801 regretted that Abercromby had carried his plan of operations no further
than the retirement of the army behind the Blackwater river on the loss of Cork.
He detailed the army's movements if the enemy attempted an advance from Cork
into Tipperary and recommended dispositions to hold the line of the Shannon or
that between Lough Erne and Lough Neagh. Likewise Colonel Thomas Graham,
later of Peninsular fame, identified a 'line of interior defence' running from Belfast
across to Lough Erne and the Shannon and from the lower Shannon across country to the Suir, and also a 'second line' covering Dublin's hinterland. Ireland's open
country, well-roaded and undefended by fortifications of any kind, gave particular
importance to the Shannon—'the greatest feature of Nature', said Graham, 'in a
military point of view'.[54] As fears of an attack from the west took hold after 1805,
the batteries guarding the Shannon bridges and fords were strengthened and even
Martello towers erected in two places.[55] The Shannon, however, defended only
Ireland's western 'front'. Dublin, the greatest prize for an invader who thought in
terms of revolution as well as conquest, was assailable from many other points.
The military planners permitted themselves to think of all Ireland lost except
control of Dublin's port—and possibly Cork harbour, which was considered equally
defensible though the city was taken. They dwelt repeatedly on the importance

---

[53] Yeomanry numbers during the Revolutionary War are given in 'Yeomanry force', 31 Oct. 1801,
Colchester MSS, PRO30/9/124, fo. 227. A return dated 24 Dec. 1805 totals 67,221 effective men.
SPOI CSO OP198/17. The yeomanry's duties are described in 'Arrangement of the Yeomanry Corps
by Major-General Morrison', Apr. 1800, Morrison MSS, NLI MS 5006/46, and in Wellesley's paper
on Ireland's defence, Dec. 1807, WO1/612/255–99. For county lists of yeomanry see *CJ* lix. 503;
lxiii. 618.

[54] Hope, 'Report on the Defence of Ireland', Nov. 1801, Murray MSS, NLS Adv. 46. 1. 6, fos. 9,
29–45; Graham, 'Memorandum concerning the present state of Ireland and the means of defending it',
Feb. 1804, Hope of Lufness MSS, SRO GD364/1/1146/26.

[55] A committee of engineers in 1805–6 recommended that £27,000 be spent on strengthening the
Shannon 'passes'. 'Abstract of . . . three reports of a committee of Royal Engineers', ibid. 1160/8.
Saunders, *Fortress Britain*, 149–50, and K. P. Ferguson, 'The Army in Ireland From the Restoration
to the Act of Union', Ph.D. thesis (Trinity Coll., Dublin, 1981), 132–3, describe the Shannon works.
The Enniskillen 'passes' were also strengthened to help contain a French drive into Ulster.

of saving the 'communication' with Britain by which troops could be landed in Ireland for its eventual re-conquest.[56] The most impressive fortification started during the wars was the Pigeon House fort extending into Dublin Bay, a work designed to provide a safe anchorage and landing place even without a garrison in the city itself. Cork harbour became similarly protected with an array of forts, batteries, and towers.[57] These two places were truly made the citadels of British power in Ireland where the success of a French invasion would be finally decided.

The interest taken in 'internal' fortresses after the 1798 rebellion further shows how unsure the military were that the country's defences would hold. Cornwallis, while lord lieutenant, first suggested these, and, soon afterwards, Colonel Hope presented firmly argued recommendations as to their location. On getting a proposal from General Dundas as well, the British government appointed William Twiss, a colonel of engineers, to assess the two plans on the basis of his own observations in Ireland. He reported back early in 1803, in time for the whole subject to be suspended on the outbreak of war when all attention was concentrated on what could be immediately provided. The discussion was renewed in 1805, with a committee of engineers making the main contribution, but seems to have died away in 1808, presumably because invasion became scarcely conceivable.[58] This itself indicates that the primary purpose of such very expensive works was to impede the operations of an invading army, not to subdue the civil population. The fortresses, as proposed, were to guard the approaches to Dublin from the south, west, and north. With garrisons of up to 6,000 men, they could not be easily bypassed by the enemy, who anyway would lack the numbers to blockade them and the artillery to capture them. As depots and magazines, they would also accelerate the army's

[56] See paper, probably by Sir George Murray when quartermaster-general in Ireland in 1805, Murray MSS, NLS Adv. 46. 1. 6, fos. 137–43; 'Abstract of . . . three reports of a committee of Royal Engineers', Hope of Lufness MSS, SRO GD364/1/1160/8. Richmond, the lord lieutenant, said the 'first object' was to secure the 'communication' between Britain and Ireland, with Dublin the most important point in this respect. Richmond to Hawkesbury, 11 Jan. 1808, Liverpool MSS, BL Add. MS 38242, fos. 162–9.

[57] Ferguson, 'Army in Ireland', 135, 137. The Pigeon House fort was proposed by the engineers in Nov. 1805, but work did not commence until 1813, perhaps because the lord lieutenant, as advised by his chief secretary, Wellesley, was not convinced. See extract of the engineers' first report, 23 Nov. 1805, Clinton MSS, NLI MS 10215; Wellesley's memorandum, 13 Dec. 1807, WO1/612/219–52; Richmond to Hawkesbury, 11 Jan. 1808, Liverpool MSS, BL Add. MS 38242, fos. 162–9.

[58] The proposal of fortresses is mainly covered in Cornwallis to Portland, 1 Nov. 1800, WO1/771/501–2; Hope, 'Report on the Defence of Ireland', Nov. 1801, Murray MSS, NLS Adv. 46. 1. 6, fos. 11–13, 47–8, 51–2; William Twiss to Lord Chatham, 15 Jan. 1803, WO30/73; Cornwallis to Duke of York, 20 Apr. 1802, Cornwallis to Chatham, 7 Apr. 1803, Hope, 'On the different systems of defence proposed for Ireland', 5 Mar. 1803, 'Abstract of . . . three reports of a committee of Royal Engineers', Hope of Lufness MSS, SRO GD364/1/1132/2, 1138/2, 1143/2, 1160/8; Chatham, 'Private memoranda for General Mann', 22 July 1805, Liverpool MSS, BL Add. MS 38359, fos. 1–4; Wellesley, 'Memorandum', Dec. 1807, WO1/612/219–52; Lord Harrington to Wellesley, 7 Jan. 1808, Wellington MSS, Univ. of Southampton WP1/187/47.

concentration against the invader or, in the event of defeat, serve as bases to fall back on for reinforcements and the replenishment of supplies.

The decision not to build 'interior' fortresses becomes particularly interesting in view of the heavy expenditure on barracks and permanent coastal defences in the latter stages of the Napoleonic War. After 1807 Martello towers were built at all the principal anchorages an invader might use—Wexford, Waterford, Cork, Bantry, Galway, Lough Swilly, and Lough Foyle. In addition, the existing forts were improved and batteries better protected with masonry.[59] At the same time the government embarked on a barrack-building programme that increased the 'permanent' accommodation for troops from 33,000 in 1806 to 44,000 by the end of the war.[60] Clearly, a military infrastructure was being created which focused on the threat of insurrection. As we have seen, it had become a principle of counter-invasion strategy in Ireland that the enemy should be prevented, if at all possible, from establishing a territorial base, since nothing would better set the conditions for a general rising. Ideally, the invader would be defeated on the coast.[61] The heavy investment in coastal defence, therefore, manifesting as it did a heightened determination to defend the perimeter, complemented the spread of barracks intensifying the army's occupation of the country. After the rebellion of 1798, and with increasing public disorder and sectarian conflict, Britain cherished no illusions that the old pre-war military establishment of 10,000 rank and file was adequate any longer for the effective government of Ireland. With little exaggeration it can be said that the eighteenth-century army used Ireland to hold the cadres on which an expansion in the event of war could be based; the nineteenth-century army was used to hold Ireland itself.

[59] Saunders, *Fortress Britain*, 147–9. The programme of works is set out in the abstract of the engineers' reports, Hope of Lufness MSS, SRO GD364/1/1160/8.

[60] 'Precis of the correspondence relative to the erection of permanent and the surrender of temporary barracks in Ireland', SPOI CSO OP239/17; 'Statement of General the Earl of Harrington's proposition for the erection of permanent barracks . . . and the proceedings had thereupon', 19 Feb. 1811, ibid. 342/5; 'Answers of General Freeman . . . on the proposed reduction of the Barrack Department', 30 Mar. 1816, ibid. 456/41. There were permanent barracks, built or in preparation, for 27,000 men in 1801. See 'Progressional increase of barracks in Ireland from the commencement, in the middle and at the close of the late war', 17 Nov. 1801, Colchester MSS, PRO30/9/172, fo. 81.

[61] The engineers' committee (see n. 58 above), recommending 'that a decided and early attention should be paid to the sea coast defence', is worth quoting: 'considering the great extent of coast and the numerous good harbours in Ireland, there is not any (maritime) country in Europe that will have, proportionably, so little of coast defence as this; and yet there are reasons which might justly induce rather a greater than a less proportion of it in this kingdom than in most others. For on the supposition that there may be disaffection in the country, while that evil exists, it is of the utmost importance to prevent, if possible, a landing of any considerable force of the enemy, as they would probably be so soon joined by large bodies of the inhabitants.' Hope was critical of 'the multiplication of sea forts and batteries' which an enemy on landing could easily isolate, and Wellesley called them 'entirely useless' with few exceptions.

Thus while the physical determinants of home defence remained the same for Ireland as for Britain—a long perimeter to defend, an interior accessible from most parts of the coast, and a capital vulnerably sited—the social determinants could hardly have been more different. Britain's defence depended on 'public spirit', the participation of the civilian mass, armed and unarmed; in this respect, of course, it looked forward to the warfare society of the twentieth century based on universal service and social consensus. Ireland's defence was built around the fact of a divided society, which severely limited civilian mobilization and required the army and government to devote considerable resources to the problem of possible insurrection. Though the country was exposed to relatively small-scale invasion in Continental terms, it was always accepted that the attack and defence were finely balanced because invasion and insurrection might combine. Nothing made Ireland more secure to Britain than the expansion of Britain's own home defence forces. Without the massive increase of volunteers in 1798, up to a third and more of the militia strength could never have been transferred to Ireland in the aftermath of the rebellion. Once the military potential of the home population had been better developed, the generals felt more confident about the security of the national base and were freer to send forces outside Britain, and also the British Isles, as the situation demanded. In the last year of the Napoleonic War of 1803–14, there were about as many regulars stationed in Britain as there had been during the peace of 1802–3—and then a sizeable proportion of them were troops waiting at their depots for passages overseas. At the same time the regular garrison in Ireland was down to what it had been (under 10,000 men) before war had started in 1793.[62]

Thus the British armed nation became the ultimate guarantee of British rule in Ireland; in this sense, there is the paradox that Ireland was held more firmly after 1798 than before. What developed during the war was a British Isles system of defence, which in turn was part of a larger strategic system for the projection of British power over much of the world. A key change was when local forces, previously confined to the separate kingdoms, accepted service outside these limits. This process began early in the war when the government in 1794 asked for 2,000 Scottish fencibles to serve in England.[63] Later the same year many new fencible regiments were raised in England and Scotland for the express purpose of replacing regulars in Ireland. The militias followed the same path more slowly. The English regiments that crossed to Ireland in 1798–9 served on condition of staying no longer than a year; afterwards, the frequent offers of the Irish to reciprocate

---

[62] On 1 Jan. 1803 there were 28,095 regular troops in Great Britain. In Oct. 1813 they numbered 33,808. I take these figures from a return dated 17 Dec. 1806 giving the effective strength of the British army, 1793–1806, WO1/903/33, and from a return giving the 'present state of the British army serving in Great Britain and Ireland', 15 Oct. 1813, WO25/3225.

[63] Lord Adam Gordon to Lord Amherst, 24 Feb. 1794, HO102/9, fos. 186–7.

were never taken up. However, in 1811 the 'interchange' of militias was passed by parliament and commenced with the transfer of twenty-five English and Scottish and fourteen Irish regiments. It was the presence in Ireland of over 10,000 'British' militia that made it possible to strip the regular garrisons there for the benefit of the army in Spain, a case in point of how freeing up the deployment of the home forces within the United Kingdom paid dividends where grand strategy was concerned.

Throughout the war the traffic of troop transports across the Irish Sea remained very heavy. Cork and the south of Ireland were important holding areas for units going to and from North America, the Caribbean, and the Mediterranean. In addition, the heavy recruitment of Irish manpower had its effect as regiments came in to replenish their ranks and were removed as soon as possible to help lower desertion rates. The three main routes linking Britain and Ireland were Portsmouth to Cork in the south, Liverpool to Dublin, and Portpatrick to Donaghadee in the north. It was not unusual for 10,000 troops to be shifted between the two countries in the course of a year, and at two tons of shipping per man a small fleet of transports must have been more or less permanently maintained outside the winter season.[64] In emergencies the distance of Ireland from the major troop concentrations in Britain—Essex and Kent—was surmounted by using the London–Liverpool canals, whose utility was perhaps discovered in 1798 when reinforcements for Ireland were rushed along this route.[65] Such an amount of troop movement over a long period had some widespread effects. The strategic union of the British Isles that the army and government wished for depended on a large infrastructure of barracks, ports, shipping, and roads; the more reliable the internal movement of troops could be made, the less critical the distribution of them on the periphery. The weakest, though still vital, link in the chain of Anglo-Irish communication was in south-west Scotland. Roads towards Portpatrick were poor, the area thinly settled, and from Portpatrick itself regiments could only be sent over in batches, 'it being impossible to dispatch more than a few of the packets each tide, and their

---

[64] The register (National Archives, Ireland M. 464) kept by the paymaster-general's office in Dublin records the embarkation and disembarkation of units coming on and leaving the Irish establishment. Not all, but most units would have arrived from or departed for Britain. This register produces the following count of arrivals in Ireland during the Napoleonic War: 1804, 12 units; 1805, 4; 1806, 18; 1807, 30 (many from the South American expeditionary force); 1808, 6; 1809, 5; 1810, 13; 1811, 27 (26 militia); 1812, 3; 1813, 42 (35 militia). The number of troops involved is harder to establish. There are returns indicating that 37,091 men embarked from Ireland from the beginning of the war until Dec. 1794 and that from then until Sept. 1795 Ireland sent away 10,420 men and 1,226 horses and received 11,988 men from England. See Pelham MSS, BL Add. MS 33118, fos. 249–55. An order of 13 Nov. 1804 appropriating transports for three infantry regiments (2,052 all ranks) lists eleven vessels totalling 4,051 tons. Leven and Melville MSS, SRO GD26/9/527/4/30.

[65] Duke of York to Windham, 10 Dec. 1806, Windham MSS, BL Add. MS 37842, fo. 195; J. W. Gordon to Sir J. Cockburn, 10 Dec. 1806, WO1/633/495–7. For 1798 see n. 69 below.

sailing is sometimes interrupted for weeks'. Loch Ryan, therefore, was developed as an alternative transit point, partly on the strength of the engineer Thomas Telford's recommendation. It offered sheltered water and enough sea room for navigation in and out of the loch in most conditions.[66]

On three occasions this Anglo-Irish strategic system was put to a stern test. The best known of these was the outbreak of rebellion in May 1798 when the government ordered reinforcements on 2 June and again on 8 June. The first wave, directed to the south of Ireland to protect Cork and Waterford, two key naval harbours, consisted of a brigade of fencible infantry from the Channel Islands and another of regulars.[67] The second wave was made up of a Guards brigade which marched from London for embarkation aboard men-of-war at Portsmouth and an infantry brigade that crossed over to Ireland from Scotland. The two battalions from Scotland had arrived by 18 June, completing the movement to Ireland of some 6,000 troops in four divisions within the space of three weeks.[68] There was an even faster and stronger response to the French landing in Killala Bay in August 1798, or, more correctly, to reports of General Hutchinson's defeat at Castlebar amid the flight of his Irish militia. Twelve English militia regiments, about 9,000 men, were immediately set in motion, requisitioning waggons and carriages and, in some cases, travelling by the canals to speed their march. Seven thousand were in Ireland in thirteen days.[69] The third episode involving a large and urgent transfer of troops to Ireland occurred in December 1806 and is less well known. The Talents administration, convinced that there was a French hand in disturbances in the west of Ireland, provided a powerful force of 5,000 men in two

[66] Alexander Dirom, 'Memoir of the Military State of North Britain in 1803', NLS MS 1754, pp. 66–7; 'Memorandum concerning papers relative to the passage of troops from Scotland to Ireland', 14 June 1808, Hope of Lufness MSS, SRO GD364/1/1184/20.

[67] Dundas to Duke of York, 2 June 1798; York to Dundas, 2 June 1798, HO30/2, fos. 30–6; Pitt to Lord Camden, 2 June 1798, Chatham MSS, PRO30/8/325, fos. 9–10. The corps were the 2nd, 29th, and 100th, and the Glengary, Nottingham, and Cheshire fencibles.

[68] Cabinet minute, 8 June 1798, Duke of York's memorandum [8 or 9 June 1798], *George III Corresp.* iii. 73–4. Ferguson, 'Army in Ireland', 182, exaggerates the strength of the reinforcements, probably accepting Pitt's statement on 2 June that 5,000 were being sent in the first wave. I get my figures from York to Dundas, 2 June 1798, HO30/2, fos. 34–6 and 'State of the infantry regiments at home', 17 July 1798, WO1/619/247–9. For the landing of the troops from Scotland see *Faulkner's Dublin Journal*, 23 June 1798. The government originally sought a brigade of fencibles from Scotland, but the Strathspey regiment was deemed too inefficient and the men of the Gordon and Breadalbane regiments refused to go. The Sutherland fencibles and the under-strength Royals (1st) made up the brigade. Camden was promised a reinforcement of 8,000. Elliott, *Partners in Revolution*, 204.

[69] Duke of Portland to the king, 1 Sept. 1798, Duke of York to the same, 2 Sept. 1798, *George III Corresp.* iii. 114, 118–19; Portland to York and memorandum, 1 Sept. 1798, Melville MSS, NLI MS 54A/147–8. For the speedy arrival of the militia see Capt. H. Taylor to Col. Brownrigg, 14 Sept. 1798, ibid. 153. I take regimental strengths from Ferguson, 'Army in Ireland', 181. A description of a militia regiment's march on this occasion is found in W. J. Cripps, *The Royal North Gloucester* (London, 1875), 70–1.

regular brigades, one of which again used the canals to reach Liverpool and cross over to Dublin. The troops received their orders on 10 December and all arrived between 4 and 8 January.[70]

After 1798, therefore, the advantages of strategic union—national defence conceived as the defence of the British Isles with all parts lending their aid as required—were patently clear to the generals who now began to prepare for invasion by having reserves and transports ready to rush reinforcements across the Irish Sea to the enemy's point of entry. Nor was this always conceived in terms of Britain's vulnerability through Ireland. In 1803 Alexander Hope, as adjutant-general in Ireland, proposed that up to 10,000 troops be sent from there if an invasion of Britain occurred; earlier, during the crisis of 1801, he had assembled transports in the south of Ireland for the same purpose.[71] Nevertheless it remains true that concern for Ireland, particularly over the reliability of the Irish militia, remained the single most important factor promoting the interchange of local forces. Cornwallis, commanding in post-rebellion Ireland, was keen to Britannicize the Irish garrison by this measure, and the politicians of the Ascendancy no less so. But at this point the debate over Catholic emancipation intervened and the issue of interchange came to turn on the larger issue of whether the state could depend on the loyalty of Irish Catholics.[72] It is not emphasized enough that, beginning with the establishment of the Irish militia in 1793, Pitt and Dundas mapped out a position that was basically hostile to the Ascendancy in the efforts they made to promote Catholic service. In despairing of an Irish Protestant particularism obstructive of the real interests of the state, their great fear was that British forces might become embroiled in an Irish civil war by a ruling class that deliberately set out to achieve this result. When in 1798 large numbers of troops were committed to Ireland, they were sent reluctantly—'Mr Dundas does not feel it possible *not* to advise your Majesty to concur in the measure now proposed and arranged'—and with specific instructions to the Irish government that their task was to defeat

---

[70] Lord Spencer to the king, 9 Dec. 1806, *George III Corresp.* iv. 494; Windham to Duke of York, 9 Dec. 1806, York to Windham, 10 Dec. 1806, Windham MSS, BL Add. MS 37842, fos. 193–5; J. W. Gordon to Sir J. Cockburn, 10 Dec. 1806, WO1/633/495–7. The brigades sent were General Hill's (1st battalions of 9th, 14th, and 91st) and Sir Arthur Wellesley's (1st battalions of 3rd, 7th, and 8th). For their strengths see the returns of 1 Jan. 1807 in Dropmore MSS, BL Add. MS 59290. Dates of arrival are given in the paymaster-general's register, National Archives, Ireland, M. 464.

[71] Hope, 'Report on the defence of Ireland', Murray MSS, NLS Adv. 46. 1. 6, fo. 46; Col. Brownrigg to Hope, 22 July 1801, Hope of Lufness MSS, SRO GD364/1/1127/3; Brownrigg to John Sullivan, 7 Aug. 1801, WO1/623/409–11; Lord Hardwicke to Lord Hobart, 20 Aug. 1801, Hobart MSS, Buckingham RO, D/MH/H/War/G13. In 1803 eight or nine large transports were to be held in Loch Ryan with a force of 3,000 men near enough to be rapidly shipped to Ireland. C. Yorke to Lord Moira, 29 Nov. 1803, Moira, *HMC, Hastings MSS* (4 vols., London, 1928–47), iii. 126; Brownrigg to Moira, 19 Dec. 1803, Hardwicke MSS, BL Add. MS 35775, fos. 62–3.

[72] See Ch. 6 for longer treatment of the militia interchange issue.

rebellion and not to wage war on the Catholic community. On announcing the reinforcement to the lord lieutenant, Pitt wrote in a private letter:

There are two conditions you must allow me to ask personally from you. One, that their continuance shall be only temporary while the real exigency lasts, as on their return may depend all chance of vigorous operations from hence during the war. The other (which I feel even of more importance) is that you shall use the force only for purposes consistent with your own principles & feelings, and shall resist with as much firmness the intemperance of your friends as you do the desperate efforts of the enemy.[73]

Dundas, especially, was master of views about strategy that took in Britain's world position and, further, related the role of local forces beyond home defence to this larger context. Probably his first thought when rebellion broke out in Wexford in 1798 was to keep possession of the harbours at Cork and Waterford for the navy. Moreover, while the British struggled to reassert their authority in Ireland he had more than half an eye on Bonaparte in Egypt, asking for precious troops to be sent to India.[74] His understanding that 'the great foundation of everything we can do offensively must rest on establishing a sentiment of perfect security at home' was what made him stage a ministerial crisis in February 1798 by offering to resign. He was already hard at work on the organization of home defence, which was really Portland's responsibility, but the absurdity of dividing management of the war between two ministers seems to have finally broken his patience when he was considering cross-Channel raids by the army in Kent; that is to say, the 'foreign' and the 'home' conduct of the war became merged.[75] Portland put up no fight. No longer war minister after 1801, Dundas looked back proudly to this period of unambivalent authority when, he said, he had ensured 'that the country should be so armed as to feel perfect security through every part', therefore allowing the army to act effectively abroad:

during the three last years I was in office I never felt a moment's concern on the subject of invasion, and never had a hesitation in sending the regular force out of the country to any

[73] Pitt to Lord Camden, 2 June 1798, Chatham MSS, PRO30/8/325, fos. 9–10; Dundas to the king, 2 June 1798, *George III Corresp.* iii. 70. Dundas's despair over Ireland is well caught in a letter to Windham: 'On the subject of Ireland, it is long since I wrote to you my sentiments which have never varied, and some recent occurrences have much confirmed [them]. But perceiving from a variety of causes that no good would ever be attempted (I mean upon the principles I entertain) I have ceased to occupy my mind upon the subject, and, unless saved by the fleet, I give up Ireland as lost.' Dundas to Windham, 10 Apr. 1798, Melville MSS, SRO GD51/1/912/2.
[74] Dundas to the king, 2 June 1798, *George III Corresp.* iii. 70; Dundas to the Duke of York, 18 June 1798, WO6/131/184–90.
[75] Dundas, 'Suggestions relative to the defence of our own coast combined with the means of annoying the enemy', [Dec. 1797], Dundas to Lord Spencer, 9 Feb. 1798, WO30/64, fos. 115–22; Dundas to Pitt, 10 Feb. 1798, Chatham MSS, PRO30/8/157, fos. 236–45; Dundas to Lord Grenville, 12 Feb. [1798], Grenville, *Dropmore MSS* iv. 79–80.

part of the world where their service was required, and I am at least entitled to look back with satisfaction to the extraordinary circumstance which took place in the last war, viz. that notwithstanding the many conquests we made we never lost a single possession during the whole of that extensive and complicated contest.[76]

The successful Egyptian campaign of 1801 was the grand epitome of Dundas's ideas because its conception ran against other views in the Cabinet in favour of defensive war or operations nearer to home and because, in the event, an invasion crisis was weathered while the pick of the army was far away.[77]

A national base fully competent to its defence by large-scale civilian mobilization was thus the foundation of Dundas's strategy. Nor was it lost on him that the Mediterranean armies of 1800–1 included numerous volunteers from the militia taken in 1798–9, strengthening his conviction that the armed nation would not only give Britain the military means to claim genuine status as a great power but would also sustain the army with the manpower it required by making the civilian population accustomed to military service and military careers accordingly more attractive.[78] On the whole, these were the ideas by which successive administrations acted for the remainder of the war. Much thought continued to be given to home defence, particularly over what might replace the volunteer mass once its efficiency and effectiveness were seriously doubted. Britain ended the war with a system of local militia which in its principles was not unlike the territorial army of the future. Dundas's predictions that the auxiliaries would become an important source of recruits for the army were largely realized, at least with respect to the militia, which after 1811 surrendered annual drafts of men. Under the pressure of the final offensive against Napoleon, the deployment of the militia widened, further breaking down its separateness from the army. Dundas had pushed the fencibles of the 1790s into serving anywhere in the British Isles and later in the Mediterranean garrisons and America.[79] His successors organized the interchange of the British and Irish militias and in the last months of the war in 1813–14 sent militia to Holland and France. This may have undermined decisively the idea that they were a home force only, for never again were they regarded exclusively so. Above all, the government, increasingly able to use the militias flexibly, was increasingly able to organize national defence so as to maximize the army's

[76] Dundas to Sir James Pulteney, 6 Apr. 1803, Melville MSS, SRO GD51/1/979. See also Dundas to Alexander Hope, 16 Dec. 1803, Chatham MSS, PRO30/8/157, fos. 294–7.

[77] The Cabinet conflicts over strategy in 1800 are detailed in P. Mackesy, *War Without Victory: The Downfall of Pitt 1799–1802* (Oxford, 1984).

[78] See e.g. Lord Melville to General Vyse, 14 July 1803, Melville to the lord advocate, 11 Aug. 1803, Hope of Lufness MSS, SRO GD364/1/1136/1–2; 'Lord Melville's Sketch of a Military System' [1803], Melville MSS, SRO GD51/1/754.

[79] 'List of the regiments of fencible infantry', Aug. 1799, WO1/620/533–5.

offensive capability. When in 1801 the army went to fight the French in Egypt, about a third of the regular force remained in Great Britain, slightly more than half in the British Isles. Towards the end of 1813 Britain retained only a seventh of the total, the British Isles under a fifth. This was what the armed nation made possible.[80]

---

[80] For 1801 see 'Return of the effectives in the British army, 1 January 1793–1 January 1806', 17 Dec. 1806, WO1/903/33. I use the figures for 1 Jan. 1802. For 1813 see 'Return of the present state of the British army serving in Great Britain and Ireland', 15 Oct. 1813, WO25/3225 and 'Return of the effective strength of the British army in rank and file from 1804 to 1813', 13 Nov. 1813, *CJ* lxix. 638 (where my total is of infantry and cavalry only).

3

The Rise and Fall of the Volunteers

FROM 1798 until the formation of the local militia exactly ten years later Britain had a system of home defence based on mass volunteering. There was a volunteer establishment of 116,000 in 1798, 146,000 in 1801, and 380,000 in 1804; numbers never less than half the total home force, and sometimes as high as two-thirds.[1] This huge mobilization, simply the greatest popular movement of the Hanoverian age, has always been regarded as the leading feature of the British armed nation, even its definition. Yet it is worth going back to the government's, or Dundas's, original conception of national defence *en masse* before it was overtaken by volunteering—not something the government planned or particularly wanted to happen. Dundas in 1797 responded to a defence plan published by an officer and acquaintance on the Scottish staff by outlining the civilian forces as he conceived them 'after the transactions which have taken place in the world within these few years'. His 'basis' for national defence, 'much the best' in the new age of warfare that had dawned, was 'general' or compulsory training of 19- or 20-year-olds, out of which trained population a militia for territorial, local, and non-combatant service, and of any size, could be drawn as the situation demanded. At this time he was already putting these views into practice with the supplementary militia and the Scottish militia which were both significant departures from the 'old' militia system instituted in 1757. Volunteers thus were incidental to national defence for which the principle of compulsory service was most apposite. The role of volunteers, according to Dundas, should be a law and order one and they should be restricted to permanently maintained county yeomanries and corps in the large towns.[2]

When the volunteer mass did come in 1798, it more or less developed itself, with Dundas accepting that volunteering was the kind of service that the public preferred. Yet even then a volunteer system was never securely established. Addington's government, it seems against the expectation of the commanding officers, disbanded most of the corps at the end of the Revolutionary War and in

---

[1] Establishment figures from: 'Volunteer corps of cavalry and infantry . . .', Chatham MSS, PRO30/8/244, fos. 238–40 for 1798; 'Abstract of the establishment of the volunteer corps . . .', Jan. 1801, WO30/65; Abstract of the return of volunteer and yeomanry corps, *CJ* lix. 501–2 for 1804.

[2] Dundas to Alexander Dirom, 7 Aug. 1797, Melville MSS, SRO GD51/1/888/2. Dirom's publication was *Plans for the Defence of Great Britain and Ireland* (Edinburgh, 1797).

1803 only wanted to revive them on a selective basis; again the volunteers largely created themselves, leaving the government to improve their organization as best it could. Shortly afterwards, in 1806, Windham as war minister declared them redundant, from which fate they were rescued only by a change of administration and by Castlereagh, who, however, proceeded to reconstruct national defence by adopting something like the militia model Dundas had started with. For the rest of the war Castlereagh's local militia was the mass auxiliary force with the volunteers reduced to a few dwindling remnants. Further, in the mid-Victorian revival of the auxiliaries a militia (1852) preceded the volunteers (1859).

Such a narrative hardly presents the volunteers as the inevitable form that civilian-based defence took. The militia idea was of long descent in European thought, its domicile in eighteenth-century England particularly continued by the act of 1757. Militia 'principles' were fiercely defended for most of the revolutionary and Napoleonic period, notably by the colonels who protected their patronage capital in the regiments by claiming that a militia independent of the army was still a necessary constitutional safeguard.[3] The colonels, however, were missing the point. In an age of mass warfare and mass revolution army versus militia mattered much less than which mode of national defence offered the best security from foreign attack and from an armed populace, seeing that the latter had become a condition of the former. Here the volunteers were not the obvious answer. From the start their inefficiency was deplored, and, worse, the main causes—low-status officers and inadequate discipline—were found not only impossible to correct but potentially dangerous to the state. Militia, in comparison, if militia principles were made to mean command by the county lieutenancies and gentry backed by military authority, were a far better alternative. At least that was how many saw it. These fears of what an armed population might portend can be particularly associated with Addington's Cabinet of 1801–3. Dundas and Pitt, on the other hand, went with the 'spirit' of the country, which they imagined would provide a sufficient defence, positively promote patriotic feelings, and overawe any disaffected elements. As with Catholic Ireland, they chose to believe in the good effects of service; that service, by attaching people to community, country, and crown, produced loyalty as much as loyalty did service. 'You will recollect,' Dundas told a general in reflecting on the Scottish volunteers of the 1790s, 'many parts of this country which were most disaffected, but were insensibly cured of it by being enrolled under arms along with others of a different description. If, on the other hand, they are not so associated, they become a prey to the intrigues of traitors and enemies,

---

[3] A good example is provided by the furore over the army's proposal in 1798 to detach light companies from militia regiments to form composite light battalions. Lord Buckingham to Lt.-Col. Hope, 22 Mar., meeting of colonels and field officers of militia, 23 Apr. 1798, HO50/30; Buckingham to Grenville, 25, 29 Apr. 1798, Grenville, *Dropmore MSS* iv. 177–81.

being debarred the privilege of bearing arms on the right side.' Pitt echoed these sentiments when supporting a mass levy in parliament in 1803.[4]

The volunteer mass, therefore, had a more complex and tenuous existence than is invariably stated or implied. By the end of 1797 the system of home defence taking shape depended on large numbers of militia for its military means (130,000, if fencibles are included) and comparatively small numbers of yeomanry and volunteers (51,000).[5] The doubling of this volunteer force in the next six months and continued growth after that imposed a very different military structure. Thanks to the volunteer expansion of 1798–1801, about half of Britain's military manpower was to remain highly independent of the army's control and allocated around literally hundreds of units that were often very small, inadequately officered, and reluctant to serve outside their localities. This need not have happened. Dundas in 1796–7, with the supplementary and Scottish militias and the provisional cavalry, did not shrink from nearly quadrupling the amount of compulsory military obligation, and, as we have seen, he was also willing to contemplate conscription for home service in the form of universal training which would provide local corps, armed and unarmed, to act with the army in the event of invasion. He further envisaged this 'national militia' as the great recruiting fund on which the army could draw; once embodied in 1798 the supplementary militia immediately began to be used in this way.[6] So we have the outlines of a tiered but entirely coherent military system; the army topmost, an immense militia for territorial defence next, with both directly or indirectly supplied from a trained reserve consisting of all available manpower.

Throughout 1797 there was no sign of a change towards the volunteer mass, even though, under apprehensions of invasion, heightened by the French expedition to Bantry Bay in Ireland, popular interest in volunteering revived and the modest expansion of 1794 was repeated. Volunteers were treated much as if they were incidental materials in the structure being created. No further appeal was

[4] Melville to General Vyse, 14 July 1803, Hope of Lufness MSS, SRO GD364/1/1136/2; *PH* xxxvi. 1644.

[5] On 1 Jan. 1798 the home force in Britain consisted of 27,918 regulars and 50,195 fencibles and militia. Return of the British army 1 Jan. 1793–1 Jan. 1806, 17 Dec. 1806, WO1/903/33. The projected size of the supplementary militia was 60,000 and the provisional cavalry 20,000. For volunteers see 'Return of volunteer companies', Jan. 1798, Windham MSS, BL Add. MS 37891, fo. 167.

[6] The plan adopted was for 30,000 (half) the supplementary militia to be called out, and men were then to be invited to join the army as volunteers to serve in Europe only until the end of the war. D. Dundas gives figures that indicate 10,000 augmented the 'old' militia, 10,000 joined line regiments, and 10,000 formed 'new corps'. 'State of the home force in Great Britain and Ireland from 1796 to 1801', WO1/407/445–55. Otherwise see Dundas to Lord Grenville, 26 Nov. 1797, *Dropmore MSS* iii. 399–400; 'Plan—army', 5 Dec. 1797, Windham MSS, BL Add. MS 37877, fos. 197–200. It is interesting that the government stuck to the point of compulsory obligation by refusing to let counties suspend the supplementary militia ballot and raise their quotas by seeking volunteers. Beckett, *Amateur Military Tradition*, 77.

made to the lieutenancies for additional corps. No new legislation was brought in to revise the original regulations of 1794. The government's promotion of local defence was aimed mainly at arrangements for driving the country and mustering civilian levies to assist the army in blocking roads and building defensive positions. Evidence is not lacking that the government soon resented the renewed growth of volunteering as a less than useful addition to the country's defences. In April 1797 the lord lieutenants were told to refuse offers of infantry outside coastal towns and towns where regulars were a necessary police. In January 1798 pay for training was reduced, then denied altogether to new corps.[7] Perhaps these restrictions were mainly aimed at Scotland, where once again the enthusiasm for volunteering easily outran England's; by the end of 1797 there were 18,124 volunteer infantry in Scotland out of 41,465 in the whole of Britain (44 per cent).[8]

How, then, did the volunteer mass, untried and unwanted for national defence in 1797, implant itself in 1798? The answer lies in the exigencies of the situation that the government faced at the beginning of the new year. By February Dundas was hard at work planning the defensive system that would be needed if France did the expected on the defeat of Austria and turned the whole of its power against Great Britain as its only remaining enemy. Before even Bonaparte's 'Army of England' was arrayed within sight of England—to provoke a display of national defence patriotism surpassed only in 1803—Dundas was informing Pitt that the yeomanry and volunteers must be called away from local duties, so that with the militia and organized civilians they might 'form one general combination of efficient strength'. If anything forced this conclusion, it was the army's weakness; 'totally exhausted' from its losses in Europe and the Caribbean, 'scarcely adequate to its defence duties', its recruiting 'palsied'.[9] The army believed that it needed 16,000 cavalry and 100,000 infantry to defend the country; in January 1798, with many of the line regiments unserviceable skeletons, it was 2,000 and 36,000 short of these figures.[10] Volunteers, if they could be persuaded to come out of their localities, together with supplementary militia, offered the only hope of bringing the home force up to strength quickly.

In eighteen months, therefore, if we recall Cornwallis's recommendation of additional militia in August 1796, the government had swung first towards compulsion

---

[7] Copy of Duke of Portland's circular letter to lord lieutenants, 10 Apr. 1797, Essex RO, Tendring Loyal Volunteers MSS, D/DHa/01/5; Portland to lord lieutenants, 15 Jan. 1798 and Dundas to same, 5 Mar. 1798, Hardwicke MSS, BL Add. MSS 35669, fos. 158, 228–31.

[8] Return, Jan. 1798, Windham MSS, BL Add. MS 37891, fo. 167.

[9] Dundas to Pitt, 10 Feb. 1798, Chatham MSS, PRO 30/8/157, fos. 236–45; R. Anstruther to Windham, 18 Nov. 1797, Windham MSS, BL Add. MS 37877, fo. 182.

[10] Return of the British army 1 Jan. 1793–1 Jan. 1806, 17 Dec. 1806, WO1/903/33. The required home defence force is cited in General Dundas, 'Considerations on the Invasion of Great Britain 1796', WO30/65.

then towards volunteering. The compulsory levies of 1797 had produced mixed results, the supplementary militia being satisfactorily raised but not the quota men, nor the provisional cavalry, nor the militia of Scotland. Yet in no sense was it accepted that 'man taxes' had failed and that other means must now be tried. Dundas's interest in the volunteer forces was tentative and pragmatic as he strove to match the country's needs with what was available and practicable. The provisional cavalry is a case in point, because there he gave up a scheme of his making once convinced that the yeomanry would be a more than adequate substitute. As this happened late in 1797, it may even have predisposed him to look favourably on the volunteer infantry as equally amenable to extra-local service and serious training.

Dundas conceded the unpopularity of the provisional cavalry as a tax on counties and a conscription of propertied individuals by bringing in legislation in May 1798 which permitted substitution and exemption on a generous scale.[11] As had always been the case with the militia infantry, the principle of personal service was to be rendered almost nugatory. But the measure also included an important novelty, in that exemption from service was given to volunteers in the yeomanry cavalry and that counties generally could choose to raise a lesser number of yeomanry in lieu of operating the compulsory scheme. Dundas thereby threw strong halters on the conscription state and its further development; the principle that volunteering should pre-empt compulsion came to be fully established when the personal exemption was extended to the volunteer infantry in 1799 and when whole counties were able to evade Addington's *levée en masse* of 1803 by raising the requisite number. Dundas did not see it quite like this at first. He did not mean to destroy the provisional cavalry, but hoped to preserve it where it was efficient and impose it where counties were slow to accept their obligations.[12] Any reprieve of the 'horse militia', however, was short-lived. The yeomanry corps had already been eager to extend their military usefulness and their hectic expansion in the first six months of 1798—from 9,750 to 22,600[13]—overturned any doubts that the 'zeal of the country' would not be equal to the needs of national defence. As early as June Dundas was abandoning the provisional cavalry, and its formal abolition followed in the next parliamentary session. He told the Earl of Westmorland, a staunch opponent of a volunteer system, that he could not compare the compulsory with the volunteer force; the yeomanry were cheaper, more amenable to

[11] Grenville, *Dropmore MSS* iv. 47–8; *CJ* liii. 582, 644.

[12] For Dundas's continuing belief in the provisional cavalry see his 'Memorandum explaining the distribution of the armed forces of the country', 17 Feb. 1798, Melville MSS, NLS MS 1048, fos. 75–9; Dundas to Windham, 10 Apr. 1798, Melville MSS, SRO GD51/1/912/2.

[13] Return, Jan. 1798, Windham MSS, BL Add. MS 37891, fo. 167; 'Volunteer Corps of Cavalry and Infantry accepted [14 Apr. 1794–14 July 1798]', Chatham MSS, PRO30/8/244, fos. 237–9.

training, ready to serve with the army, and so numerous that the total number of cavalry in Great Britain had reached the maximum that was useful.[14] So the case continued to stand: a forced levy of cavalry passed beyond contemplation.

The Defence Act passed in April 1798 was designed to add the volunteer infantry, along with the yeomanry, to the force available for national defence. The incentives for corps to serve outside their localities which it authorized included pay for training, a clothing allowance, and a sergeant and drummer permanently attached.[15] They were to be properly armed and disciplined bodies on which the district commands could call for military, not simply police, purposes. Dundas therefore had laid out his plan, but at this stage he was given a first taste of the incorrigible localism that was to plague all dealings with the volunteers. For Bonaparte's army, apparently poised to invade, provoked the most basic defensive instincts of the population, exactly as was to occur in similar circumstances in 1803. In just four months, between April and July 1798, the volunteer establishment increased from 54,600 to 116,000.[16] This was mostly a response from below, long seen in the war-exposed societies of the Continent, in which localities acted to secure their own safety out of their own resources. Well over half the volunteer infantry in England by mid-1798 were either unwilling or not known to be willing to serve further than twenty miles away. The government did not oppose such formations because it could not; but it reacted quickly to avoid, as Dundas put it, diminishing 'the means which might otherwise be appropriated to the greater object of national defence against foreign invasion'. Even so, the very rapid proliferation of 'local defence' volunteers continued for several weeks until the government flatly refused to accept further proposals of this kind, though only in the inland districts.[17]

The sheer size of the volunteer mass seems to have astonished all beholders. Dundas referred to the 'armed nation' almost as if it created itself, and he fended off criticism of volunteering by claiming that the proof lay in its popularity: 'I know no other way of doing it but in the way it is now going on, nor do I conceive it either prudent or practicable in any other way.'[18] The whole experience convinced him and Pitt, and others besides, that the public in its wisdom had chosen the mode of defence most suitable for Britain. Volunteering, it was going to be

---

[14] Dundas to Westmorland, 10 June 1798, WO1/942/255–60.

[15] 38 Geo. III, c. 27. In March the volunteer corps had been invited to serve over their military districts. See Dundas to Lord Hardwicke (circular), 12 Mar. 1798, Hardwicke MSS, BL Add. MS 35669, fos. 246–8.

[16] The April figure is taken from 'Memo—Invasion Book', SPOI Westmorland MS 138. The July figure is in Chatham MSS, PRO30/8/244, fos. 238–40.

[17] For Dundas's official correspondence with lord lieutenants see Dundas to Lord Hardwicke, 10 May 1798, Hardwicke MSS, BL Add. MS 35670, fos. 42–6; to Duke of Manchester, 15 May 1798, Manchester MSS, Cambridge RO, Huntingdon, DDM 80/11/20.

[18] Dundas to Windham, 10 Apr. 1798, Melville MSS, SRO GD51/1/912/1.

pointed out again and again, mobilized public spiritedness without trespassing on the multitudinous private interests of a commercial society; it also was genuinely indigenous and therefore more soundly based than any imposed service the state could devise; last but not least, it reconciled satisfactorily an armed population and public order in that local communities were presumed to be the best judges of their own security. The volunteers were the fullest manifestation of the patriotic feeling that Dundas and Pitt believed would most save the country. How seriously the government took the question of public morale at this time needs to be understood. Pitt made patriotic incitement one of his 'great objects'. Beginning with the thanksgiving for naval victories in December 1797, the ministers worked hard on public opinion, demonizing opposition, feeding reports of the country's military 'strength' to the press, and launching the great public subscription known as the 'voluntary contribution'. Dundas, too, constantly urged the importance of carrying the attack to the French, which led to the raid on Ostend in May 1798.[19] Many doubts surrounded Britain's ability to show national resistance to an invader. The rapid expansion of the volunteers in 1798, particularly in England where numbers had been low, gave the lie to the idea that Britain's 'military spirit' had been stultified by commerce and freedom from the ravages of war.

The scale of the mobilization was never contested by the generals; the army at last began to feel it possessed means equal to the threat of French attack, and that it was also less tied to defence of the national base. In spite of rebellion and continuing danger in Ireland, there was no withdrawal of troops from abroad in 1798–9 to better secure the British Isles; indeed, by January 1799 reinforcements were on their way to the Mediterranean and India.[20] Admittedly, the volunteers were too untrained at this stage for the government's hand to be greatly freed and another year or so passed before their presence began to have significant effect. Volunteers were included in defence plans for the first time in April 1799 when the quartermaster-general set out the stations and patrol areas of the 'established and trained' London corps numbering 11,332 men. In the depressing days after

---

[19] Pitt to Lord Mornington, 26 Jan. 1798. Lord Rosebery, *Life of Pitt* (London, 1891), 204–5; Cookson, *Friends of Peace*, 100–1, 166–7. *The Times*, 15 Jan. 1798 added up the military force in Britain to arrive at a total of 227,450 men. Dundas in a paper held raids on the enemy's coast to be 'essential to the support of the war at home, namely as affording the most effectual means of counteracting the manoeuvres of the disaffected and the alarms of the desponding, of shewing the energy of the nation, and above all of keeping alive the *spirit of enterprize* by which alone our *public spirit* (now fortunately raised by the late conduct of the enemy) can be maintained in a disposition suitable to the difficulties of our situation [*Dundas's italics*]', 'Suggestions relative to the defence of our own coast combined with the means of annoying the enemy' [Dec. 1797], WO30/64/115–18.

[20] There were 42,412 troops abroad on 1 Jan. 1798 and 45,323 a year later. Return of British army, 17 Dec. 1806, WO1/903/33. For the government's efforts to create a 'disposable force' see [Duke of York], 'Disposable force when relieved' [30 Sept. 1798], York to Colonel Brownrigg, 30 Sept. 1798, Brownrigg to William Huskisson, 3 Oct. 1798, Melville MSS, SRO GD51/1/687, 688/1, 3.

Marengo Dundas argued warmly, and eventually successfully, with his colleagues that Britain had never been so strongly defended and ought to continue with offensive operations. When next invasion was actually threatened—in 1801—the army assumed there were about 30,000 volunteer infantry and 7,000 yeomanry to assist it in the field.[21]

These preparations by the army were substantiated by the sweeping conversion of the volunteers themselves to the idea of national defence. By early 1799 there were few corps left restricted to local service; nearly one-tenth came to offer service outside their military district anywhere in England.[22] We can imagine how intensive training and the blandishments of inspecting generals had some effect in persuading the corps that they should take themselves seriously as a military force. But the change occurred mainly at the insistence of their own officers, just as volunteering was to remain for the next ten years subservient to the officers' requirements. The local notables in command, particularly, matched local opportunities to national needs. They devoted considerable time and money to their corps, clearly regarding them as an important new area of public action through which they could assert their social leadership and mark the consequence of their communities. Volunteering during the Revolutionary War was concentrated in towns, and it was town élites who were most forward in the later eighteenth century in upholding ideals of public service and in expanding public authority, often through voluntary bodies. Military volunteering was to prove highly susceptible to urban concerns about social improvement, community-building, and status-fixing, including a 'bourgeois' sensitivity to 'county' or aristocratic overlordship.[23]

So the emergence of the volunteer mass is misrepresented if it is taken to be merely the reflex response of a society to threatened invasion, the old 'wave of patriotism' explanation. Though corps were invariably initiated at the local level, the spontaneity of what occurred in 1798 is qualified by the fact that the government had already recognized that some system of civilian-based defence was needed and contested the localism of the volunteers from the start. In the localities themselves, volunteering was shaped by much else besides instincts of self-defence or patriotic appeals. The continued growth of volunteer numbers after Bonaparte's army dispersed is interesting on this account. The establishment increased by nearly 25 per cent between November 1798 and August 1800, a period when Britain was not on the defensive at all but part of the Second Coalition. Moreover, further growth

---

[21] General Dundas, 'Proposed general arrangement for the defence of the capital', Apr. 1799, WO30/65; Henry Dundas, 'Secret memorandum on the present disposable force', Aug. 1800, Melville MSS, SRO GD51/1/725/1; General Dundas, 'Supposed number of troops that might be assembled in any particular district attacked by the enemy', Jan. 1801, WO1/407/491–9.

[22] C. Sebag-Montefiore, *A History of the Volunteer Forces* (London, 1908), 199 n. 2; 'Abstract of troops in . . . Great Britain', Jan. 1801, WO1/407/489. [23] See below, 237–42.

was curtailed and effective strengths declined in 1800–1, which coincided with a crisis of public order under the impact of high food prices.[24] On this evidence volunteering enthusiasm came to bear little correlation to wider developments, whether the war situation, social tension and popular disorder, or the fading of popular loyalism. Indeed, the amount of urban interest in volunteering better indicates the social forces that commandeered it; outside the south-west about two-thirds of the new corps were town-organized.[25] And if not this the expansion may be attributed to the militia exemption granted volunteers in January 1799, a valuable privilege to possess in view of how the supplementary militia had greatly increased the individual's chances of being caught by the ballot.[26] Exemption certainly promoted recruitment while requiring nothing further of a volunteer than his enrolment in a corps. It therefore can stand as a satisfactory explanation of volunteer growth in 1799–1800 and the stabilization of establishment numbers and decline of effective numbers in 1800–1.

Coming as the exemption did at the tail-end of the huge expansion of 1798, it represented the government's acknowledgement that the volunteers had graduated to an effective role in national defence. For the moment that role was limited to police, convoy, and guard duties in the rear of the field armies. But by 1801 the army was giving thought to the problem of building battalion-sized fighting units out of the generally smaller corps, and the volunteers were being considered in operational planning at the level of the district commands; in the event of an invasion of Suffolk, for example, Colonel Hope in the eastern district wanted a large volunteer force positioned on the enemy's flank to turn him southwards towards the main defences at Chelmsford.[27] The army's high expectations, however, were not less than the volunteers' own military enthusiasm. Many corps started as Hitchin's did, pledging to support 'civil order and government, and the suppression of riot and tumult' within their immediate locality if the magistrates were left without adequate police resources. Yet they soon assumed an entirely different and military character; first, by placing themselves at the disposal of the district generals to become part of the counter-invasion strategy; and secondly, by adopting many of the forms of military organization, including even colours and 'musick'.

[24] 'Invasion book', SPOI Westmorland MS 138 gives strength of yeomanry and volunteer infantry as 118,500 in Nov. 1798, 146,138 in Sept. 1800, and 128,038 in Mar. 1801. See also 'Volunteer and yeomanry establishment' [Aug. 1800], Melville MSS, SRO GD51/1/725/11; Abstract of the establishment of the volunteer corps, Jan. 1801, WO30/65.   [25] Cookson, 'Volunteer Movement', 873.

[26] For the rather involved history of the exemption see Beckett, Amateur Military Tradition, 84. The exemption given volunteers in 1799 (by 39 Geo. III, c. 14) was from the supplementary militia, which of course was a much larger establishment than the old militia.

[27] Alexander Hope to the Duke of York, July 1801, Hope of Lufness MSS, SRO GD364/1/1130/ 2. Hope had been Howe's adjutant-general in the eastern district in 1797–8 and had produced a detailed 'memoir' for its defence.

Their chaplains constantly reminded them of their task of national defence. The 'rules' drawn up by their officers instructed them in their duty to become soldier-like in discipline and habits.[28] The greatest occasion for the Hitchin corps came in 1800 when it joined the other volunteers and militia of the county in a royal review at Hatfield. It showed off, in the most impressive way possible, the volunteers as an 'army', genuinely part of the military force of the country.[29] The 'disgust very generally excited' by the disbandment of the volunteer infantry in 1802 is therefore understandable; for it shut many local notables out of a form of public enterprise that they valued and believed was useful and efficient.[30]

Disbandment is usually linked to Addington's attack on public expenditure at the conclusion of the Revolutionary War. In fact, it was much more a decision of military policy, about which the new Cabinet possessed firm views and the determination to pursue them. Still too often Addington's government is regarded as captive to or captivated by Pitt, when actually it was genuinely strong in parliament and politically resourceful.[31] On coming to power, Lord Pelham, the home secretary, Charles Yorke, the secretary at war, and Lord Hobart, Dundas's successor, immediately embarked on reform of the volunteers and militia. They held the volunteer force to be generally inefficient and wanted an expansion of the militia at its expense. All three ministers may have been predisposed against the volunteers by their associations with the army and militia. Hobart had risen to high rank in the army before beginning his political career; further, he had close connections with Buckingham and Westmorland, two peers who were intensely hostile to large-scale volunteering. Both Pelham and Yorke were active militia colonels. Pelham and Hobart, as former chief secretaries in Dublin, also shared a concern about an armed population from Irish experience. All Irish administrators were haunted by the memory of the Irish volunteer movement whose threat of armed force during the American War had extracted sweeping concessions from the British government. Hobart himself had put down attempts to revive the volunteers in 1792 while Pelham had found no answer to the problem that whatever

---

[28] R(?) Fraser, *Hints to the Volunteers of the United Kingdom* (London, 1801); 'When he becomes a Volunteer, he quits, in some degree his private, to enter into a public station; he stands forward with the profession of being a disciplined soldier, fit for all purposes of war . . .'. See also *Rules Bristol Volunteer Association*.

[29] On the Hitchin corps see Hitchin Volunteers MSS, esp. letters to and from William Wilshere in 1798, Hertford RO; *Cambridge Chronicle*, 13 Oct. 1798; J. H. Busby, 'Local Military Forces in Hertfordshire, 1793–1814', *J. Soc. for Army Hist. Res.* 31 (1953), 16–17, 20–1. See also my article 'Patriotism and Social Structure: The Ely Volunteers, 1798–1808', ibid. 71 (1993), 160–79.

[30] 'Of the expedience of a reformed establishment of the late volunteer army' [1803], WO1/407/503.

[31] Glover, *Britain at Bay*, 20. A measure of rehabilitation has been achieved through P. Ziegler, *Addington* (London, 1965); C. D. Hall, 'Addington at War: Unspectacular but not Unsuccessful', *Bull. Inst. Hist. Res.* 61 (1988), 306–16.

auxiliary forces were created in Ireland they imbibed, to a greater or lesser degree, the sectarian passions of Irish society.

Hobart was seeking opinions about volunteer reform as early as December 1800 and seems to have produced a paper on the subject in May 1801, a few months after coming into office.[32] By this time no one could deny the popularity of volunteering; from 1798 it had added huge numbers to the armed force of the country, providing one answer to the problem which was coming into sharper and sharper focus, that Britain must adapt to a new age of warfare in which, as one undersecretary put it, 'a nation which attacks en mass can only be repelled by a defence en mass'.[33] The question was whether the volunteers were a sufficient answer. Experience of them during the Revolutionary War suggested that they were spasmodic in their commitment, haphazardly organized, and frustratingly impervious to outside control, hardly qualities to make them part of a 'permanent' system of defence. One general claimed that because of 'party influence' almost every corps he had inspected was 'a chaos of discord and confusion'.[34] These doubts certainly showed in Hobart's memorandum. His criticisms were the more powerful in that he praised the yeomanry on all counts; as public-spirited, well-trained, well-led, a force the military and the magistracy found equally serviceable. In contrast, the infantry were 'by no means so well composed or so well regulated'. To Hobart the 'inferior class' of men in the ranks mattered less than the absence of 'gentlemen of rank and property' in command. The new government collectively had a noticeably strict attitude on this subject, among other things favouring a militia because it exemplified the gentry's military leadership. Hobart considered the gentry's participation all the more important because the volunteers were trained and organized outside 'army discipline', so that the efficiency and reliability of the corps mostly depended on the informal authority of the officers. If he could not have gentlemen of the county, he wanted half-pay officers, who at least could offer to the corps their experience and the army's standards. How problems of discipline could be solved otherwise taxed him. Since the corps were voluntary organizations they acted by their own rules and, in the final analysis, had to respect the individual's right to resign. The worst consequence Hobart sought to address was the sharp fluctuation in volunteer numbers as men joined to escape the militia ballot and then left, often adding to the evil by failing to return the arms issued them.[35]

[32] General Vyse to Hobart, 4 Jan. 1801, Hobart MSS, Buckingham RO, D/MH/H/War/G1; memorandum, May 1801, WO1/407/549–61. The latter does not appear under Hobart's name, but it closely follows part of the text of another paper of Mar. 1803 (ibid. 533–46), which was certainly Hobart's work.

[33] Paper by Sir George Shee, 16 Mar. 1803, Pelham MSS, BL Add. MS 33120, fos. 104–9.

[34] General Vyse to Lord Hobart, 4 Jan. 1801, Hobart MSS, Buckingham RO, D/MH/H/War/G1.

[35] 'Memorandum on volunteers', Jan. 1801, WO1/407/609–12 had already drawn attention to this problem.

Hobart's strictures produced few practical results, mainly an act of parliament which penalized volunteers who did not return their arms and attempted to make the militia exemption dependent on regular attendance at drill.[36] This meagre legislative effort has to be compared with the attention the government devoted to revising and consolidating the militia laws until they were able to produce the comprehensive and long-lasting act of 1802. On the arrival of peace disbandment of the volunteers was the easier because of what were felt to be fundamental flaws in their organization. It was the harder because Dundas had created expectations among them that they would be continued. Hence the outcry when it happened. But the unpopularity of the decision to disband is further evidence of the ministers' determination to do away with the system they had inherited from Pitt's government.[37] It cannot be imagined that the army made any objections. As late as September 1801 only about a quarter of the total volunteer strength was organized in bodies larger than one hundred cavalry and two hundred infantry, all that the army could use to form the battalions and half-battalions fit for field service. 'In their present detached form they are unmanageable', General Dundas had warned.[38]

The weaknesses in the volunteer system identified in 1801 formed the substance of every future attack. Once the volunteers became an issue, most that was brought against them boiled down to their inefficiency in meeting the army's requirements. Their discipline was inadequate because 'military subordination' was required of a military force; yet they continued to accommodate civilian sensitivities. Nor were volunteers soldiers for a fixed term; they could withdraw from service at any time, and did so, producing a considerable turnover of men in many corps.[39] Above all, they were constituted as a force for home defence but remained outside the army's control. An informal relationship might have developed had numbers of half-pay officers accepted commissions, but these, inevitably, were more interested in full-pay service in the militia and fencibles, if not the army. As it was, army officers held no power of command over the volunteers until they were called out for 'actual service', so that the training of the men was largely unsupervised and little could be done beforehand to form the local corps into the battalions which the army required.

In 1801 Addington's ministers inaugurated a shift in policy away from volunteering back towards the sort of 'national militia' Dundas had earlier envisaged,

---

[36] 42 Geo. III, c. 66.

[37] Dundas, at the very least, encouraged the yeomanry to think they would be continued, as they mostly were. Sebag-Montifiore, *History of the Volunteer Forces*, 220 n. 1. In 1803 he kept deploring the disbandment to correspondents. Melville to Sir James Pulteney, 6 Apr. 1803, Melville MSS, SRO GD51/1/979; to Addington, 29 July 1803, Hope of Lufness MSS, GD364/1/1136/6.

[38] 'Abstract of the strongest yeomen and volunteer corps', Sept. 1801, WO30/65 (no. 30); General Dundas, 'Memorandum of Circumstances to be determined . . . previous to, and at the Moment of Invasion', Feb. 1801, Hope of Lufness MSS, SRO GD364/1/1134.   [39] See below, 233–4.

based on building up a reserve of trained men who could be called out of their localities in any number as the occasion demanded. The Training Act of the much maligned Windham, it should be noted, stood in the same line of descent. Pelham and Yorke agreed on enlarging the militia, with a proportion embodied and serving outside the county at any one time; thus most militiamen would stay at home where they would attend training but otherwise pursue their civilian avocations. Their scheme was an obvious alternative to the volunteers, designed as it was to promote personal service in place of substitution (down to removal of the exemption for volunteers—though this was never pressed). Its merits *vis-à-vis* the volunteers were also implied; gentlemen of 'considerable property' would find their 'private interests' compatible with holding commissions, and the men would be trained in battalion or brigade camps for two periods of the year. Yorke, in introducing his militia legislation, spoke of a combined English and Scottish force up to 72,000 strong, disposable as he and Pelham recommended.[40] The major work on the eighteenth-century militia sees the act of 1802 as the finale of its development. It was, in fact, a plan for a mass militia through which Britain could have come close to conscription for home defence. Pelham knew exactly what he was doing; he sent to Prussia to find out how that country struck a balance between conscription and production.[41]

Neither was this preference for militia over volunteers quickly discarded soon afterwards in the crisis of 1803. The ministers, in the end, succumbed only to Pitt's populist patriotism with a loss of political nerve, which ever since has been turned into an accusation that they were confused and dilatory in organizing home defence. Given a few years of peace, not unreasonable to have expected, the government might have implemented its militia reforms to good effect and even been in possession of the reserve of trained men the militia was intended to produce. As it was, the volunteer mass of 1803 was never pre-ordained. Lord Eldon recalled a Cabinet 'to consider the propriety of allowing of volunteer regiments; and the ministers avowed that they were afraid of incurring such an expense.'[42] When Anglo-French relations deteriorated in March, the new, enlarged militia was immediately called out; but Hobart also declared it 'less desirable to have a very numerous body of volunteers than a well-regulated one'. He linked government assistance to the corps more firmly than ever to service, training, and size, and was most anxious that those of the 'large towns and manufacturing districts',

[40] *PH* xxxvi. 537, 540. See also Yorke to Hobart, 19 Feb. 1802, Hobart MSS, Buckingham RO, D/MH/H/War/B24.

[41] Western, *English Militia*, 236–8; Pelham to Addington, 23 Sept. 1801, Pelham MSS, BL Add. MS 33120, fos. 41–52. Also ibid. 33048, fos. 361–3 for paper by Pelham dated Mar. 1802 and Lord Buckingham to Hobart, 24 Jan. 1802, Hobart MSS, Buckingham RO, D/MH/H/War/G25, for the approval of one of the most influential militia colonels.

[42] H. Twiss, *Life of Lord Eldon* (3 vols., London, 1844), i. 416.

relatively large and efficient as they had been, should re-establish themselves. Furthermore, he returned to the point that the 'principal disadvantage attending the infantry companies' was the low social rank of many who held commissions. To abolish officers' pay in order to improve their respectability was an absurd proposition; but Hobart saw the change as the key one needed to make the volunteers efficient, and there his mind was concentrated.[43] As offers of corps flooded in during spring and early summer, the government even acted to restrain the growth of numbers. Most applications were held over until the ballot for the supplementary militia had been completed; and quotas were imposed on Scotland, Devon, and Cornwall, where volunteering again proved exceptionally popular.[44] As late as August the volunteer strength in England and Wales was only 60,000, half of what it had been at the close of the Revolutionary War and a fifth of what it was to become.[45]

Meanwhile Pitt began his cautious path back to power. He wanted to return as the indispensable war leader, so that it suited him to continue the show of eschewing party opposition while having a position on matters of national importance. National defence, of course, was the issue he could use to best effect; for it did not lend itself to partisan politics, and in the circumstances of 1803 there was inevitable anxiety about the state of the country's defences, of which the volunteer offers were one symptom. Pitt saw obvious advantage in promoting mass arming against the wishes of the government, making the most, too, of his own close involvement in the volunteer movement. Out of the public gaze, moreover, he used his growing political strength to force advice on the ministers. There is no reason to doubt Wilberforce's account of how the levy en masse was initiated by Pitt and accepted by the government under threat of independent parliamentary action; Dundas, at the time far away in Scotland, knew the scheme as Pitt's work, down to its 'doing more than can be practically well done'.[46] This defeat probably marked the beginning

---

[43] Memorandum on volunteers, 18 Mar. 1803, WO1/407/533–46. Addressed from Downing Street, this was almost certainly from Lord Hobart's office. The government sent out 'Proposed conditions of service for corps of volunteer infantry' on 31 Mar. See Sebag-Montefiore, History of the Volunteer Forces, 239–40.

[44] Memorandum on volunteers and 'Progress of measures respecting volunteers', n.d. [1803], WO1/407/513–18, 521–31.

[45] The figure of 60,000 is an estimate taken from the parliamentary return of corps dated 9 Dec. 1803. SP 1803–4, xi.

[46] Earl Stanhope, Life of William Pitt (4 vols., London, 1862), iv. 68–9; Lord Melville to his son, 26 July 1803, to the lord advocate, 11 Aug. 1803, Hope of Lufness MSS, SRO GD364/1/1136/5, 1136/1. A memorandum on the subject signed by Pitt survives. See 'Further considerations on the plan for a general enrolment and array of the people', 2 July 1803, Sidmouth MSS, Devon RO, 152M/C1803/OM15. Dundas thought the number of volunteers to be unmanageable and 'would much rather have had 200,000 on the footing of Lord Hobart's first letter in June than double that number selected and formed in the loose and desultory manner they have more recently been', Dundas to Alexander Hope, 16 Dec. 1803, Chatham MSS, PRO30/8/157, fos. 294–7.

of the end for Addington's administration; it had lost its freedom of action by losing confidence in its own power. Men as well as measures may have been at Pitt's mercy; in July, Yorke, whom Pitt had been advising, replaced Pelham at the home office (and therefore became responsible for the volunteers). Pelham had remained an unrepentant advocate of a 'stationary militia'.[47]

So an interesting sub-theme to the increasing tension between Addington's ministers and their Pittite shadows is their 'hard' and 'soft' attitude to volunteering. The former disliked a large volunteer movement as 'popular' and unserviceable, and preferred to expand the militia principle. The latter believed that war in their age increasingly required governments to mobilize the will of societies and that numbers of volunteers created the sort of armed nationalism which would ultimately defeat any invader. The idea of unconquerable moral force arising out of the 'national spirit' made questions of organization and technique lesser concerns; though it was argued in favour of the volunteers that they were economical, rapidly formed in time of crisis, and, anyway, by definition, the kind of military service most congenial to the public.[48]

The practicality and efficiency of the huge volunteer mass—380,000 by the end of 1803—became an issue immediately. In August its size was limited to six times the militia establishment when it was realized that training and arming within the full scope of the Levy en masse Act would make impossible demands. Yorke wanted to treat the volunteers much as militia, drafting the separate corps into county battalions and subjecting them to army training and command.[49] But no government was able to make any such impression on their localism and civilianism. All the old problems re-emerged in the Napoleonic movement; numerous small corps which stubbornly resisted amalgamation; less than satisfactory applicability to the strategy of home defence; service, in the final analysis, only on terms that suited the individual; the existence of armed bodies which were operating outside the control of military law. The volunteers were, essentially, the armed nation, but making them into a national army proved an impossibility. Parliament's long study of the volunteer consolidation bill over the session of 1804 identified the many defects without producing any substantial reform. Out of the wreck of their views on national defence, Addington's ministers salvaged very little except the condition of territorial service placed on two-thirds of the volunteers under the regulations of August 1803 and the 'permanent duty' which about a quarter of the corps accepted; the first enabled the army to include the volunteers fully in its defence

---

[47] For Pelham's views see the paper probably dated June 1803 in Pelham MSS, BL Add. MS 33120, fos. 104–9.

[48] As Melville argued in a letter to Addington, 29 July 1803, Hope of Lufness MSS, SRO GD364/1/1136/6.

[49] 'Communication received from Mr Secretary Yorke concerning volunteers', [1803], ibid. 1139/5.

plans; the other gave them short periods of training under army discipline.[50] But the Addingtonians, while submitting to the *force majeure* of Pitt, retracted nothing. And in the wings waited Windham, who was about to emerge as war minister and the next great proponent of compulsory over voluntary service.

Windham's reputation as war minister badly needs some restorative work. Though Fortescue years ago declared Windham's reforms to have been based on 'sound principles', the prevailing verdict today condemns them for being impracticable or incapable of having the effect intended. According to these critics, the army's recruitment continued to languish in spite of his best efforts, the volunteers never recovered from the damage he inflicted, and his proposals for compulsory training were inoperable.[51] A first defence to put up on Windham's behalf is that no government of the period solved the army's recruiting problems. A second is that he acted with respectable backing within the army; even inside the Horse Guards, though the Duke of York could not forgive him for bringing in short-service enlistment, his agenda for reform was generally accepted. A third is that Windham stood in a line of ministers who preferred militia to volunteers, particularly a local militia which would not impede army recruiting, yet which could, if need be, contribute huge numbers to national defence out of a trained population. The home defence force Cornwallis advised and Dundas adopted in 1796 was the same basic plan that Windham advanced ten years later. Dundas, it is worth adding, whatever his praise for the volunteers, continued to believe that the patriotism that distinguished them could be inculcated more widely still through some permanent scheme of universal training. He was calling for something very like Windham's notorious Training Act in 1803 and publicly reiterated his support for compulsory training in the debates on the bill.[52]

Neither did Windham come 'cold' to the subject of national defence or to military policy generally. He had been a member of the Cabinet in Pitt's war administration (1794–1801), but, more significantly, as secretary at war during this time he served as the civilian head of the army and knew its concerns, assiduous and intelligent as he was, better than most other politicians. In particular, he had wrestled with the army's recruiting problems; and in 1806 we can believe his avowals to the king that the major object of his reforms was 'the increase and improvement of the regular army'. This review of the country's military system

---

[50] The proportions come from J. W. Fortescue, *The County Lieutenancies and the Army 1803–14* (London, 1909), 79, where it is stated 211,000 out of 342,000 volunteers were liable to serve in any part of Great Britain; and from my article, 'Volunteer Movement', 883.

[51] R. Glover, *Peninsular Preparation: The Reform of the British Army 1795–1809* (Cambridge, 1963), esp. pp. 240–5. Fortescue, *County Lieutenancies*, 284, maintained that Windham's reforms were based on 'sound principles' (and pointed out how Castlereagh followed his ideas).

[52] Melville to Charles Yorke, 27 June 1803, Hope of Lufness MSS, SRO GD364/1/1136/7; *PD* 1st ser. vii. 1086 (11 July 1806).

was produced within weeks of taking office. Windham knew what he wanted to do, and he was the first war minister whose plans attempted to impose a unity on Britain's diverse military forces, especially in linking regulars and non-regulars. (Castlereagh, interestingly another who had spent time at the war office, was the second.) Dundas had made an *ad hoc* response to the changing strategic situation, enlarging the militia in 1796, then opposing it with huge numbers of volunteers in 1798, then raiding it for men in 1799 in order to create an army for offensive operations. The Addingtonians returned to home defence based on the militia principle, but in the crisis of 1803 they balloted men for the army in competition with the militia (their Army of Reserve scheme) and revived the volunteer mass. Pitt's second administration continued this illogical and incoherent system where the volunteers starved the militia, the militia starved the army, and the army had negligible authority over the bulk of the country's fighting men. Windham understood these absurdities very clearly. He also understood the importance of putting the army's needs first, since it was the only offensive force and formed the core around which home defence would be organized. As conscription into the army was out of the question, the nation's manpower should be channelled towards it by making service more attractive and by reducing the militia and the volunteers. At the same time universal training would both establish a large pool of potential recruits and provide for home defence.[53]

Windham's reforms, moreover, deserve to be recognized as a considerable political achievement: Cabinet approval was swiftly won; the king, always particular about army matters, disliked only short-service enlistment and graciously gave way in due course;[54] parliament passed the necessary legislation to effect the changes in a single session.[55] The triumph of compulsory over voluntary service in home defence was never seriously contested, in spite of the potential threat of a volunteer interest in parliament and the powerful social forces concentrated in the corps. Windham, to some degree, divided this opposition by declaring that he had no objection to volunteers who could support themselves, which meant wealthy, 'respectable' urban corps. But he also knew that the enthusiasm of 1803 had run its course, that numbers were well below establishment, that training had become slacker, and that subscriptions were bringing in declining amounts. Perhaps 10 per cent of volunteer officers resigned when savage reductions in government support

---

[53] Windham's memorandum to the King, 27 Mar. 1806, *George III Corresp.* iv. 416–19. 'An army is at this moment the first concern of this country', Windham to Thomas Amyot, 23 Jan. 1806, Earl of Rosebery (ed.), *Windham Papers* (2 vols., London, 1913), ii. 283.

[54] King to Windham, 29 Mar. 1806, *George III Corresp.* iv. 419–22.

[55] The key acts were 46 Geo. III, cc. 51 and 63 (repeal of Additional Force Acts), c. 69 (military pensions), c. 90 (military training), c. 91 (suspension of the militia ballot), and c. 124 (volunteering from the Irish militia). The reduced allowances for volunteers were announced on 17 July and regulations dealing with army recruitment on 7 Oct. See Fortescue, *County Lieutenancies*, 159–73.

were announced; yet in doing so they could be accused of putting politics ahead of public service, and, worse, of bearing out the view that volunteering was incompatible with a stable and permanent system of defence. Though the point cannot be proved, there are grounds for supposing that so many officers resigned in 1806–7 mainly because a fit opportunity presented itself.[56] The Training Act further attests to a loss of faith in the volunteer system. However much the opposition in parliament insisted that it was calculated to destroy the volunteers, they did not dare to try a division on the principle.[57] This legislation provided for the training of 200,000 men each year and was the strongest assertion so far of the state's power to compel military service.

No one has considered the army's reception of Windham's ideas, warmer than might have been expected. We can almost certainly read the Duke of York's views at one remove in the attitude of his father; the king approved 'general' training without comment, wished only that the volunteers be let down lightly, and confined all criticism to measures affecting the army itself, particularly enlistment for a limited term. The commander-in-chief indeed found Windham's proposals for improving recruitment generally 'bad and absurd'.[58] He was also loathe to give up balloted recruitment, begun in 1803 as the 'Army of Reserve', because of the inadequacies of other recruiting methods.[59] Otherwise he agreed with Windham's basic intentions; that the militia should be regularly used to feed men into the army, that the volunteers were only worth saving where they could be made efficient, and that a trained population had become a necessity under the new conditions of war. Apart from the army proposals, York would have deemed the waste of the volunteers, whom he thought could be converted into 'volunteer militia', as Windham's greatest practical mistake. In a 'military plan' drawn up in February 1807 he envisaged a three-layered military system. The bottom layer consisted of the mass of trained men who could be organized into corps of 'armed peasantry' if and when required, exactly as Windham wanted. The next layer, however, perhaps reflected the Duke's 'Prussian' inclinations, for he wanted regularly organized local forces, which Windham had not provided for, interposed between the irregular 'armed

---

[56] I get the figure of 10 per cent from my Ely study. Effective volunteers were about 10 per cent down in Jan. 1806 compared with Jan. 1804. See Sebag-Montefiore, *History of the Volunteer Forces*, 335 n. 1. Windham said in parliament that officers were not prepared to put any more money into the corps, having made heavy advances in the past, and that they 'now wished to find some point of honour that would give occasion for a quarrel, which would enable them to resign with a better grace', *PD* 1st ser. vii. 915 (3 July 1806).

[57] Sir Henry St John Mildmay, a volunteer commander, led the opposition to the Training Act, but he was an insignificant politician. *PD* 1st ser. vii. 904–7, 1105–6.

[58] King to Windham, 29 Mar. 1806, *George III Corresp.* iv. 419–22; York to Colonel J. W. Gordon, 7 Sept. 1806, J. W. Gordon MSS, BL Add. MS 49472, fos. 52–3.

[59] York to Windham, 18 Mar. 1806, WO1/632/157–80.

peasantry' and the army. These battalions were to be militia, in the sense of being based on counties and commanded by gentry, but service was to be voluntary, therefore taking over the existing volunteers. The remaining layer, of course, was the army, which was to comprise first battalions as the 'disposable' force and second battalions at home. The home battalions were to be raised by ballot and enlistment, and created in the first instance by merging the old militia with the line, surely a soldier's rather than a politician's proposal in view of the value the militia colonels placed on their patronage.[60]

How Windham received this plan is not known because George III dismissed the ministers soon afterwards.[61] He certainly would have saved the militia, which was politically untouchable and, anyway, supplied the army, if indirectly, by ballot. He remained sceptical that ill-trained auxiliaries could operate successfully in the line alongside regulars and therefore scrapped local militia and volunteers in favour of irregular warfare, not without support from some notable military men.[62] He would have wondered, too, how training the population could be carried on if a large volunteer force was also maintained. But the point to be emphasized is that, along with the Duke of York, Windham put the needs of the army, especially the offensive army, first, and believed that adequate numbers of men could be drawn into the first battalions from the home service battalions (militia and regulars) which, in turn, would be supplied from a trained population. Under the existing system, while the volunteers might pass for a trained population, they also blocked the vital flow of men any further. Windham's Training Act, therefore, the most ridiculed of all his reforms, was, in fact, the one most acceptable to the army. Castlereagh, it should be added, adopted the essentials of Windham's plan when he succeeded him as war minister; he began the practice of taking annual drafts from the militia into the army, and his local militia scheme was based on the principle of compulsory service at the expense of the volunteers.

1806 was a major *conjuncture* in the development of the Napoleonic military system. For one thing, the British army began to be accorded the priority it deserved—even before the Peninsular War commenced—though the numbers transferring from the auxiliaries into the regulars proved never quite sufficient and in the last years there was increasing resort to foreign troops. For another, the voluntary principle in home defence was discounted by politicians, the military, and, seemingly, volunteer officers themselves, and the search began for an altogether

---

[60] 'Memorandum of Duke of York to Lord Grenville relative to augmenting the army', 15 Feb. 1807, ibid. 634/125-38. A 'military plan' elaborating on this paper is found in Dropmore MSS, BL Add. MS 59288, fos. 60-9.

[61] Grenville may have responded. Buckingham, at least, offered comments, including the view that the militia officers would have none of it. Paper and Buckingham to Grenville, 3 Mar. 1807, ibid. 58879, fos. 42-7.

[62] Sir James Pulteney and Craufurd 'of the Light Infantry', for example. *PH* xxxvi. 1647-56; *PD* 1st ser. i. 966-72; vii. 814.

different basic force. A local militia went back to the supplementary militia that Cornwallis had cogitated on and Dundas had legislated for in 1796 and to Pelham's schemes of 1801; militia stationed in their counties of origin had long been held up as the more 'pure' or 'true' form, mostly on the grounds that such would keep commissions in the hands of the gentry and encourage personal service instead of substitution. Castlereagh never hesitated about rejecting the idea of an armed peasantry, the alternative model for home defence which Windham had espoused.[63] Proponents of militia tended to fear popular military power and wanted control to be exercised through propertied officers and formal organization and discipline. The successes of Americans, the *chouans* of the Vendée (who may have converted Windham),[64] and Tyroleans against regular military force, which were often adverted to, only confirmed the point that an armed peasantry was equally dangerous to established authority. And yet great interest was taken at this time in universal training and irregular warfare, the resurgent radicals, in particular, exploiting discontent over the ballot as a selective tax especially oppressive on the middle classes.[65] The idea of the mass levy was seductive because it not only conjured up a vision of national resistance to the tyrant who dared to invade but also fitted in with notions of light infantry having proved themselves the new élite in war. Castlereagh did not have to decide on the constitutionality, or even public acceptability, of subjecting the whole eligible population to compulsory service: that had already been decided by the failure of volunteering. But in the context of mounting criticism of the ballot and public promotion of a mass levy, his local militia proposals were definitely a conservative riposte to radical views.

Nevertheless, Castlereagh's home defence organization in its final form was politically ingenious, which largely explains its continuation until the end of the war. Unlike Windham, who hastened to effect the programme of reform he had announced to parliament over the previous three years, Castlereagh bided his time, pondering the possibilities and determined to be one war minister who got the details right. He eventually went to parliament a year after taking office. Meanwhile he had attended to the army's needs, his main concern, by arranging a huge draft from the British and Irish militias. Pitt's successors perfected the strategy, seen to most advantage in Lord Liverpool's long administration, of identifying

---

[63] See Castlereagh's criticisms of an armed peasantry in ibid. vii. 821.

[64] Windham was the minister closest to the *émigrés* during the 1790s, and consistently supported military intervention on behalf of the French counter-revolution. In the debate on the volunteer consolidation bill, 22 Mar. 1804, he used the example of the Vendée to attack the volunteers as being trained for, but useless for, regular warfare. See ibid. i. 988.

[65] S. C. Smith, 'Loyalty and Opposition in the Napoleonic Wars: The Impact of the Local Militia, 1807–15', D.Phil. thesis (Oxford, 1984), 21–5. Lord Selkirk's scheme for a mass levy was the most widely publicized, produced as a pamphlet, *On the Necessity of a More Effectual System of National Defence and the Means of Establishing the Permanent Security of the Kingdom* (London, 1808). On opposition to the ballot see below, 103.

powerful bodies of opinion, or 'interests', involved in an issue and then finding a policy that minimized conflict between them and strengthened public confidence in the executive and parliament.[66] One example of this mode of political management was Castlereagh's decision to reinforce the army from the militia instead of reviving the ballot for the Army of Reserve. As he appreciated, either method would have excited 'the opposition of some considerable class of interests, both in and out of parliament',[67] but it was deftly avoided by gratifying the militia colonels with the right to recommend their subalterns for commissions in the army. Exactly the same strategy was adopted with respect to the local militia scheme. Two bodies of opinion he was anxious to conciliate were the volunteer officers, heavily represented in parliament,[68] and the advocates of a compulsory mass levy, who did not lack spokesmen there either. Each of these 'interests' was overlapped by broad public dislike of the ballot formed out of its intensive use in 1803. Castlereagh's adroitness in the business was that he managed to produce a force that made ample provision for voluntary service while possessing the means of compulsion if ever and wherever this proved insufficient.

At first the new war minister's idea was to develop a more practicable version of Windham's training scheme, balloting from this trained population to form a 'sedentary' or local militia, which in turn would supply the army, possibly to the extent that the 'regular' militia could be abandoned altogether. The volunteers were to be treated much as Windham had proposed, reduced in strength to about 100,000 and concentrated in the 'great towns and populous manufacturing districts' as largely self-supported corps of the well-to-do.[69] Such a plan was almost the reverse of that which he later recommended to parliament; it emphasized compulsory service, and makes it easy to believe Castlereagh when he admitted that in principle he preferred a mass levy to volunteering.[70] Both options—a mass levy or a volunteer force—were ways of avoiding the ballot, and Castlereagh's second thoughts seem to have revolved mainly around this consideration as public apprehensions on the subject deepened.[71] The decision to incorporate the existing volunteer

---

[66] B. Hilton, 'The Political Arts of Lord Liverpool', *Trans. Royal Hist. Soc.* 5th ser. 38 (1988), 147–70; J. E. Cookson, *Lord Liverpool's Administration* (Edinburgh, 1975), 400–1.

[67] 'Measures proposed for Improving the State of the Military Force', 12 May 1807, Marquess of Londonderry (ed.), *Memoirs and Correspondence of Viscount Castlereagh* (12 vols., London, 1848–53), viii. 54.

[68] Smith, 'Local Militia', 32–3, using Joshua Wilson, *A Biographical Index to the Present House of Commons* (London, 1808). Perhaps 110 out of 558 British MPs held commissions in the volunteers.

[69] 'Memorandum on the system of defence, more particularly on the formation of a sedentary militia and the training of the people', WO1/407/303–37.   [70] *PD* 1st ser. xi. 856.

[71] The five-year term of militia men recruited in 1803 was due to expire, though the government hastened to obtain a ruling from its law officers to the effect that substitutes were bound to serve to the end of the war. Castlereagh's revised views on home defence organization are faintly visible in his speech in the Commons introducing his plans on 12 Apr. 1808, ibid. xi. 39–48.

corps as far as possible into the now-named 'local' militia owed little to the volunteer officers themselves. Unlike the militia colonels, they never formed an organized 'interest' able to negotiate directly with the government; and they knew, anyway, as the local subscriptions supporting them dried up, that they would have to exist on the government's terms. Castlereagh calculated that many officers would no longer balk at transferring their services into county-organized militia if they could also transfer their rank, and that plenty of their men would follow them. This would have the excellent effect of preserving already trained manpower, as the Duke of York wanted, and of relieving most of the country of a particularly burdensome ballot in view of the large number required. So Castlereagh turned decisively to a plan which would maximize the volunteer component of the new force and minimize conscription by ballot. At the same time he gave up the idea of subjecting the rest of the population to compulsory training, for reasons that probably had much to do with the practical difficulties involved and his own dislike of an armed peasantry existing outside the formal military structure. He certainly remained confident that the local militia would have much of the effect of any training scheme, with men being replaced as they joined the army or as their term of service expired.

Castlereagh introduced his local militia proposals to parliament in April 1808. They excited little debate and no protest was heard from the volunteers, which is a fair indication of Castlereagh's success in finding the middle ground on the issue. Most points of view were accommodated. Conservatives welcomed the creation of a county force which would remain in the county and consist of county men, thereby reinforcing local hierarchies. The interest of urban élites in patriotic service, long expressed through volunteering, far from being stifled, was offered fresh opportunity in the conversion of volunteer corps into local militia. Even radicals and those who wanted a mass levy had the consolation of seeing the principle of personal service established for the first time by the prohibition of substitution. More than this, Castlereagh judged well the social realities behind participation in home defence. There was general complaint that the cost of home defence was not shared equitably when local forces relied on voluntary contributions and especially when the ballot operated as a selective tax whose amount was determined by the market price of substitutes. The replacement of the volunteers by a force wholly supported out of public funds was therefore one improvement. Another was to establish the cost of non-service by fine, though fixed at a level only the wealthy could afford (from £10 to £30 on a scale graduated according to income) and which therefore became a tax only the wealthy paid. Castlereagh's object in abolishing substitution while allowing some to buy their way out was to emancipate gentlemen from a service they would have found intolerable and at the same time impose it on the better sort among the lower classes. The artisanry of some property and respectability generally shunned the army and regarded any kind of military service as an imposition; but they had been attracted into the volunteer corps in significant numbers and were such excellent soldiering material that it was desirable to include them in any mass force. One of the considerations behind the local militia, with its closer links with the army than the volunteers possessed, was to open up this class to more intensive recruiting. Castlereagh sought to win them by offering them service on much the same terms as the volunteers; local training, minimal disruption of their civilian avocations, and exemption from the 'regular' militia.[72]

Lasting until the war's end, the local militia was the nearest the politicians got to the 'permanent system of home defence', or mass reserve, they had long considered necessary. It quickly reached a strength of over 100,000 men, and exceeded 200,000 by 1812,[73] all organized in battalions and bound to a four-year term of service, which overcame the worst defects of the volunteers. Whether the training of the local militia was more effective is harder to determine; the real difference was that men trained when ordered, just as men could no longer please themselves how long they served or even, if sufficient volunteers did not offer, whether they would serve at all. Britain, for the first time during the wars, adopted conscription for home defence; the state was empowered and, more to the point, properly organized to arm, train, and send into the field large numbers of civilians as it deemed necessary.

In the event, the government never used anything like the full conscriptive power it had acquired. Castlereagh wanted the local militia to take as many volunteers as offered and as many conscripts as needed, which turned out to be a highly successful blend of choice and compulsion. At least three-quarters of the men enrolled in 1808–9 were volunteers, mostly obtained from volunteer corps transferring their services, so that relatively light balloting sufficed to make up the numbers.[74] The second ballot held in 1812 was more widespread, though again without producing any sign of popular opposition. Even when ordered out for

---

[72] The training requirements were the greatest imposition on the armed civilians of the volunteers and local militia. The volunteers, according to the act of 1804, were required to train at least 24 days each year. The local militia required 42 days the first year, 28 days each the second and third, with no training at all for the fourth and last year of enrolment. This was, on average, the same requirement.

[73] The establishment totalled 185,161 men in 1808 and 240,388 in 1812. In 1811 195,556 men assembled for training. Sebag-Montefiore, *History of the Volunteer Forces*, 350; York to Lord Liverpool, 11 Oct. 1811, WO1/407/705.

[74] Castlereagh told the Commons on 27 Mar. 1809 that out of 195,161 men in the local militia 125,000 were 'old' volunteers and 50,000–60,000 'new' volunteers, *PD* 1st ser. xiii. 818. A parliamentary return of 10 Apr. 1810 shows 32,811 balloted and 153,138 'otherwise enrolled' in 76 of the 87 counties, *CJ* lxv. 620. Another return of 22 Apr. 1810 totals 109,949 privates as transferring from volunteer corps, ibid. 625–6. Smith, 'Local Militia', 147–52, examines figures from diverse and scattered subdivisions relating to various years.

training, perhaps a better test of popular attitudes, the regiments reported a low rate of non-attendance.[75] The artisan classes remained well represented in the local militia, showing that they could be made to serve on terms more favourable to the state than the old volunteer code had been.[76] Castlereagh's scheme, indeed, was durable basically because, conscriptive in principle, it was benign in practice; it antagonized none of the broad social groups necessarily part of any national mobilization. For the poorer classes the local militia was another haven from the hated 'militia tax' and from the army whose power to draft men continued to terrorize the popular imagination. In addition, the labourer and servant welcomed the supplementary earnings military service brought, while the artisan placed importance on the modest cost to himself—time was his money, and the small obligation was worth a great deal more if it also excluded him from the 'regular' militia. As for the gentry, including the urban gentry, many of whom took colonelcies, they seized the opportunity to concentrate local military leadership in their hands. About 1,300 volunteer corps were replaced by about 270 local militia units,[77] destroying most of the independent commands lower-status people had created for themselves. Those on the margins of the élite—prospering tradesmen and professionals— undoubtedly took the lion's share of the lower commissions, the hope being vain that all could be reserved for gentlemen. But the point to be made is that the local militia gave the county gentry a larger military role than they ever possessed under mass volunteering, establishing a close correspondence between property and power in an area where it had been rather elusive.[78]

Not that the gentry were able to protect the local militia from the economies that were forced on it almost from the beginning. Their appeals were in vain as reduced training and reduced establishments impaired the efficiency of the regiments and whittled away the colonels' patronage.[79] No sooner did the country make a remarkably satisfactory settlement of the political and social issues of home defence than the demands of offensive war came to the fore, and these, as far as the non-regular forces were concerned, were translated into demands that they shed

[75] Smith, 'Local Militia', 357–8. There was a 95 per cent turn-out for training in 1811 (228,418 men out of 240,388) according to a parliamentary return, *CJ* lxvii. 669–70.

[76] Smith found that 51 per cent of the men belonged to the 'artisan and shopkeeper class', with the reservation that this figure may be a little high because Cheshire and Lancashire figured prominently in his data. Smith, 'Local Militia', 153–6.

[77] The return of volunteers in *SP* 1806, x. 229–31 lists 1,307 corps. A local militia return of 1810 lists 269 units. *CJ* lxv. 621–4.

[78] Smith, 'Local Militia', 42–91, deals with the selection of officers for the local militia, including the absorption of volunteer officers into the new force. About two-thirds of the local militia officers were from the volunteers.

[79] Ibid. 313–42; Sir A. Muir Mackenzie to Melville, 16 Dec. 1809, Sir Patrick Murray to Mackenzie, 29 Jan. 1810, Delvine MSS, NLS MS 1501, fos. 60–2, 64–9; Duke of Atholl to Spencer Perceval, n.d., Melville MSS, NLS MS 1048, fos. 184–6.

much of their expense. It would have helped the local militia if it had lived up to expectations as a source of recruits; the results here were immediately disappointing, and the government turned instead to the 'regular' militia and foreigners. A long period of almost constant war and alternatives to life enlistment still could not overcome civilian aversion to army service; nor, for that matter, a reluctance to undertake anything other than local service, as was discovered in 1814 when some local militia were invited to assume guard and garrison duties for the purpose of sending English militia to Ireland.[80] The state therefore, since it could not use its manpower reserves as freely as it required, was quite ready to redistribute military expenditure in support of foreign levies and subsidies. Though conscription into the army never eventuated during the 'Great War' with France, the British state met the enormous demands of the later offensives by assuming much fuller powers over the military organization it possessed, including cavalier treatment of the militia and local militia; the militia were ordered to Ireland, where they had previously gone as volunteers, and were pressed to serve in Europe; the local militia suffered heavy reductions in their training and establishments. Whatever the gentry's interest in them, the home forces could no longer function as effectively as independent entities within the military system even if they preserved the name.

The changes described in this chapter have a longer perspective, since the development of the modern state is associated with the extinction of independent military authority within its boundaries and the imposition of compulsory military service on its citizens. Great Britain is an interesting case because the state's military monopoly remained imperfect much longer than elsewhere and because conscription occurred much later. During the Revolutionary and Napoleonic Wars, as earlier in the eighteenth century, the state, in a real sense, set up conflict between its war needs and powerful social interests by basing its military expansion on forces which the latter dominated and which highly prized their independence from the army. The militia, formed in 1757, quickly underlined the relative unimportance of the army as a vehicle of social opportunity in Britain by becoming a key county institution controlled by county magnates. Once militia colonels the same magnates protected their commands from outside interference by keeping alive the idea that the militia was the 'constitutional force' as a counterweight to the regular army, necessary to prevent military power from being concentrated in one part of the state. In 1798–9, first to get militia to serve in Ireland, then to recruit militiamen for the army, required delicate negotiation with the colonels, who also at this time successfully blocked a proposal to amalgamate their light companies as light battalions under the command of army officers. The volunteer mass of the French Wars represented a much, much greater amount of armed

---

[80] Smith, 'Local Militia', 287–304; Beckett, *Amateur Military Tradition*, 119–20.

force whose availability to the state depended on how far the corps themselves decided to extend their obligations. To a significant degree, they were organized, financed, and their officers chosen without reference to the state. Despite the mainly financial inducements held out to them, their particularism and civilianism were never eradicated or even controlled to the state's satisfaction.

Britain was the only European power that based its defence on a volunteer force. Elsewhere the miltary demands made on governments during the eighteenth century strengthened the principle of compulsory service, and the advent of mass warfare greatly reinforced this trend. From the 1757 Militia Act there was in Britain observable development towards the conscription state, but it was a slow and halting process beset with compromises and often disguised by the promotion of volunteering by the state itself. Britain's exceptionality can be understood better if we appreciate the special conditions under which Britain had to organize defence *en masse* in the Napoleonic age. For one thing, Britain's army remained comparatively small, with a large proportion stationed overseas in imperial garrisons, so that there was a greater than usual dependence on a civilian contribution to defence; the militia, almost certainly, was the most efficient in eighteenth- and nineteenth-century Europe. There was also an abiding concern for economy in war expenditure because military costs had to be added to the cost of maintaining Europe's largest navy. Thirdly, Britain was perceived as having a complex and sophisticated commercial economy which was highly sensitive, among other things, to any interference with the labour supply; there was always concern that mass mobilization, even for the purpose of training civilians, would adversely affect production, ultimately diminishing the country's means for war. Volunteering especially commended itself in these economic terms, its local organization mediating between the state's and the population's priorities and the private contributions in support of corps relieving the public funds.

Yet volunteering was not only seen to be appropriate to the country's circumstances; it was genuinely a popular movement. Its officers were often lesser men than the gentry who built their standing out of the lesser pickings of local influence and power. Its rank and file formed from the artisan and labouring poor could derive significant material benefit from their service. This self-interest was overtopped by the concern of local communities to provide for their own defence and other psychological satisfactions of service, and these further by fears, developing the old Francophobia of British society, of what successful invasion portended for the nation. The volunteers were certainly encouraged to regard themselves as national defenders, and they were increasingly organized as a force for national defence. However, their localism was always more conspicuous than their readiness to serve the state on the state's terms. This should not come as any surprise. Much public enterprise in the eighteenth century originated at the local level and volunteer corps were modelled closely on the forms such enterprise usually took. Like so many commissions and charitable bodies, the corps received statutory recognition but their activities were subject to little interference from the centre. They also began typically with extensive support from the propertied classes, especially through subscriptions and public meetings, but who were then content to delegate management to the small body of officers. The country gentry, where they wielded influence over provincial towns or industrialized countryside, mostly seem to have taken a passive role, allowing lower-status groups (down to prosperous shopkeepers) to add to the large area of public life they already occupied.[81]

The failure of the volunteer system, then, does not have an obvious explanation: it was cheap, popular, based on local communities, and appeared to strike the right balance between the military service the state required and that which society was prepared to offer. Yet in both wars the volunteer mass was short-lived. Moreover, both in 1802 and 1808 the government reverted to militia, breaking up the local interests involved in the volunteer corps and advancing the principle of compulsory service. The change to militia showed, in the first place, that the state wanted to alter the local agency of its military authority. Indeed, it can be represented as part of a trend in late eighteenth-century local government for county bodies to interfere more in and be more assertive against the parishes.[82] Though public enterprise was usually locally organized, in this case the corps too often could not finance themselves adequately, keep up the establishments they had been assigned, or fulfil their training obligations. 'Declining zeal', slackness, and inefficiency characterized many public bodies of the time; the difference was that in the important matter of national defence these deficiencies could not be ignored. This brings us to the other aspect of the change to militia, the centre's urge to control local organizations serving national purposes—which most did not. The machinery of supervision over the volunteers soon eventuated: general legislation, inspection, and audit. (Were early Victorian bureaucratic methods anticipated in military administration?) On the other hand, the state's demands kept expanding, until in the full tide of the Napoleonic War what was required was a civilian force which would supply the army and also make it possible for an increasing proportion of the army to be dispatched overseas. The first the volunteers never did; the second remained doubtful in their case because individuals served as they wished and the varying size and discipline of the corps made it difficult to integrate them with other home forces. Volunteering failed both in the localities and at the centre; failed as a devolution of public authority onto local rulers and failed as a policy of central direction and control.

As an alternative way of organizing a mass force a militia was persistently

---

[81] Langford, *Public Life*, 177.   [82] Eastwood, *Governing Rural England*, ch. 3.

attractive; not for nothing did the armed nation begin with Dundas's supplementary militia in 1796 and end with Castlereagh's local militia. Indeed, the 'large' militia established in 1802 sets up a pattern in which volunteering appears as an *ad hoc* response to the crises of 1798 and 1803 and only a short-term solution to deeper military problems. Such a view understates the strengths volunteering was conceived to have, notably its popular appeal and unifying effect on the wartime society; but the regular revival of militia schemes does point out how Britain struggled to meet the new conditions of war with an effective civilian force. At the government level military, not political, considerations were always paramount. Dundas, Windham, and Castlereagh all accommodated their conservatism to the idea of a trained population. While Castlereagh's local militia returned the control of local forces into the hands of the gentry, the government proceeded to treat the colonels' interests with such little respect that we cannot possibly accept its institution as only a conservative backlash against *parvenu*, socially less reliable elements. Rather, the gentry were indispensable to a county-organized force like the militia, so that the militia was seen not so much as existing for them as they for it. They were the means of effecting the changes the state desired; they alone had the social authority needed to operate the ballot, or any kind of compulsory service, and to form and discipline battalions drawn from disparate communities; and they probably offered the best hope of opening up the local auxiliaries as a source of army recruits.

Contemporaries often bewailed the 'old' militia dating from 1757 as having become nothing better than an adjunct of the army; hence the sardonic reference, 'regular' militia. By the war's end the state had indeed severely encroached on its independence, not only keeping the regiments out of their counties for the duration but also imposing annual drafts for the army and obligatory service in any part of the British Isles. The change from volunteers to local militia could be said to have followed the same trail. This new militia was a force brought into being by the state, paid for by the state, and with its terms of service decided by the state— these latter included subjection to courts martial and military law at all times, which the volunteers had managed to avoid. Further, the local militia advanced the principle of personal conscription by disallowing substitution, thereby breaking open manpower reserves to which previously the state had access only on sufferance; the ballot of 1812 was clearly the largest compulsory levy yet seen.[83] Such measures indicate that the obstacles to conscription were not as great as some have supposed. As one official put it: 'if the armament cannot be accomplished without trenching on constitutional principles, the principles of the constitution ought, as

---

[83] We can assume this because relatively few from the 1808–9 enrolment offered to continue their service. Smith, 'Local Militia', 320.

far as they affect the case, to be changed; for a government that in these times does not possess the means of its own protection or the power of compelling the people to embody for their own defence is not likely long to stand.' The will to conscript for the army even existed. To the Duke of York in 1807 and General Dundas in 1810 the army's endemic shortages of men made 'a forced inlistment' only a matter of time.[84]

Yet the idea of compulsory training and service was still refracted through the prism of a pre-bureaucratic state or *ancien régime*. The same official above who argued for conscription for home defence believed that the trained men could be most effectively formed into military bodies by 'the revival . . . of something like the feudal principle' by which 'men of great estates' equipped and commanded 'as large a proportion of their tenants and followers as they could afford to pay'. The decisive shift to a modern system occurred not with conscription, which was actually an idea as old as the state. It occurred when the state no longer mediated its authority through local rulers but utilized its manpower resources through its own centralized power. This becomes the clearer when we understand that in the Napoleonic age the militia quotas were determined not by the size of the actual population but by the returns of the parishes themselves. Furthermore, the British militia system, although conscriptive in principle, imposed unequal obligations through substitution, fine, and exemption, so that the state recognized that, in general, it could exact service only from the lower orders. Even the local militia as a mass force continued to relieve the propertied classes. No conscription democracy operated, only submission to the realities of the hierarchical society. This, then, remained a pre-bureaucratic system in that it worked through and was only workable through the powerful local interests concentrated in the county lieutenancies. Nor did it rest on pretensions of military citizenship; the poor could be compelled to serve, the rich could not because their conscription would have suborned their social position and therefore their authority. An armed nation might seem to imply centralism and modernism, but it was, in fact, something conjured out of an *ancien régime* whose military aspects tell us much about its essential character.

---

[84] Western has a section on obstacles to conscription and claims that it was an impossible proposition. But see the paper by Sir George Shee, 16 Mar. 1803, Pelham MSS, BL Add. MS 33120, fos. 104–9; memorandum of Duke of York to Lord Grenville, 15 Feb. 1807, WO1/634/125–38; General Dundas to Lord Liverpool, 8 June 1810, WO1/644/195–201. See also Sir James Craig to Brownrigg, June 1804, Sir Charles Grey to same, 6 July 1804, ibid. 902/119–22, 138–9.

4
The Manpower Ceiling

'IT is a curious fact which deserves to be made known, that we have at this moment in arms in this country a military force greater than ever France had during any time of the Revolution.' So the newspapers said in 1803, as the volunteer mass swelled way beyond the proportions of the previous war. There were predictions at this time of over two million men marching against the invader—a figure perhaps conjured up from the 'military census' of able-bodied men the lieutenancies were undertaking.[1] Once the age of mass warfare had been ushered in, the amount of military manpower a society possessed or could tap became of increasing interest to governments and publics. In Britain especially, where nothing like it had occurred before, the sheer scale of armed preparation was taken as the most visible evidence of the country's commitment to the war and its patriotic spirit. Already, in 1801, the public had been invited to marvel at the 469,188 men the country had mobilized.[2]

National comparisons were an even better index of Britain's military expansion. Lord Liverpool's papers during the Napoleonic War include an 'account' of the great powers which was obviously compiled as a sort of league table of their military strength, national efficiency, and 'national spirit'. In it the number of the armed forces is ratioed to the 'male active population'. France, Russia, and Austria are ranked as having almost one in fourteen under arms, Prussia almost one in ten (with the observation that the Prussian army 'is in great part composed of foreigners and cannot therefore be considered merely as a national army'), while Britain:

Population	Proportion capable of bearing arms	Army	Navy
15,000,000	3,750,000	266,621	120,000
		386,621	

more than 1 in 10 of the male active population

add volunteers		385,151
sea fencibles		30,000
above 1 in 5		803,772.[3]

[1] *Cambridge Chronicle*, 13 Aug., 3 Sept. 1803.   [2] *The Times*, 14 July 1801.

[3] 'Account of the military and naval force of the following countries in the proportion they bear to their respective populations', Liverpool MSS, BL Add. MS 38358, fo. 230. I date this paper to 1805 because on 8 Mar. Hawkesbury made much of the fact that Britain had 810,000 men under arms. *PD* 1st ser. iii. 808–9. See him again for the 'extent of the armed force', 25 May 1809, where a mobilization of 786,521 men is set against a British Isles population of 14,942,646. Fortescue, *County Lieutenancies*, 306.

In the eighteenth century the connection between population and state power
had been assumed rather than explained, and then in terms of national productive-
ness.[4] Now, during the titanic struggle with Napoleon, populousness acquired an
explicit military significance; great powers were great powers by virtue of possessing the manpower reserves out of which could come the new-size armies. Britain's
good fortune in this changed military order was not her wealth so much as her
island situation. A relatively small army, a large part of which necessarily remained
overseas, did not matter; for a prepared civilian population would possess an overwhelming advantage of numbers over an invader operating across the sea. Benjamin
Bell, the Edinburgh surgeon and 'calculator', described this strategic balance between Britain and her more populous neighbours as early as 1797. Universal training, he said, would furnish 'upwards of twelve hundred thousand, perhaps even a
million and a half of able-bodied men . . . a number more than sufficient to repell
the attack of all Europe were it possible for them ever to combine against us'.[5]

Was the census of 1801 an attempt to establish more definitely the size of
Britain's manpower reserves, belonging therefore to the development of the armed
nation? Nobody said as much in parliament. According to the very meagre reports
of discussion on the census bill in November 1800, attention focused rather on the
current 'scarcity' and whether it indicated an increasing imbalance between food
supplies and population. Yet John Rickman, the chief instigator of the census,
when listing its practical benefits, mentioned first the importance in wartime of
knowing the number available for armed service, particularly home defence. He,
moreover, drew up his proposal in 1796, at a time when Britain was forced back
on the defensive after the collapse of the First Coalition and Austria's defeat. A
similar situation existed in 1800—Russia had withdrawn from the Second Coalition, the Austrian alliance was faltering, and an invasion attempt was expected
once France was free of Continental enemies. Rickman made some play of the
public confidence a census would engender. While the census certainly was not a
response to a manpower crisis—the army had solved its recruiting problems for the
moment by taking drafts from the militia, and the volunteers had become a sufficient force for home defence—it was agreed to during a period of great anxiety.
The government, too, may well have been taken with the idea that a census would
demonstrate that the national resources were too often underestimated and that,
in fact, Britain's economy was more than equal to the struggle with France.

Indeed, the census was conceivably a shot fired in the developing psychological
war with the Napoleonic regime. When he published his memorandum of 1796 in
June 1800, Rickman noted: 'France has certainly encouraged her own subjects, and

[4] A. J. Youngson, *After the Forty-Five: The Economic Impact on the Scottish Highlands* (Edinburgh, 1973), 54 ff.   [5] Bell to Dundas, 19 July 1797, Melville MSS, SRO GD51/9/120.

alarmed Europe, by her vaunted 27 millions'.[6] This remark had a background in the steadily intensifying statistical effort of the Revolutionary governments. The Brumaire coup brought about a new phase in the collection of data which could be used to point up national progress and national power inasmuch as the Consulate quickly established a bureau of statistics which began planning for a population census and a massive national survey. It is most unlikely that these developments passed unnoticed in Britain. A number of private individuals were striving to refute the view that Britain's population and production were declining, and the French government's interest in statistical verification of national resources made it even urgent that the British government do something similar to secure public confidence. In this context concern about 'scarcity' seems to have been merely the public face the ministers assumed to put the case for a census.[7]

Rickman in 1800 hailed Sir John Sinclair's *Statistical Account of Scotland*, completed the previous year, as an invaluable compendium of information useful to the state. Since the *Account* was also an attempt to take a census, it, almost certainly, helped to form views about how a census might be conducted and for what purposes.[8] The accuracy of Sinclair's population totals had been affected by his collecting returns from the parish ministers over a period of seven or eight years. Rickman, presumably to avoid the same problem, wanted to extrapolate from three or four parishes in each county. The government, however, decided in favour of an 'actual enumeration'—which shows that it wanted figures of the greatest possible exactness and authority despite the 'trouble and expence'. Possibly the totals Sinclair turned in had much to do with this decision. He began the rout of the population 'pessimists' which the census of 1801 completed. His figures indicating that Scotland's population had increased 23 per cent in forty years (a rate of growth even more impressive in view of the notorious out-migration of Scots) offered the best guarantee yet that a census would deliver proof of an expanding population to put alongside evidence of an expanding economy. Furthermore, the number available for military service was immediately extracted from the population total Sinclair offered.[9] At over 300,000, this would have indicated that one man in

---

[6] 'Thoughts on the Utility and Facility of Ascertaining the Population of England', *Commercial and Agricultural Magazine*, ii. 391–9 (June 1800). The article has been reprinted in D. V. Glass, *Numbering the People: The Eighteenth Century Population Controversy and the Development of Census and Vital Statistics in Britain* (Farnborough, 1973), 106–13.

[7] French statistical endeavours are covered in Jean-Claude Perrot and Stuart Woolf, *State and Statistics in France 1789–1815* (New York, 1984) and Woolf, *Napoleon and the Integration of Europe* (London, 1991). Glass covers the population controversy in 18th-cent. England. See also my article 'Political Arithmetic and War in Britain 1793–1815', *War and Society*, 1 (1983), 37–60.

[8] Glass, *Numbering the People*, 109; Sir John Sinclair, *The Statistical Account of Scotland 1791–1799*, ed. D. Withrington and I. Grant (repr., 20 vols., East Ardsley, 1977–83), i, p. xlii.

[9] 'General view of the population of Scotland drawn up from Sir John Sinclair's statistical account . . . compared with the returns made to Dr Webster in 1755', Jan. 1798, Melville MSS, SRO

nine was serving in the militia and volunteers, establishing against the doubters that the country, even its heavily recruited Scottish part, was well short of being at the limits of military expansion.

It was the localities, allocated quotas for the militia and other compulsory levies, who were most immediately interested in the manpower demands of the war. During the Revolutionary War much discontent began to emerge over the manifest 'inequality' of the county quotas in relation to population,[10] and it might be imagined that the census was intended to end these disparities, especially as Rickman saw this as yet another benefit it would confer. However, curious though it is, the data the census provided were never used to ensure that manpower reserves were drawn on equitably. When the supplementary militia was raised in 1796, the contribution of each county was determined by the number of taxed houses, reckoned to be a reasonably accurate index of total population.[11] And when the old quotas of the 1757 Militia Act ended in 1799, the new ones were calculated by the proportion a county provided when the number of men serving was added to its supplementary militia quota. As the change was meant 'to equalise, as accurately as possible, the burthen to be borne by each county respectively, according to its actual state of population',[12] it is somewhat surprising to find that further revision of the quotas in the 1802 Militia Act took no account of the census figures. Instead the government chose to base the calculation on the lieutenancy returns of age-eligible men, the same that had been done when the Scottish militia was first organized in 1797.[13] The Army of Reserve of 1803 was also allocated according to these returns. In principle, quotas derived from regular censuses of 'military age' men conducted by parochial officials were as fair and exact as the *ancien régime* could make them. In practice the system gave every locality an interest in and ample opportunity for understating the numbers[14]—though this mattered less and less because, as it happened, the 1802 quotas were never revised regardless of the provision in the Act.

GD51/5/244. I suspect Sinclair himself drew up this paper. Webster's population figure was taken as authoritative.

[10] The different ratios of men serving to men available are listed in Chatham MSS, PRO30/8/244, fos. 96–101.

[11] Glass, *Numbering the People*, 107. The data used were probably taken from a return of 1790. See *House of Commons Sessional Papers of the Eighteenth Century*, ed. S. Lambert (19 vols., Wilmington, Del., 1975), ii. 257.　　　　　　　　　[12] Dundas to Lord Rivers, 2 Nov. 1799, HO30/2, fos. 369–71.

[13] Alexander Dirom, 'Scheme for forming the Scotch militia into 12 regiments', 4 Feb. 1798, HO102/16, fo. 83. The act of 1802 laid down that the privy council was to revise the quotas once every ten years, the first occasion to be not later than 25 June 1805.

[14] A good idea of how inaccurate the lists could be is given in Sir A. Grant to Duke of Gordon, 21 Dec. 1802; 'Objections and protest by Sir Archibald Grant against proceedings of lieutenancy'; minutes of general meeting of lieutenancy, Aberdeen, 24 Aug. 1803; resolutions of Huntly district, 26 Aug. 1803, Gordon MSS, SRO GD44/47/28–9; W. Sinclair of Freswick, 'Some general observations on persons liable to be balloted for the militia and army of reserve', Sinclair of Freswick MSS, SRO GD136/1253/1.

At first, then, the population census was not conceived as bearing in any way on the actual administration of manpower resources. Afterwards the idea that the size of the compulsory levies ought to be proportionate to population became a dead letter, so that in 1808 even the local militia, the nearest to a conscript force the war produced, merely multiplied the old quotas by six.

If the census was not put to practical use, it still had the effect the government probably hoped for, of bolstering the nation's confidence against the enormous might of France. The population total returned—almost eleven millions—was well clear of the pre-census estimates of the 'pessimists'; over another four millions, parliament was immediately told, could be allowed for Ireland.[15] Further, Rickman's calculations on the eighteenth-century population revealed sustained growth at an increasing rate, a trend confirmed by the next census in 1811. The imbalance in population terms between France and Britain was now seen to be of the order of two to one.[16] This might have been a discouraging enough disparity had not the census also been valuable for work on the national income. There had been lively interest in the 'true extent of national resources' in the later 1790s as war expenditure and borrowing mounted, and with the census data at their disposal the calculators, led by Patrick Colquhoun, were able to produce an authoritative estimate of national income to emphasize Britain's economic power. Colquhoun particularly drew attention to the figure Gregory King had ventured about a century earlier and the difference with his own, some five times greater.[17]

The census offered no information about the age structure of Britain's population, which would have made possible a more exact calculation of manpower reserves. The Defence Act of 1803 changed the definition of 'military age' by requiring the registration of men aged from 17 to 55; the militia class since 1757 had been men 18 to 45. It seems to have been accepted that this class equalled one-fifth of the total population, probably on the basis of Alexander Webster's Scottish census of 1755.[18] The expanded 'military population' in 1803 was taken to comprise one-quarter—hence the calculation cited at the beginning of this chapter showing that over one in five of the population 'capable of bearing arms' was serving.[19] Military participation on this scale was totally new to eighteenth-century society.

[15] *SP* 1801–2, vii. 451 (Summary of Census).
[16] Liverpool in House of Lords on 8 Mar. 1805. *PD* 1st ser. iii. 808.
[17] Cookson, 'Political Arithmetic', 38–45.　　[18] Sinclair, *Statistical Account*, i. 8, 101, 127.
[19] Cf. Sir George Shee's paper, 16 Mar. 1803, Pelham MSS, BL Add. MS 33120. fos. 104–9, where the population fit to bear arms, 'according to the ordinary mode of computation', was given as 3,500,000 out of a total British population of 10,500,000. But I have found this 1 >:< 3 ratio nowhere else. The Defence Act of 1803 (s. 24 and Schedule D) required the lieutenancies to send in annually abstracts of the subdivision rolls. These returns could have served as a census of the military population, but they were not even complete in 1803–4 and were hardly made afterwards. See 'General abstract of the subdivision rolls for various counties', *SP* 1803–4, xi. 296–9; 1806, x. 333.

Even if we cannot accept the contemporary figure as very accurate, more careful analysis of the age structure of the population suggests that about one in ten was serving in 1794 and one in six in 1809.[20] In specific localities, of course, the ratio could be very much higher.

Yet opposition to military service rarely disturbed the wartime society, least of all during the Napoleonic War, when recruitment reached new heights. The worst disorders occurred in the 1790s with respect to the militia; in Ireland (1793), England (1796), and Scotland (1797).[21] On these occasions the sort of communal hostility to conscription was manifested that was also found in France, though the militia levy designated men only for home service and—with the exception of Scotland—bore relatively lightly on the eligible population. It was apprehension of a severe and damaging man-tax that caused the trouble; opposition rapidly dissipated into more or less grudging acceptance once the true measure of the burden was taken. The militia, anyway, continued to take up the kind of men who otherwise joined the regular army. Both were understood to relieve, and did relieve, society of those who did not fit easily into its structures—the mobile poor, the unemployed, family mavericks, bastard-getters, adventurers, and so on. Whatever the army's demands for men during the prolonged struggle with France, the general attitude remained largely one of indifference, as indeed it had been throughout the eighteenth century and would continue to be under a regime of voluntary enlistment. The remarkable constancy in the size of the annual intake of recruits seems to indicate that the army was drawing on a fairly unvarying proportion of the population, which could be expected when such a multifarious group of 'outsiders' felt its attraction.[22]

Conscription in France was a gigantic onslaught on the peasant society, invading the deeply felt autarky of the village community and upsetting the labour supply of the local economy. Sometimes the tension between the traditional antipathy to military service and the new demands of the state broke into open violence against the *gendarmerie*. More usually, it was translated into the assistance and protection offered to young men on the run from the authorities—during the Napoleonic regime several hundred thousand evaded service either by desertion or disobedience of the conscription law.[23] France's experience, therefore, stands in stark contrast to

[20] Emsley, *French Wars*, 33, 133.

[21] These disorders are covered in T. Bartlett, 'An End to Moral Economy: The Irish Militia Disturbances of 1793', *Past and Present*, 99 (May 1983), 41–64; J. Bohstedt, *Riots and Community Politics in England and Wales, 1790–1810* (Cambridge, Mass., 1983), 173–84; K. J. Logue, *Popular Disturbances in Scotland 1780–1815* (Edinburgh, 1979), 75–115.

[22] Interestingly, the army after Waterloo raised a similar number of men per annum, an average of 12,885 recruits. See H. Strachan, *Wellington's Legacy: The Reform of the British Army 1830–54* (Manchester, 1984), 56.

[23] The authoritative study is A. Forrest, *Conscripts and Deserters: The Army and French Society during the Revolution and Empire* (Oxford, 1989).

Number of Recruits, 1803–13
(excluding Army of Reserve and Additional Force men, militia volunteers,
and recruits for foreign and colonial corps)

1803	11,253	1809	11,720
1804	9,430	1810	9,095
1805	11,677	1811	11,472
1806	11,875	1812	14,432
1807	19,114	1813	11,285 (for nine months)
1808	12,963		

Source: *CJ* lxix. 635.

Britain's, and for mostly obvious reasons—conscription, first of all, but also conscription aimed at a narrow social group (single men of 20–5) with the requirement of unlimited service. But it is still worth asking why the little compulsion there was in Britain did not cause more trouble for the government. After all, in 1803 about 100,000 men were raised by the militia and Army of Reserve ballots without serious opposition, though the size of the levy exceeded anything previously attempted and the demand for men drove up the price of substitutes and volunteers to record levels. The local militia legislation of 1808 went further and required a force of over 200,000 to be raised, if necessary by ballot without substitution being allowed.

The saving grace of the militia system in both Britain and Ireland was that personal service was inflicted on only small numbers. Regiments were always largely filled by substitutes whom individuals or groups of individuals paid for and by volunteers whose expense was met by parishes. Irish regiments consisted almost totally of volunteers because there the ballot was usually inoperable in view of the defects of the parochial organization and fear of popular resistance. The proportion of 'principals' (that is, balloted men serving in person) was highest in the northernmost Scottish counties, where the population often turned to soldiering to escape a survival economy. It was lowest in the urban and industrial districts, which were also the army's richest recruiting grounds.[24] Generally, personal service declined over time, once the prospect of a long war and therefore long service set in, and also as the government became increasingly reluctant to use the ballot.

---

[24] The high rate of personal service in northern Scotland is noted in Sir J. St C. Erskine to Lord Melville, 4 May 1804, Chatham MSS, PRO30/8/133, fos. 75–80. A return to parliament on militia recruitment 1807–8 shows that the ten counties with the highest rates were: Hereford, Sussex, Berkshire, Huntingdon, Dorset, Somerset, Suffolk, Wiltshire, Norfolk, and Devon. The ten lowest were (excluding Rutland): Middlesex, London (Tower Hamlets), Derby, North Yorkshire, Leicester, Nottingham, East Yorkshire, Cumberland, Staffordshire, and West Yorkshire. See *SP* 1808, vii. 201.

The Leicestershire militia took in 143 principals out of 560 in December 1792 and only 12 out of 480 in 1808. The Edinburgh regiment had 179 principals out of a total of 601 men in 1799, 155 out of 622 in 1802, 41 out of 944 in 1804 and 39 out of 1,009 in 1812. In 1804 over the whole of the Scottish militia one man in twelve was a principal; in the recruiting of 1810 one in fifteen was; in that of 1812 one in twenty-seven.[25]

How the poor avoided personal service to this extent is an interesting question, especially in view of the high price of substitutes, averaging over £27 in the 1807–8 ballot according to a parliamentary return.[26] Of course, the exemption allowed volunteers must have had an appreciable effect, and evasion of the authorities cannot have been difficult in large communities or where wage labourers were mobile—the militia lists, which were the only registers of eligible men, remained with the parishes and subdivisions. Furthermore, the whole cost of avoiding service rarely devolved on individuals; militia 'clubs' were organized to find substitutes in return for a small premium from each member, and, under the militia laws, parishes could subsidize the cost of substitutes to the poor, and even the modestly wealthy, out of the rates.[27] Employers and gentry were also often willing to help their workmen and other dependants.[28] Probably a great many communities took collective action to protect their own, using the rates and subscriptions to create a fund which was then drawn on either to raise men or pay fines. How often officials falsified the lists or certificates of exemption is anybody's guess, but such practices were an obvious way of doing favours or serving the interests of the parish.[29] Since allowances were paid to the wives and children of serving militiamen, every parish could save itself expense if it controlled militia recruitment. However, the difficulties individuals and parishes had in finding suitable men soon told, particularly when parishes began to be fined for not filling their quotas. They seem to have found the cheapest and most convenient arrangement to be thus: to pay or collect

---

[25] Leicestershire figures from ibid. and Western, *English Militia*, 256. Edinburgh figures from Erskine's letter (previous note) and regimental roll books, Buccleuch MSS, SRO GD224/426/1, 5; 427/1. Figures for Scotland are from Erskine's letter; 'Account of the number of men raised for the militia', *CJ* lxvi. 561–2; W. Wynyard to Lord Liverpool, 26 Oct. 1813, WO25/3225.

[26] 'Account of the sum fixed in each county as a bounty for substitutes', *CJ* lxiii. 614.

[27] Western, *English Militia*, 245–54.

[28] For example, the expenses of the militia club at Bellie, Aberdeenshire, for the 1807–8 ballot totalled £231. 19s. 4d., of which the Duke of Gordon contributed £30. Gordon MSS, SRO GD44/47/32.

[29] Sinclair of Freswick in Caithness expanded on the skulduggery perpetrated when lists were compiled and exemptions considered. See his paper in Sinclair of Freswick MSS, SRO GD136/1253/1. In one district of Aberdeenshire in 1803 the deputy-lieutenants deliberately and illegally altered the lists to achieve a lower militia quota. Gordon MSS, SRO GD44/47/29. Four Lewis parishes in 1807 exempted 124 men on the grounds that they were constables. Whetstone, *Scottish County Government*, 107.

the fines for non-service (which were limited to £10 per man), adding to this sum the bounties for volunteers they were authorized to levy, but leaving it to the county regiment to raise the men, which it could do more easily and more cheaply than could a parish acting on its own.[30] So personal service became a rarity, and the battalions came to be filled with militia volunteers whose recruiting costs were met by parish communities rather than unlucky individuals.

Not surprisingly, it was the wealthy who most came to resent the militia levies; they bore the brunt of the militia costs charged to the rates, made the largest contributions to parochial subscriptions, and might also have to buy their servants and dependants out of service. To them the militia was a 'tax', second only to the property tax as an onerous burden of war. Its amount was unpredictable, depending on the market price for substitutes or volunteers. Its 'partiality' was notorious, worse than the property tax, no account being taken of ability to pay. For this last reason particularly, it helped fuel a 'middle class' animus against war taxation and was duly incorporated in the radicals' litany attacking the aristocratic state.[31] Grievance over the militia was surely at its height in 1803–4 when there were in close succession ballots for the militia, supplementary militia, and the Army of Reserve, sending the prices for substitutes to sums exceeding the annual income of labouring families; even in Scotland, where men were easiest to come by, while a third were recruited for no more than the fine for non-service, the remainder cost more than £15 per man and sometimes as much as thirty guineas.[32] After such heavy levies, the government avoided general ballots as much as it could. In spite of the very large numbers who enlisted into the army from the militia, general ballots were held only in 1807 and 1810. This was managed by reducing the militia establishment (from 86,000 in 1804 to 61,000 in 1806, and from 78,000 in 1808–10 to 61,000 in 1812) and by allowing the regiments to take in boys and beat for recruits in direct competition with the army. The declining importance of the ballot, though obvious, is difficult to enumerate because before 1812 no record was kept of the number of principals and substitutes (the direct products of the ballot system) as distinct from volunteers and recruits. When the information was procured,

[30] See Sir J. St C. Erskine to Lord Melville, 4 May 1804, Chatham MSS, PRO30/8/133, fos. 75–7: 'in truth a very large proportion of the Scotch militia has been raised in the manufacturing towns by the very same modes by which the army is usually recruited; and I know that to Glasgow, in particular, officers and parties have been sent from almost every regiment that was in want of men and in possession of funds arising from the penalties for not serving'.

[31] For a general account of war taxation as a political issue see Cookson, *Friends of Peace*, 78–82, but for specific mention of the militia 'tax' see 'On the inequality of our taxation and the importance of sustaining the middling class of the community', *Examiner*, 1 May 1808. The introduction of the local militia brought a fresh barrage of complaint, e.g. *Leeds Mercury*, 10 June 1809, *Stamford News*, 22 June 1810, *Examiner*, 7 Oct. 1810.

[32] Sir J. St C. Erskine to Lord Melville, 4 May 1804, Chatham MSS, PRO30/8/133, fos. 75–7.

the first return revealed that in 1812 the difference was between 370 in the former category and 6,393 in the latter.[33]

Ireland, as suggested earlier, is an even better case of how enlistment prevailed over the ballot. Modelled though the Irish militia was on the English, its establishment in 1793 provoked so violent a response from the peasantry that most local rulers quickly concluded the ballot was unworkable.[34] Within three months of the passing of the first militia bill, a second allowed parishes to provide volunteers, and the practice began immediately whereby parish fines and bounties were transferred to the regiments which did the actual recruiting.[35] It was often complained that the very large complement of enlisted men made the Irish militia a derogation of the militia ideal and more like fencibles, in that they were less the product of any communal effort than the property of their colonels who found the men and generally used the regiment as a source of influence and patronage.[36] Again it is difficult to say precisely how much the ballot was used. During the Revolutionary War, according to an act of 1802, the ballot was 'not generally adopted', and in the crisis of 1803 the Irish government accepted that both the militia and the Army of Reserve would be largely raised by enlistment, passing a 'speedy enrolment' bill to expedite the process.[37] When in 1807 it was proposed to add 9,905 men to the militia establishment, twenty out of thirty-five counties and cities wanted 'enrolment' under the colonels as opposed to the ballot or parochial allocations of volunteers.[38] There is no doubt that the ballot was used more extensively in 1807 and 1809 than at any other time, as very large augmentations were demanded and the pressure on Ireland's manpower resources was by this time beginning to tell; perhaps 1,138 principals and substitutes out of a total of 8,288 men were raised in 1809–10. Even so, almost all of the 1,138 were drawn from five counties, and a return of balloted men in 1813 indicates a similar concentration.[39] We can be the surer that the ballot was scarcely operative in Ireland because too few gentry would

---

[33] W. Wynyard to Lord Liverpool, 26 Oct. 1813, WO25/3225. There is an incomplete return to parliament which shows that 8,898 out of 14,921 men (60 per cent) were raised as principals or substitutes in 1810, a year when a general ballot operated. See *CJ* lxvi. 561–2. However, the counties and regiments are unlikely to have made a careful distinction between substitutes and volunteers and recruits until instructed in 1812. Another return, purportedly of recruits raised by beat of drum but referring to volunteers and recruits, gives a total of 27,360 raised in Britain, 1809–13. *SP* 1813–14, xi. 265–7.   [34] Bartlett, 'End to Moral Economy', 41–2.

[35] H. McAnally, *The Irish Militia 1793–1816* (Dublin, 1949), 39–51.

[36] Ibid. 285–6. Lord Hardwicke saw the Irish militia as being 'rather of the description of fencible men raised by bounty for home service'. Hardwicke to C. Yorke, Feb. 1804, Hardwicke MSS, BL Add. MS 35705, fos. 139–41.   [37] McAnally, *Irish Militia*, 172–4.

[38] *CJ* lxiii. 617; 'County replies to Littlehales's circular letter of 19 August 1807', SPOI CSO VIIIA/ 1/13.

[39] McAnally, *Irish Militia*, 235–6, 252–3. There is a detailed survey of the use of the ballot in 1807–8 in *SP* 1808, vii. 275–332 (summarized in McAnally, 326).

act at the subdivisional level and the machinery of parochial government did not always exist; in his county, the major of the Carlow regiment told the chief secretary, 'there are parishes without any resident clergyman, churchwardens, or even a church, in consequence of which no vestry could be held or the money legally assessed off the inhabitants'.[40] Below the county, therefore, central authority could rapidly lose its effectiveness. It is interesting that in Ireland the county, not the parish, paid the family allowances for militiamen and carried the liability for deficient numbers.

As a levy on available manpower, the Irish militia was but a small imposition. The original quotas of 1793 were fixed on the basis of twenty-one men per thousand hearths. A thousand hearths, in the understanding of contemporary authorities on Ireland's population, translated into at least 5,500 people, therefore an eligible population of 1,100, and therefore a service ratio of one man in about fifty.[41] England's ratio was worked out at between one in forty and one in fifty,[42] and it may well be that the calculations for Ireland were done so as to match the English figure. All this becomes interesting because when it was decided to press ahead with a Scottish militia in 1797, the government took an entirely different course, confining the ballot to a small age group (19–23-year-olds), with the result that each man on the lists stood an almost one in four chance of being called. A conscription of this ferocity was certainly never intended. The disappointing number on the lists—24,663, perhaps half of what had been expected—was the effect of heavy military recruitment in Scotland from the commencement of the war, which doubtless carried over into a determination by many places to doctor the returns in their favour.[43]

Henry Dundas, it seems, must bear most of the responsibility for the militia plan adopted. He ignored his Scottish advisers who much preferred to develop volunteer corps, and altered his original idea for a force of 12,000 drawn from the 20–30 age group only to the extent of halving both. 'King Harry the Ninth' would not pass an opportunity to carry through in his realm what he could never accomplish in England. The English militia he disliked as merely another enlisted force alongside the army, the volunteers as providing numbers but too local-minded and perhaps not really controllable. While the supplementary militia was more in accord with his ideas, it was an addition grafted on to an already flawed system. National defence, said Dundas, ought to rest on the compulsory induction of all young men

---

[40] R. Cornwall to Sir A. Wellesley, 1 Aug. 1807, WO1/774/409–11. See also Lord Clancarty to Sir E. Littlehales, 16 Aug. 1809, SPOI CSO OP283/46; McAnally, *Irish Militia*, 236, 252, 258.

[41] Ibid. 24, 316; D. A. Beaufort, *Memoir of a Map of Ireland; Illustrating the Topography of That Kingdom, and Containing a Short Account of Its Present State, Civil and Ecclesiastical* (Dublin, 1792).

[42] A. Dirom to the lord advocate, 4 Feb. 1798, HO102/16, fos. 85–7.

[43] Dirom, ibid., stated that 'many of the counties have not returned their just proportions'.

into military service, so that the army would always be backed by a reserve of trained civilians. In Scotland the soundness of these principles was about to be tried. Although substitution was permitted, it was taken for granted that most men would serve personally, both because of the youth of the draft and Scotland's comparative poverty.[44] In the event, Dundas entirely misconceived the situation. The attempt to ballot the militia provoked popular resistance reminiscent of that put up in France to conscription, which was equally burdensome on a small age cohort; and, when the levy was finally under way, there was a rush to avoid personal service little different from England's experience.

The Scottish militia disorders in the summer of 1797 were concentrated in the arable farming areas of the Lowlands where small farms and family economies could little afford a loss of labour or supplementary income. Larger farmers, though careful not to engage in open protest, must have been equally concerned about the effect of such a militia on the labour market, they mostly hiring farm servants from year to year. At the time it was pointed out that agricultural workers would largely fill the ranks because in the towns, and wherever there were well-populated trades, young men could often claim exemption as apprentices.[45] Beyond present necessities loomed ineradicable fears that sons, friends, and neighbours lost to military service were lost for ever; late in the American War several Scottish regiments had been shipped to India in violation of their terms of enlistment and at least two others refused to embark when given the orders; the Scottish fencible men, originally raised for the defence of Scotland, had mostly ended up in Ireland, another passage marked by mutinies and executions; the Duke of York's decision in 1795 to reduce many newly raised corps in order to bring the old regiments up to fighting strength was not only a breach of faith with the colonels and men but sent numbers off to the West Indies.[46] In the popular imagination, the army never yielded up its own; there was ample disbelief that a Scottish militia would remain in Scotland and that the men would be released back into civilian life after a short

---

[44] Dundas to the Duke [of Montrose], 15 Nov. 1796, Melville MSS, SRO GD51/1/888/2; Dundas to the lord advocate, 7 Mar. 1797, printed in Meikle, *Scotland and the French Revolution*, 276–81; A. Dirom to the lord advocate, 27 Mar. 1797, lord advocate to Dundas, 29 Mar. 1797, Melville MSS, NLS MS 7, fos. 150–7.

[45] G. Paterson to lord advocate, 3 Oct. 1797, Laing MSS, EUL La. ii. 501.

[46] J. Prebble, *Mutiny: Highland Regiments in Revolt, 1743–1804* (London, 1975) deals with the American War mutinies and the fencible mutinies of 1794. Memories of the bad treatment the American War regiments had received adversely affected recruiting in 1793. F. H. Mackenzie to Lord Adam Gordon, 19 May 1793, HO50/2, fos. 150–1; D. McLeod to R. Blair, 23 May 1793, HO102/8, fos. 238–40. Alan Cameron's 79th mutinied in Belfast in 1794 on a rumour that the colonel had sold the regiment to the East India Company. T. Bartlett, 'Indiscipline and Disaffection in the Armed Forces in Ireland in the 1790s', in P. Corish (ed.), *Radicals, Rebels and Establishments* (Belfast, 1985), 117. Col. Alexander Hay's correspondence with the Horse Guards over the reduction of the 109th (Aberdeenshire) regiment in 1795 is in Leith Hall MSS, SRO GD225/1044/21/104, 106–7.

period of service. As in France, military levies which threatened to destabilize families and communities met with massive opposition. The crowds which acted to interrupt the handing in of the militia lists frightened the authorities to the extent of postponing the ballot for nine months and reducing the call-up to half the projected force. The subtler response of *insoumission*—non-co-operation—was also evident in Scotland. So many men were believed to have left their counties or 'gone south' to England that it was doubted whether the lists could include more than 18,000 effective names.[47] Labour was highly mobile in Scotland, and since the ballot was delayed over the slack time of the agricultural year, it was relatively easy for men to move away from their parish of registration and avoid service under cover of the normal itineracy.

Yet we can be over-fascinated by Scottish opposition to the militia in 1797, perhaps under the influence of 'crowd history' which focuses on the most spectacular protest elements in popular culture, or even dislike of the 'Dundas system' as the subordination of Scottish interests to the metropolitan power. After all, in 1798–9 the militia was successfully established in Scotland, though it was not the militia Dundas had wanted or envisaged. As in England and Ireland, men were very ready to join a home force once the market for substitutes and volunteers was operating. The ballot and embodiment of half the force after May 1798 was followed by further encouraging reports from the lieutenancies that public feeling had 'totally changed' and that men were now 'desirous' to serve.[48] So the regiments were brought up to full complement at the beginning of 1799. This, moreover, was done on the basis of the original lists and therefore without extending the eligible age (though legislation soon afterwards altered the age requirement to 19–30, which nearly tripled the size of the ballotable population). Because the chances of being drawn were so high, the cost of substitutes and volunteer bounties soared, proportionately well above English levels—the premiums charged by militia clubs, it was observed, averaged half a guinea in England and three guineas in Scotland.[49] On the other hand, the levy was small in population terms, and the subscriptions of the wealthy or parishes thus had to cover relatively few individuals. This effect was still not enough to prevent the regiments at the outset from being heavily loaded with principals; the Edinburgh (Midlothian) regiment, drawn from an exceptionally wealthy and populous part of Scotland, contained 179 principals out of 601 rank and file in 1799.[50] A Scottish militia, prevented by statute from marching out of Scotland, was a generally attractive form of military service to young men, many

[47] A. Dirom to the lord advocate, 4 Feb. 1798, HO102/16, fos. 85–7; Duke of Buccleuch to Dundas, 6 July 1798, Buccleuch MSS, SRO GD224/30/5/17.
[48] Dundas to the Duke of Atholl, 26 Dec. 1798, HO50/29.
[49] A. Dirom to the lord advocate, 4 Feb. 1798, HO102/16, fos. 85–7.
[50] Regimental roll book, 1799, Buccleuch MSS, SRO GD224/426/1.

of whom were used to taking employment on the opportunity of the moment. The addresses and advertisements put out by the lieutenancies made much of the security the militia offered—regular pay and all found—and promised the protection and patronage of the officers both during service and on discharge.[51] Such advantages, like the chance for non-principals to gain a small capital sum, held significant value for that part of the proletariat which had to improvise an existence.

The market for substitutes and other recruits rapidly expanded in Scotland, as it did everywhere else. In the heavy balloting for the militia and Army of Reserve in 1803–4, only one man in twenty offered personal service in the counties below Inverness. These levies, drawn now from the usual militia class of 18–45-year-olds, tripled the number that had been required in 1797, and the localities seem to have reacted vigorously to avoid the charges for family men and the fines for deficient quotas. Agents of militia clubs and parishes, and regimental recruiting parties with the non-service fines in their pockets, descended on Glasgow and the surrounding manufacturing towns to which large numbers of Highlanders and disbanded soldiers had gravitated during the short peace.[52] The market operated with similar efficiency in the ballot of 1810, for which we also have relevant information. Outside the north, where again the number of principals remained exceptionally high, twenty-seven in twenty-eight recruits were enlisted men.[53]

The militia acts in practice, therefore, whether in England, Ireland, or Scotland, paid lip service to the idea of personal conscription. Apart from the generous list of exemptions, there was ample scope for the community to accept the obligation on the individual's behalf or for the individual himself to discharge it onto somebody else. The omnipotent wartime state imposing its demands on its citizens, regardless of their interests and convenience, is still some time away. Paul Langford has emphasized how much in the eighteenth century the public good came to be identified with the interests of the propertied classes, and how much freedom the localities continued to enjoy *vis-à-vis* central authority.[54] The militia system provides a classic example of such a political structure. Conscription was incompatible with the distinctions of the social hierarchy, and, in view of the service demanded, with the avocations of the established part of society—the latter recognized, for instance, in the exemptions allowed to the members of certain professions. There was also the wider disruptive effect of conscription on the relationships of propertied principals and their subordinates and on local communities where the ballot, left to run its course, could cause great hardship and kindle animosities against

---

[51] J. R. Western, 'The Formation of the Scottish Militia in 1797', *Scot. Hist. Rev.* 34 (1955), 13.
[52] Sir J. St C. Erskine to Lord Melville, 4 May 1804, Chatham MSS, PRO30/8/133, fos. 75–7.
[53] *CJ* lxvi. 561–2, an incomplete return from 25 Scottish, 30 English, and 7 Welsh counties.
[54] Two of the basic themes of his Ford Lectures, published as *Public Life and the Propertied Englishman, 1689–1798*.

the rich. Thus the militia acts upheld the private contracts of apprentices and articled clerks against the military needs of the state and excluded from service poor men with large families, the second provision further operating to keep down the cost of poor relief. Thus, too, the acts made it easy for the propertied to protect their dependants or transfer the burden of actual service away from their parishes altogether.

It seems to have been generally accepted that defending private and local interests against the militia obligation was worth the considerable expense. The rationalization usually advanced was that the free operations of property protected the productive base of society, which additionally promoted the idea of the volunteers, and later local militia, as the appropriate form of service for the settled and possessing classes.[55] Conversely, the long-term, extra-local service the crown expected of the militia proper directed that it should be recruited from the same, less stable social elements as the army was. The greatest opposition to the 'regular' militia, as it came to be called, came from the army, which saw itself competing for recruits without the advantage of local associations; on at least two occasions its abolition in favour of home service, second battalions was seriously suggested.[56] But the propertied classes fashioned the militia system, as everything else, as best suited them, which included a readiness to tax themselves heavily to defend the order they had created. Enlistment was used to negate the conscriptive power residing in the militia ballot, a power inimical to their interests and concerns; yet enlistment also established the type of militia that was more fully disposable for national defence and more useful for imperial strategy and the recruitment of the army than a conscript force would ever have been. As the local militia showed, the compromise between conscription and property could extend no further than part-time, locally stationed and maintained battalions.

Little satisfactory work has been done on the social composition of the British army and auxiliaries of the Napoleonic age, nothing comparable to Samuel Scott's survey of the royal army in France at the beginning of the Revolution.[57] The regulars, in fact, remain *terra incognita*, while the volunteers and local militia have been sampled only in a very small way. Some of the volunteers in the metropolis and large towns were socially quite exclusive, but, in general, the local auxiliaries appear to have been a varied mix of the artisan and labouring classes. While

---

[55] As a paper in favour of the volunteers pointed out: 'The money so spent completely reverts into the national wealth; and no material subtraction from the useful industry of the nation would be sustained'. WO1/407/501–8. Lord Melville praised Castlereagh's local militia scheme for instilling 'military feelings and habits' without interfering with production. Melville to Sir A. Mackenzie, 30 Sept. [1810], Melville MSS, SRO GD51/1/996/3.

[56] Memorandum of Duke of York to Lord Grenville, 15 Feb. 1807, WO1/634/125–38; H. Calvert, 'Scheme for recruiting and new modelling the army', 10 Nov. 1809, WO25/3224.

[57] *The Response of the Royal Army to the French Revolution* (Oxford, 1978), 5–19.

unambiguously artisan corps were found in many towns during the 1790s,[58] the great volunteer expansion of the Napoleonic War, and later the local militia as the successor force, enormously extended the military participation of the labouring population. Contemporaries agreed that their readiness to serve went beyond exemption from the militia ballot to the material rewards: 'the clothing is clear gain; and so is the shilling on Sunday, which forms the little sum to the poor man which may be freely spent on happiness in any shape'.[59] However, a rank and file drawn from skilled and unskilled labour in not too unequal proportions hardly made the auxiliaries socially distinctive from the line army. The artisan element in the army was always prominent, partly because recruitment was concentrated in the towns, but also because the small trades were highly vulnerable to economic fluctuations. Scott has shown that artisans and shopkeepers made up roughly 60 per cent of the French army in 1789, and there is no reason to think the British army would have been significantly different.[60]

Yet the problem of army recruitment increasingly became the problem of extending the catchment to include the sort of men who filled the ranks of the local auxiliaries. Their social denomination aside, volunteers and local militiamen proved highly resistant to service in the army. The local militia acts expressly allowed the regulars to recruit from the regiments, with a notable lack of success; and the volunteers were separated from the army even more by their intense localism and civilianism.[61] In contrast, the 'old' militia provided increasing numbers of men, almost 50 per cent of recruits once regular transfers began, totalling 83,207 men, 1807–13.[62] This suggests that the army (and the militia, likewise an enlisted force raised by bounties), while drawing from the artisan and labouring population in general, attracted those who were not established in civilian society or who felt disaffected with that society to the point where the conventional aversion to soldiering no longer operated on them. In Continental Europe the state had to extract recruits from autarkic peasant communities, and mostly resorted to conscription to do it. In Britain the problem for the army was to compete successfully for men in a free

---

[58] Beckett, *Amateur Military Tradition*, 84–5; Cookson, 'Ely Volunteers'; Smith, 'Local Militia', 153–69. The first Edinburgh corps formed was described as consisting of 'the most respectable young and middle-aged men in town, lawyers, writers, bankers, merchants, the principal tradesmen and shopkeepers, mixed according to their size and figure, nor should I forget the medical profession'. George Home to Patrick Home, 23 Mar. 1795, Home of Wedderburn MSS, SRO GD267/1/18/14–15.

[59] 'Of the expedience of a reformed establishment of the late volunteer army [1803]', WO1/407/505.

[60] Scott, *Response*, 16–17. J. R. Western, 'The Recruitment of the Land Forces in Great Britain 1793–9', Ph.D. thesis (Edinburgh, 1953), 222–3, found that about a quarter of British soldiers were drawn from the 'artisan and shopkeeper class', a 'good half' were 'labourers', and a 'large part of the remainder "weavers"'. A 'preponderance of men' came from industrial areas.

[61] Beckett, *Amateur Military Tradition*, 115, says an average of 2,600–4,000 local militiamen per year joined the army 1809–13. There are no figures for volunteers.

[62] Return of men raised for the regular army, 1803–13, *CJ* lxix. 635.

and individualistic society which showed the same basic antipathy to the military life as the European peasantries.

The popular image of the soldier was of one who existed in a kind of exile from the ordinary world, bereft of the ties of social existence and deprived of the felicities and securities that these conferred; if the soldier did return, he returned as if from the dead, too often without the means of earning a livelihood. Enlistment for life emphasized the divide that was crossed in the act of recruitment. From that moment a man placed himself under different authority, different protectors, different 'habits'; the regiment became his community, the officers his patrons, his comrades his friends. The army from outside was less understood as an alternative society which could provide its own satisfactions than as cruel and oppressive, an insult to the idea of 'free-born Englishmen'. An engagement for life, even if practically rather than technically that, ran contrary to a man's freedom to advance his interests by selling his labour where he chose. 'Military discipline', the superiority that rank bestowed and the punishments inflicted for actions which civilian authority ignored, likewise imposed an abhorrent degree of servility and servitude. The most keenly felt 'tyranny', however, was 'foreign service', which in peace as well as war immured men for long periods outside the home country, most notoriously in the West Indies and India, alien and insalubrious places. No other European army had to devote so much force to such far-flung responsibilities; none therefore required such arduous service. Popular hostility to military recruitment may have deepened in the 1780s as the imperial garrisons were expanded and the practice of drafting men from regiments ordered home into those remaining became commonplace. The large expeditions to the West Indies during the first years of the war, brought up to strength by arbitrarily transferring men from regiment to regiment, certainly raised fears that the army would hold no guarantees of home service sacred.

In Napoleonic France resistance to conscription appears to have lessened as policing measures became more effective and as society became acclimatized to its demands.[63] In Britain, however, prolonged war and the extensive military participation of civilians in the local auxiliaries apparently did nothing to weaken civilian prejudices against the army. As mentioned before, the volunteers and local militia proved a disappointing source of recruits. The 'ordinary recruiting' (the very phrase indicated a continuing dependence on other methods) by regimental parties and district recruiting staffs brought in a fairly unvarying number both during the war and long afterwards. If the army did become more popular and a vehicle for patriotic feeling, it shows up but faintly in these particular figures. While the yield

---

[63] I. Woloch, 'Napoleonic Conscription: State Power and Civil Society', *Past and Present*, 111 (May 1986), 101–20.

of recruits was high in 1800–1 and 1812–13, years when the army enjoyed a rising reputation because of its long-awaited victories in the field, military success
happened to coincide with severe social distress, which must also have been an
important factor. Furthermore, the best year of all was 1807, when the country was
isolated and defeated, and the terms of the Convention of Cintra caused national
outrage. This recruitment was clearly founded on exceptional effort, a very large
increase in the number of parties and individuals working the ground.[64]

'Ordinary recruiting' invariably failed to supply the manpower the army required, not even sufficient to make good annual losses; in the Napoleonic War
these averaged 21,000 per year against 12,500 recruits. Other ways of raising men
were crucially important, though they soon brought diminishing returns and the
army's strength in the last years of the war was mainly supported by the expansion
of foreign and colonial corps. By 1811 the conclusion was drawn 'that the army at
present in existence . . . of about 211,000 effectives is as large a force, combined
with the regular militia and navy, as the population and finances of the country
could well support'.[65] It does seem that the army, in trying various alternatives,
pressed quite hard on available resources and could have significantly increased the
take of men from the home society only by resorting to conscription. The generals
certainly spoke in such terms,[66] and their sense that some ceiling of effort had been
reached is perhaps borne out by the fact that from 1808 the 'British' army (British
corps and militia) stabilized its numbers at around 270,000. If this is right, the
civilian society's resistance to army recruitment hardened at a low level in comparison with Napoleonic France. A reasonable estimate of the total number raised
during the Napoleonic War would be about 300,000 out of a British Isles population of 16,000,000 in 1801 and 18,000,000 in 1811. Conscription in France over the
same period is said to have produced 2,600,000 men out of a population of over
30,000,000. Even accepting that perhaps only 1,500,000 conscripts actually joined
the army and that Britain also supported a large navy, the difference of military
effort is striking.[67] Again, the generals were aware of the situation. Apart from the

---

[64] For the annual totals of 'ordinary recruiting', 1803–13, see Fortescue, *County Lieutenancies*, 292.
There are also totals for 1798–1803 in Hope of Lufness MSS, SRO GD364/1/1159/16, but it is noted
that the numbers are inaccurate because they include 'drafts from one regiment to another as well as
[men] originally enlisted'. However, the success of recruiting after the difficult years of 1795–9 is often
mentioned, e.g. York to Dundas, 23 Jan. 1801, Melville MSS, SRO GD51/1/654/25. For post-war
recruiting see Strachan, *Wellington's Legacy*, 56. The number of recruiting parties in Britain and
Ireland, 1803–6, varied between 361 and 453. By May 1807 there were over 1,100. *SP* 1806, x. 350–
1; 1807, iv. 331.

[65] Fortescue, *County Lieutenancies*, 291–3; [Paper on army recruitment, Jan. 1811?], Liverpool MSS,
BL Add. MS 38361, fos. 66–9.

[66] 'Memorandum of Duke of York to Lord Grenville relative to augmenting the army', 15 Feb.
1807, WO1/634/125–38; General Dundas to Lord Liverpool, 8 June 1810, ibid. 1/644/200–1.

[67] The return printed in Fortescue, *County Lieutenancies*, 292 presents a total of 249,851 men raised,
but it does not include the Army of Reserve (45,492) or the 'new' levies of 1804–5 (5,158). For the

absence of 'forced enlistment', they explained the army's difficulties in terms of the high wage economy and economic opportunities generally of a 'commercial', as opposed to an agrarian, society.[68]

The three main methods, outside 'ordinary recruiting', of raising men were: first, where private individuals recruited for their own interest; secondly, where a compulsory obligation was placed on individuals or communities; thirdly, volunteering from the militia. In a broad sense, these were pursued consecutively, initially appropriate but losing their usefulness as the demand for men went on increasing. Some account of them makes the point better than anything else that the army really did work its manpower resources to depletion, short of introducing conscription.

The heyday of private recruiting occurred during the first years of the war when the government knew no other way of finding large numbers quickly and variously commissioned notables and army officers to levy new corps, 'independent companies' (which would later be drafted into existing regiments) or a stipulated number of men in return for rank. Success depended on local influence, often in different parts of the country, and sufficient money to make a bold show and add to the government's bounty. The Duke of York hated the practice for deprofessionalizing the officer corps, but its time was past once the continued demand for recruits removed the easy pickings and drove up costs to the point where the returns became doubtful. Recruiting for rank was increasingly pushed back into areas where vast suzerainties survived, notably the Scottish Highlands and Ireland.

It had a last gasp in the crisis of 1803–5 when there were plans for expanding the 'general' or 'foreign service' force by about 21,000 men (two troops added to cavalry regiments, ten second battalions, and eight 'new levies', two in Scotland and six in Ireland).[69] After a year, only 1,088 men had been raised for four second battalions in England, indicating, as the Duke of York noted, the importance of local connections for this kind of recruitment. Meanwhile the 78th (Ross-shire) and 79th (Cameron Highlanders) added battalions,[70] and the Irish levies, reduced to four corps, particularly worked the less-touched western areas—Tipperary,

Napoleonic conscription see G. Ellis, *The Napoleonic Empire* (Basingstoke, 1991), 62–4. W. B. Hodge, 'On the Mortality Arising from Military Operations', *J. of Stat. Soc.* 19 (1856), 232, 264–5, claims 793,110 men were recruited during the entire war. But this figure is grossly inflated by including foreign and colonial corps in the calculation and by making an insufficient deduction for transfers between regiments.

[68] Sir J. Craig to Col. Brownrigg, June 1804, WO1/902/115–28; York to Windham, 18 Mar. 1806, ibid. 1/632/157–80.

[69] York to Lord Hobart, 13 Jan. 1804, Hobart to York, 25 Jan., 24 Mar. 1804, WO1/627/37–58, 371–3; Hobart to York, 21 Mar. 1804, WO6/132.

[70] Returns dated Jan. 1805 showed the progress made: *CJ* lx. 620. W. H. Clinton to John King, 10 May 1804, Hardwicke MSS, BL Add. MS 35774, fos. 39–40. Many of the Scots were again raised in north-east Scotland. Fortescue, *County Lieutenancies*, 154. Stewart of Garth was in charge of the recruiting of the 78th and described his success in his *Sketches of the Character, Manners and Present State of the Highlanders of Scotland* (repr., 2 vols., Edinburgh, 1977), ii. 253–6.

Galway, and Mayo. Even so, it was always hard going. The Dublin government struggled in the first place to find promoters—twelve magnates, at least, were approached and declined—and the promoters then struggled to find recruits; the period of the levy was originally for six months, but after nine only one of the corps was complete and two were no better than half-strength. And the cost had become prodigious in anyone's money: one of the Irish colonels claimed that he needed to find five thousand guineas over and above what the government provided—a believable figure.[71] There was just one other attempt at private enterprise recruiting in the light of this experience. The Hon. Henry Augustus Dillon, former colonel of the Irish Brigade and MP for Mayo, was permitted to return to the Connaught ground in 1805–6, though once again the results were hardly won.[72] Even on the periphery, the influence of local magnates to promote large-scale recruiting had been worked to exhaustion.

The establishment of the Army of Reserve at the outset of war in 1803 bore its own testimony to the inadequacies of private enterprise recruiting; for it was hailed by one minister as 'the basis of a future permanent plan' for replenishing the infantry 'on a consistent and regular system'.[73] This new force raised a home service army by ballot, closely following the militia organization, though, unlike the militia, the men were left free to opt for 'general service' at any time. The introduction of the compulsory principle into army recruitment was an important departure; the nearest the government had previously approached compulsion was in the Quota Acts of 1795–6, but these had been short-lived expedients to rebuild the regiments shattered in the Low Countries and the Caribbean and had laid the obligation on parishes, not individuals.

Whatever hopes there were that a permanent reserve could be created to feed men into the active battalions, the Army of Reserve proved to be a 'one-off' solution to the army's problems. Almost 32,000 men were enrolled in two months; thereafter diminishing returns set in, despite ever higher bounties and accumulated

---

[71] The story of the Irish levies can be followed in 'Circumstances to be attended to on the formation of the proposed new regular regiments', SPOI CSO OP198/19; Hardwicke to Hawkesbury, 7 Nov. 1804, Hardwicke MSS, BL Add. MS 35774, fos. 82–3; 'Memo relative to the levies undertaken in Ireland', 7 Jan. 1805, H. Browne to Col. Gordon (extract), 9 Jan. 1805, York to Lord Camden, 14 Jan. 1805, WO1/630/17–27; Camden to York, 28 Jan. 1805, WO6/132/250–2. The lord lieutenant's dealings with likely promoters, March–April 1804, are mentioned in Hardwicke MSS, 35705, 35775 *passim*. See also Hardwicke to C. Yorke, 10 May 1804, ibid. 35774, fo. 37. Burke's levy became the 98th regiment, Lord Mathew's the 99th, and Falkiner's the 100th. Browne's was drafted into the 87th.

[72] Dillon to Hardwicke, 19 Sept. 1804, ibid. 35774, fo. 68. Dillon's levy was established as the 101st regiment in Aug. 1806 when it was 650 strong. *CJ* lxiii. 601.

[73] C. Yorke to Melville, 10 July 1803, Hope of Lufness MSS, SRO GD364/1/1136/8. I suspect that Yorke, secretary at war, was the main author of the scheme. But see Lord Westmorland to Lord Hobart, Feb. 1802, C. Yorke to Hobart, 14, 19 Feb. 1802, Hobart to the King, 17 June 1803, Hobart MSS, Buckingham RO, D/MH/H/War/G26, B23–4, A68.

fines on the parishes for deficiencies. The final total in May 1804 was 45,492 enrolments in Britain and Ireland, of whom 37,136 were effective.[74] Pitt, in replacing Addington's government about this time, accepted that the ballot was spent but clung to the idea of a permanent reserve by supposing that the Army of Reserve, as largely a force of substitutes, had drawn on the same old catchment and that another, little touched, existed among the 'country population'. His Additional Force, as it was called, returned to parish quotas, with the costs controlled to encourage their co-operation—bounties of a set price were paid by the government, and the fines were no longer levied quarterly. The leading feature of the scheme, however, was a stipulation that parishes were not to go outside their neighbourhoods for men. Furthermore, these local recruits were to be placed in the regiments associated with their county or district. It marked the first serious attempt to get away from urban-based recruiting and what were perceived to be the social elements traditionally attracted into the army. At the same time as he put up these proposals, Pitt required the army to investigate the feasibility of short-service enlistment as a further way of breaking down civilian antipathies.[75]

A new recruiting ground was not to be, however. Parish recruiting under quotas and fines proved even less successful than the ballot, producing only 15,000 in two years when twice that number was asked for. The government, naturally, blamed the counties and parishes; a fierce circular sent out at the end of 1805 noted that twenty-five English and Scottish counties had produced no men, and that five-sixths of those which had been raised belonged to just twenty counties.[76] There undoubtedly was much passive disobedience, but the larger truth was that local rulers were responding in a time-honoured way to a measure which they disliked, waiting to see what, or if any, further executive action would follow. They knew the impracticability of parish recruiting and knew better that the settled, 'industrious' population was impervious to 'military ideas' and that the recent ballots had swept most available men into the army. As the Duke of York said: 'In going back to the same parishes which had failed to raise their men under the Reserve and militia laws, little was to be expected'.[77] Only 2,533 men were found by the parishes in the first six months of the Additional Force, including Ireland, and the

[74] For these figures see the returns dated 30 Sept. 1803 in Hope of Lufness MSS, SRO GD364/1/1141/10–11 and York's paper, 31 Jan. 1805, Liverpool MSS, BL Add. MS 38358, fo. 260.

[75] *PD* ii. 265–79. Pitt repeated his interest in short-service enlistment in June, ibid. 510. Meanwhile, Brownrigg, the Duke of York's secretary, had sent out letters to thirteen generals. See Chatham MSS, PRO30/8/116, fos. 305–6 and WO1/407/127–33.

[76] Fortescue, *County Lieutenancies*, 299–301; Hawkesbury to the lord lieutenants, 31 Dec. 1805, Chatham MSS, PRO30/8/240, fos. 117–18.

[77] See J. J. Edmondstoune, A. Moore, and J. Blain to Lord Bute, 19 Aug. 1804, ibid. 118, fos. 222–4. The Duke of York's remark is in his memorandum on recruiting, 6 Feb. 1807, Dropmore MSS, BL Add. MS 59288, fos. 28–35.

gradual, though far from adequate, improvement in the rate after this owed much
to the regular regiments who recruited for themselves using the fund produced
from the fines on defaulting parishes. Even with the local officials, the best results
came from urbanized and industrialized areas. The official return of March 1806
showed that the parishes had raised 8,975 and the regiments 3,950 men. But the
claims made in parliament that the parishes had gone outside their localities can be
readily believed; it would have been surprising if they had not stitched up deals
with the regimental officers and availed themselves of the services of the crimps
and other middlemen they had used during the militia and Army of Reserve
ballots.[78] Such only underlined the futility of trying to extract recruits from the
larger part of the country short of outright personal conscription; no sooner was
a lesser form of compulsory obligation imposed than the burden was effectively
transferred to the traditional recruiting reserves.

Pitt had wanted 19,782 men within a month, and got a few hundred; another
instance of how great the distance could be between London and the localities.[79]
The prime minister appears to have accepted that compulsion had failed after the
Additional Force had been operating for a few months because in February 1805
he decided the situation was urgent enough to require a draft from the militia.
Eventually, from 1811, annual transfers of men from the militia into the army were
to be arranged, but it took many years and many trials before recruiting in this
way was recognized as the best practicable solution to the army's problems. Pitt's
desperation in 1805 equalled his desperation on an earlier occasion in 1799 when
he also dared the wrath of the militia colonels and lord lieutenants in order to
create the army he needed to support Britain's part in a new anti-French coalition.
At that time the militia magnates were simply bulldozed into compliance; while
they were still protesting the government introduced the necessary legislation—
perhaps with some satisfaction, for the colonels had also opposed a proposal for
light infantry battalions to be formed by detaching their light infantry companies.[80]

[78] For returns Sept. 1804–Feb. 1805, see Hope of Lufness MSS, SRO GD364/1/1159/15. The
rate then was 543 men per month, but was 822 in Oct.–Dec. 1805 and 933 in Jan.–June 1806. By Jan.
1806 about a third of the men had been raised by the army. See Chatham MSS, PRO30/8/240, fos.
119–20. The same return gives the county totals of parish enlistments, headed by Lancashire, Surrey,
Middlesex, Leicestershire, the West Riding, Lanark, Renfrew, Cheshire, and Nottingham. The return
of March 1806 is in *CJ* lxi. 624–7. For the parliamentary claims see *PD* vi. 1001–2, 1010–12, 1014.

[79] Fortescue, *County Lieutenancies*, 299–300.

[80] For the opposition put up in 1799, see Western, *English Militia*, 231–2 and Col. Brownrigg to Sir
C. Grey, 17 June, 29 July 1799, Univ. of Durham Library, 1st Earl Grey MSS 1847, 1904. Much is
also found in HO50/30, including a report of a meeting on 24 June, by which time the bill was before
the House. The previous year the enlistment of supplementary militia men had not been well supported by the colonels and lord lieutenants. The government sought 10,000 men and got under 2,000.
Western, *English Militia*, 225, 269; Dundas to Lord Grenville, 30 May 1798, Grenville, *Dropmore MSS*
iv. 223–4; York to Dundas, 2 June 1798, Dundas to [Duke of Portland], 18 Nov. 1799, HO30/2, fos.
34–6, 380–2. The protest against militia volunteering in Mar. 1805 is covered in Chatham MSS,
PRO30/8/117, fos. 136–45, J. H. Strutt to Pitt, 19 Mar. 1805 (and paper), 181, fos. 106–9.

However, it was also quickly understood that recruiting from the militia depended, above all, on the colonels and that they required compensation if the army drew on their regiments, which were an important investment in status and local influence.

The more the practice went on, in fact, the more attentive the government became to these interests. The colonels' patronage was extended by a second act in 1799 which allowed them to recommend their officers for commissions in the line, provided a sufficient number of rank and file men transferred. During the war hundreds of young gentlemen contracted obligations in this way by being given a chance in the army they might not have had otherwise and the prospect of a permanent pension in the form of half-pay.[81] The colonels further benefited whenever the militia establishment was increased. Castlereagh's large drafts for the army in 1807 and 1809 were compensated for by even larger augmentations; and in this connection it needs to be remembered that all regimental appointments, down to the NCOs and drummers, could be useful when the regiment was considered as a nexus of local influence. The colonels opposed drafts on the grounds that they disabled efficient battalions, but the depth of their dislike was the damage done to their personal empires when so much patronal capital had to be given away. This was why the government gave them what protection it could. When establishments were reduced, surplus officers and NCOs were allowed to be kept on as supernumeraries.[82] The number of NCOs who could transfer was carefully controlled, and the colonels were even given power to retain men of their choice; in 1805 up to half the battalion could be so reserved.[83] Recruitment from the militia, therefore, was not as straightforward as the large numbers taken might suggest. It was a contentious matter involving local magnates who formed a 'militia interest' in parliament and who were often political allies of the ministers themselves. Indeed, if the much vaunted 'independence' of the militia from the army is to be found anywhere during the wars, it is in the desire of the colonels to protect their regimental fiefs.

---

[81] For an example of these aspirations, see Lt. Alexander McGregor's journal (typescript), 11, John Macgregor MSS, SRO GD50/110. Col. Littlehales, the military secretary to the lord lieutenant in Ireland, believed this patronage was more useful than bounties in getting men to volunteer. Littlehales to W. W. Pole, 3 Feb. 1811 (and memo of same date), WO1/946/25, 81–6. After 1799–1800 it became standard practice to allow a colonel to recommend for an ensigncy for every 50 men transferred. Hardwicke to Hawkesbury, 23 Mar. 1805, SPOI CSO VIIIA/1/13; [Castlereagh] to York, 7 Aug. 1807, WO1/635/347–59; circular to Irish colonels, 24 Apr. 1809, SPOI CSO OP283/2; instructions for volunteering, 20 Apr. 1811, WO3/585/27–42. According to the general orders given in Kilmainham MSS, NLI MS 1330, 152 ensigns were appointed to the line from the Irish militia in 1800.

[82] 39 & 40 Geo. III, c. 1, s. 19; 51 Geo. III, c. 20, s. 33.

[83] 45 Geo. III, c. 31, s. 4; 45 Geo. III, c. 38, s. 4. The second 1799 act gave colonels the power to stop the enlistment of musicians, armourers, and clerks, and indeed any man on showing 'sufficient cause' to the general of the district. For restrictions on the enlistment of NCOs, see 45 Geo. III, c. 31, s. 2; 49 Geo. III, c. 4, s. 13; 51 Geo. III, c. 20, s. 13; 54 Geo. III, c. 1, s. 12. There is ample evidence that colonels endeavoured to keep their best men: e.g. 'A staff officer' to Windham, 20 Feb. 1807, Windham MSS, BL Add. MS 37886, fos. 68–9; Col. J. Irwin to Major C. O'Hara, 20 Jan. 1808, O'Hara MSS, NLI MS 20330.

Militia Transfers

		British	Irish
1798	38 Geo. III, c. 17	c. 2,000	
1799	39 Geo. III, c. 106	15,712	
	39 & 40 Geo. III, c. 1	10,414	
1800	40 Geo. III, c. 1 (Ireland)		8,138
1805	45 Geo. III, c. 31	8,963	
	45 Geo. III, c. 38		4,617
1806	46 Geo. III, c. 124		2,968
1807	47 Geo. III, c. 55		8,353
	47 Geo. III, c. 57	19,152	
1808	48 Geo. III, c. 64		3,378
1809	49 Geo. III, c. 4	16,092	
	49 Geo. III, c. 5		4,879
1810	49 Geo. III, c. 56		2,914
1811	51 Geo. III, c. 20	8,657	
	51 Geo. III, c. 30		2,795
1812		6,676	3,251
1813		6,246	2,669
	54 Geo. III, c. 1	8,285	1,318[a]

[a] For the British militia: 1798: Dundas to [Portland], 18 Nov. 1799, HO30/2, fos. 380–2; 1799: *CJ* lxi. 636; 1805: return of 24 May 1810, WO1/946; 1807: *CJ* lxiv. 502; 1809–12: York to Lord Bathurst, 20 Oct. 1813, WO25/3225; 1813: *CJ* lxix. 638. For the Irish militia: 1800–11: McAnally, *Irish Militia*, 151–2, 189, 208, 216–17, 230, 250; 1812–13: as above.

Yet a permanent system of taking men for the army did eventuate; the colonels did become the 'drill sergeants' they once vowed they never would.[84] The 1811 act provided for annual transfers amounting, in effect, to one-seventh of a regiment's establishment. It is interesting that such a scheme had been introduced in Ireland in 1806, where the ballot was generally dispensed with and the colonels found it relatively easy to raise men by enlistment. For the British colonels there was more conflict between the government's requirements and their ambitions. By 1811, however, a working arrangement seems to have evolved in which men were offered to the army without unduly disturbing the good order of the regiment and the local interests it contained. It also mattered that recruitment by beat of drum, first allowed in 1809, provided the militia with the means of finding men directly, continuously, and in favourable competition with the army where the ballot was a

[84] Lord Carnarvon to Dundas, 18 June 1799, HO50/30.

cumbersome and unpopular operation. Even so, conversion of the militia into a kind of army reserve was another significant encroachment on its independence by the state. There was no return to a situation where recruiting from the militia was a measure adopted *in extremis*, put to the colonels with some diffidence. In the next crisis of military manpower, at the commencement of the Crimean War, the army immediately began to draw lavishly on the militia to the point where the very idea of its being the 'constitutional force' became a travesty.[85]

About 36,000 militiamen, including the supplementary militia volunteers of 1798, 'transferred their services' during the Revolutionary War, and 110,000 during the Napoleonic War. To these could be added the fencible men who joined the army after the disbandment of their corps in 1799–1802. A small number also enlisted from the militia on the disembodiment of the regiments in 1802.[86] Probably a good third of the army in the later years of the Napoleonic War had served previously in the auxiliaries, and the steady influx of trained men into the ranks must have had its own effect on the British army's quality and improved performance. Yet the militia was never an infinite resource. Throughout 1813 the commander-in-chief worried about the diminishing returns of volunteering; the quotas were almost completely met in 1807–8, but by 1812 the deficiency was as high as 30 per cent (50 per cent in the case of the Irish militia).[87] The downwards trend was arrested only at the very end of 1813 when the government sought to throw all the reinforcements it could into Europe and Wellington's victories made the army exceptionally popular. It is doubtful whether the colonels can be blamed for the increasing shortfalls. More likely, the turnover of men in the regiments had become so great that an increasing proportion of the rank and file were either new recruits or men unfit for army service. Thus, as with other schemes additional to 'ordinary' recruiting, a resource was worked beyond the rate of natural replenishment.

Britain, therefore, always was pressing against the ceiling of available manpower for its essentially volunteer army. Since the army's own efforts could never be adequate, local magnates, local officials, and militia colonels were called into play at various times; but even their influence faltered, faltered inevitably, as the drain

---

[85] Strachan, *Wellington's Legacy*, 57; E. M. Spiers, *The Army and Society, 1815–1914* (London, 1980), 162–3.

[86] McAnally, *Irish Militia*, 168; memorandum by the Duke of York, 14 July 1804, WO1/628/226–7.

[87] York to Lord Bathurst, 31 Jan. 1813; H. Bunbury, 'Memorandum submitted for Lord Bathurst's consideration', 30 Aug. 1813; York to Bathurst, 20 Oct. 1813, WO25/3225. The British quotas (deficiencies in parentheses) were 19,823 (3.5 per cent) in 1807–8; 21,784 (27 per cent) in 1809–10; 11,039 (22 per cent) in 1811; 9,450 (30 per cent) in 1812; 10,055 in 1813. The Irish quotas were 8,556 (2.3 per cent) in 1807; 3,495 (4 per cent) in 1808; 6,708 (28 per cent) in 1809; 3,735 (22 per cent) in 1810; 5,096 (46 per cent) in 1811; 6,543 (51 per cent) in 1812; 7,546 in 1813. See return of 1 July 1808, WO1/904; McAnally, *Irish Militia*, 230; Fortescue, *County Lieutenancies*, 223; York to Bathurst, 20 Oct. 1813, WO25/3225.

of men continued. Once the country was engaged in a major conflict on the Continent, in Spain after 1808, the army's losses, running at over 20,000 per year, kept threatening to outpace the intake of recruits.[88] This resumption of offensive war was supported by a remarkably modest expansion of the total army, and then the greatest growth occurred among the foreign corps in British pay. It is interesting that 115,407 were added to the army from the British Isles population in 1805–8 and 91,984 in 1809–12.[89]

The problem of tapping greater manpower reserves invariably came back to popular attitudes towards the army. Politicians and generals agreed that what was wanted was 'a more intimate connection between the army and the mass of the people'.[90] Up to the war the increasing disparity between the earnings of civilians and soldiers had emphasized the army's isolation, but during the 1790s the soldier's wage was raised above subsistence level, initially by adding allowances to cover increased costs and then in 1797 by calculating his expenditure so as to give him a disposable sum of 2*d.* per day, with guarantees against further inflation.[91] In addition, the war provided large bounties on enlistment or for extension of service, and, probably more to the soldier's advantage, ample opportunities for supplementary employment as regimental and garrison tradesmen, as labourers on defence works, or even as harvest workers when local farmers found labour in short supply. By the time of the Napoleonic War the army clearly had shaken off the image of a miserably impoverished rank and file. In 1804 General Sir James Craig went so far as to say that 'the increased pay and comforts of a soldier's situation have left to the friends of a young man who would oppose his entrance into the service scarcely any argument but that of the folly of entering for life'.[92] Yet at the same time the generals firmly believed that men were pushed rather than pulled into the army, that most potential recruits did not rationalize the decision to enlist by weighing up the advantages and disadvantages but were impelled instead by some 'embarrassment' or dissatisfaction in civilian life.[93] The challenge, therefore, was to create powerful

[88] [Paper on army recruitment, Jan. 1811?], Liverpool MSS, BL Add. MS 38361, fos. 66–9. For the army's losses of men see Fortescue, *County Lieutenancies*, 291.

[89] Ibid. 293; return of number of men raised for the regular army exclusive of foreign and colonial corps 1803–13, *CJ* lxix. 635.

[90] Sir James Craig's words in a letter to Col. Brownrigg, June 1804, WO1/902/115–28.

[91] Sir W. Fawcett, 'Proposal for relieving the present necessitous situation of the private soldier', 24 Aug. 1791, Chatham MSS, PRO30/8/243, fos. 1–2; 'Observations upon the proposed arrangements respecting the pay of the soldier', [May 1797], Windham MSS, BL Add. MS 37903, fos. 215–19; York to the king, [22 May 1797], *George III Corresp.* ii. 575–6.

[92] Craig to Col. Brownrigg, June 1804, WO1/902/115–28. Sir David Dundas maintained that the soldier was 'well and sufficiently paid' and that it was unnecessary 'to hold out to him any farther daily and money advantage'. See his paper dated 15 Apr. 1806, Windham MSS, BL Add. MS 37883, fos. 218–21.

[93] Earl of Stanhope, *Notes of Conversations with the Duke of Wellington 1831–51* (London, 1938), 18; Lord Chatham to Col. Brownrigg, 7 June 1804, WO1/902/75–85.

positive inducements which might be expected to operate on a wider population, counteracting popular antipathy to the army.

Two major changes in recruitment had long occupied the attention of the army, and indeed were implemented partially and occasionally during the Revolutionary War. The first was to associate line regiments with particular counties or districts, giving them appropriate names and concentrating their recruiting parties in the hope of establishing a permanent connection based on their local identity. The second was to offer recruits 'limited' service in terms of the period of their enlistment. Both had been tried during the American War as a result of recruiting difficulties. From 1775 the augmented establishment was largely raised on the basis of service for the duration of the war; the county names that regiments carried were introduced in 1782. Having apparently worked so well at that time, short-service enlistment became a much favoured nostrum whenever recruiting faltered in the future. The army command, however, seems to have soon settled into a conviction that it was incompatible with the army's imperial responsibilities, a conclusion no doubt brought on by what happened at the close of the American War when limited-service soldiers had to be denied their discharge in order to fill the overseas garrisons. Besides the needs of a far-flung empire, a long-service army appealed to very deep feelings about an army being no stronger than its separate regiments were cohesive units or even bonded communities; the foundations of discipline were seen to lie in the trust between officers and men, ideally built up to the point where the soldiers 'look to their corps as their country, and to their officer as their only protector'. Life enlistment, therefore, was not only defended by conservative 'Prussians'. Sir John Moore stoutly opposed short-service as he thought it removed every incentive on the soldier to turn his back on civilian society and adopt the military life unequivocally.[94]

Only two partial attempts were made to revive the county affiliations of the regiments decided on in 1782. In 1796 many of the 'quota men' were to be allocated to the regiment of their county, though in the end so few were raised the result was totally insignificant. Pitt's second government returned to the idea with the Additional Force, again unable to follow it very rigorously and, anyway, not raising the numbers that might have created the identities sought for.[95] Mostly, then, county-based regiments remained nothing more than a pious hope, frequently commended but never acted upon.[96] Militiamen intent on transferring

---

[94] Ibid., Moore to Brownrigg, 11 June 1804, 75–95.

[95] For the regimental allocations in 1796 see Melville MSS, BL Add. MS 43770, fos. 88–9; in 1805 see Chatham MSS, PRO30/8/240, fos. 119–20.

[96] e.g. paper by Lt.-Col. R. Anstruther [Nov. 1797], Windham MSS, BL Add. MS 37877, fos. 183–7. In the Napoleonic War the Horse Guards wanted to convert the militia into a local force, which, with the ballot if necessary, would supply the second, home service battalion of the county regiment, and

to the army were given a wide choice of regiment, itself evidence that they were unparticular about local loyalties. The units assigned to receive Army of Reserve men in 1803–4 seem to have been almost casually chosen.[97] This does not mean that there were no regiments with a pronounced 'local' character—some Irish and Scottish-raised regiments particularly belie this—but these were untypical over the army as a whole. The chief difficulty in the way of implementing such a policy was the pressure the army was always under to have the maximum number of regiments at 'effective' strength. Recruiting parties needed to be sent where men could be found, and the best recruiting areas were areas of high population mobility where migrants and transients were the most likely catches. By 1803 the county names were admitted to be a dead letter, 'done away by the necessities of the recruiting service'.[98]

The idea of the county regiment can easily be linked to interest in short-service enlistment; for limited service was frequently recommended as one means by which regiments could gather men of a 'better description' and thus acquire a proper local identity. The Duke of York would never have admitted the connection. He had resisted the principle of short-service up to the time Windham forced it on him in 1806.[99] Even where service for the duration of the war had been conceded—as in the case of the 'quota men' in 1796 and the militia recruits of 1798–9—he expressed uneasiness that the 'life' soldiers would be rendered permanently dissatisfied; worse, that on the return of peace the government might be forced to safeguard the defence of the empire and risk mutiny by keeping the limited-service men overseas.[100] After 1806 he continued to be vehement on the subject, asking for repeal and feeding a receptive Castlereagh with data from the

thence the line battalion. [Memorandum by Duke of York], 15 Feb. 1807, Dropmore MSS, BL Add. MS 59288, fos. 37–42; H. Calvert, 'Scheme for recruiting and new modelling the army', 10 Nov. 1809, WO25/3224. Windham, in his training scheme, wanted to use the regular regiments in their particular counties to establish 'a connection . . . between the army and the mass of the people', *George III Corresp.* iv. 416–19.

[97] In 1807 the Duke of York argued that the success of militia volunteering depended on the soldiers having the widest possible choice of regiment. Memorandum [for Castlereagh], 20 Nov. 1807, WO1/636/307–8. This policy was adopted hereafter. For the destinations of militia volunteers in 1809 see the return in WO1/904/613–14; in 1812 see WO1/946/141. The regiments allowed to receive recruits from the local militia in 1811 are listed in WO3/585/81–5. For the Army of Reserve see Hope of Lufness MSS, SRO GD364/1/1141/10–11. On the other hand, some attempt was made to protect the Irish or Scottish character of certain regiments.

[98] 'Of the expedience of a reformed establishment of the late volunteer army', WO1/407/502.

[99] Most notably in 1804, when Pitt raised the possibility of introducing short-service enlistment in parliament, and asked the army to report on its feasibility. The Horse Guards consulted thirteen generals (see WO1/902/9–139). Opinion was divided, but the Duke was adamant in his opposition. Duke of York memo, 14 July 1804, WO1/628/209–39.

[100] York to the king, 4 Dec. 1796, *George III Corresp.* ii. 522; memorandum by York, 14 July 1804, WO1/628/209–39.

returns as 'proof' that recruiting had suffered severely.[101] The fact of the matter was that fluctuations in the numbers taken in depended mainly on the competition that the militia or other forces offered at particular times.[102] Yet essentially the Duke was right and Windham was wrong; short-service enlistment did not do much to make 'joining the army an attractive proposition against other occupations'.[103] When life-enlistment was restored in 1808, the proportion preferring it to the seven-year term steadily rose to about five-sixths, a trend also observable in the case of the militia volunteers.[104] Short-service always meant, in fact, service until the end of the war, or for ten years at most, by which time most would have been safely inducted into 'military habits'.[105] Its greatest appeal was the additional bounty collected when the transfer to 'unlimited' service was made; militiamen, presumably handsomely rewarded on first joining that force, especially favoured transfer to the army initially on short-service.[106]

So Windham's reform never had anything like the effects predicted for it. But the debate which it excited and assessment of the measure once it had been implemented did have important consequences. For the conviction solidified that the army could not, short of a resort to conscription, extend its social catchment to 'men of a better description' and that the wiser policy was to increase its attractiveness to those who were susceptible by showing that the soldier's well-being was taken seriously and that the military life had much to commend it alongside a civilian existence.[107] It does not look like coincidence that the Duke of York paid increasing attention to the rank and file's welfare from 1804 after he had heartily denounced short-service enlistment in defiance of the politicians' interest in the question and the opinion of some generals. As early as 1805 he wanted to extend

---

[101] See the papers in WO1/903/1, 29; memorandum on recruiting, 6 Feb. 1807, Dropmore MSS, BL Add. MS 59288, fos. 28–35; York to Castlereagh, 1 Feb. 1808, WO1/637/157–212.

[102] A conclusion obviously to be drawn from the figures presented in 'State of the recruiting of the regular army since 1803', WO1/946/125.

[103] Windham, memorandum to the king, 27 Mar. 1806, *George III Corresp.* iv. 416–19.

[104] The numbers of 'limited' service and 'unlimited' service recruits are given in *CJ* lxv. 599 (1807–9); WO1/645/473 (Dec. 1808–Nov. 1810); York to Lord Bathurst, 20 Oct. 1813, WO25/3225, Return no. 3 (1811–Aug. 1813). About 15 per cent of British militiamen and 50 per cent of Irish militiamen joined the army on 'unlimited' service in 1807–8. The figures were about 50 per cent and 95 per cent in 1812. See *CJ* lxv. 502, lxviii. 771.

[105] Windham to the king, 29 May 1806, Windham MSS, BL Add. MS 37842, fos. 33–4; Calvert to Bunbury, 13 July 1813, WO1/656/69–70.

[106] Militia volunteers were paid a bounty of 6 guineas on enlistment for limited service and 10 guineas for enlistment for life in 1807. By 1811 these sums had risen to 10 guineas and 14 guineas.

[107] 'The great difficulty has always been to make a man first engage in a military life, after which he is easily induced to extend his services unlimitedly'. 'Memorandum of Duke of York to Lord Grenville relative to augmenting the army', 15 Feb. 1807, WO1/634/125–38. The army's inability to break open new reservoirs of manpower was particularly evident after 1806–7, when Windham and then Castlereagh raised the number of recruiting parties from 380 at the beginning of 1806 to 3,102 at the end of 1807, with very disappointing results. See the abstracts of recruiting returns, WO1/637/181, 185.

the family allowances paid to the militia and Army of Reserve to the regulars, something he kept pressing on the government for the remainder of the war.[108] Windham, too, on coming to office, took over the Duke's proposal for more generous pensions.[109] But these improvements preceded a welter of others promoted by the Horse Guards relating to such matters as the provision of barracks, hospitals, and regimental schools, the removal of chaplain sinecurists, greater toleration of Roman Catholic worship, and the replacement of corporal punishment by imprisonment and fines. Army reform during the Revolutionary War had concentrated on the inadequacies of the fighting army and the officer corps. The attention later paid to the conditions under which the soldier lived and served converted the regulars into a force which was essentially the Victorian army before its time. The idea of the soldier as citizen may have appealed to some radicals, but remained totally alien to the British military ethos. At home, as well as in imperial garrisons abroad, the army from 1815 was a barracks army, formed around regiments that were veritably self-contained communities, its rank and file not only increasingly self-conscious about these regimental identities (much of the material for which came out of the French wars) but also presenting themselves to the rest of society pretty much as members of a caste.[110]

The change, then, was from an eighteenth-century army which existed on the margins of society to a nineteenth-century army which created its own world and confidently met society on its terms. In 1787 the adjutant-general commented on the 'miseries of [the soldier's] situation when compared with any other class of men'; 'everything tends to discourage him, to mortify his spirit and vanity . . . it is impossible to suppose that any eligible man in his sober senses will enlist as a soldier'.[111] The Duke of York's greatest achievement was to give the soldier a 'profession'. The word recurs in his memoranda: the idea emerges clearly from the changes he implemented.[112] The professional soldier entered the army for life; he made his NCOs the model for his conduct, aspiring for their rank and the now considerable rewards attached to it; he wore his regimental uniform with pride; he

---

[108] York to J. W. Gordon, 22 Aug. 1805, J. W. Gordon MSS, BL Add. MS 49472, fos. 9–10; memorandum by the Duke of York, 26 Mar. 1808, WO1/637/475–82; 'Memorandum on the establishment and keeping up of the British army' [1811], Liverpool MSS, BL Add. MS 38361, fos. 70–80.

[109] Windham to the king, 27 Mar. 1806, *George III Corresp.* iv. 416–19.

[110] Stewart, *Highlanders*, i, p. vii says the Duke of York asked him to write the history of the Black Watch, one indication that an enhanced regimentalism was being encouraged from above.

[111] Memorandum on recruiting by Sir W. Fawcett, 10 Aug. 1787, Chatham MSS, PRO30/8/242, fos. 5–6.

[112] The best place to approach this idea of a long-service, professional army is through the generals' discussion of short-service enlistment in 1804. See WO1/628/209–39; WO1/902/9–139. William Stewart, 'Remarks', 10 Apr. 1806, Windham MSS, BL Add. MS 37883, fos. 193–8, and his *Outlines of a Plan for the General Reform of the British Land Forces* (London, 1806) come close to the Duke's vision for the army. Stewart was colonel of the 95th, the Rifle Brigade.

was surrounded by his family at the depot; his sons were encouraged to follow him; he could look forward to a pension in recognition of his long service, which was a 'better fate' than the one handed out to his civilian contemporaries. Few men, it still had to be admitted, chose the military profession; in a society such as Britain's it was not to be expected that men would readily surrender their freedom for a life of military subordination. But once in the army 'military habits' were soon formed; the advantages of the 'military life' over one of labour and insecurity were soon recognized, as the number of volunteers from the Army of Reserve and the militia convincingly demonstrated. And British freemen made good soldiers, if well treated, protected by their officers, inspired by their NCOs. In their view of what the army's 'constitution' should be, the generals at the Horse Guards began with the army's imperial responsibilities, responsibilities which were seen to be increasing as the country's imperial destiny took further shape during the Napoleonic War. Only a long-service army, as professional in its 'internal government' as in its fighting calibre, could provide for a 'military system' of remote and isolated outposts. Armed nation British society may have become during the French wars, but the army itself carried into peacetime a sense of self-confident detachment.

5
Scotland's Fame

A LEADING feature of the Victorian army was the size of the Celtic component; the proportion of Scots among the rank and file exceeded Scotland's proportion of the United Kingdom population until about 1870; the proportion of Irish remained greater almost to the end of the century. In 1830 55 per cent of the NCOs and men were either Scottish or Irish-born.[1] Such an army virtually sprang into existence after 1793. The British army since the 1760s had been predominantly Anglo-Scottish (where it had not been German);[2] but on the outbreak of hostilities with Revolutionary France, while it was true Scots were immediately recruited in large numbers, the government also began drawing heavily and continuously on Ireland's much greater manpower reserves. Of fifty-six regiments added to the line in 1794, for example, twenty-two were Irish.

The national composition of the army during the wars of 1793–1815 is difficult to state precisely because the historian is dependent on the regimental returns which are often incomplete, particularly for the army overseas. However, one can present some tentative findings using the inspection returns for 1806, 1811, and 1813. The 1813 returns are easily the most useful, surveying about 40 per cent of the army, excluding foreign and colonial corps, and more fairly distributed than the other returns are between the garrison force in Britain (which exaggerates the English proportion of the army) and the regiments abroad. These returns reveal that the army was about one-half English, one-sixth Scottish, and one-third Irish. The 1806 and 1811 figures yield similar results for the line infantry, which provides the most reliable sample.[3] In view of the deficiencies of the data, it seems reasonable

---

[1] Spiers, *The Army and Society*, 50.

[2] L. M. Cullen, 'Scotland and Ireland, 1600–1800: Their Role in the Evolution of British Society', in R. A. Houston and I. D. Whyte (eds.), *Scottish Society 1500–1800* (Cambridge, 1989), 240. Dislike and suspicion of Catholic soldiers, especially among Ireland's rulers, continued to prejudice the recruitment of Irish. See F. G. James, *Ireland in the Empire 1688–1770* (Cambridge, Mass., 1973), 179, 264–5; R. E. Burns, 'Ireland and British Military Preparations for War in America in 1775', *Cithara*, 2 (1963), 47–9.

[3] The precise results over 77,185 privates in 1813 are: English 51.5 per cent, Scottish 15.3 per cent, Irish 32.0 per cent, 'foreigners' 1.1 per cent. I exclude the 60th regiment from the calculations as effectively a foreign corps. A sample based excessively on British-stationed battalions distorts the result because it gives undue weighting to the Guards, the cavalry, and the units recruiting from the English population, all English-dominated. The 1806 and 1811 returns survey 14 per cent and 22 per cent of the line infantry. In 1806 47.0 per cent are found to be English, 18.5 per cent Scottish, 33.1 per cent

to suppose that the actual English and Scottish proportions would have been slightly lower and the Irish slightly higher. In 1811 England made up 57 per cent of the United Kingdom population, Scotland 10 per cent, and Ireland 33 per cent.[4]

Scotland shows up in these figures as grossly over-represented in the army's rank and file. This was even more the case with respect to the officers. Again relying mainly on the data that the 1813 returns provide, we can say the Scots kept about a quarter of all military commissions in their grasp, the share they seem to have possessed throughout the eighteenth century.[5] The significant fact, however, is that they kept that share in spite of a massive expansion of the officer corps— from 3,328 'regimental' officers in 1790 to over fifteen thousand on full or half-pay in 1814.[6] By these figures, the small gentry and other families of quite modest wealth in Scotland must have provided huge numbers of officers. Besides the proportion of Scots in the army, the evidence is overwhelming of Scottish military participation on a scale that far exceeded England's or Ireland's. Scotland raised over 15,000 men as fencibles at the beginning of the war (1793–5), equal to nearly half the strength of the English militia and three-quarters of the strength of the Irish militia. Nor was Scotland behindhand in 1798–9. The 10,000 men provided at that time for the militia and new fencible corps was an amount proportionately not less than the 50,000 of England's supplementary militia.[7] So many communities reported that their manpower reserves were heavily depleted, if not near exhaustion, it is tempting to regard these as canny attempts to protect the supply of labour to local employers. But a key figure bearing out the complaints can be extracted from the militia returns of 1797 giving the numbers in the eligible age-group of males, 19–23-year-olds. The total for Scotland as a whole was returned at 24,663 men or

Irish, and 1.2 per cent foreign. In 1811 49.6 per cent were English, 11.4 per cent Scottish, 36.7 per cent Irish, and 2.3 per cent foreign. The more comprehensive data for 1813 shows that 48.1 per cent of the line infantry were English, 16.5 per cent Scottish, 34.4 per cent Irish, and 1.0 per cent foreign. The returns are found in WO27/90, 102, 121–3.

[4] N. McCord, *British History, 1815–1906* (Oxford, 1991), 78.

[5] For the proportion of Scottish officers in the 18th-cent. army see J. Hayes, 'Scottish Officers in the British Army 1714–63', *Scot. Hist. Rev.* 37 (1958), 23–33; P. E. Razzell, 'Social Origins of Officers in the Indian and British Home Army, 1758–1962', *Brit. J. Sociology*, 14 (1963), 250; G. A. Steppler, 'The British Army on the Eve of War', in Guy, *The Road to Waterloo*, 11. My calculations from the 1813 returns show 38.9 per cent of the officers as English, 24.3 per cent as Scottish, 35.0 per cent as Irish, and 1.8 per cent as 'foreign'.

[6] The 1790 figure is given by T. H. McGuffie, 'The Significance of Military Rank in the British Army Between 1790 and 1820', *Bull. Inst. Hist. Res.* 30 (1957), 214. For 1814 see *CJ* lxix. 643–4.

[7] I get the total of 15,000 fencibles from the inspection returns for 1795 in WO27/76–7 which produce a total of 14,587 men in 23 regiments, but excluding the West Lowland and Northern regiments which were in England. The nine new Scottish fencible corps of 1798–9 were the Clan Alpine, Lochaber, Ross and Cromarty, McLeod, Regiment of the Isles, 3rd Argyll, Tarbet, Banffshire, and Wallace, each, it appears, with an establishment of 600. A list of fencible infantry in the British Isles dated Aug. 1799 (WO1/620/533–5) shows half the strength to have been Scottish. Add at least 5,000 for the Scottish militia.

about 1.5 per cent of the total population, a little above a third of the size of the cohort as far as it can be established.[8] Scotland's 'military spirit' is also attested by the volunteers. With around 15 per cent of the British population, Scotland provided 36.4 per cent of the volunteers in 1797, 21.9 per cent in 1801, and 16.7 per cent in 1804.[9]

It is not difficult to formulate a generalized social explanation for the success of military recruitment in Scotland—though any such explanation may be more a comment on the lack of authoritative work on the local and regional texture of Scottish history than the opposite. The key factor would have to be the increasing mobility of the Scottish population in the eighteenth century, which itself was fuelled by many other factors, all of which tended to strengthen from the middle of the century.[10] The pressure of population on resources was felt most keenly in the Highlands, where it caused seasonal and permanent migration out of the area and kept numbers who remained at little better than subsistence living. North of the Highland line substitution in the militia fell away because it was less affordable; and, by all accounts, even the small pay due volunteers became an important consideration.[11] Highland migrants and seasonal workers often ended up in the southern towns, where some attempts were made to form them into military corps.[12] The Scottish towns surpassed the Highlands as recruiting areas because as well as receiving migrants from the north they drew in people from the rural districts of the Lowlands. Indeed, agricultural and accompanying social changes in the Lowlands provided the main conditions promoting military recruitment in Scotland

[8] For the county distribution of the total of eligible men (24,659) see 'Mr Chalmer's scheme of 12 battalions', HO102/16, fo. 20. I arrive at a cohort size for males in the age-group 19–23 by averaging out Webster's percentages for the age-groups 10–19 and 20–9. See Flinn, *Scottish Population History*, 256–7. If the census figure of 1801 is taken as the Scottish population total (1,625,000) and the male-age group under study equals 4.25 per cent of that total, the size of the group works out at 69,000. This is, admittedly, a crude procedure, but the data hardly permit greater accuracy and the discrepancy is so huge that the point is safely made.

[9] For numbers see return of volunteers, Jan. 1798, Windham MSS, BL Add. MS 37891, fo. 167; Abstract of the establishment of the volunteer corps, Jan. 1801, WO30/65; 'General state and view of H.M. forces', 1 Nov. 1804, Hope of Lufness MSS, SRO GD364/1/1151/3.

[10] It is now established that migration abroad from Scotland was relatively and absolutely greater in the 17th than in the 18th cent. T. C. Smout, N. C. Landsman, and T. M. Devine, 'Scottish Emigration in the 17th and 18th Centuries', in N. Canny (ed.), *Europeans on the Move: Studies On European Migration 1500–1800* (Oxford, 1994), 76–112. But population movement within Scotland and from Scotland to England has not received the same attention, and its quantification is exceptionally difficult. My statement refers to this internal migration.

[11] J. M. Bumstead, *The People's Clearance: Highland Emigration to British North America 1770–1815* (Edinburgh, 1982), 157, says that the lairds used volunteer allowances as an inducement to keep intending emigrants at home. They also proposed additional units for the same purpose.

[12] The Edinburgh volunteers included a 'Royal Highland' regiment. In 1794 there was a proposal to raise a corps from Macdonell clansmen in Glasgow, but the lord provost feared that they would 'look up to their chieftain rather than to the magistrates'. A. MacDonell to Dundas, 9 Nov. 1794, J. Dunlop to [lord advocate?], 28 Nov. 1794, Melville MSS, SRO GD51/1/849/1–2.

since Lowlanders were far more numerous than Highlanders. The continued com-mercialization of farming, known at the time as 'improvement', had the general effect of increasing the size and reducing the number of farmholdings, thus tend-ing to drive out small occupiers for their replacement by wage labourers. Because of the hiring practices that were preferred, these labourers came to form a large, highly mobile workforce, inevitably attracted to the opportunities towns offered and once there prone to end up as military recruits. Scottish recruitment, therefore, was related to Scottish urban growth which was mostly driven by rural immigra-tion and which, along with England's, was the fastest in eighteenth-century Europe.[13]

During the wars, as we shall see, the Highland regiments and the Highland soldier were made (mainly by Lowlanders) into proud symbols of Scotland's ancient nationhood and of her equal partnership with England in a British empire. To this day Scotland's identity, including her military identity, remains largely defined by the Highlands.[14] It seems important, then, to emphasize that martial Scotland in the Napoleonic age was predominantly Lowland in substance, if not in spirit. Again consulting the inspection returns, we find that in 1795 eleven fencible regiments whose names identified them with clans or districts north of the High-land line were filled almost exactly half with Highlanders and half with others. In three Lowland regiments whose details are also recorded, Lowlanders outnum-bered Highlanders eight to one.[15] Two fencible regiments of 1798 belonging ostens-ibly to the most remote parts of the Highlands—the Clan Alpine regiment and the Regiment of the Isles—were 48 and 70 per cent Highlander.[16] There is no reason to think that line regiments mainly recruited in Scotland were markedly different

[13] The best general descriptions of social change in 18th-cent. Scotland are included in T. M. Devine and R. Mitchison (eds.), *People and Society in Scotland: vol. 1, 1760–1830* (Edinburgh, 1988); R. Mitchison, 'Scotland 1750–1850', in F. M. L. Thompson (ed.), *The Cambridge Social History of Britain 1750–1950* (3 vols., Cambridge, 1990), i. 155–208 and in Houston and Whyte, *Scottish Society*, 1–36.

[14] H. Trevor-Roper, 'The Invention of Tradition: The Highland Tradition of Scotland', in E. Hobsbawm and T. Ranger (eds.), *The Invention of Tradition* (Cambridge, 1983), 15–41; L. Leneman, 'A New Role for a Lost Cause: Lowland Romanticisation of the Jacobite Highlander', in L. Leneman (ed.), *Perspectives in Scottish Social History* (Aberdeen, 1988), 107–24; P. Womack, *Improvement and Romance: Constructing the Myth of the Highlands* (Basingtoke, 1989); C. Withers, 'The Historical Creation of the Scottish Highlands', in I. Donnachie and C. Whatley (eds.), *The Manufacture of Scottish History* (Edinburgh, 1992), 143–56.

[15] The returns (WO27/76) include the following fencible infantry regiments: 8th (Rothesay and Caithness), 3rd battalion of the 4th (Breadalbane), Mackay Baillie's (Reay), John Baillie's (Inverness), Balfour's, Campbell's (Dumbarton), Clavering's (2nd Argyll), Douglas's (Angus), Dunbar's (Caithness Legion), Lord Elgin's (Elgin), James Fraser's (Fraser), Leith's (Princess of Wales's or Aberdeen High-land), MacDonell's (Glengarry), and Morrison's. In the eleven 'Highland' regiments Highlanders made up 49.7 per cent of the troops, Lowlanders 36.3 per cent, English and Irish 13.6 per cent. These figures cast some doubt on the often cited estimate of 37,000 men raised in the Highlands for the militia and army, 1793–1815. E. Richards, *A History of the Highland Clearances: Agrarian Transformation and the Evictions 1746–1886* (London, 1982), 148. [16] Western, 'Recruitment', 226.

from this in their composition. Indeed, even in the Highland regiments the pro-portion of Highlanders steadily diminished over time, partly a consequence of dimin-ishing supply after the great numbers taken in 1793–5. In 1809 the 71st, 72nd, 74th, 75th, 91st, and 94th were all ordered out of the kilt and deprived of their designation as Highland regiments. Of 330 recruits received in 1798 by the Black Watch 51 per cent were born in the Highlands; in the period 1807–24, out of 268, 32 per cent were.[17] The overall numerical superiority of Lowlanders in Scot-tish regiments should come as no surprise: it was simply the effect of a population base perhaps three to four times larger. The Edinburgh recruiting district which extended from Dumfries and Berwick to Stirling and Perth usually employed the largest number of officers and men making up the regimental recruiting parties, which itself is an indication of where most recruits were to be found.[18]

Whatever appeals to clan loyalties were made by Highland magnates, they cared little about reviving the lordship of the chiefs; for them raising a regiment was essen-tially a political act directed towards the centre of power in London. Often they avowed that they wished by these means to declare their abhorrence of revolution and support for the war, and it is true that both parties, magnate and government, regarded the undertaking as a public sign of their political union. As a finan-cial transaction, this kind of enterprise was usually profitless and could be heavily expensive, especially at the outset of a war when the rush for men drove the cost of bounties well beyond the official sum; the 90th and 79th, raised in 1793–4, were said to have cost their proprietors £5,000–£6,000 and over £15,000.[19] Financial

[17] D. M. Henderson, *Highland Soldier: A Social Study of the Highland Regiments 1820–1920* (Edin-burgh, 1989), 7–8; Stewart, *Highlanders*, i. 508; E. and A. Linklater, *The Black Watch: The History of the Royal Highland Regiment* (London, 1977), 227. In 1794 the first recruits for the Gordon High-landers included only 354 men drawn from the Highland counties out of a total of 895. J. M. Bulloch, *Territorial Soldiering in the North-East of Scotland During 1759–1814* (Aberdeen, 1914), 230. The 98th (later 91st, Argyllshire), also raised in 1794, was very similar. S. D. M. Carpenter, 'Patterns of Recruitment of the Highland Regiments of the British Army 1756–1815', M.Litt. thesis (St Andrews, 1977), 79.

[18] Return of recruiting parties 1801–6, *SP* 1806, x. 350–1. See also return of recruiting parties 1808–9, WO25/3224, where Edinburgh over a twelve-month period not only had the most parties but also was the most productive district in terms of recruits raised per party. This return is appended to a memorandum on recruiting by Calvert, the adjutant-general, dated 19 Oct. 1809, which lists the recruiting districts and their boundaries.

[19] L. Maclean, *The Raising of the 79th Highlanders* (Inverness, 1980), 7; T. Graham to R. Graham, 22 Feb. 1796, *HMC, Graham of Fintry MSS* (London, 1942), 7. Cox and Greenwood, the army agents, informed the Marquess of Huntly that his recruiting fund for a regiment of over 1,000 men would amount to £28,436, £22,850 if he sold the commissions at the current market price and £5,586 for the levy money the government provided. This worked out at £26 per man, well above the £15. 15s. od. bounty other colonels were trying to keep below. However, Huntly was warned the price of sulbaltern commissions was likely to fall and a 'reserve' needed to be provided for the contingencies of recruiting. He would also have known that colonels had to provide certain items for each soldier out of the levy money as well as payments to recruiting parties. See Cox and Greenwood to the Duke of Gordon, 1 Mar. 1794, Gordon MSS, SRO GD44/47/13/46–7.

loss, however, was only bearable because the other returns were so valuable; in particular, the endowment of patronage that came with a regiment raised in this way. The avidity with which some magnates turned to military recruitment after 1793 cannot but catch the historian's attention. Between them the Earl of Breadalbane, the Duke of Gordon, the Countess of Sutherland's interest, Sir James Grant, and the chief of the Mackenzies raised six fencible and five line battalions in the first two years of the war. Such does, of course, say something about the resources the greatest among the Highland aristocracy commanded; but it also indicates the profound changes that were taking place as clan chiefs were converted into London-looking county grandees scarcely distinguishable from others of this kind.

The growing concern about Highland emigration articulated during the war has a context in the military clientages the magnates looked to and were able to build up when the demand for recruits was continuous and heavy over a long period.[20] Raising a regiment not only helped to provide for a magnate's own relatives and kinsmen but could also bring other powerful interests under his influence and, still more important, conferred obligations on families of the minor gentry who were especially numerous in the Highlands and whose clan loyalties had faded as they lost their position as intermediaries between the chiefs and their tenants. The typical Highland gentleman by the end of the eighteenth century was impoverished alongside his Lowland and English brethren, deprived of access to patronage and power, and only too ready to see the army as his remaining vehicle of social opportunity. Lord Macdonald, 'Lord of the Isles', who had dealt with the 'half pay gentry' in raising a regiment during the American War, passed on the benefit of his experience to Mackenzie of Seaforth in 1793. Seaforth, he said, should not depend 'upon his influence among his own people' but go further abroad for his officers:

There are upon all highland estates descendants and friends of the respective families residing upon them who look upon a war as a sure means to rise upon the auspices of their superior, and it is amazing to think what a zest the appointing a few officers gives to an adventure of this sort. An *esprit de corps* instantly arises among the multitude, and the superior is well seconded, for let me assure you that without a great deal of ardour and every auxiliary power to excite it, a body of men is not to be had all at once upon any given estate be it ever so numerous. Add to this that many young gentlemen would follow their relatives as volunteers in hopes of getting commissions which the fortune of war would throw in their way, and let it be further remarked that young people in that part of the world have not the same occasional advantages of recommendation or the same means to acquire commissions that their southern neighbours enjoy.[21]

---

[20] Bumstead, *The People's Clearance*, 157; A. MacDonell to Lord Pelham, 31 Mar. 1802, HO102/18, fos. 151–2; Duke of Kent to H. Torrens, 17 Apr, 1811, WO1/646/513–16.

[21] Lord Macdonald to A. Brodie, 22 Feb. 1793, Seaforth MSS, SRO GD46/6/25/13. There are informative lists of officers in H. B. Mackintosh, *The Grant, Strathspey or 1st Highland Fencible Regiment 1793–9* (Elgin, 1934), 82–95; Mackintosh, *The Inverness-shire Highlanders or 97th Regiment of*

Military patronage thus could create quite extensive networks of obligation—and in this respect even NCOs rank could be sought after as a stepping-stone to an officer's commission.[22] Any colonel proprietor had an eye for the regimental establishment that gave him most advantage; when some of the fencibles found themselves with surplus men their colonels asked for permission to form additional companies against the government's insistence that they augment those already existing.[23] A second battalion was even more attractive for the amount of patronage it conferred, and a regular regiment more attractive still because the officers gained a half-pay entitlement, a sort of permanent annuity.[24]

There was little clan sentiment in what the Highland magnates were doing in 1793–4. If Sir James Grant raised his fencibles in three weeks, he also found a third of the men for his line regiment in London, Bristol, and Belfast, and put few Highland officers in command. Breadalbane was not above selling sixty-two of his fencible men into the army; Robertson of Lude transferred men in the same way, to recoup, so his officers said, some of the expense he had incurred in raising his corps. Colin Campbell sought permission to enlist three or four hundred Prussian deserters to get around his recruiting problems.[25] While the magnates used regiments to demonstrate their local power and standing, they valued them even more for the credit they gave them in London and the opportunity they presented of confirming their access to the inner circles of power. Two in particular who used their military services at this time to consolidate their alliance with the government were Sir James Grant and Mackenzie of Seaforth. Grant, whose estates were heavily encumbered, was rewarded with a Scottish sinecure worth £3,000 a year and the lord lieutenancy of Inverness in 1794. Mackenzie, who also had financial

Foot 1794–6 (Elgin, 1926), 51–62; J. Mackay, *The Reay Fencibles* (Glasgow, 1890), 42–52. A good idea of how officers were chosen is given in Lord Breadalbane to ——, 25 Feb. 1793, 'List of names given in to the Earl of Breadalbane', 'Appointments by whom recommended', 8 Mar. 1793, John MacGregor MSS, SRO GD50/18. Ibid. 110 is the journal of Lieutenant Alexander McGregor, East Middlesex militia, an interesting example of how a Highlander embarked on a military career.

[22] Mackintosh, *Grant Fencibles*, 96 ff. notes four of the original sergeants and four privates, one a 'volunteer cadet', who won ensign's commissions in various fencible, militia, and regular regiments.

[23] The augmentation can be followed in Sir J. Grant to Lord Amherst, 9, 11 Apr. 1793, Lord Adam Gordon to Dundas, 19 Apr. 1793, HO102/8, fos. 147–8, 151–3, 162; Amherst to Grant, 26 Apr. 1793, Seaforth MSS, SRO GD248/213/2/8; Amherst to Dundas, 17 Apr., 11, 14 June 1793, HO50/2, fos. 108, 154, 156.

[24] See e.g. Sir James Grant's concerns about his patronage in raising his line regiment. Fraser (of Ainslie and Fraser) to Grant, 16 Jan. 1794, Grant to Lord Amherst, 24 Jan. 1794, Amherst to Grant, 11, 14 Feb. 1794, Seafield MSS, SRO GD248/213/2/1, 17, 26, 33.

[25] Grant to Revd James Grant, 15 Apr. 1793, ibid. 190/3/21; Mackintosh, *97th Regiment*, 21 n. 2; Stewart, *Highlanders*, ii. 215–16; Maclean, *79th Highlanders*, 12–13; various letters, Breadalbane MSS, SRO GD112/52/1; Major D. Macdonald, Perth Highland Fencibles to Dundas, 19 Mar. 1796, Colonel Campbell, Dunbartonshire Fencibles to [Dundas], 3 Jan. 1795, Melville MSS, SRO GD51/1/860, 874. In 1795 the Duke of Gordon, at Dundas's request, transferred men to Baillie's Inverness Fencibles at 5 guineas a man. Bulloch, *Territorial Soldiering*, 171.

problems, was made lord lieutenant of Ross in 1794 and given permanent rank in the army and an English peerage. In 1800 Lord Seaforth, as he now was, was appointed governor of Barbados.[26]

The plot thickens when Henry Dundas is shown to have been the leading hand behind Scottish military preferment, in the process dealing with 'multitudes' of applicants.[27] Dundas's purposes are not easy to discover—the full exposure and exposition of the 'Dundas system' is still awaited—but, in general, apart from looking after his family and their many connections, he seems to have wanted 'government', in the sense of order and loyalty to established authority, to be upheld by the widest possible coalition of powerful families. Scotland possessed few independent towns, and therefore the dominance of the great proprietors was all the greater; indeed, it has been compared with Denmark, where 1 per cent of the population in 1789 owned over half of the national wealth.[28] Dundas thus preferred consensus, an abolition of politics confirmed by the judicious distribution of patronage, to any divide and rule strategy. Local rivalries between magnates were deplored because they forced the crown to take sides and weakened the confederation he was anxious to build. However, he was quite prepared to make tactical alliances with his opposition if this was a means of applying pressure on a magnate who preferred independence to inclusion in Dundas's system.[29]

From 1784 Dundas used his position on the board of control for India to direct Indian patronage towards Scotland. The same happened with respect to colonial office-holding when he became the minister in charge of colonies in 1791. Once war had commenced, while he had no formal authority to issue letters of service for the recruitment of new regiments—this belonged to the secretary at war— the Scottish applications were either solicited by him or taken up on his recommendation. But the most important addition to the actual mechanisms of control in Scotland occurred with the introduction of county lieutenancies in 1794. Dundas would have established them the previous year if his Scottish militia bill had not been abandoned, and he seems to have found an opportunity to resurrect the

[26] R. G. Thorne (ed.), *The House of Commons 1790–1820* (5 vols., London, 1986), iv, *sub* Sir James Grant, F. H. Mackenzie.

[27] Dundas to Montgomerie of Coilsfield, 11 Oct. 1794, Melville MSS, SRO GD51/1/830/2.

[28] Houston and Whyte, *Scottish Society*, 10.

[29] Examples are the electoral truce of 1787 in north-east Scotland negotiated by Dundas with Lord Fife, the Duke of Gordon, the Grants, and Lord Findlater and Dundas's alliance with the whig Earl of Breadalbane in 1793–4 against the Duke of Atholl in Perthshire. Thorne, *House of Commons*, ii, *sub* Banffshire, Perthshire. The militia of the Revolutionary War caused many disputes between magnates, organized as it was into regiments drawn from several counties. In 1803 most of Scotland reverted to single county regiments. Whetstone, *Scottish County Government*, 111. It is interesting that in setting up the lieutenancies in 1794, Dundas advised that they should exercise their patronage 'so as to avoid and prevent any difference or competitions between the heritors', Dundas to the Duke of Gordon, 14 May 1794, Gordon MSS, SRO GD44/47/14.

Scottish lieutenancies *sans* militia when the government adopted his plan for volunteers in the English counties.[30] The lieutenancies, he told the Scottish magnates,
would 'lay the foundation for some permanent system' of police and home defence
by creating an authority in the counties able to unite the heritors and organize and
command local forces.[31] The effect, not stated, was to give magnates of Dundas's
choice opportunities to extend their influence over the body of the gentry, exercised particularly through the appointment of deputy-lieutenants and the militia patronage they possessed after 1797. Indeed, the lord lieutenants for a while
came closest to fulfilling Dundas's ideas concerning the governance of Scotland,
the office acquiring great prestige and tending to concentrate local power in the
hands of those of whom the crown approved.[32]

Dundas's dealing in military patronage can be tracked in some detail over the
first year of the war. When the government decided to substitute the regulars in
Scotland with a fencible force of about 4,800 men, Dundas turned immediately
to seven magnates—the Dukes of Argyll and Gordon, the Countess of Sutherland, Lords Breadalbane, Hopetoun, and Eglintoun, and Sir James Grant. Gordon,
together with Hopetoun and Eglintoun—the only Lowlanders of the seven—were
close allies of Dundas; in the case of Hopetoun the relationship was made even
closer in 1793 by Dundas's marriage into the family. Argyll and Sutherland were
unassailable interests in their parts of Scotland with whom every government
had to deal. Grant and Breadalbane are the more interesting cases. Grant was an
important magnate in the north-east whom Dundas was anxious to integrate into
his system. They had made an electoral agreement in 1787, which included a
promise that Grant should have the 'first good office that falls in Scotland', and the
alliance was further cemented by the two regiments—one fencible, one regular—
Grant raised in 1793–4.[33] Dundas's alliance with Breadalbane was purely tactical.
Breadalbane never renounced his whig politics and yet he was permitted to raise
two fencible battalions in 1793 and another in 1794. The explanation is that Dundas
owned a Perthshire estate and wished his son to represent the county, to succeed

---

[30] For the projected militia see Lord Douglas to [Dundas], 16 Jan. 1793, Melville MSS, SRO
GD51/1/821; A. Brodie to Mackenzie of Seaforth, 31 Dec. 1792, 30 Jan., 11 Feb. 1793, Seaforth MSS,
SRO GD46/6/25/1–2, 5. At the end of the session in June 1793 Dundas obtained leave to bring in a
Scottish militia bill. *CJ* xlviii. 945. Amherst, at Dundas's request, produced recommendations for
volunteers on 13 Feb. and these were given a trial at a Berkshire meeting on 4 Mar. Two days later
Dundas sent the king a draft warrant for the appointment of lord lieutenants in Scotland. See Amherst
to Dundas, 13 Feb. 1794, HO42/28, fo. 269; Lord Radnor to Pitt, 4 Mar. 1794, PRO30/8/245, fo. 107;
George III Corresp. ii. 183.

[31] Dundas to the lord lieutenants, 14 May 1794, HO102/11, fos. 26–34.

[32] Whetstone, *Scottish County Government*, 95–115. The king wanted 'the persons of most rank and
weight in the respective counties' appointed, 'unless their political principles are such as would render
their nomination improper', *George III Corresp.* ii. 183.

[33] Thorne, *House of Commons*, ii, *sub* Banffshire; iv, *sub* Sir James Grant.

in which he needed the support of Breadalbane as the most powerful interest that could be brought against the Duke of Atholl.[34]

Only two line regiments were raised in Scotland in 1793—the 78th by Mackenzie of Seaforth and the 79th by Alan Cameron of Erracht. Otherwise recruiting was directed towards independent companies which were then drafted into regiments as required. The fact that greater favour was shown exclusively to two of Dundas's clients says much about his interest in military patronage and success in channelling it through himself. Mackenzie's alliance with Dundas was brokered by Alexander Brodie, prominent in the East India Company and Dundas's close friend. A staunch whig throughout the 1780s, Mackenzie began his defection to Pitt in 1790 by offering a regiment at the time of the Anglo-Spanish crisis and completed it in February 1793 by accepting Dundas's invitation to raise 'the only (at least the first) regiment of Highlanders on the British establishment'.[35] Dundas's association with Cameron of Erracht was of an altogether different character. Cameron was an American loyalist exile with little more than a pension and debts to his name who had, however, married into an immensely wealthy planter family. He was determined to make a military career for himself and his sons, his father-in-law backed him with £20,000, and he literally bought the men, against competition and the disapproval of his clan superior, all over Scotland. Dundas's partiality for Cameron extended to being godfather to one of his sons and doing his best to keep the 79th within his fiefdom by getting it sent to India. Cameron's second-in-command also was married to Dundas's sister-in-law.[36]

After 1793 careerists like Cameron and entrepreneurs seeking a profit became more prominent in Scottish recruiting as the government's demand for troops kept on increasing and its terms became more generous. While Argyll, Gordon, Grant, and Eglintoun's heir raised line regiments in 1794 and Mackenzie and Breadalbane additional battalions for their existing corps, the efforts of these magnates have to be put alongside the four line and fourteen fencible regiments raised under other auspices. The fencibles of 1794 had nothing to do with the defence of Scotland but were for service elsewhere in the British Isles, making possible further transfers of regulars abroad, partly or even mainly in support of Dundas's Caribbean strategy. Dundas still tried to direct this patronage, writing 'private applications' to 'persons whom he thought he was likely to influence' in October.[37] Yet the list of

[34] Thorne, *House of Commons*, sub Perthshire.

[35] See Brodie's letters, Seaforth MSS, SRO GD46/6/25; Thorne, *House of Commons*, iv, sub F. H. Mackenzie. .

[36] Maclean, *79th Highlanders*; C. G. Gardyne, *The Life of a Regiment: The History of the Gordon Highlanders from its Formation in 1794 to 1816* (London, 1929), 12; Duke of York to Pitt, 28 June 1795, Chatham MSS, PRO30/8/106, fos. 54–5. Cameron gives an account of his military career in Cameron to Lord Castlereagh, 30 Jan. 1808, WO1/637/285–7.

[37] Dundas to the king, 6 Oct. 1794, *George III Corresp.* ii. 251–2.

those issued with recruiting letters includes some who later claimed that they had lacked powerful connections or whose appointment upset established interests. The Inverness fencibles, for example, were raised by John Baillie. A long-serving Indian officer, 'unprotected by interest or indeed anything but my own character', he was introduced to Dundas by the ever-attentive Alexander Brodie. James Leith was another professional soldier, apparently held in high regard in the Duke of York's circle. Such patronage got him the precious letter of service and permission to name his corps after the Princess of Wales, but in his native county of Aberdeen his 'friends' were already committed to helping his brother-in-law raise a regiment for the line: 'I believe I may say that my regiment is one of the few which has been raised in Scotland without the patronage of some individual of large landed property.' The recruiting activities of the Leith–Hay family in north-east Scotland have a wider political significance in that they were carried on in competition with the Gordon interest; and this rivalry anticipated the formation of an opposition in Aberdeenshire to the Gordons which destroyed the balance of power that Dundas had worked to his advantage.[38] Dundas also seems to have been outmanœuvred in Forfarshire where he first approached William Maule, the greatest landowner in the county, only to be overtaken by the Douglas interest.[39]

Scottish military recruitment during the Revolutionary War began as an extension of Dundas's system but rapidly showed signs of exhausting the resources of the great families and bringing forward other interests to complicate the politics involved. The depletion of the manpower reserves that territorial influence could command is seen in the dwindling proportion of Scots-born when the fencibles of 1794 are compared with those of 1793. The early regiments were nearly 98 per cent Scots; the next year's 84 per cent Scots. In 1798 when the Leith–Hay family raised another fencible regiment in Aberdeenshire, their colonel took pride in the fact that he had enlisted sufficient Scots to make up half his numbers.[40] Since

[38] Baillie to [Dundas], 9 Aug. 1795, Leith to Dundas, 29 Nov. 1794, 10 Dec. 1795, Melville MSS, SRO GD51/1/852, 870, 872; Bulloch, *Territorial Soldiering*, 253–6, 263. Leith's military career is given in the *DNB*. For Aberdeenshire politics and the alliance of the Earls of Fife and Aberdeen against the Duke of Gordon see Thorne, *House of Commons*, ii, *sub* Aberdeenshire. Aberdeen helped Alexander Hay to recruit his regiment, the 109th, and then intervened to restore Hay's relations with the Duke of York after it was drafted in 1795. Shortly afterwards Hay was promoted to major-general and appointed to the staff in Scotland. See Leith Hall MSS, SRO GD225/1044/21/104, 106, 110–11, 130, 140–1, and the Duke of Gordon to Dundas, 3 July 1800, Melville MSS, NLS MS 5, fo. 131.

[39] Maule to Dundas, 18 Oct. 1794, Melville MSS, SRO GD51/1/838; memorandum on Angus fencibles, unnamed to D[avid] Scott, n.d., NLS MS 14299, fos. 154–7. Dundas's friend and wealthy East Indian director, David Scott of Dunninald, was the county member; his position would have been very secure with Maule's continued support. Another account fitting the Angus fencibles into county politics is in R. Sunter, *Patronage and Politics in Scotland 1707–1832* (Edinburgh, 1986), 134–47.

[40] The inspection returns for 1795 (WO27/76–7) cover eight regiments and battalions raised in 1793–4 (4,643 Scots out of 4,742) and thirteen raised in 1794–5 (6,511 Scots out of 7,752). Colonel Hay to Dundas, 24 Dec. 1798, Melville MSS, NLS MS 7, fos. 114–15.

the home service of fencibles always made them a more popular option than the regulars, the individuals recruiting for the regular army did well if they could find even a majority of Scots. As early as 1794–5 the corps of Simon Fraser, one of Scotland's most famous living soldiers, was only 57 per cent Scottish and the equally famous Scotch Brigade only 54 per cent. Thomas Graham admitted that in his 90th or Perthshire regiment either Manchester or Birmingham invariably provided twice as many men as the county; in 1794 he had recruiting parties out in London, Manchester, Nottingham, Shrewsbury, and Leicester.[41] Graham epitomized the enterprise and hard work that was needed once the task of recruitment passed out of the hands of the magnates. The magnates had the easy pickings because of their territorial influence and because they were first. Their successors inevitably made it into more of a business, the government, in effect, providing them with a contract which they could only fulfil by subcontracting to other officers, by finding patrons and working connections, and by building a far-flung organization of seasoned army men on the ground, always with a careful eye on the accumulating cost.[42]

Dundas none the less clung to ideas that the Highlands were an underutilized resource of men and the Highlander superior soldier material, especially in comparison with townsmen. If three-quarters of the corps he promoted in 1793–4 carried Highland or northern names, in 1798 he was back to asking for 'Lochiel or any other real Highland chieftain' to raise additional fencible regiments. The results were much the same. Behind a façade of Highland loyalty and military enthusiasm, careerism and patronage were the driving forces and professional recruiting the recipe for success; the Loyal Macleods or Prince of Wales Own, for example, was raised by a long-serving East India Company officer ('having no other property in this country but my *ready gold*, to it alone I must trust for success') and the regiment had to be purged of suspect Irishmen before it could be sent to Gibraltar.[43] Dundas's admiration of the martialness of Highland society seems to be another instance of the way in which Lowlanders towards the end of the eighteenth century were conferring an identity on Highlanders which mostly reflected the identity

[41] For Simon Fraser's corps and the Scotch Brigade see the 1795 inspection returns. The Royal Glasgow regiment was only 47 per cent Scottish. For the 90th see T. Graham to R. Graham, 1 Feb. 1812, *Graham of Fintry MSS*, 161; Lynedoch MSS, NLS MS 16197 (vii).

[42] An excellent account of a recruiting officer's duties is found in Gordon MSS, SRO GD44/47/13, which include the almost daily letters of Captain Finlayson, based in Aberdeen in 1794, to the Duke of Gordon, his employer, and his secretary.

[43] Macleod of Colbecks to Dundas, 11 May 1798, Dundas to the lord advocate, 15 May 1798, *Laing MSS* ii. 656–7; J. Macleod to Lord Seaforth, 22 Aug. 1798, Seaforth MSS, SRO GD46/6/25/81; Lt.-Col. R. Matthews to W. Huskisson, 29 Sept. 1799. WO1/620/615–16. Major Andrew Hay, who raised the Banffshire or Duke of York's fencibles, was described as being without 'either cash or connections', having only 'an estate [of] about £300 a year and much encumbered' with 'not above half a dozen tenants', Lord Fife to Dundas, 3 Aug. 1798, Melville MSS, SRO GD51/1/903/7.

they wished for themselves. It is interesting how easily Dundas was taken in by a scheme to embody the clans in 1797. Put to him by Captain Macpherson of the 17th foot, with palaver about the loyalties of clansmen to their chiefs and their hostility to 'levelling and dangerous principles', he wrote off to various magnates all eagerness for the 'restoration of clanship' and the further regiments it might provide for Ireland. Not so the replies. Some told him the authority of the chiefs had all but gone; some the same indirectly by declaring that few of their people would offer themselves for service in Ireland. Everyone agreed that volunteers for the defence of Scotland would be the most popular form of service, reducing the military patriotism of Highlanders to the level of everywhere else in Great Britain. Moreover, what could be tacitly understood from the responses was that the clan chiefs disliked Macpherson's plan for reviving their inferiority to the superior chiefs. Better volunteer corps which they could command independently, and better county lieutenancies for making them like all other gentry than the old clan hierarchies. Dundas, in common with many of his contemporaries, had sentimentalized the Highlands to the point of being unable to see how Lowlandized the Highlands had become.[44]

Most clan chiefs within the very loose clan confederations of the magnates were comparable to those Lowland gentry who could not afford to live in London but who asserted their local leadership instead. Particularly in the counties and particularly through volunteering and home defence, the war provided the lairds with a windfall of opportunities to extend their public roles and local consequence, all of which has to be placed in the context of the increasing effectiveness of county government in eighteenth-century Scotland.[45] The Scottish counties, it is worth noting, began to form themselves into defence communities in 1794 before the new lord lieutenants had received their official instructions or presented their commissions.[46] Dundas can be believed when he said that he appointed the greatest man

[44] 'Plan for raising 16,000 men for internal defence by embodying the Highland clans', Feb. 1797, Dundas to Mackenzie of Seaforth, 22 Feb. 1797, Seaforth MSS, SRO GD46/6/34–5; Duke of Gordon to Dundas, 1, 25 Mar. 1797, Melville MSS, NLS MS 5, fos. 95, 101–2; W. Ogilvy to Dundas, 4 Mar. 1797, ibid. 1048 fo. 63; Macpherson of Cluny to the Duke of Gordon, 6 Mar. 1797, A. Mackintosh to Gordon, 16 Mar. 1797, Gordon MSS, SRO GD44/47/24, 49/24; Duke of Argyll to Dundas, 10 Mar. 1797, GD51/1/670/2; [Macpherson of Cluny] to Sir James Grant, 20 Mar. 1797, Macpherson of Cluny MSS, SRO GD80/938; J. Ross to J. Wilson, 24 Mar. 1797, Seafield MSS, SRO GD248/3408/9/12. Captain Macpherson urged his plan on the government again in 1803–4. 'Memoir . . . submitted to Duke of York', E. Macpherson to Windham, 27 June 1803, Windham MSS, BL Add, MS 37881, fos. 195–200; W. H. Clinton to Lord Hobart, 2 July 1803, Hobart MSS, Buckingham RO, D/MH/H/War/ G57; Macpherson to Pitt, 15 May 1804, Chatham MSS, PRO30/8/154, fo. 315; Macpherson to Lord Melville, 17 Dec. 1804, EUL Gen. 1995/51.   [45] Mitchison, 'Scotland 1750–1850', 163–4.

[46] The first circular letter to the lord lieutenants, with other papers on home defence, was sent on 14 May 1794, HO102/11, fos. 26–43. County meetings before this date are recorded in the *Edinburgh Evening Courant*, 17 Apr.–7 June 1794: Ayr met on 10 Apr., Roxburgh 15 Apr., Dumfries 23 Apr., Lanark 25 Apr., Argyll, Forfar, Dunbarton, Inverness, and Selkirk 30 Apr., Stirling and Linlithgow 9 May.

in each county to be lord lieutenant,[47] and the power to make deputy-lieutenants was a valuable addition to a magnate's local patronage, though not as valuable as the militia appointments. But it is easy to exaggerate the dominance of Scottish magnates within their counties. Lieutenancies and county meetings were communal forms of authority, something emphasized in virtually all Scottish counties by the practice of collecting defence subscriptions from individuals according to their cess (or land-tax) assessments.[48] Moreover, lord lieutenants were often absent from their counties which meant an alternative authority had to be created out of the deputies. The distinct status of these deputies within the county was recognized by the uniforms they came to wear. In short, home defence during a period of prolonged war causing an inordinate amount of county activity intensified the long eighteenth-century trend cutting back the power of the magnates in favour of gentry rule.[49]

By and large the relationship between the magnates and the developing county élites remained uncomplicated because there continued to be vast differences in the scale of wealth of the two and the magnates made the support of the other the fulcrum of their local position. An important factor was that there were few families of real consequence in any county. Populous Lanarkshire had only thirty-nine deputy-lieutenants in 1799; Aberdeen, about the same time, thirty; and Perth and Ayr, twenty-five each. No more than fifteen people ever attended a county meeting in East Lothian. In Selkirk in 1794 just four contributed £20 upwards for county defence; half the total sum raised was given by the Duke of Buccleuch. In Aberdeen in 1803 on a similar occasion twelve gave £20 upwards, with the Duke of Gordon and his heir providing a third of the total. Compare Lincolnshire's subscription in 1794, when sixty-nine individuals gave at least £20; or Somerset's, when eighty-one gave £50 or more.[50] With close co-operation between magnates and the wealthier lairds more typical than not, the most powerful elements of Scottish

[47] Lord Melville to the lord advocate, 13 July 1803, HO102/64, fo. 430.

[48] See the reports of county meetings in *Edinburgh Evening Courant*, 17 Apr.–25 Aug. 1794. The peculiar Scottish practice of 'assessing' what were voluntary contributions may be attributed to the relative poverty of Scottish counties and perhaps the large number of non-resident landowners. Printed letters were sent to cess-payers asking them to comply with the meeting's decision. If an ordinary subscription proved insufficient, as happened in Stirling and Clackmannan in 1804 over the volunteers, there was resort to 'assessment'. In Clackmannan's case, only one person refused to pay. See circular letter to heritors of Fife, 5 Apr. 1794, Melville MSS, NLS MS 3834, fo. 26; circular from Stirlingshire meeting, 26 Jan. 1804, Central Region Archives, Stirling, Stirling burgh MSS, B66/25/388/24; meeting of Clackmannan lieutenancy, 21 Jan. 1804, J. Jameson of Alloa to J. McGibbon, 6 May 1804, ibid. 26.

[49] Whetstone, *Scottish County Government*, 99–100; T. Burnett to the Duke of Gordon, 26 Oct. 1803, Gordon to Burnett, 28 Oct. 1803, Gordon MSS, SRO GD44/47/29.

[50] Whetstone, *Scottish County Government*, 100–1; *Edinburgh Evening Courant*, 7 June 1794; subscription list for internal defence, 8 Aug. 1803, Gordon MSS, SRO GD44/47/29; Brownlow MSS, Lincoln RO, 4BNL Box 5; W. G. Fisher, *History of Somerset Yeomanry, Volunteer and Territorial Units* (Taunton, 1924), 17–18.

landed society easily became select oligarchies through whom the most important business of the county was decided. What is more only the larger towns could maintain a significant degree of independence against landed power and authority; many of the smaller towns were so weak as to be nothing more than appendages.

The pattern of volunteering in Scotland enforces the idea that the magnates and the lairds acting together, not the urban élites as in England, were the main beneficiaries of this kind of military activity as well. While powerful concentrations of volunteers quickly emerged in Edinburgh and the area around Glasgow in 1794, by the end of the year an equal number were to be found distributed among the small coastal towns from Dunbar to Thurso and the islands and inlets of the west. By 1796 there were over sixty volunteer companies on the outer coasts against under fifty on the central lowlands. This difference, broadly one of north against south, only intensified with further expansion of the volunteers in 1797–8. By July 1798 almost half and by January 1801 over half of Scotland's total volunteer force was found in thirteen counties positioned north of a line running roughly from Dumbarton to Aberdeen.[51] There were 228 corps formed during the Revolutionary War.[52] Most Scottish corps, then, belonged to quite small places. They were commanded by lairds or lairds' men and were usually initiated by a county meeting or the lieutenancy, sometimes under the lord lieutenant's direct patronage as happened in Banffshire and Caithness. Even the larger towns could not always prise themselves free of landed power. In Aberdeen the county passed resolutions for organizing the city's defence, and command of these volunteers went to Alexander Moir of Scotstown, a county gentleman who had no military experience and who, in fact, resigned his commission after a year to become sheriff-depute of the county. Edinburgh, moreover, in 1803 supported the dignity of the Duke of Buccleuch to the extent of giving him the colonelcies of its 2nd and Royal Leith regiments.[53] In England volunteering was not nearly so county-organized and controlled, and towns of any size were more likely to act on their own and resist all outside interference. One measure of this was the relative ease with which Scotland amalgamated its many small corps into larger formations; in 1801 over 40 per cent of the infantry were organized in corps of over two hundred rank and file where under 25 per cent of the English were.[54]

The other outstanding feature of Scottish volunteering was the numbers that

---

[51] Lists of the volunteer establishment are found at Chatham MSS, PRO30/8/244, fos. 205–10, 237–40; Melville MSS, SRO GD51/1/725/11; WO30/65 unfoliated.

[52] Fortescue, *County Lieutenancies*, 59–60.

[53] *Edinburgh Evening Courant*, 14 Aug. 1794, reporting meeting of 6 Aug.; J. Abercromby to Duke of Gordon, 26 Aug. 1794, Moir to Duke of Gordon, 14 Feb. 1795, Gordon MSS, SRO GD44/47/35; Bulloch, *Territorial Soldiering*, 294; Buccleuch to Charles Yorke, 15 Sept. 1803, Melville MSS, NLS MS 1048, fos. 128–30.

[54] 'Abstract of the strongest yeoman and volunteer corps', Sept. 1801, WO30/65.

came forward. The size of Scotland's volunteer force at any time during the Revolutionary War far exceeded England's in population terms, and in 1803 the flood of offers forced the government to impose county quotas in June two months before it was done in England. Scotland had 52,000 volunteers in 1804 (compared with 30,000 in 1801), with well over half of these on the June allowances. If the June allowances are made an index of volunteer enthusiasm, the point being that these corps were the first formed in 1803, Scotland with 29,000 'June' men easily outshone England with 61,000.[55] Even these figures do not do justice to the Scottish response to the threatened invasion because many more than joined volunteer corps offered their services. In Aberdeenshire, for example, there were 1,120 'embodied' volunteers by September 1803 and over 11,000 'voluntary offers' had been received. Argyll returned over 12,000 volunteers; Perth over 9,000. Lowland Scotland may be represented by Renfrewshire, which in 1798 found 5,071 men willing to serve or already serving. Against the census totals for 1801, Aberdeenshire's total of volunteers represented 10 per cent of the population, and Argyll's 15 per cent. These percentages were comparable with anything found in the front-line counties of the south-east; the northern division of Pevensey Rape in Sussex, for instance, was ready to mobilize 11 per cent of its population in 1803. Perthshire's rate of 7.5 per cent was the second highest for any inland county. In the earlier invasion crisis of 1798, the 6 per cent of relatively safe Renfrewshire compares favourably with Lincoln's 7 per cent and Essex's 10 per cent. All English figures given here are based on totals that include those offering unarmed service, which significantly inflate them; Argyll and Perth's relate to armed volunteers only, and over much of northern Scotland there would have been little point in organizing other service. Thus it needs to be borne in mind that in the coastal English counties home defence embraced a wider range of activity and, therefore, similar Scottish percentages indicate how much of Scotland's defence was seen to depend on civilian soldiers defending their own communities.[56]

Contemporary Scots eagerly found evidence of their nation's 'military spirit' in the great volunteer mobilizations of the wars which thus assume importance in

[55] Draft memorandum on volunteers [1803], WO1/407/513–18; 'General State and View of HM's forces', 1 Apr. and 1 Nov. 1804, Hope of Lufness MSS, SRO GD364/1/1151/1, 3. The corps of 1803 on or not on the June allowances are listed in *SP* 1803–4, xi.

[56] 'List of voluntary enrolments' [2 Sept. 1803], Gordon MSS, SRO GD44/47/36 and Bulloch, *Territorial Soldiering*, 308–19 for Aberdeen; Colley, *Britons*, 380 for Argyll and Perth; 'Return according to Dundas's letter of 6 April 1798', Tods, Murray and Jamieson MSS, SRO GD237/192/3 for Renfrewshire; *Sussex Militia List, Pevensey Rape 1803: Northern Division* (Eastbourne, 1988); 'Statistical Map' of 1798, Essex RO, L/R 1/3 for Essex; chart of 1798, 'Military Lincolnshire', Kesteven Quarter Sessions MSS, Lincoln RO for Lincolnshire. In contrast to Colley, I prefer to assess mobilization rates against census totals rather than against returns of the eligible population, which were surely less accurate.

the formation of a Scottish national consciousness. But rather than pronounce a panegyric on Scottish patriotism, the historian will search for the conditions that made volunteering particularly attractive in this part of Britain. One factor was the need for many places to provide for their own defence since there was virtually no naval presence north of the Forth and Clyde and the army in the same area maintained posts (mainly for recruiting purposes) only at Aberdeen, Inverness, and Fort William.[57] Small ports and settlements along the extensive coasts of Scotland felt particularly exposed to enemy raids across the North Sea from Holland and Germany. It was increasing enemy activity in the North Sea that produced the rapid growth of volunteering in Scotland in 1797, but not in England.

The other main incentive was the material benefits the corps offered in a generally poor society. Scotland's gentry tended to be rich only in military experience and the numerous retired and half-pay officers were obvious substitutes for the civilians who took most of the volunteer commissions in England. The early burgeoning of the Scottish movement probably started the practice of restoring half-pay officers to full pay when they joined the volunteers, with a lesser emolument for ex-officers of the army and militia. This arrangement was regularized in 1798, though confined to officers up to the rank of captain. When after 1803 the privilege was limited to one officer per company, the Scottish corps, significantly, began to find it difficult to fill their commissions.[58] A sad, but as was said at the time not untypical, case was James Bartlett, an ex-army officer and lieutenant-colonel of the 1st Banffshire battalion, who asked to be reduced to the rank of 'eldest captain' because he had only a 'small pittance' to support himself and his family and could not afford to serve without pay.[59] While officers often funded their pay for the benefit of their unit, there was still advantage for them if they could cover its costs in this way without encroaching on their private income, something the Scots were better placed to do.

The importance of pay to Scottish officers no doubt made them equally alive to the similar concerns of their rank and file. In 1798 there was uproar in the Scottish corps when the government reduced the weekly allowance to the men from two shillings to one shilling. It was pointed out that in Edinburgh these earnings were

[57] A list of barracks dated 6 Mar. 1806, Dropmore MSS, BL Add. MS 59286, fos. 32–9, indicates the stations of troops. The peculiar problem of Scotland's defence is considered in Dundas to the lord advocate, 7 Mar. 1797, Meikle, *Scotland and the French Revolution*, 276–81, and C. Hope to Lord Cathcart, 27 Sept. 1806, Melville MSS, SRO GD51/1/986.

[58] Sebag-Montefiore, *History of the Volunteer Forces*, 212 and n. 2, 239; Fortescue, *County Lieutenancies*, 114; Bulloch, *Territorial Soldiering*, 313, 351. It is hard to find evidence of volunteer officers receiving half or full army pay before the regulations of 1798. In 1795 the Royal Edinburgh Volunteers asked for their major, an ex-army officer, to be given full pay, though what precedents there were for this remain obscure. Officers to the lord provost, 9 Dec. 1795, Melville MSS, NLS MS 1049, fos. 58–9.

[59] Bulloch, *Territorial Soldiering*, 358–60.

a 'material consideration' to the 'lower and working classes of people', 'many of their masters having very liberally engaged not to deduct anything from their working hours during their attendance at the drill'. In the country areas where wages were lower, volunteering as additional paid work was even more welcome. The same issue of making training a bargain Scots would close with arose in 1803 when the government first offered volunteers pay for eighty-five days and then reduced it to twenty days.[60]

These general conditions favouring volunteering in Scotland also account for its particular appeal in the Highlands. It was a form of self-defence along the isolated coasts and a service quite unlike the militia which could take men away from home or tax individuals and communities heavily. A correspondent of Sir James Grant's believed that a place in the volunteers was worth £5 a year to a man.[61] One laird commanding the company at Moidart in western Inverness caught the economic deprivation of Highland society nicely by noting that the men were anxious for the pay and the officers that the government allowances should cover their costs. In the furore over Highlands emigration in 1801–3 it was seriously suggested that the agents could be thwarted and 'the attachment of the people to their king and country' restored by reinstating the volunteer corps.[62] If we take the Highland counties to have been Perth, Argyll, Inverness, Ross, Cromarty, Sutherland, and Caithness, with a quarter of the Scottish population they provided over a third of Scotland's volunteers towards the end of the Revolutionary War. Later in the Napoleonic War when county volunteer strengths were tied to militia quotas, the same discrepancy no longer occurred.[63] But since the need to believe in the martial reputation of the Highlanders was becoming ever stronger as Scotland searched for a national identity and an imperial role, the Highland volunteers were powerfully reassuring in the face of their people's abiding dislike of the militia.[64]

In the Lowlands the volunteers were hailed as the recovery of Scotland's 'ancient military spirit' and of its 'independence' within the context of the Union.[65] As

---

[60] Duke of Buccleuch to Duke of Portland, 4 Feb. 1798; memorial of field officers and captains of 1st battalion, 2nd regiment Royal Edinburgh Volunteers, Melville MSS, SRO GD51/1/905/2, 906; J. Brodie to Portland, 30 Jan. 1798, HO102/16, fo. 67; Fortescue, *County Lieutenancies*, 82–3. Many letters of complaint in 1798 are found in HO102/16, though commanding officers preferred to take the line that their men were serving out of patriotism and only wished to recoup their costs.

[61] Average wages over much of the Highlands and Isles were £4 p.a. North of Inverness wage rates were generally 50 per cent lower than for the rest of Scotland. V. Morgan, 'Agricultural Wage Rates in Late Eighteenth-Century Scotland', *Econ. Hist. Rev.* 2nd ser. 23 (1971), 184–93.

[62] A. Macdonald to Dundas, 22 July 1797; Sir J. Grant to Lord Melville, sending paper by Ranald Macdonald, 1 Mar. 1803; H. Mackenzie, 'Short remarks on the present emigration from the Highlands', 28 Feb. 1803, Melville MSS, SRO GD51/1/889, 51/5/52/4, 6–7.

[63] Volunteer establishments for the different counties are given in ibid. 51/1/725/11 (Aug. 1800); WO30/65 (Jan. 1801); *SP* 1803–4, xi; 1806, x. 319–27.   [64] Fortescue, *County Lieutenancies*, 48–9.

[65] G. Home to Home of Wedderburn MP, 23 Mar. 1795, Home of Wedderburn MSS, SRO GD267/1/18/14–15.

in England, the largest expansions, in 1797 and 1803, occurred under threat of imminent invasion. Scotland's reaction to these threats was especially intense because the regular army was necessarily drawn off to the south-east of Britain and because previously in the eighteenth century the most the country had had to fear was the occasional small-scale raid. In 1797 the Scots suddenly found themselves in the front line with the enemy in firm possession of the opposite North Sea coast and about to disengage elsewhere in Europe. Volunteers in Scotland, therefore, became an integral part of the home garrison, more so than their English comrades ever were. Colonel Dirom of the Scottish staff, who mainly planned the defence of Scotland, immediately looked to them to provide the numbers required for an adequate field force. The particular fear was that within four days of leaving the Dutch or Belgian ports an invasion force could appear in the Firth of Forth and capture the capital.[66] From 1799 the volunteers of the counties around Edinburgh were trained alongside the permanent forces in preparation for forming the mixed divisions which would meet a French attack. As part of the 'first line' in 1803 these corps were to be among the first to receive arms.[67] This was the situation that so noticeably subdued volunteer localism. So few regular or English regiments were kept in Scotland, it was easy for the volunteers to regard the country's defence entrusted into their hands, and they had the further 'proud satisfaction' of knowing that England in an hour of need would call on a Scottish volunteer army to march south to her aid.[68] England thus was no longer able to provide for her own defence, much less Scotland's.

Scotland's assumption of responsibility for her own defence was a process begun in a very small way during the Seven Years War with the raising of two fencible regiments. Up to then, the English government had been profoundly hostile to giving Scotland any means of independent military power lest it get into the wrong hands. As it was, care was taken to raise the fencibles of 1759 in well-affected areas, namely the Duke of Argyll's and the Sutherland domains. Only four Scottish

---

[66] Dirom to the lord advocate, 27 Mar. 1797, Melville MSS, NLS MS 7, fos. 154–6; Dirom, 'Memoir of the Military State of North Britain in 1803', ibid., MS 1754.

[67] Quartermaster-general's department memorandum, 25 July 1803, WO1/625/547–51; Lord Moira to C. Yorke, 18 Dec. 1803, Hardwicke MSS, BL Add, MS 45040, fos. 94–7; 'Disposition for concentrating the regulars, militia, yeomanry and volunteer forces for the defence of the southern district in North Britain', 10 Apr. 1804, Buccleuch MSS, SRO GD224/628/3/12. This last paper mixed 16,686 volunteers with 2,736 regulars and 8,119 militia in three brigades. The Edinburgh Volunteer Light Dragoons went into quarters at Musselburgh for two weeks in March 1799. See their minute book, NLS MS Adv. 22. 2. 21.

[68] C. Hope to Lord Cathcart, 27 Sept. 1806, Melville MSS, SRO GD51/1/986. Hope commanded a battalion of Edinburgh volunteers. The plans of the Horse Guards for a convergence of volunteer brigades on the south-east in the event of invasion referred to 20,000 men marching from Scotland. 'Distribution of the volunteers in Great Britain shewing the moveable force', Hope of Lufness MSS, SRO GD364/1/1147/1.

fencible regiments were raised during the American War, in spite of the severe pressures on the army and plenty of applications; then they seem to have been scattered in small garrisons across the country from the south-west to the Shetlands.[69] When the fencibles of 1793 took up their stations, the defence of Scotland for the first time was consigned, almost entirely, into Scottish hands. Later, the militia made the garrison just as emphatically Scottish. In light of the anguish expressed for nearly a century over the country's loss of its martial heritage, this amount of self-reliance in defence contributed enormously to the retrieval of Scottish nationhood in the age of Ossian and Scott.

During the American War a rough balance of strength had been preserved between (mainly English) regulars and Scottish non-regulars.[70] In contrast, in 1795 fencibles outnumbered regulars five to one; in 1797 seven to one; in March 1801 the garrison consisted of 1,685 regulars (the infantry only a few invalid companies), 1,076 English militia, and 5,120 Scottish militia, with 30,000 volunteers available as an auxiliary force. During the Napoleonic War the Scottish militia were invariably the major part of the garrison, usually two-thirds or more.[71] With these numbers, Scottish troops could not be kept away from the towns and their regiments broken into small detachments—if they had been, anyway, they would have been useless for battlefield service. The practice of the Napoleonic War was for Scottish line battalions to be stationed in the country in order to replenish their ranks; often they were not strong enough to occupy the most important local garrisons.[72] The sternest test of the policy of Scotticizing the military force in Scotland came in 1797 with the widespread disorder over the militia. These protests caught the country without any regular cavalry; but the fencibles were not found wanting by Lord Adam Gordon, the commanding general, nor the yeomanry and volunteers. Several Scottish fencible regiments were included among the reinforcements ordered into Scotland from northern England. English militia were sent not so much because they were 'southern' but because they were the troops immediately available in a dangerous and still uncertain situation.[73]

---

[69] Whetstone, *Scottish County Government*, 96; Robertson, *Scottish Enlightenment*, 106, 161.

[70] Mackesy, *War for America*, 524–5, assuming 2,000 troops were the normal regular garrison and the four fencible regiments also equalled about 2,000 men.

[71] For 1795 see Chatham MSS, PRO30/8/245, fos. 176–83; for 1797 WO30/64/57; for 1801 WO1/407/489 and WO30/65/23. For the Napoleonic War see the returns in Hope of Lufness MSS, SRO GD364/1/1137/30/2; 1141/2, 21, 25; 1148/1, 5, 11; 1158/5, 10; 1163/4, 10; 1184/4, 6.

[72] See the distributions of troops in ibid. 1163/10 (Dec. 1806), 1184/6 (Dec. 1809), 1202/12 (Dec. 1810).

[73] Duke of York to Pitt, 3 Sept. 1797, PRO30/8/106, fo. 190; Duke of Portland to R. Dundas, 3 Sept. 1797, R. Brownrigg to Lord Adam Gordon, 5 Sept. 1797, Laing MSS, EUL La ii. 501; York to the King, 7 Sept. 1797, *George III Corresp.* ii. 621; Lord Adam Gordon to Portland, 18 Sept. 1797, HO102/15, fos. 158–9. See also H. Dundas to Portland, 4 Sept. 1797, ibid., fos. 35–40: 'I have not a conception of there being any difference in this case between a regiment of English and Scotch cavalry,

What of the army, or at least the Scottish regiments, most of them new formations? Did they too contribute to the reassertion of Scottish nationhood that
occurred in the late eighteenth and early nineteenth century? As already suggested,
martial achievement directed attention beyond Scottish success within the Union
to the more distant past, whether the ancient warrior society still represented by
the Highland soldier or the small country that down the centuries had successfully
defended its independence against more powerful kingdoms. It reinforced a Scottish patriotism which celebrated national identity through antiquarianism, nostal-
gia, and myth without challenging the idea of Scotland within the Union or British
empire.[74] Unlike after the American War, the Scottish regiments continued on the
establishment, indeed were permanently incorporated into the army with their
traditions laid in the greatest and most glorious war Britain had ever fought; they
were perfect vehicles for revering Scottish deeds of arms while affirming Scottish
loyalty to the crown and empire. Regimental history as a genre originated in
Scotland soon after Waterloo with the publication of Colonel David Stewart's
Sketches of the Highlanders (1821). This work was initially conceived as a history of
the 42nd regiment, the famous Black Watch, but was expanded into a chronicle of
all the Highland regiments and a description of the old clan society to become a significant text for the cult of the Highland soldier in nineteenth-century Scotland.[75]

The concentration of Scottish soldiers in a few regiments to form distinctively
Scottish units was a feature of the army that originated during the French Wars.
The extant inspection returns for 1813 reveal that 70 per cent of Scots serving in
the line infantry were found in just ten regiments, in contrast to the Irish, who
spread themselves much more evenly. Five of these regiments—42nd (Black Watch),
78th, 79th (Cameron Highlanders), 92nd (Gordon Highlanders), 93rd (later Sutherland Highlanders)—were over 80 per cent Scottish in their rank and file; the
other five—26th (Cameronians), 71st, 72nd, 91st, 94th—were over 60 per cent.
Perhaps fifteen regiments were as proportionately Irish, but then they often lacked

---

and therefore if sending an efficient force there without delay is of moment (which I think it is) there
ought to be no hesitation on that ground of sending a Scotch regiment *immediately* in place of waiting
for an English one till a more distant period.'

[74] The development of a Scottish national identity in this period has been much studied in recent
years, though the role of the military has not received the attention it deserves. See R. Mitchison, 'Patriotism and National Identity in Eighteenth-Century Scotland', in T. W. Moody (ed.), *Nationality and
the Pursuit of National Independence* (Belfast, 1978), 73–95; Leneman, 'A New Role for a Lost Cause';
T. C. Smout, 'Problems of Nationalism, Identity and Improvement in Later Eighteenth-Century
Scotland', in T. M. Devine (ed.), *Improvement and Enlightenment* (Edinburgh, 1989), 1–21; Womack,
Improvement and Romance; M. Fry, 'The Whig Interpretation of Scottish History', in I. Donnachie
and C. Whatley (eds.), *The Manufacture of Scottish History* (Edinburgh, 1992), 72–89; C. Kidd, *Subvert-
ing Scotland's Past: Scottish Whig Historians and the Creation of an Anglo-British Identity 1689–c. 1830*
(Cambridge, 1993).

[75] Perhaps the earliest unit history was *Some Account of the 26th or Cameronian Regiment* (1828).

Irish officers and had only casual connections with Ireland, besides which there were double the number of Irishmen in the army.[76] This emergence of 'national' regiments (as they were called) was not a foregone conclusion. However Scottish the Scotland-recruited regiments of the period originally were, they had to take their chance with the reductions and drafts of 1795–6; and those that survived might easily have been made into the undefinably 'British' corps, which most marching regiments became, by long years away and the failure of the territorial base to sustain the flow of men. This, for example, was the fate of the 74th and 75th, unambiguously Scottish when they were raised for service in India in 1787 but deprived of their designation as 'Highlanders' on their return because they proved unable to recruit back to strength in Scotland.[77]

The army, certainly, showed little interest in creating national regiments in the 1790s. The reorganization the Duke of York planned in 1795–6 would have broken up most of the 'young' Irish and Scottish corps, including the 79th, the Argyll Highlanders, and Gordon Highlanders.[78] In the event, those that were saved owed their survival to a number of fortuitous factors, mainly whether the Duke of York approved of the terms on which they had been raised under his predecessor, Lord Amherst, and whether they could immediately assist the army overseas. The Gordon Highlanders, originally numbered the 100th, should have been reduced but escaped, less because of Dundas's intercession than because it was part of the Corsica garrison in 1795 as a full-strength, efficient regiment.[79] Alan Cameron's 79th, on the other hand, were given the choice of being drafted or going to the West Indies.

[76] For the 1813 inspection returns see WO27/121. In the mid-Victorian army the predominantly Scottish regiments remained the 42nd, 71st, 72nd, 78th, 79th, 92nd, and 93rd. H. J. Hanham, 'Religion and Nationality in the Mid-Victorian Army', in M. R. D. Foot (ed.), *War and Society* (London, 1973), 159–81.

[77] The 75th in 1811 was a typical 'mixed regiment', 45.5 per cent Scottish, 32.1 per cent Irish, 21.8 per cent English (WO27/102, pt. 2). The 74th drew many more men from the English and Irish militias than the Scottish militia in 1811. Hope of Lufness MSS, SRO GD364/1/1214/35–6, 1229/25. For a brief history of these two regiments see Stewart, *Highlanders*, ii. 164–76. The 26th also attracted few Scottish recruits when it returned from Canada in 1800. The 90th was looked on as a 'national' regiment, but struggled unsuccessfully to maintain this character. S. H. F. Johnston, *History of the Cameronians: vol. 1, 1689–1910* (Aldershot, 1957), 193, 217, 225.

[78] Dundas to the Duke of Portland, 14 Aug. 1795, HO30/1, fos. 188–91; Portland to lord lieutenant of Ireland, 16 Aug. 1795, Kilmainham MSS, NLI MS 1003; 'Scheme of the West India service', 19 Aug. 1795, Windham MSS, BL Add. MS 37891, fos. 57–9; R. Brownrigg to the Duke of York, 24 Aug. 1795, Brownrigg MSS, WO133/1. Early in 1796 the Duke of York decided on the further reduction of all regiments numbered above the 90th. The Argylls and the Gordons were spared, becoming the 91st and the 92nd. There was no firm policy of drafting Scots into Scottish regiments (cf. Western, 'Recruitment', 50). The 79th, for example, was to be divided between the 40th, 54th, and 59th. The 109th Aberdeenshire ended up as part of the 53rd. Even the Black Watch, the most famous Highland regiment, was heavily diluted by Lowlanders and some English from the 97th, 116th, 132nd, and 133rd. Stewart, *Highlanders*, i. 415–16, mentions these four, but calls them Highland corps.

[79] Stewart, *Highlanders*, ii. 223–4; Duke of Gordon to Dundas, 6 Jan. 1796, Melville MSS, NLS MS 5, fo. 79; Dundas to Lord Huntly, 3 Dec. 1796, Gordon MSS, SRO GD44/47/15.

They went, returned as a cadre of officers and NCOs in 1797, and managed to recruit themselves back into existence with the help of their colonel's private fortune.[80] The fate of the Strathspey Highlanders (numbered 97th, 1794–5) shows how the Duke of York's thinking went above 'clan regiments' and the politics of the Dundas system. Raised by Sir James Grant, chief of the Grants, this corps was unceremoniously disbanded after serving several months as marines, too poorly officered to be worth saving. It encapsulated all the evils of recruitment for rank and private military patronage that the Duke so disliked as interfering with the claims of career officers and which was a major motive for his attack on the 'young corps' at this time.[81]

However, once the Duke had consolidated the army more to his liking, he seems to have accepted the idea of national regiments, though less evidently for the Irish than the Scots. Scottish sensitivities, anyway, were stronger, if we can believe a memorial of some fencible privates: 'As we are all Scotch men, we would wish to be distinguished as such.'[82] Perhaps York was encouraged by further evidence of Scotland's recruiting zeal in 1798–1800 when not only was a militia successfully established but the fencibles also expanded, including the addition of six new corps.[83] At this point, certainly, the army began the deliberate building of Scottish regiments. Volunteers for the line who came forward from the Scottish fencible infantry in Ireland in 1800 were allocated to the 21st (Royal North British Fusiliers), 71st, and 72nd (these three skeleton regiments recruiting in Ireland), and to the 79th and 92nd.[84] Similarly, in 1803 the Army of Reserve recruits in Scotland were so distributed as to establish second battalions of the 26th, 42nd, and 92nd. As the Duke of York slowly realized his policy of dividing every regiment between an 'active service' first battalion and a 'home' second battalion to receive and train recruits, the Scottish garrison came largely to consist of these depot battalions. They gave the Scottish regiments an uninterrupted presence in the country over much of the Napoleonic War, surely an important part of the process whereby they came to carry Scotland's national honour and martial heritage.[85] The Irish

---

[80] Duke of York to Pitt, 28 June, 3 July 1795, Chatham MSS, PRO30/8/106, fos. 54–6; Cameron to Dundas, 23 Jan. 1799, Melville MSS, SRO GD51/1/695/1; Cameron to Lord Castlereagh, 30 Jan. 1808, WO1/637/285–7. See also Maclean, *79th Highlanders*.   [81] Mackintosh, *97th Regiment*.

[82] William Anderson, etc. to Lord Huntly, 2 Apr. 1800, Gordon MSS, SRO GD44/47/16.

[83] Stewart, *Highlanders*, ii. 373 n. Stewart includes the Banffshire corps, which was partially raised in Scotland (Colonel Hay to Dundas, 24 Dec. 1798, Melville MSS, NLS MS 1048, fos. 114–5)— probably like the Tarbet and Wallace regiments, which he does not mention.

[84] Circular to general officers, 25 June 1800, NLI MS 5073; 'General return of the number of men from the Scotch fencible regiments of infantry who have volunteered', Kilmainham MSS, NLI MS 1330.

[85] e.g. in Dec. 1807 the line battalions stationed in Scotland belonged to the 1st, 26th, 42nd, 72nd, 73rd, 74th, 75th, and 91st; in Oct. 1811 to the 1st, 21st, 25th, 26th, 78th, 79th, and 91st. 'State of the Infantry', 7 Dec. 1807, WO1/636/363–5; Duke of York to Lord Liverpool, 11 Oct. 1811, WO1/407/

regiments, sent away from Ireland as soon as they were formed, were never so visible. Whatever the army did, Scots, reflecting the self-consciousness of their society,
would mostly have joined Scottish regiments. But because the army went out of its
way to encourage such feelings, this happened more emphatically and extensively
than would have been the case. Even the number of 'foreign' recruiting parties in
Scotland seems to have been kept down and militia volunteers presented with a
limited choice of regiment.[86]

The Scottish regiments were the product of Scottish national feeling: they, in
turn, became such important representations of Scotland that the development
of Scottish nationhood in the nineteenth century cannot be separated from them.
The irony is that, almost without exception, these regiments were Highland regiments by name and of fairly recent creation. Many of the new corps raised during
the Revolutionary War denoted themselves as 'Highlanders' for the purpose of
recruiting generally in Scotland; but if any one event made the Highland regiments part of conscious nation-building it was the prominence given the 42nd,
79th, and 92nd in the Egyptian campaign of 1801. Victory in Egypt caught the
public imagination as a victory against the odds, restoring the honour of British
arms over France after the defeats in Flanders in 1794 and Holland in 1799.[87] In
London the Highland Society, already anxious that Highlands emigration could
damage the country's military revival, moved immediately to recognize the services of the regiments, beginning with the issue of a special medal to the Black
Watch. When this regiment returned from Egypt to Edinburgh in 1802, it marched
through cheering crowds in an extraordinary display of public interest.[88]

693–5. Returns, such as these, indicate that in the period 1807–13, the 1st, 26th, and 91st always had
units in Scotland, the 25th, 71st, 78th, and 79th for five of the seven years, the 42nd for four, the 21st
for three, and the 92nd for two.

[86] Returns of recruiting parties at Musselburgh and Dalkeith, 18 Jan. 1808, Inverness district,
25 Aug. 1810, Aberdeen district, 2 Sept. 1810, Leven and Melville MSS, SRO GD26/9/146. Out of
68 parties, one could say eleven were 'foreign' in belonging to regiments which had not originated
in Scotland (with the exception of the 95th or Rifle Brigade, a specialist unit). Returns of volunteers
from Scottish militia regiments have not been found, but in 1811 local militia volunteers were to be
allocated to either 'Lowland' regiments (1st, 21st, 26th, 71st, 72nd, 73rd, 74th, 75th, 90th, 91st, 94th)
or 'Highland' regiments (42nd, 71st, 78th, 79th, 92nd, 93rd). WO3/585/81–5. In 1808–9, excluding
those who joined the Royal Marines, 231 volunteers from the Edinburgh militia out of 282 went into
regiments of Scottish origin or with Scottish connections (i.e. 1st, 21st, 25th, 26th, 71st, 72nd, 74th,
75th, 78th, 94th). See the regiment's description book, Buccleuch MSS, SRO GD224/440.

[87] Stewart, *Highlanders*, i. 446–90, describes operations in Egypt, in which he participated. The
British, he wrote, were 'opposed to a veteran enemy, greatly superior in numbers, elated with their
former victories, and believed unconquerable, because hitherto unconquered. In the distant region
where the contest was now carried on, no support could be expected by either of the parties, appointed
as it were, to decide the palm of prowess and military energy, while their respective countries were
anxiously looking for the result.'

[88] Ibid. 492, 497. The medal depicted the head of Abercromby. For a representation see L. L.
Gordon, *British Battles and Medals* (London, 1979), 18.

Much remains to be investigated about how nationalist perceptions were projected through Scotland's war experience. The Black Watch received another
rousing reception after Waterloo, as did the Gordon Highlanders.[89] Two Scots—
Sir Ralph Abercromby and Sir John Moore—provided models of heroic leadership for succeeding generations; for a long time they ceded a higher place only to
Wellington in the British military pantheon. Each gladly associated himself with
'Highland' bravery and endurance; on becoming a Knight of the Bath, Moore
included a Highland soldier on his coat of arms as a particular compliment to the
92nd but also divulging pride in his Scottish ancestry. Perhaps the confluence
of the war and a Scottish national identity is seen most clearly in the plans for a
national monument on Calton Hill, Edinburgh to commemorate the country's
contribution to victory. A committee was formed, in the first instance, because a
similar project was being pursued in London. The original concept went beyond
the idea of a memorial for the valorous and famous—'a Westminster Abbey of the
North'—to that of a 'hallowed place of record' of the services of all Scotsmen,
officers and other ranks, the world over; this, too, presumably explains the circular
addressed to the commanding officers of local corps soliciting copies of their
muster rolls. Subscriptions sought from every parish and from the 'colonies' gave
further force to the idea that it was to be, essentially, the nation's tribute to the
nation.[90] As an expression of Scottish nationhood at an interesting time of its
development, the national monument has been largely overlooked, probably largely
because of its incompletion. In fact, its failure was mostly political. The project
became divisive among the élite once it was appropriated by the whig-dominated
intellectual and artistic establishment of Edinburgh; a last show of unity was the
laying of the foundation stone during the royal visit in August 1822 in an impressive freemason ceremony.[91]

Looking back a decade, Henry Cockburn, himself a member of the committee
of subscribers, considered the idea of a national monument had been floated on

[89] Stewart, *Highlanders*, i. 593–4; Gardyne, *Life of a Regiment*, 392.

[90] *Prize Essays and Transactions of the Highland Society of Scotland* (14 vols., Edinburgh, 1799–1843),
v (1820), lxi; *Scots Magazine*, lxxviii (1816), 34–40; *Blackwood's Edinburgh Magazine*, iii (1818), 234–5;
Edinburgh Magazine, ii (1818), 485, iv (1819), 178, 269; printed circulars, 8 Sept. 1819, 25 Dec. 1821,
24 Jan. 1822, 11 Apr. 1823, Minto MSS, NLS MS 11747, fo. 113; Airth MSS, ibid. 10958, fos. 304–
5, 10959, fo. 128; ibid. 15973, fos. 12–13.

[91] The division became centred on the proposed design of the building, the whigs wanting a replica
of the Parthenon, their opponents a large-domed Corinthian church. Each party supported different
architects. See Minto MSS, NLS MS 11747, fos. 114–15; *Blackwood's Edinburgh Magazine*, v (1819),
377–87, 509–12, vi (1820), 76–8, 137–48, 370–5; *Edinburgh Magazine*, vi (1820), 99–105, 304–12, ix
(1821), 49–52; 'Application and Intent of the Various Styles of Architecture', *Quarterly Review*, xxvii
(1822), 308–36; Earl of Aberdeen, *An Inquiry into the Principles of Beauty in Grecian Architecture* (London, 1822); [A. Alison], 'Restoration of the Parthenon', *Edinburgh Review*, 38 (1823), 126–44; H. W.
Williams to C. R. Cockerell, 18 Mar. 1823, W. Burn to Cockerell, 18 Mar. 1823, Cockerell MSS, NLS
MS 638, fos. 36–7, 84–5.

'the prevailing effervescence of military patriotism' at the moment of victory.[92] This was a sneer which perhaps deliberately misrepresented the extent to which Scotland had become allied to the tory state; its national tradition militarized, its role within the empire based on military service. In 1830, about the time Cockburn was writing, Scotsmen remained heavily over-represented in the army, and continued so for some time after. Twelve line regiments carried Scottish titles from the Napoleonic period into the Victorian army, where just two had borne them in the eighteenth century.[93] Moreover, once the regimental depots were reinstituted in 1825, the Scottish regiments were able to maintain a physical presence in their country to give substance to the perceptions of nationhood that had developed. The prolonged post-Union concern over the dissipation and loss of the old 'military spirit' only makes more striking the strength of the martial tradition in nineteenth-century Scotland.

Until it got into the hands of the whigs, the national monument project was intended to celebrate Scotland's great mobilization in her own defence as well as her contribution and sacrifice for the larger imperial cause. It therefore evoked that version of the nation's past that many were finding increasingly attractive: the virtues of an ancient warrior society—loyalty, service, courage—the same that had united and defended Scotland for centuries, had been shown to live on in the present. Another outlet for these reflections was found at this time in proposals to erect monuments to Wallace and Bruce.[94] So, while Sir Walter Scott and others may have articulated the country's martial heritage, the events of the war gave their material particular point and substance. The war produced Scottish armies that had not been seen for a century, and armed Scotsmen, in a sense, had ended the English occupation of their country by taking over its defence themselves. Indeed, the permanence of the militia, as compared with the earlier fencibles, and the retention of the new Scottish regiments after the war signalled an important change in the balance of the Union, gradually effected but now finalized, England's dependence on Scottish arms for her own security and for defending her international position. Revival of the Scottish military tradition therefore underlay a more equal relationship because it played up Scotland's status as an ancient kingdom and the

[92] H. Cockburn, *Memorials of His Time*, ed. K. F. C. Miller (Chicago, 1974), 291.

[93] Strachan, *Wellington's Legacy*, 51. The regiments bearing Scottish names in the mid-Victorian army were: 21st (Royal North British Fusiliers), 25th (King's Own Borderers), 26th (Cameronians), 42nd (Royal Highland Regiment), 71st (Highland Light Infantry), 72nd (Duke of Albany's Own Highlanders), 78th (Highlanders), 79th (Cameron Highlanders), 90th (Perthshire Light Infantry), 91st (Argyllshire), 92nd (Highlanders), 93rd (Highlanders).

[94] The whigs, in contrast, continued to measure national achievement in terms of 'improvement', valuing their Pantheon primarily as a way of educating public taste and encouraging artistic excellence. The military context of the monument came to be all but ignored. See *Edinburgh Review*, 38 (1823), 126–44. For the Wallace and Bruce monuments see *Edinburgh Magazine*, ii (1818), 378, 580, iv (1819), 368; Airth MSS, NLS MS 10896, fos. 223–4, 230–1.

Scottish contribution to British imperial power. While the wartime contribution was never tallied precisely, and could not have been, the country's service was taken to have honoured Scotland and to have reasserted the equality of her relationship with her sister kingdom. The most arduous war Britain had ever fought did much to allay sensitivities that Scotland had entered the Union only to become England's province. As Colley has pointed out, it was these sensitivities which encouraged Scots to promote Britain's imperial identity because this reduced the English 'to a component part of a much greater whole'.[95] In the same way, war, by forcing an increasing resort to Scottish resources, emphasized Scotland's partnership in a larger British nation.

[95] Colley, *Britons*, 130.

6

Ireland's Fate

MUCH about the Anglo-Irish military relationship in the last third of the eighteenth century seems to counterpoise the increasing difficulties of the political relationship. Ireland's military expansion in this period paralleled Britain's, her military establishment and administration were progressively assimilated, and her forces freely applied to imperial purposes. From 1770 Britain kept about 15,000 troops on the Irish establishment, 4,000 of which were made available for overseas service. This army represented the kind of arrangement that the imperial government had wanted the American colonies to accept in the 1760s and it was most valuable for adding to the total forces kept up by Britain in peacetime on which any augmentation in the event of war had to be based. During 1775, for example, on the outbreak of war in America, seventeen infantry regiments in four reinforcements recruited up to strength and sailed from Ireland.[1] In 1792 under a quarter of the British army was stationed in Ireland but a third (twelve cavalry and twenty-one infantry) of the regiments. Except for five of the cavalry units, all of these regiments had left Ireland by June 1794, having doubled their strength to over 16,000 men.[2] Furthermore, such increases were based to a significant degree on Catholic recruitment. This had begun *sub rosa* during the Seven Years War but was inhibited during the American War by the crown's sensitivity on the issue of employing Catholic Irish to subdue Protestant Americans.[3] When the Revolutionary War began, Catholic recruitment became heavier than ever before and more open, partly under the influence of the Relief Act of 1793 which relaxed the prohibitions against the arming of Catholics and their appointment to military commissions.

Ireland, therefore, even Catholic Ireland, was being steadily drawn into an imperial military system in a period when the country's political subordination to Britain was increasingly resented and challenged. Catholic relief in 1778, as a

[1] Burns, 'Ireland and British Military Preparations for War in America', 42–61.

[2] Regiments stationed in Ireland and their departure can be traced in the paymaster-general's register, National Archives (Ireland), M. 464. See also 'State of the Army in Ireland', 1 Nov. 1793, HO50/453; 'Army and Militia in Ireland', 24 Mar. 1794, Chatham MSS, PRO30/8/331, fo. 211; 'Demand on England for embarkations up to December 1794', Pelham MSS, BL Add. MS 33118, fos. 253–5; return of effectives in the British army, 1 Jan. 1793–1 Jan. 1806, WO1/903/33.

[3] T. Bartlett, '"A Weapon of War Yet Untried": Irish Catholics and the Armed Forces of the Crown, 1760–1830', in T. G. Fraser and K. Jeffrey (eds.), *Men, Women and War* (Dublin, 1993), 69–71; James, *Ireland in the Empire*, 161, 168, 179–80. There was quite heavy recruitment of Irish for the East India Company from 1776. L. Cullen, 'The Irish Diaspora of the 17th and 18th Centuries', in Canny (ed.), *Europeans on the Move*, 141.

political measure initiated by the British government, was intended to recognize Catholic loyalty and consolidate the anti-American consensus of Catholic and Protestant opinion in Ireland. Instead the Protestant élite took it to show that London henceforth would deal with the Catholics as suited its interests. When in the same year the outbreak of war with France produced an armed volunteer movement for home defence independent of the lord lieutenant's authority, the Protestant leaders were able to unite Irish opinion against London, first behind demands for the removal of restrictions on Anglo-Irish trade and then in favour of a devolution of power to the Irish parliament. Once the 'constitution of 1782' had been conceded by Britain, the issues of Irish politics proved too intractable for a harmonious working relationship to develop between the British ministers and the Irish legislature. Apart from continuing British control of Ireland, Britain's primary concern was that Ireland should add to rather than absorb imperial military resources—hence the 'commercial propositions' of 1785 (unpassable in the Dublin parliament), the Catholic relief acts of 1792–3, and the Irish militia of 1793, all British-initiated. Such a policy might have been built on the sort of loyalist or anti-revolutionary consensus that emerged in Britain after 1789, had Irish opinion not also been concentrated around concern for 'independence' and 'Protestant ascendancy'. The Protestant self-interest of the Irish parliament in the end proved to be incompatible with Britain's need to avoid alienating the Catholic majority of the population in the midst of war with France, rising agrarian and sectarian disorder, and the separatist nationalism of the United Irishmen.

The great irony of these events is that when rebellion did break out in 1798 and Anglo-Irish relations came to a point of crisis Ireland's military contribution to the empire had never been so lavish and the Irish Catholic presence in the armed forces of the crown never larger. The heavy recruitment at the beginning of the war probably made the army, officers as well as rank and file, about one-third Irish. This army, we need to remember, was a *British* army in that its ethos primarily focused on the loyalty and service owed to the crown. Protestant opinion was early snubbed in the 1790s when commanding officers in Ireland were permitted to send their men to mass.[4] Sir Ralph Abercromby, who as commander-in-chief in Ireland soon ran foul of the 'Protestant interest' and resigned, was immediately appointed to another command by the Duke of York; significantly, the issue at the centre of the Abercromby affair was whether the army should be distracted from its task of defending Ireland against French attack by internal disorder caused by problems and animosities the Irish ruling class refused to address.[5] A case can be made out

---

[4] See below, 173–4.
[5] Three key letters on the Abercromby episode are Abercromby to the Duke of York, 17 Feb. 1798, Abercromby to [Dundas], 24 Mar. 1798, Alexander Hope to Dundas, 3 Apr. 1798, Melville MSS, NLI MS 54A/121, 125, 132.

that even the Irish militia set itself above Irish contentions to be subordinate to British and imperial interests. Whatever apprehensions and alarms there were, the evidence indicates that, despite its Catholic numbers, the militia remained largely impervious to seditious activity.[6] Irish militia colonels, quite unlike their British counterparts, regularly offered their regiments for service out of Ireland and accepted annual drafts of their men into the army as early as 1805, six years ahead of the British. As for the men themselves, they can be shown to have volunteered for the army in proportionately greater numbers than their English and Scottish comrades.[7]

Appearances, however, can be deceptive; the integration of Irish military forces into a British-imperial strategic system was not as complete as their service might suggest. To keep desertion rates down and generally to avoid problems with the civilian population, regular regiments with large numbers of Irish recruits were removed from Ireland as soon as possible, most never to return while the war lasted.[8] It was only after 1815 that predominantly Irish regiments, by this time thoroughly part of the professionalized army which prolonged war and global empire both required and created, were rotated through Ireland on a regular basis.[9] During the war the balance of Irish troops in some key garrisons—Gibraltar, for example—was closely watched, and their very presence caused concern in Lower Canada with its French Catholic population.[10] In Ireland itself the same careful attention was given to the stations of the militia, which was always distrusted because of the lower competence of the officers and the strong Catholic component in the ranks. The militia was mainly kept in hand by posting the county regiments to 'foreign' parts of Ireland and by having those that were predominantly Catholic overlooked by regulars or 'Protestant' units.[11] After the rebellion of 1798 a Britannicization of the permanent forces in Ireland occurred; until then the Irish militia had constituted over half of the Irish garrison; subsequently it was reduced to between a third and a half, and, when the interchange with the British militia commenced in 1811, to less than a third.[12] At the same time barrack-building was unabated, providing the infrastructure for military occupation; the 'permanent'

---

[6] Bartlett, 'Indiscipline and Disaffection', in Corish, 115–34; P. Karsten, 'Irish Soldiers in the British Army, 1792–1922: Suborned or Subordinate?', *J. of Soc. Hist.* 17 (1983–4), 41–4.

[7] I say this on comparing the number of British and Irish militia volunteers with the average strength of the British and Irish militias, 1799–1813—55,000 against 20,000. The British militia delivered 102,197 men to the army, the Irish militia 45,280.

[8] See below, 196–7. For the general policy of excluding Irish troops from Ireland see Dundas to Lord Camden, 22 Apr. 1797, HO100/69, fos. 218–19; Duke of York to the king, 22 Apr. 1797, *George III Corresp.* ii. 565; York to Dundas, 11 Nov. 1797, Melville MSS, NLS MS 6524.

[9] The 83rd, for example, was in Ireland 1830–4 and 1845–9; the 89th served there 1833–5 and 1848–54.

[10] Dundas to Lord Cornwallis, Mar. 1799, *Cornwallis Corresp.* iii. 78–9; extract of letter from Sir J. Craig to the adjutant-general, 8 June 1810, WO1/644/499–500.   [11] See below, 198–9.

[12] See below, 198.

accommodation for troops doubled between 1801 and the end of the war and was distributed across the interior as well as along the coasts.[13]

All this makes it possible to argue that Protestant rule in Ireland became in the course of the wars an armed hegemony. The Irish yeomanry, started in 1796 and over 60,000 strong during the Napoleonic War, is usually allowed to stand for the Protestant Ascendancy in arms; but the militia interchange of 1811 was such a key development in the de-Catholicization of the armed forces in Ireland, it is well to remember that it was promoted by a British government which included Perceval, Ryder, and Liverpool, all opponents of Catholic emancipation and all in key positions where the management of Irish affairs was concerned. In other words, conservative anxieties about the armed nation outlined in an earlier chapter also extended to Ireland, the difference being that there the problem came to focus not on civilian volunteers but on Catholic militiamen. Furthermore, these anxieties and the policies formulated out of them were associated with the same politicians who generally resisted the line of Pitt and Dundas that military necessity was the political argument of greatest importance and that armed mobilizations for the sake of home defence presented opportunities for reducing social tension and conflict. As with Britain, so with Ireland; in both countries we can trace the defeat of Pittite conceptions of the armed nation and in the United Kingdom from 1807 the uninterrupted dominance of ministers who were deeply concerned to find ways of controlling popular military power.

Britain's Irish policy under first North and then Pitt has been firmly placed in the context of the increasing demands of war.[14] Britain and France twice within thirty years renewed the global conflict of the Seven Years War, and the British state was inevitably attracted to Ireland as a valuable strategic resource as yet under-exploited. North's concessions to Irish Catholics and Irish trade in 1778–9 established a pattern that Pitt followed; Catholic relief offered the prospect of readier access to Ireland's considerable reserves of military manpower and freer trade between Britain and Ireland furthered the idea of one state with three kingdoms. Pitt in 1785 offered commercial advantages to Ireland in return for an Irish contribution to imperial expenses. Catholic relief in 1792–3 was agreed to in the midst of rapidly deteriorating Anglo-French relations, and the second relief act actually went through parliament with the militia legislation which gave practical effect to the right to bear arms and access to public office that the other declared. Against the strong reservations of Dublin Castle, Pitt and Dundas were determined to improve on the minor reforms of the previous year in an attempt to build

---

[13] See above, 58.
[14] Donovan, 'Roman Catholic Relief Programme', 79–102; T. Bartlett, *The Fall and Rise of the Irish Nation: The Catholic Question 1690–1830* (Savage, Md., 1992).

a permanent loyalty to Britain among the Catholic gentry and Catholic opinion generally. They would have none of the Castle's advice that the new militia should be an exclusively Protestant force, instead using the proposal as a sign of their good faith to Catholic Ireland. Protestant fears that to admit Catholics to social and political power would lead inevitably to the expropriation of Protestant property and Irish independence were incomprehensible to them, dismissed as 'obstinacy and blindness'. Britain could not feel secure in Ireland until it had won the loyalty of 'that body which comprises the effective mass of the people of Ireland': Dundas called it 'the plainest of all political truths that a country where a parliament and a free constitution is allowed to exist never can submit to the practice of three-fourths of the country being sacrificed to the whims, prejudices or opinions of the other fourth'—the alternative was to occupy Ireland with military force. In view of Protestant stubbornness, the process of Catholic integration depended on a pragmatic response to circumstances as they arose. In 1793 Pitt, faced with imminent war with France, was most concerned to draw the teeth of Catholic protest against the penal laws and the organization behind it, thus to isolate the United Irishmen whose radicalism, Irish nationalism, and revival of volunteering were directly opposed to British interests. Timely concession would make possible the same loyalist, anti-French consensus that was taking shape in Britain, a connection of 'all lovers of order and good government in a union of resisters to all the abettors of anarchy and misrule'.[15]

Pitt's government hoped to put the Catholic question aside after the 'revolution' of 1793, only too well aware that to many Irish Protestants their action looked like tame submission to the threat of organized Catholic politics. Anyway, the conduct of the war was their first priority. Ample assurance, therefore, was given that the settlement was final. When Catholic hopes revived during Lord Fitzwilliam's brief lord lieutenancy and as social disorder spread through the activities of the Defenders, United Irishmen, and Protestant vigilantes, Dublin Castle was firmly instructed to stand by the Protestants. The British ministers made no worthwhile intervention as the terrible cycle of outrage and retribution ran to the point of open rebellion. Yet we can easily exaggerate the extent to which Pitt and Dundas's Irish policy floated on circumstances. Their attitude to Ireland was always 'British', if by 'British' we mean that they maintained a profound contempt for the Irish ruling class and its 'bigotry' and equally strong convictions that the Catholic majority could be and must be converted to loyalty to Britain for the sake of national security, and indeed Britain's world position. This was ultimately the 'British' context in which

---

[15] Quotations are from Pitt to Dundas, 8 Nov. 1792, cited Bartlett, *Irish Nation*, 154; Dundas to Pitt, n.d., Chatham MSS, PRO30/8/157, fo. 230; Lord Grenville to Dundas, 24 Oct. 1791, Grenville, *Dropmore MSS* ii. 215; Dundas to Lord Westmorland, 7 Jan. 1793, cited Bartlett, 'Catholics and the Armed Forces', 73.

Pitt and Dundas viewed Ireland. No one knew better than they that they had not solved the Catholic question in 1793. Sometime in the future the Catholics would have to be conceded full political rights, but meanwhile Britain could only steer a narrow course between Catholic demands and Protestant alarm with an eye to moderating both until the time was right.[16] The breakdown of social order in the 1790s made such a policy increasingly difficult because the government was thrown into dependence on the Protestant gentry and the military force they could organize. Even so, throughout this period Pitt and Dundas continued to look for ways of promoting the idea of Catholic loyalty, not least through Catholic contribution to the war.

A list of Catholics 'of most importance' drawn up in 1806 included eight nobles and nineteen 'country gentlemen'.[17] The small numbers in themselves attest to the limited influence of the Catholic magnates in Irish society, the effect multiplied by the reverse fact of Protestant ownership of most of Ireland's land and the prominence of the large estate within the agrarian economy. This point has to be made because there is an immense difference between the Highland magnates of Scotland and the Catholic magnates of Ireland in respect of their assimilation into the British state through their patronage of British miltary recruitment. If Catholics raised troops during the Revolutionary and Napoleonic Wars, they did it inconspicuously and individually, never as a statement of Catholic loyalty to the crown. In the recruitment of 1794—probably the heaviest Ireland had ever experienced— no less than twenty-two line regiments were raised without a single Catholic patron being prominent.[18] Yet previously Catholic nobles had made some notable offers, even if these had not always been taken up. Lord Trimleston's offer in 1762 of six regiments of Irish Catholics to serve Hanover or Portugal was declined, but early in the American War Lord Kenmare successfully applied to raise 1,900 men in Kerry and Cork.[19] These instances suggest that in 1794 and afterwards the problem was not so much the limited social resources of the magnates as Catholic politics which by this time were based on a rising Catholic consciousness and were increasingly directed by more militant urban-based merchants and lawyers. Under such men Catholic opinion remained unsatisfied by the gains of 1793. While Catholics took some advantage of the opening of military commissions to them by the reforms, they objected to 'Catholic' corps as opposed to the principle of civic equality in that they required Catholics to support, indeed positively welcome, their separate treatment from Protestants. The changes of 1793 also had the effect of focusing attention on distinctions that remained. Catholics might be commissioned

[16] G. O'Brien, *Anglo-Irish Politics in the Age of Grattan and Pitt* (Dublin, 1987), 164–6.

[17] 'Notes as to Irish Catholics 1806' signed by R. M., Richmond MSS, NLI MS 60/264.

[18] D. A. Chart, 'The Irish Levies During the Great French War', *Eng. Hist. Rev.* 32 (1917), 499–503.   [19] Bartlett, *Irish Nation*, 58; Burns, 'Ireland and British Military Preparations', 48–9.

in Ireland but as soon as they were moved to Britain their possession of rank certainly became improper without being strictly illegal.[20]

Dundas, we know, had wanted to add Catholics to the military resources of the state since 1778, and at the time an Irish militia was being projected he told the Irish government very firmly that he could see 'no reason why in respect of arms [Catholics] are to be distinguished from the rest of his majesty's subjects'. His attitude is caught in a reply to Lord Fife in Scotland who had sounded the alarm on hearing the MacDonells, a Catholic clan, were raising a fencible regiment on their Glengarry lands: 'No service can at present be more acceptable than fencibles who will serve in Ireland, and [if] Glengary chuses to raise Catholicks in his corps we shall certainly not prevent him'.[21] At the insistence of Dundas and Pitt, the Irish militia of 1793 gave effect to a new principle, that of the inclusion of Catholics in the Irish home forces of the crown. But while most Irish militia regiments soon had a predominantly Catholic rank and file, the command of these soldiers remained just as decisively in Protestant hands, even down to the NCOs. One careful inquiry made between 1808 and 1811 counted thirty-six Catholic officers in eleven regiments, with none in a further thirteen, and an unknown number in the remaining fourteen.[22] The regular army had a significantly higher concentration of Catholic officers than this, since the Duke of York and successive ministers extended the practice, long applied to the army, of letting Catholic gentlemen unhindered into military office, at least in the lower ranks. George III intervened to prevent the appointment of Catholics to military commissions only when the individual was known to him.[23]

If it could be done, Pitt's government was not averse to forming Catholic regiments commanded by Catholic officers. Because Catholics in the army generally lacked seniority, it is interesting that the ministers seized an opportunity when émigré officers from the disbanded Irish regiments of the old royal army of France arrived in the country. With the idea of placing these officers in command, the Cabinet in August 1794 adopted a plan for raising an Irish Brigade from the Irish Catholic population, excluding Protestants completely; eventually six regiments, each of 600 men, were envisaged. As it happened, these were vain expectations, though the government persevered until 1797 when the establishment of the Brigade was

[20] Bartlett, 'Catholics and the Armed Forces', 76–7.
[21] Donovan, 'Roman Catholic Relief Programme', 89, 92; Bartlett, 'Catholics and the Armed Forces', 73; Lord Fife to [Dundas], 7 Oct. 1794, Melville MSS, SRO GD51/1/831; secretary's minute book noting letter to Fife, 1 Sept. 1794, Melville MSS, NLS MS 21.
[22] E. Wakefield, *An Account of Ireland, Statistical and Political* (2 vols., London, 1812), ii. 592–631.
[23] Bartlett, 'Catholics and the Armed Forces', 77; J. R. Western, 'Roman Catholics Holding Military Commissions in 1798', *Eng. Hist. Rev.* 70 (1955), 428–32. Sir Henry Sheehy Keating is said to have been the first Catholic officer promoted to general rank. In 1811 he, then a colonel, was mentioned in parliament as an officer whose religion prevented his promotion. *PD* xx. 416.

reduced to two regiments. One problem was that to satisfy Protestant prejudices the troops were to serve outside the British Isles, specifically the West Indies; another, the small amount of 'interest' and influence the colonels possessed in Ireland, not to say their lack of money; yet another, the Irish government's unhelpful attitude, once Camden replaced Fitzwilliam as lord lieutenant. Finally, as we have seen, Catholic opinion itself was never reconciled to the idea of exclusive corps, however tempting the opportunity of service under the crown. But the experiment of an Irish Brigade deserves more attention than it has received as one example of how Pitt's government was quite prepared to tread on Protestant sensitivities after 1793 in order to have improved access to Ireland's manpower reserves. Pitt and Dundas, too, doubtless would have agreed with Portland that the Brigade offered far-reaching political as well as military advantages in standing as a symbol of Britain's desire to secure Irish Catholic loyalty.[24]

Also unobserved has been the expansion of the Irish militia during the 1790s which greatly increased the number of Catholics in the ranks and thus Protestant suspicions as to its reliability. Pitt's government not only rejected Dublin's advice of a Protestant-only militia in 1793 but afterwards proceeded to double its size and allowed Catholic majorities in most of the regiments. The initial rank and file establishment was increased from 14,948 to 21,660 in 1795. A further augmentation in 1797, permitting colonels to place up to one hundred men in each company and to apply for additional companies, had raised the total establishment to 28,500 by the end of the Revolutionary War.[25] The first of these increases was effected by Fitzwilliam during his brief tenure of Dublin Castle and was part of his determination to make Ireland more secure against French attack. Before Fitzwilliam went to Ireland he and Pitt discussed the general topic of Ireland's defences, and, since the ministers had decided that the war situation required the regular force in Ireland to be reduced to the bare minimum, it can be assumed that Pitt wanted the Irish militia to be strengthened.

But this has a political context as well. On the same occasion the formation of a yeomanry was certainly discussed and Fitzwilliam must have been told of the plan for an Irish Brigade at this or some other time. The whole cast of the discussion,

---

[24] Pitt to the king, 4 Aug. 1794, *George III Corresp.* ii. 229; Duke of Portland to the colonels of the late regiments of the Irish Brigade, 29 Sept. 1794, WO1/766/245–9; Dundas to Portland, 13 Feb. 1795, HO30/1, fos. 200–6; Portland to [Dundas], 17 Jan. 1796, WO1/768/73–6; Portland to Lord Camden, 10 Apr. 1797, Kilmainham MSS, NLI MS 1004. Fitzwilliam wrote on 15 Jan. 1795: 'I feel much inclined to give the Irish Brigade a fair chance in the outset, and to make the experiment of the loyalty and zeal of the Catholicks, and therefore, within the scope of the catholick religion, not to give them any competitors, or in any way to impede their success', HO30/1, fo. 209. Eventually, after service in the West Indies, the Brigade was reduced in 1797. Duke of York to Dundas, 11 Nov. 1797, Melville MSS, NLS MS 6524.

[25] McAnally, *Irish Militia*, 322, for 1793 and 1795 establishments; return of militia, 1 Nov. 1801, Hope of Lufness MSS, SRO GD364/1/1128/4 for 1801 establishment.

moreover, was the idea that if Ireland provided more for its own defence and indeed contributed more to Britain's war effort in general, a favourable setting for Irish reform might be created. This, it should be remembered, came after other conferences in which Pitt seems to have reiterated his pragmatic approach to the Catholic question, that circumstances would determine whether and what action should be taken.[26] There can be little doubt that Fitzwilliam departed for Ireland convinced that the government wanted him to promote Catholic service through the militia, the yeomanry, and the Irish Brigade, that he and they were agreed that the war was the paramount concern, and that Catholic emancipation was to be decided on the exigencies of the case. He was right on the first two counts but failed to understand that Pitt regarded the 1793 settlement as satisfactory in the meantime and that, while the encouragement of Catholic service lay within its terms, to go further would destabilize Ireland and convert the country into the strategic liability Britain was anxious to avoid.

Pitt's caution about further antagonism of Protestant feeling appears contradictory to the second large expansion of the militia which began early in 1797.[27] By then the amount of social violence—though its causes embraced much more than religious enmities—was poisoning Catholic–Protestant relations. There was also accumulating evidence that militiamen in various garrisons had been suborned by the two main subversive groups, the Defenders and the United Irishmen. In this situation it was doubtful what could be expected of the militia in a crisis.[28] But the appearance of a French fleet in Bantry Bay in December 1796 exposing the weakness of Ireland's defences disposed both London and Dublin to find reinforcements where they could. The increase of the militia belonged to a number of measures taken in 1797 to strengthen Ireland against French attack which culminated in the appointment of the best British general of the day, Sir Ralph Abercromby, as commander-in-chief. Under the twin threat of invasion and rebellion,

---

[26] 'Memorandum of conversation with Lord Fitzwilliam, Sir J. Parnell, Mr Grattan, Sir W. and G. Ponsonby', 27 Nov. 1794, Chatham MSS, PRO30/8/331, fos. 289–90. This meeting has not been noticed in J. Ehrman, *The Younger Pitt: The Reluctant Transition* (London, 1983), 422–7; E. A. Smith, *Whig Principles and Party Politics: Earl Fitzwilliam and the Whig Party, 1748–1833* (Manchester, 1975), 184–6; R. B. McDowell, 'The Fitzwilliam Episode', *Irish Hist. Studies*, 15 (1966), 115–30. The decision to increase the militia was announced to the Irish parliament on 9 Feb. 1795, so early in the session that McAnally speculates that it may have been made 'before Fitzwilliam came upon the scene at all', McAnally, *Irish Militia*, 71–2. Trade concessions in return for Ireland's war contribution were further discussed by Fitzwilliam in a letter of 31 Jan. 1795, HO30/1, fos. 211–15.

[27] From 1 Feb. 1797 to 1 Feb. 1798 the number of effective rank and file in the Irish militia increased by a quarter (from 18,219 to 22,917 men). McAnally, *Irish Militia*, 106. The augmentation order, authorizing an increase of company strength from 70 to 100 men, was dated 15 Feb. 1797 and was made on the lord lieutenant's initiative. See 'Extracts from General Orders respecting the augmentation of the Militia', Morrison MSS, NLI MS 5006/6; Lord Camden to Pitt, 10 Feb. 1797, Chatham MSS, PRO30/8/326, fos. 144–50.   [28] Bartlett, 'Indiscipline and Disaffection', 122–9.

Pitt's Irish policy degenerated into military preparation and support for the counter-insurgency operations judged necessary by the men on the spot.

Pitt's interest in forming an Irish yeomanry as a force which would pay political as well as military dividends was undone by the same crisis. When he discussed the idea with Fitzwilliam in November 1794, his intention surely was to extend Catholic–Protestant co-operation in home defence, much as Fitzwilliam said when he discussed the proposal from Dublin a few weeks later.[29] Ideally, volunteer corps organized under the crown and cutting across sectarian lines would have been equally hostile to Orange, Defender, and United Irish disorder, and would have embodied the pro-British loyalism, the party of order and national defence led by a united élite, that the British government saw as the best guarantee of its authority in Ireland. Events, however, kept overtaking these aspirations. The importance Fitzwilliam placed on Catholic participation in the yeomanry associated the idea with his doomed Catholic policy; and Fitzwilliam's successor, Lord Camden, had no wish to anger Catholic feeling further by foisting a Protestant force on the Catholic population. Also there was always concern in Dublin Castle that the arming of civilians might produce an independent military force as had happened with the volunteers during the American War. When in 1796 a yeomanry did come to be established, it was a capitulation to sheer necessity. As the possibility of French invasion loomed, the army found itself pinned in the north by the breakdown of order over large areas and signs of imminent insurrection. With no more than 32,000 troops in the whole of Ireland, additional force was desperately needed if any realistic concentration against an invader was going to be achieved. Thus to find the immediate origins of the yeomanry we have to look no further than a paper drawn up in August by Camden's commander-in-chief. This began by reflecting on the 'late success of the French in Italy and on the Rhine' and concluded with an appeal for 'many thousands of well affected persons, who properly armed and under regulation . . . would enable Government to liberate the greater part of the troops', none but 'baggage guards' being left behind if invasion occurred.[30]

---

[29] See n. 26. For Fitzwilliam's proposal of a yeomanry, see Smith, *Fitzwilliam*, 195; Fitzwilliam to Portland, 15, 29 Jan. 1795, Fitzwilliam MSS, Sheffield Central Library, F5/14–16, 30–2.

[30] [General Cunninghame], 'Thoughts on the Defence of Ireland', 10 Aug. 1796, SPOI CSO OP23/9. Cunninghame's authorship of this report is established by Cunninghame to W. Elliot, 16 Aug. 1796, HO100/62, fos. 170–82, cited in Ferguson, 'Army in Ireland', 150. Camden asked for the army to be 'drawn together' on 28 August, ibid. 157. A 'Yeomanry Plan' dated 22 Sept. 1796 is found in HO100/61, fos. 112–15. For accounts of the formation of the yeomanry, which lay too little importance on the army's situation, see R. G. Morton, 'The Rise of the Yeomanry', *Irish Sword*, 8 (1967), 58–64; McDowell, *Ireland*, 557–9; H. Senior, *Orangeism in Ireland and Britain, 1795–1836* (London, 1966), 41–7, 53–60; A. Blackstock, 'The Social and Political Implications of the Raising of the Yeomanry in Ulster, 1796–8', in D. Dickson, D. Keogh, and K. Whelan (eds.), *The United Irishmen: Republicanism, Radicalism and Rebellion* (Dublin, 1993), 234–7. For the number of troops in Ireland in July 1796 see Ferguson, 'Army in Ireland', 149.

Even at this stage the Irish government was still under pressure to wear a 'British' face because when the formation of a yeomanry was announced in the Irish parliament Catholics were invited to enrol.[31] However, as is well known, the Irish yeomanry raised in 1796–7 was and continued to be predominantly Protestant. Some corps were vehemently Orangeist in their attitude, and indeed sometimes originated out of local armed associations formed to repel or revenge the attacks of Defenders; but many more simply reflected the insecurity of a minority as social conflict became increasingly violent. Apprehensions about arming Catholics existed deep in the Protestant Irish psyche, particularly in remembrance of the massacres of 1641.[32] The cavalry, drawn mainly from the substantial tenantry, was probably less affected than the infantry; officers, in recruiting from the lower orders, could be expected to make a careful selection of men, but it was also not unknown for the rank and file to insist on the exclusion of Catholics. As the infantry increased, therefore, the Protestant attitudes of the force may have become more pronounced. At first, the yeomanry were about one-half cavalry, one-half infantry. After the 1798 rebellion the government wanted stronger local garrisons, and infantry numbers expanded rapidly to reach seven-eighths of the total during the Napoleonic War.[33] Nevertheless, we can draw too close an association between the yeomanry and an aggressive Orangeism. As with the volunteers in Britain, the dominant feature of the corps was their localism. The small single company corps, reluctant to serve outside its own area, was especially prevalent in Ireland; as late as 1809 there were just thirty-two corps with a strength of three hundred men or more out of perhaps eight hundred.[34] It follows that the yeomanry must have mirrored the complexity of Irish society itself, where levels of politicization and social conflict varied enormously and where local rulers approached the problem of order in a range of ways, often including an unwillingness to act at all.

Unlike the Catholic militia, the readiness of the yeomanry to support British authority in Ireland was never in question. The alternative of a local militia to volunteers was never contemplated in Ireland because any force raised on the principle of compulsory service was exposed to disaffected or potentially disloyal elements in society.[35] Yet the Irish yeomanry must count as one instance where the British

[31] Pelham's speech, 14 Oct. 1796, *Faulkner's Dublin Journal*, 15 Oct. 1796.
[32] Senior, *Orangeism*, 58–60, 182–8; Bartlett, *Irish Nation*, 220–3.
[33] 'Yeomanry force—number and duties', 31 Oct. 1801, Colchester MSS, PRO30/9/124, fo. 227. The effective strength of the cavalry and infantry, 1803–7, is given in a parliamentary return, *CJ* lxiii. 618.
[34] Sir A. Wellesley to Duke of Richmond, 16 Mar. 1809, Richmond MSS, NLI MS 58/69. At the close of the Revolutionary War there were about 450 corps and an establishment of 45,000 men. By 1804 there were 800–900 corps and an establishment of 80,000. Memorandum by Sir E. Littlehales, 1 June 1804, Hardwicke MSS, BL Add. MS 45037, fos. 113–19.
[35] Lord Castlereagh to Sir A. Wellesley, 28 Dec. 1807, WO1/612/305–22.

state failed in its long-established practice of using military service to diminish Celtic particularisms. When a national constabulary was established in Ireland in 1822, partly as an alternative to the yeomanry, it was pointedly recruited from Catholics as well as Protestants.[36] Ten years earlier, Sir John Hope, arriving to take command in Ireland, had interested Peel in his proposal to disband the yeomanry and remove an impediment to Catholic service, 'one great means of introducing order among the people of this country'.[37] Hope was right in understanding the yeomanry as the Protestant Ascendancy in arms; no other perception was possible to Catholics, just as many Protestants were made nervous by the number of Catholics in the militia. On the other hand, his soldier's confidence that military service could smother sectarian conflict was entirely misplaced. The British and Irish governments made some attempt to engineer this result for the sake of the larger interests of the state, but the divisions in Irish society had become too deep for any civilian-based force to bridge. In the perspective of the war, the yeomanry was effective; in the perspective of Irish history, it added to Ireland's travails as perhaps the first of the Protestant paramilitaries.

The yeomanry became firmly identified with the Protestant Ascendancy in the aftermath of the 1798 rebellion, they taking a leading part in the 'terror' that forced the countryside into submission. Its importance was emphasized all the more by the militia's poor showing on practically the only occasion it went into action against French troops. The 'Castlebar races', General Humbert's rout of Hutchinson's force in September 1798, upheld all the prejudices entertained against the Irish militia—that it was ill-disciplined, unreliable, and of little use in Ireland. There was such serious talk of disbanding the militia or sending regiments away from Ireland that the fact neither happened becomes significant. Thomas Bartlett could be said to take an 'Irish' view of the yeomanry and militia in the post-rebellion period when he states that the former became the main auxiliary force and the latter was relegated to supplying recruits for the army.[38] In a 'British' perspective the Irish militia as a trained and permanent territorial force continued to make an important contribution to the defence of the British Isles and to the military resources of the empire. Furthermore, to Pitt and other supporters of Catholic emancipation, the militia demonstrated Catholic service and loyalty, particularly, be it noted, if it stayed in Ireland. The point will be explained later at greater length, but this was essentially why Pitt and Dundas kept the Irish militia in Ireland for the rest of the Revolutionary War though fourteen regiments in the first six months of 1799 offered to serve abroad and legislation was passed to

[36] G. Broeker, *Rural Disorder and Police Reform in Ireland 1812–36* (London, 1970), 156–7.
[37] Hope to Alexander Hope, 17 Oct. 1812, Hope of Lufness MSS, SRO GD364/1/1222/10; S. H. Palmer, *Police and Protest in England and Ireland 1780–1850* (Cambridge, 1988), 196.
[38] Bartlett, 'Catholics and the Armed Forces', 76.

permit it.[39] Neither was the militia whittled down after 1798 as part of a policy to Protestantize the Irish garrison. On the contrary, it gave over 8,000 men to the army in 1800 and still reached the maximum of its strength during the entire war—over 25,000 effectives—in 1801. While it is true that this increase of the Irish militia was intended to gratify the colonels at a time when the delicate matter of the Union was being negotiated, it also shows the continued resistance of Pitt's government to the Protestant Ascendancy by keeping up Catholic military participation in Ireland.[40]

Pitt again showed his colours on the issue in 1804 when his party opposed an increase that accompanied a proposal to interchange the British and Irish militias. Interestingly, once in office he promoted an augmentation, but then this was to prepare the way for a further draft of militiamen into the army.[41] In Pitt's scheme of things the Irish militia existed for larger purposes than the perpetuation of Protestant rule in Ireland. However, it was Lord Grenville who was the chief keeper of the Pittite policy of concession and integration after 1801. In 1791, recently minister for Ireland, he had extolled 'the benefit of attaching to English government that body which composes the effective mass of the people of Ireland', and when prime minister in 1806–7 he returned to the promotion of Catholic military service as politically the safest way of advancing the principle of civil equality. He proposed to appeal to the Catholic gentry to help recruit the second battalions of established Irish regiments (the 83rd, 87th Prince of Wales, 88th Connaught Rangers, and 89th were mentioned) and to appoint Catholics to the field commissions as a further gesture of confidence in Catholic loyalty. To enable such corps to serve in Britain, he needed to do no more than extend the military provisions of the 1793 act; but in order to head off a developing Catholic agitation he was persuaded to try for the larger concession—the opening of positions on the staff to Catholics—that provoked the king and brought down his administration.[42]

The connection, therefore, between relief and recruitment remained the same from 1793. The military aspects of the penal laws were, in fact, a small sum of Catholic grievance; yet they became the main focus of emancipationist effort, at least from the British side. Pitt, Dundas, and Grenville, facing unprecedented

[39] See below, 200; McAnally, *Irish Militia*, 145–8; correspondence relating to the offers of fencible and Irish militia corps to extend their services, WO1/778.

[40] The rank and file strength of the Irish militia was 22,356 men in Feb. 1799, 14,970 in Feb. 1800, and 25,451 in Sept. 1801. Figures from McAnally, *Irish Militia*, 151; monthly return of militia, 1 Sept. 1801, Hope of Lufness MSS, SRO GD364/1/1128/3.

[41] McAnally, *Irish Militia*, 183–6, 192–4. For the militia debates of Mar.–Apr. 1804 see *PD* i. 1072–98, ii. 40–90, 131–40. Lord Hardwicke accused Pitt of 'inconsistency' in opposing interchange. Hardwicke to C. Yorke, 28 Apr. 1804, Hardwicke MSS, BL Add. MS 35705, fos. 288–93.

[42] Grenville, *Dropmore MSS* viii. 253, 270, 328–9, 486–8, 491–4, ix. 4–6, 7, 12–13, 21, 31–2, 107–10; P. Jupp, *Lord Grenville* (Oxford, 1985), 399–410.

manpower demands by the army, displayed a consistent interest in the Catholic population as a source of recruits; and they had a rather naïve faith that raising the men would be facilitated by the good offices of the Catholic gentry. However, military necessity provided the occasion rather than the motivation of their Irish policy. Their abiding concern was to convert an aggrieved élite into a loyal service class in order to remove a dangerous particularism within the state. The French wars presented opportunities in this direction that did not normally exist in peacetime: the service requirements of the state increased manifold and there could be no better proof of Catholic loyalty than their co-operation in the military effort of the empire. Catholic service and patriotism were seen as saps that could be pushed forward inexorably to undermine Protestant defence of the penal laws. Lord North once spoke of using military careers and patronage to 'attach the *noblesse*'.[43] So, in successive wars, beginning with the Seven Years War, had the Highland chiefs been largely assimilated. In 1793 the attempt began to absorb the Catholic gentry of Ireland into the same process, possibly encouraged by the fact that the fall of the French monarchy had finally closed an alternative avenue of service. As Lord Grenville defended himself to the king in 1807: 'no measure should more effectually promote the general interests of the empire than one which will accustom the gentry of Ireland to look for their promotion and advancement in life to your Majesty's service, and which by mixing them in habits of intercourse with the great body of your Majesty's officers, will gradually infuse into their minds the same spirit and principles by which that body is animated.'[44]

The fall of Grenville's administration and its replacement by Portland's restored to power men who were warier than Pitt of where the armed nation might lead and who definitely preferred to trust the loyalty of Irish Protestants to the loyalty of Irish Catholics. Many were former ministers of Addington's government, including Hawkesbury, Westmorland, Portland, Eldon, and Castlereagh, so that we might say they shared an Addingtonian response to social order based on the Protestant state and the securities any society needed against the armed force it created to defend itself. This previous administration, we need to remind ourselves, was not only resolutely opposed to Catholic emancipation but also sought to substitute volunteers with militia as the more reliable species of armed force. Holding these views, the Addingtonians were the last to be kindly disposed towards the Irish militia. To them armed Catholics in Ireland were a case of the cure being worse than the original complaint, and they quickly seized on Cornwallis's suggestion of a militia interchange as the most effective solution. The long debate over interchange is covered in the next chapter; but Lord Hardwicke as Addington's lord

---

[43] Donovan, 'Roman Catholic Relief Programme', 91.

[44] Grenville, *Dropmore MSS* ix. 108. About 525 commissions were filled by Irish Catholics in the armies of France, Spain, and Austria in the 18th cent. Cullen, 'Irish Diaspora', 135.

lieutenant pressed for it very earnestly and it almost certainly would have been implemented by the Cabinet had the war situation permitted. As it was, the Irish militia, when revived by Addington's government in 1803, was confined to the 'small' establishment of 1795 and as late as 1806 was still only 18,000 strong.[45] Lord Hawkesbury, and in Dublin the Duke of Richmond and Sir Arthur Wellesley, all good anti-emancipationists, took up the issue of interchange again in 1807. When it was finally enacted in 1811, Richmond was still lord lieutenant, Hawkesbury (now Lord Liverpool) was war minister, and the fervent 'Protestant', Spencer Perceval, was prime minister.

An Addingtonian, anti-emancipationist dislike of the Irish militia translated into an equally strong affirmation of the Irish yeomanry as indispensable for the defence of the Protestant Ascendancy and British sovereignty over Ireland. In contrast to the fate of the British volunteers at the conclusion of the Revolutionary War, the Irish corps were largely kept up, making clear their importance as a 'law and order' force. When war resumed, moreover, while Addington's government restored only a 'small' Irish militia, it presided over an expansion of the yeomanry force from 45,000 men in 450 corps to 80,000 men found in over 800 corps by 1804. Hardwicke wanted to exceed even these numbers; Castlereagh believed a yeomanry of 100,000 was needed, and in 1804 thought was being given to a possible establishment of 12,000 cavalry and 80,000 infantry in as many as 1,165 corps.[46] In Britain after the threat of invasion receded the volunteers and local militia were maintained on declining establishments, but in Ireland as late as 1811 the yeomanry establishment stood at 86,725 all ranks.[47] It needs to be appreciated that in terms of a Protestant population under a million such figures must have represented close to the maximum possible, a mobilization of at least one in three serviceable males. In Ulster it seemed that 'almost every Protestant' was a yeoman.[48]

---

[45] The 1795 establishment set company strength at 70 rank and file. The augmentation to 100 rank and file per company, ordered by Pitt's government in 1805, began to take effect from the beginning of 1806. For figures see militia returns, 1 Sept. 1805, SPOI CSO OP198/12 (18,104 effectives); 1 Jan. 1806–1 Mar. 1807, Dropmore MSS, BL Add. MS 59290 (18,750 to 22,730 men).

[46] 'Continuation of the private memorandum of certain military arrangements, etc., prepared by Sir Edward Littlehales', 1 June 1804, Hardwicke MSS, BL Add. MS 45037, fos. 113–19; Castlereagh to W. Wickham, 9 Aug. 1803, Wickham MSS, Hampshire RO, 38M49/1/6/33; 'Abstract of effective strength of the yeomanry, 24 Mar. 1803, SPOI CSO OP412/9; 'Number on estimates from December 1803 to December 1804', ibid. 174/19. A parliamentary return of volunteers 1803–8 showed 36,790 in all ranks in March 1803 and 76,574 in June 1804. See *CJ* lxiii. 619. The case for a 'small' militia and 'large' yeomanry is put in Wickham to Castlereagh, 14 Aug. 1803, Wickham MSS, Hampshire RO, 38M49/1/7/17.

[47] 'State of supplementary [yeomanry] establishment, April 1811', SPOI CSO OP342/11. The 'total regular establishment' on 23 May 1811 is pencilled on the back of this document.

[48] Wakefield, *Account of Ireland*, ii. 826. Wickham, when chief secretary, believed the 'loyal inhabitants' could not mobilize a yeomanry of more than 80,000–90,000. Wickham to Castlereagh, 14 Aug. 1803,

Yeomanry and militia, therefore, provide an Irish variation of the opposition between an Addingtonian and a Pittite conception of the armed nation in which the Addingtonians with their emphasis on the political dangers inherent in militarization eventually prevailed. It is wrong, though, to see the yeomanry as a counterweight to and eventually largely a replacement for the militia in Ireland.[49] Rather the militia was conceived and operated as a substitute for regular forces, thus permanently in service anywhere in the country, properly trained, and under military authority. When the Irish militia began to be sent to England, they were replaced by larger numbers of British militia who proceeded to relieve regulars in garrison, making the point of the militia's strategic value over and above the yeomanry's. In an Addingtonian view, interchange, not a yeomanry, solved the problem of the Irish militia because it strengthened the British (and 'Protestant') component of the permanent force in Ireland at the expense of the Irish (and 'Catholic').

At the time the yeomanry was easily understood as existing mainly outside the broader strategic concerns of the war; first, because it was concentrated in Ulster and weakest towards the south and west, the areas most exposed to invasion; secondly, because it was never successfully brigaded and continued to be based on literally hundreds of company-strength local corps fit only for subordinate military tasks.[50] The term 'yeomanry' was adopted in emulation of the English yeomanry set up to police the localities in 1794, and also in preference to 'volunteers' which in the Irish context referred to the volunteer movement of the American War. At the height of the invasion crisis in 1804 the army told the Irish yeomanry that their 'primary and most important object' was to protect property and maintain order in their areas, if necessary acting with neighbouring corps 'for mutual security, and for putting down any considerable rising of the disaffected'. Outside times of threatened invasion, the Irish government preferred to use the yeomanry as sparingly as possible.[51] Though Dublin Castle from the outset exercised control by

Wickham MSS, Hampshire RO, 38M49/1/7/17. In 1834 the first reliable 'religious census' showed that Catholics made up 80.9 per cent of the population. S. Connolly, *Religion and Society in Nineteenth-Century Ireland* (Dundalk, 1985), 3.

[49] Bartlett, Indiscipline and Disaffection', 130–1.

[50] For Ulster's dominance of the yeomanry see above, 56. The attempt to brigade the yeomanry had failed by 1805. Wellesley had them formed into battalions for training in 1808 and tried to make this a permanent organization, though without destroying the independence of the contributing units. Memorandum for Sir E. Littlehales, 23 June 1808, SPOI CSO OP290/6/38.

[51] Circular letter to the commanding officers of yeomanry corps from the adjutant-general, Oct. 1804, ibid. 232/2. In this document, the third and fourth services required of the yeomanry were to provide 'such military duties as they can afford, in aid of, or to replace the Stationary Force' and to join 'the Army acting in the field when it is judged necessary for the general security of Ireland'. For Dublin Castle's reservations about the yeomanry see W. W. Pole to Lord Harrington, 21 Oct., 4 Nov. 1811, SPOI CSO VIIIA/1/13.

appointing the officers and providing pay and clothing and also by keeping the units under the eye of the army and its own officials, the yeomanry corps were basically locally ordered responses to a general escalation of social tension and violence.[52] If the yeomanry had not been established in 1796, post-rebellion Ireland would have seen the proliferation of some similar form of local self-defence organized by property-owners and Protestants. The very scale of the mobilization within these groups indicated the yeomanry's localness, the fact that it represented a militarization from below rather than from above. All the more reason, then, for seeing the yeomanry and militia as holding little relevance for each other. The militia was indispensable to the actual conduct of the war and did not outlast the war. The yeomanry, reinforcing local order, was seen as indispensable to the authority of government in Ireland and continued at significant strength into the 1820s.

'Though it is very desirable to have Protestant yeomanry', Hardwicke told his chief secretary, 'yet the less that is said about it the better.' Shortly afterwards Emmet's rebellion produced a backlash of Protestant loyalism in which Catholics were excluded from yeomanry corps and Catholic notables prevented from raising new units. Catholic corps, said the chief secretary, 'would not be *cried* but *roared* out against throughout all Ireland'.[53] Explicitly Protestant in membership and attitude, the yeomanry 'came to epitomize the spirit of the Protestant nation'. The Dublin yeomanry who rushed to their posts to defeat Emmet's rising were the same who the next year paraded of their own volition on William of Orange's birthday, setting up a long-lived Protestant ritual in opposition to the government's attempts to install non-sectarian, broadly approved public observances.[54] Such a response can be made to stand for what happened to the yeomanry's perception of themselves all over Ireland. The conviction quickly took root that Emmet's rising was another 'papist' rebellion, further proof, if proof

---

[52] Brigade majors, responsible to the chief secretary through a yeomanry office in Dublin, were appointed to each county; but the supervision of training and discipline by civil officers was given up for the Napoleonic War when inspectors, holding colonel's rank, and brigadiers-general were placed in the military districts. The relegation of the brigade majors to purely administrative tasks indicates that the army was not satisfied that the yeomanry had been sufficiently 'decivilianized'. The administration of the yeomanry is described in the adjutant-general's circular to COs, Oct. 1804, SPOI CSO OP232/2 and Lord Hardwicke to Lord Hawkesbury, 29 Oct. 1805, ibid. VIIIA/1/13. For the army's interest in greater control see 'General remarks on the yeomanry lately inspected by Lieutenant-General Floyd', 8 Sept. 1801, Colchester MSS, PRO30/9/172, fos. 65–7; Brownrigg to the Duke of York, 21 Aug. 1802, Brownrigg MSS, WO133/2; Col. Beckwith to Lord Cathcart, 25 Oct. 1803, Beckwith MSS, NLI MS 14303.

[53] Wickham to Castlereagh, 14 Aug. 1803, Wickham MSS, Hampshire RO, 38M49/1/7/17.

[54] Hardwicke to Wickham, 12 Nov. 1802, ibid. 5/10/90; Bartlett, *Irish Nation*, 276; Sir E. Littlehales to Lord Hardwicke, 1 and 2 Nov. 1804, Hardwicke MSS, BL Add. MS 35721, fos. 127–30; J. R. Hill, 'National Festivals, the State and "Protestant Ascendancy" in Ireland, 1790–1829', *Irish Hist. Studies*, 24 (1984–5), 30–51.

were needed after 1798, of the disloyalty and treacherous intentions that characterized the Catholic population. Against malice on this scale, the only sure defence available to outnumbered Protestants, whether in Dublin or elsewhere, was to have as many arms as possible in their own hands. The yeomanry was so total a mobilization of Protestant manpower in locality after locality that it was a supremely important expression of Protestant strength and solidarity. It is difficult to think of an institution that better manifested Protestant community or nationalism. While the Dublin corporation became the leading voice of the Protestant Ascendancy, the yeomanry corps were the Ascendancy's physical embodiment and its security, the main means by which confidence in the future of the Protestant state in Ireland could be preserved amidst local weakness and vulnerability. The ultimate test the yeomen imagined for themselves was a massive Catholic rising, very possibly linked to a French invasion and as horrifying as the massacres of 1641. Continued disorder in the 1800s and for another two decades did nothing to relax these fears or dispel the notion that Protestant Ireland might be saved only by its armed vigilance.

Like the earlier volunteers of the American War, then, the yeomanry exemplified and helped to intensify Protestant consciousness in Ireland, though after 1801 Irish Protestantism rapidly eschewed the idea of an independent Ireland. The question arises whether widespread military participation had a similar effect in promoting Catholic nationalism or indeed the sort of broader national identity found in Scotland. During the Napoleonic War the Catholic leadership increasingly drew attention to the Catholic military contribution and they also pressed issues of Catholic treatment in the army and militia. On the other hand, the rank and file soldiery may easily be portrayed as remote from Catholic politics and even indifferent to church religion, mainly finding in the regiments an alternative community which offered protection and security they could find nowhere else. An Irish military tradition in the eighteenth century was associated with the 'wild geese', those Catholic gentry who took commissions on the Continent, especially in the royal army of France. But this form of service came to an abrupt end with the revolution, with the result that all Irish military achievement now came to be expressed through the British army. Unlike Scotland, Ireland lacked a proud military history as a nation holding off conquest and finding unity against the English invader. The Irish identity that was developed in the eighteenth century rather related to the oppressions and humiliations of British rule; therefore contemporary and political rather than nostalgic, mythical, and historical.[55] Yet perhaps the huge recruitment of Irishmen in the revolutionary-Napoleonic period did

---

[55] M. Elliott, 'Ireland', in O. Dann and J. R. Dinwiddy (eds.), *Nationalism in the Age of the French Revolution* (London, 1988), 73–4.

have an effect. After all, a number of recognized Irish regiments bearing proud reputations emerged out of the war and never before, whether in Ireland or away from Ireland, had contingents of Irishmen been brought into such frequent and close proximity with contingents of Scotsmen and Englishmen. In the army, in contrast to parliament, the monarchy, and the Church, the Union as the union of three constituent kingdoms was most evident; the wreath of shamrock, thistle, and rose on every regimental colour, as indeed the Union flag itself, exactly and fittingly symbolized the soldiery who marched under them.

There is a view of Irish society before the nineteenth century which emphasizes local and regional affinities ahead of, and sometimes in lieu of, any larger identities. Ireland, beginning as a congeries of tribal authorities, never acquired a sense of its unity before the English arrived in force to exploit its divisions. The regional complexion of some Irish regiments when first raised can be noted in this context. Of the four most famous regiments dating from 1793, the 83rd was linked to the Dublin area (eventually becoming the County of Dublin regiment), while the 87th and 88th looked to the west of Ireland and the 89th to the south. The 88th took the name of Connaught Rangers from its establishment, and it was said that all but two of its officers were from Galway and relatives and clients of the Earl of Clanricarde. It is also interesting that the 18th (Royal Irish) and the 27th (Inniskillings), whose origins went back to the Williamite wars, were able to maintain their strong associations with Ulster by the government assigning them the Ulster recruits for the Army of Reserve and Additional Force.[56]

The Irish militia regiments with their strong county associations particularly convey the depth of regionalism in Ireland which often made fellow countrymen into strangers or foreigners. Many affrays between regiments, passed off as Catholic–Protestant incidents or as soldiers' brawls developing out of the bonds of comradeship, must also have included the antipathies induced when groups of men from different parts of Ireland came together.[57] But the same hostility was even more evident in the way militiamen permanently stationed far away from their native places preyed on the civilian population. Edward Wakefield observed the treatment meted out to the people of Co. Wicklow when one of the Mayo regiments marched from Arklow; peasant families drove their cattle into the mountains and woods and hid

[56] G. B. Laurie, *History of the Royal Irish Rifles* (London, 1914), 9; H. F. N. Jourdain and E. Fraser, *The Connaught Rangers* (3 vols., London, 1924–8), i. 1–2. The regional affiliations of these regiments also seem to appear in 'Return of parties destined to receive the Royal Army of Reserve in Ireland', 4 Aug. 1803, Kilmainham MSS, NLI MS 1331; return of Additional Force men, 3 Jan. 1806, Chatham MSS, PRO30/8/240, fos. 119–20. The inspection returns for 1813 (WO27/122) show that 83 per cent of the privates of 87th/1 were Irish, 86 per cent of 88th/2, and 73 per cent of the 89th.

[57] Though the worst incident occurred at Tullamore in 1806 when men of the Sligo militia took the lead in attacking men of the King's German Legion. See D. S. Gray, '"A Gross Violation of the Publick Peace": The Tullamore Incident 1806', *Irish Sword*, 12 (1976), 298–301.

their horses and carts in an attempt to save their property from being taken or to avoid the payments extorted from them as the price of being left alone:

These militia regiments are accompanied with such an extraordinary weight of luggage, that it cannot be removed in the number of cars allowed them, without overloading them in this unfeeling manner; and besides, the women and children, for whose use there ought to be separate cars, are placed upon them as close as they can sit; the soldier *proging* on the horse with the point of the bayonet, while the wretched owner is sweltering in his trusty, at such a distance as to keep the animal in sight, but sufficiently near to hear the curses of those who are abusing and destroying his property.

Conversely, when militiamen were among their own people they could show signs of supporting them against the magistrates and the soldiers of other corps. A mistake was made when the Co. Limerick regiment was posted to the disturbed districts of Westmeath in 1813 because it turned out that most of the men came from 'that part of the County of Longford which borders upon Westmeath'; some detachments were as 'near as four miles from the places where they were princip- ally raised'. The army first removed the regiment to the large garrison town of Athlone and then, on 'a familiar intercourse with many of the ill-disposed part of the townspeople' becoming 'observable', it was marched out of the area altogether. This course of action was close to the advice offered by one general that 'Catholic' regiments should always be placed in Protestant districts and vice versa.[58]

Granted that at the time the Irish militia was constantly written off as pre- dominantly Catholic, it is still a good question to ask how Catholic it actually was. 'Irish soldiers', the chaplain-general claimed, 'often make their religion a pretext for idleness on the Sunday. Many who claim the right of going to mass prefer the alehouse.' The Duke of Richmond when lord lieutenant believed that 'in a Cath- olic regiment comprising of 500 or 600 perhaps not 200 attend church'.[59] Since Catholic clergy sought to conduct a vigorous missionary effort among the troops, this too may count as evidence of widespread religious indifference. The Irish Catholic bishops were very alive to the need to protect Catholic worship in the army, but it is almost certain that most of the complaints they received about

[58] Wakefield, *Account of Ireland*, ii. 819 n.; Peel to Sir John Hope, 31 Aug. 1813, Peel to Sir George Hewitt, 6 Jan. 1814, SPOI CSO VIIIA/1/13; T. Bartlett, 'Indiscipline and Disaffection in the French and Irish Armies during the Revolutionary Period', in H. Gough and D. Dickson (eds.), *Ireland and the French Revolution* (Dublin, 1990), 194. Wakefield added: 'This is no overcharged statement; such scenes are common; and, as I am informed, occur every year, after parties of soldiers have scoured the country, demanding contributions for "letting the beast off". The money, thus collected in the course of the day, is divided on their return at night.'

[59] John Owen to Lord Palmerston, 1 Dec. 1812, WO7/61/215–16; Richmond to W. W. Pole, 17 Mar. 1812, Richmond MSS, NLI MS 62/450. See also Sir A. Wellesley to J. Villiers, 8 Sept. 1809, Duke of Wellington, *Dispatches During His Various Campaigns*, ed. Lt.-Col. Gurwood (12 vols., Lon- don, 1837–8), v. 134–5: 'Any man may go to mass who chooses, and nobody makes any inquiry about it. The consequence is that nobody goes to mass.'

obstructive commanding officers came from priests, not from the soldiers themselves. When Irish militia began serving in England there were protests that
Catholic chaplains should be appointed to the regiments.[60] These attempts to
promote Catholicism in the army coincided with the institution of brigade and
garrison chaplaincies, Anglican of course, in place of the old, usually sinecurist
regimental chaplaincies. It is doubtful whether this change gave Protestantism a
more effective presence in the army (there were only thirty-eight chaplains all told
in 1814), much more depending on the religious concerns of the colonels. Again
and again, anyway, it was they who were reminded of the provision made for
Catholics to attend mass.[61]

However, nothing is more certain than that Catholic consciousness in the militia went from strength to strength the longer the war lasted. Militiamen were
more exposed than most to the climate of sectarian bitterness that developed in
Ireland, moving as they did the length and breadth of the country. For example,
from July 1807 to June 1813 the Longford regiment was successively at Galway,
Killarney, Roscrea, Cork, Wexford, and Waterford.[62] There were countless occasions when the militia became involved in disorders which had a definite religious
element, as when Donegal men rioted on St Patrick's day at Tuam or the Tyrone
band played 'party tunes' at Wexford at the time of the 1807 election. At Cookstown,
Co. Armagh, the local commander had to ban the wearing of orange ribbons while
the Kerry militia marched through. In 1813 the government placed a general
prohibition on regimental bands taking part in processions.[63]

Yet all this may have mattered less than the treatment of Catholics within
the regiments themselves where men of quite low social status encountered the
barriers of Protestant Ascendancy. Once the freedom to attend mass had been

[60] C. Long to Dr Troy, 20 Dec. 1805, 13 Jan. 1806, Hardwicke MSS, BL Add. MS 35775, fos. 134–
5; Sir E. Littlehales to Sir A. Wellesley, 24 May 1808, SPOI CSO OP269/5/43; Wakefield, *Account of
Ireland*, ii. 820–1. Thomas Hussey, Catholic bishop of Waterford, styled himself 'Vicar-Apostolic over
all the Catholic military in Ireland' and attempted to make compulsory Protestant worship into a public
issue. Ferguson, 'Army in Ireland', 177–8; T. P. Power, *Land, Politics and Society in Eighteenth-Century
Tipperary* (Oxford, 1993), 307–8.

[61] Duke of Portland to Lord Camden, 21 Oct. 1796, Kilmainham MSS, NLI MS 1004; P. E.
Kopperman, 'Religion and Religious Policy in the British Army c. 1700–1796', *J. of Relig. Hist.* [Aust.]
14 (1987), 390–405; Pelham to Portland, 26 Oct. 1796, Pelham MSS, BL Add. MS 33113, fo. 59, cited
Ferguson, 'Army in Ireland', 177; adjutant-general's circular letter to generals commanding districts,
14 May 1806, Leven and Melville MSS, SRO GD26/9/527/5/78; Wellesley to Littlehales, 31 May
1808, SPOI CSO OP290/6/31–2. For the number of chaplains in 1814 see WO7/61/433.

[62] Longford Militia record book, NLI microfim P. 5556. The Longford regiment was described as
wholly Protestant in John Dubourdieu [Jan. 1812], 'Detached observations on the comparative numbers of Protestants and Catholics in Ireland', SPOI CSO OP366/3.

[63] Littlehales to Lord Harrington, 22 Mar. 1811, Littlehales to Sir John Hope, 3, 5 July 1813, SPOI
CSO VIIIA/1/13; Lt.-Col. Leslie's order, 15 July [1798?], Leven and Melville MSS, SRO GD26/9/
527/1/117; L. Brien to W. Taylor, 21 May 1807, SPOI State of the Country papers, 4175/1–2.
Bartlett, *Irish Nation*, 322, provides a number of examples of Catholic militia fighting yeomanry.

conceded—something that happened early in the war[64]—the 'Catholics' of the regiment were probably identified as those who stayed away from Protestant worship, and a division was created around which grievances could develop. The key issue was over NCO promotions, their rank of course carrying impressive authority and standing in the regiment. In the light companies of thirty regiments in 1802, two-thirds of the sergeants were Protestants when over two-thirds of the men were Catholics. During the Napoleonic War it is not unlikely that the private men became increasingly Catholic while Protestants continued to dominate and in some cases monopolize the NCO ranks. By 1811 the Waterford militia, for example, included forty Protestants as corporals and sergeants (half the complement) and just sixty-nine as privates; in the Roscommon regiment the colonel insisted on none but 'loyal' men holding rank though it was seven-eighths Catholic.[65] Colonel John Irwin operated a similar ban in the Sligo militia and consequently faced constant opposition from a Catholic 'party' among his soldiers. As he explained himself to his second-in-command over the case of one Brett:

He assumes to be the head of the Roman Catholics of the regiment and to be their champion; on that account I will shew him and them, that he never rises in the Sligo. If he sought for promotion only, he might be certain of it either in the line or any other militia regiment. But he won't leave us, forsooth why—because he is the head of a party, and as the head of that party, higher he never gets with me. I do not agree with you either as to the expediency or propriety (from the part I have taken in the Roman Catholic business) of my appointing them n.c.o.s or acting towards them in any other degree than I have allways and hitherto done. It would by them be only considered as temporizing and a petty effort at conciliation; both of which lines of proceeding I feel to be inconsistent [with] my general character and accordingly deprecate . . . The only man I object to is Brett; at the same time I would not pass over a deserving Protestant to appoint a Roman Catholic—that would be *time serving* indeed.[66]

If this colonel's attitude was extreme, there were plenty of others who rationalized their preference for Protestants by pointing to their advantages of education over Catholics; also, 'having been accustomed to orderly habits, [they] are neater and

[64] A public notice issued in May 1793 promised 'the free exercise of each religion'. McAnally, *Irish Militia*, 38, 59. There was trouble early in the life of the Tyrone regiment when officers tried to stop their men from attending mass. Bartlett, *Irish Nation*, 324. Catholic chaplains were appointed to the regiments encamped at Loughlinstown in June 1795, and the government enforced the same arrangements the following year. McAnally, *Irish Militia*, 81; Bartlett, *Irish Nation*, 324. A witness in a court-martial in 1796 described the practice at the Chapelizod barracks: 'those who go to mass turn to the left, and it is free for the exercise of religion, every man does as he pleases.' Ferguson, 'Army in Ireland', 75. The army's policy on this matter is given in Brownrigg to General Fox, 15 June 1797, Brownrigg MSS, WO133/3/227–8.

[65] Brigadier-General W. Scott to Lord Hardwicke, 18 Jan. 1802, Hardwicke MSS, BL Add. MS 35675, fos. 1–4. For the Waterford and Roscommon militias see Wakefield, *Account of Ireland*, ii. 621, 624. Ibid. 592–631 for Wakefield's survey of the Catholic presence in the Irish militia.

[66] Irwin to C. O'Hara, 16 Sept. 1812, O'Hara MSS, NLI MS 20330.

cleaner in their persons, and more easily formed into good soldiers'.[67] In short, a Protestant officer class in the militia succeeded in kindling all the resentments against Protestant Ascendancy, whether by appropriating office and authority mainly for Protestants or by implying Catholic inferiority and disloyalty.

Catholic military participation promoted Catholic consciousness on a broader level when the leaders of Catholic opinion in renewing their bid for emancipation from 1804 began employing the argument of Catholic Ireland's war contribution. This line tallied with the old Pittite view that Protestant bigotry and self-interest were greater problems in Ireland than Catholic disloyalty and that the power of Catholic numbers could not be denied indefinitely in any system of government which purported to observe the principle of representation. The number of Catholics offering armed service to the crown drew attention at one and the same time to Protestant injustice, Catholic strength, and the wider strategic interests of the empire.[68] While Britain's heavy dependence on Irish military manpower was beyond argument after 1793, it helped to provoke much interest, not to say dubious research, in the comparative size of the Catholic and Protestant populations as each side tried to testify to its importance in the national scale of things.[69] The actual proportions remain speculative; nor can we be certain about the number of Catholics in the army at any one time. Still, there are good reasons for thinking that Protestant Ireland was under-represented in the army, mainly because the yeomanry appropriated so much of its manpower and because Protestant opinion, increasingly exercised about the demographic balance of the two communities, was able to see positive advantages in Catholic recruitment. When new regiments were about to be raised in Ireland in 1804, the home secretary and the lord lieutenant agreed that they should be recruited from Catholic areas 'as it was by no means desirable to bring away any of the *Protestants of the North* upon whom must be your great dependence, under God'. If Irish made up one-third of the army's rank and file, the Catholic Irish component is likely to have been over a quarter. Grattan,

---

[67] Wakefield, *Account of Ireland*, ii. 633.

[68] Bartlett, *Irish Nation*, 309–10; D. Scully, *The Irish Catholic Petition of 1805: The Diary of Denys Scully*, ed. B. MacDermot (Dublin, 1992), 141–7; resolutions of the 'Catholics of Ireland', 24 May 1809, SPOI CSO VIIIA/1/4; Catholic petition presented 20 May 1811, *PD* xx. 207–9.

[69] Resolutions of the 'Catholics of Ireland', 24 May 1809, SPOI CSO VIIIA/1/4, where it was claimed that at four or five millions the Irish Catholics comprised one-quarter of the United Kingdom population. In contrast, a 'Protestant' paper argued that the Protestant proportion of the Irish population was one-third or two-fifths and that the Catholics therefore were no more than one-sixth of the UK total. Duburdieu, 'Detached observations', SPOI CSO OP366/3. Patrick Duigenan in a debate on the Catholic question on 31 May 1811 claimed that there were two million Protestants in Ireland out of a total population of 3.5 millions, *PD* xx. 412. Wakefield, *Account of Ireland*, ii. 630–1, using Beaufort's population figures for 1792, divided his total into 522,023 Protestants and six times as many Catholics (3,211,297). Edward Hay, a leading Catholic, sought to organize a census of Catholics in 1795. Hay to Lord Fitzwilliam, 16 Sept. 1795, Fitzwilliam MSS, Sheffield Central Library, F30/52; Bartlett, *Irish Nation*, 295.

therefore, hardly exaggerated when he told parliament Irish Catholic numbers were great enough 'to turn the scale of empire'.[70] Like Scottish nationalism in this period, Catholic nationalism thrived on a sense of possessing the means to subvert English supremacy and thus of having entered a more equal relationship.

A sizeable Catholic Irish presence in the army can also be inferred from the heavy drafts taken from the Irish militia, and it might be speculated that Catholic consciousness was imported into the army by men who had first-hand experience of Protestant intolerance and oppression. It is interesting, too, that the best recruiting returns for the army came from a belt of country running north-west from Dublin, taking in north Leinster (including Dublin), the Ulster borderlands, and Connacht. Edward Wakefield produced both official totals of recruits for the various recruiting districts 1802–11 and estimates of county populations. When this data is used to ratio recruits to population, the most productive districts are shown to have been Dublin (Dublin, Meath, Wicklow, Kildare, Queen's), Enniskillen (Donegal, Sligo, Leitrim, Fermanagh, and parts of Tyrone and Cavan), and Athlone (Mayo, Roscommon, King's, Galway, Westmeath, Longford, and part of Tipperary).[71] County totals exist for the recruitment of the Army of Reserve in 1803 and the militia in 1808, both of which took men for long-term service and therefore were not too different from the army. Outside Antrim, Down, and Londonderry, where county and parochial administrations were definitely more efficient than elsewhere, the areas quickest to fill their quotas were again in the same broad region.[72] North Leinster, north Connacht, and south Ulster were where sectarian antagonisms and violence were fiercest from the time of the Defenders in the 1790s to the Ribbonmen who became active about 1810.[73] These conditions produced considerable movement of people and a generally unstable society which must have been conducive to military recruitment. But again a situation may have been created by which a significant amount of Catholic grievance and hostility was transferred into the army.

On the other hand, to the extent that the army was prepared to allow regiments

---

[70] Lord Hardwicke to C. Yorke, 3 Feb. 1804, Yorke to Hardwicke, 11 Feb. 1804, Hardwicke MSS, BL Add. MS 35705, fos. 84–5, 95–8; *PD* xx. 385.

[71] Wakefield, *Account of Ireland*, ii. 630–1, 834. C. O'Grada, *Ireland: A New Economic History 1780–1939* (Oxford, 1994), 21, surveying the regional origins of 5,598 East India Company recruits 1802–14, does not contradict this finding. Dublin and the rest of Leinster provided the most recruits on the basis of Wakefield's population figures. This agrees with Cullen, 'Irish Diaspora', 141–2.

[72] See return of the Army of Reserve, Dec. 1803, *CJ* lix. 524–5 and militia return, 1 Mar. 1808, WO1/612/379. I have calculated the percentage of the quota filled by these dates, and divided the list into a successful and unsuccessful half. The following counties and cities belonged in each case among the successful: Dublin city and county, Meath, Louth, Longford, Cavan, Fermanagh, Tyrone, Sligo, Mayo, Cork city.

[73] M. Elliott, 'The Defenders in Ulster', in Dickson, *United Irishmen*, 223–4; T. W. Moody, F. X. Martin, and F. J. Byrne (eds.), *A New History of Ireland* (5 vols. pub., Oxford, 1976–), v. 19–20.

to express an Irish identity, this would have been made to supersede religious and other divisions. The army officially recorded its men as 'English', 'Irish', 'Scottish', or 'foreign'—religious adherences were included in the inspection returns only as late as 1861. Sent away from Ireland, unprovided with Catholic chaplains, probably unoffended, for the most part, by army Christianity with its emphasis on martial virtues, the Irish troops seem likely to have found less comradeship and *esprit de corps* in religion than in their Irishness. An Irish identity was an obvious loyalty to develop in coexistence with large numbers of Scots and English. Moreover, if some Irish regiments started out with strong regional characters, they must have soon lost them or had them much weakened as men were drafted on overseas stations and recruits taken where they could be found. Militia volunteers, at any rate, were given a wide choice of regiment and there were instances where these men made particular corps compositely Irish in the best sense of the term. In 1800 the 68th took 2,269 men from twenty-seven different militia regiments, the 85th 958 from ten, the 54th 895 from twenty-four, and the 64th 861 from fifteen.[74] We can even exaggerate the localism of the county militias because, in view of the inoperability of the ballot in Ireland, men were sometimes enlisted far away from the county; returns from the Wexford regiment in 1806 show that of 109 recruits raised, 66 were found in Ulster; at the same time the Wicklow regiment found 45 out of 47 in Co. Mayo.[75] The army, certainly, but also the militia to a lesser extent, served as a melting-pot of regional populations, as armies often have, with the result that regiments were not loathe, if they could do it, to build a loyalty to themselves as Scottish, English, Irish, or (in the single case of the 23rd) Welsh.

The four line regiments that most successfully promoted their Irishness during this period were the 18th (Royal Irish) and 27th (Inniskillings)—both of which went back to the Williamite wars—and two new corps raised in 1793, the 87th (Prince of Wales Irish) and 88th (Connaught Rangers). Like all other units with large Irish contingents, they were almost permanently absent from Ireland as long as the war continued; the 18th returned to Ireland in August 1802 but left in October 1803; the 27th left in April 1793 and, except for recruiting by the 3rd battalion in 1806–8, was never again on the Irish establishment until after the war; the 87th left in 1794 never to return; the 88th likewise, though its 2nd battalion was stationed in Ireland to recruit in 1807–9 and 1813–15. Nevertheless, figures provided by the inspection returns strongly suggest that in the war's latter stages these regiments were at least 75 per cent Irish. In part this was the product of deliberate

---

[74] 'General return of men from the Irish militia who have volunteered in 1800', Kilmainham MSS, NLI MS 1330.
[75] Returns of men raised for augmentation 27 Dec. 1805–1 June 1806, WO1/774/129–30, 175. See also above, 172, for Longford men in Co. Limerick militia. However, the other returns included in WO1/774 (for six regiments) show that the men were largely raised in the home county.

policy, as the army became interested in building up 'national' regiments; Army of Reserve and Additional Force men raised in Ireland were directed into all four regiments. Yet these regiments also possessed drawing power of their own. Lord Moira, the 27th's colonel, asked for a 4th battalion to be formed in 1809: 'On an average our parties get about 15 men every week. Many of these are men who would not enlist in any other regiment, the Enniskillen being a popular corps.' One test of their popularity we can apply is their success in attracting volunteers from the Irish militia. In 1800 twenty-seven line regiments received drafts and the 27th's at 713 men was the sixth largest without the regiment even being present in Ireland; in 1808 sixty-six regiments participated and the 88th headed the list of the number taken in, with the 27th third and the 87th tenth; in 1809 the 88th was second out of seventy-two regiments.[76]

The adjutant-general in Ireland in 1805 claimed that there were only two Irish regiments 'that have any pretentions to be called national', he meaning the 18th and the 27th. Both were the main bearers of Irish military pride into the 1800s, having won public acclaim (and battle honours) for their part in the Egyptian campaign of 1801, up to then easily the British army's most glorious moment in the war. The same victories instantly translated Abercromby into an Irish national hero in remarkable contrast to the odium which had attended his departure from the Irish command three years before.[77] But by the end of the Peninsular War the 87th and 88th were even better known than the old regiments, in particular the 87th for its 2nd battalion's capture of an imperial eagle at Barossa and the 88th for its conduct in numerous actions—Bussaco, Fuentes de Onoro, Badajoz, Ciudad Rodrigo, Salamanca, Vitoria. Ireland related to them because they promulgated their Irish identity unashamedly in the army. On its colonel's orders the 87th went into action with its band playing 'Garry Owen' and 'St Patrick's Day', the most popular Irish airs of the day. The regiment's 'Barossa Song', said to have been composed by a private after the battle, recounted the bravery of the 'Faugh-a-Ballaghs'; 'Long live our Irish lads to cheer on each Barossa Day.' In the same spirit, the 88th observed St Patrick's Day by wearing the shamrock and adopted the tune 'St Patrick's Day', soon to be regarded as Ireland's 'national anthem', as its regimental march.[78]

---

[76] Extract of letter from Moira to Lt.-Col. Gordon, 3 Mar. 1809, WO1/640/167–8; general return of men from the Irish militia who have volunteered to serve in the line in 1800, Kilmainham MSS, NLI MS 1330; state of the volunteering from the Irish militia, 15 Feb. 1808, WO1/612/369; state of the volunteering, 10 Aug. 1809, WO1/1119/511.

[77] Memorandum by Col. Anstruther, 25 Mar. 1805, Chatham MSS, PRO30/8/241, fos. 104–7. See the toasts to Abercromby on various occasions in *Dublin Evening Post*, 12 Oct., 2 Nov. 1809; *Freeman's Journal*, 27, 30 Oct. 1809; *Faulkner's Dublin Journal*, 20 Oct. 1810.

[78] M. Cunliffe, *The Royal Irish Fusiliers 1793–1950* (London, 1952), 107–8, 449–50; Jourdain and Fraser, *Connaught Rangers*, ii. 558, 564.

The 87th laid up its colours in St Patrick's cathedral perhaps as early as 1811. So began the association of Irish regiments with St Patrick's which itself began to be restored and embellished to serve as an ancient, national shrine.[79] While the cathedral never quite managed to become the temple of military fame and national symbol hoped for, it was at this stage clearly part of a developing Patrician tradition intended to build a separate Irish identity within the Union and also, as promoted by liberal Protestant opinion, to oppose the festivals of Protestant Ascendancy centred around William III and the events of 1688–90. The lord lieutenant withdrew from Williamite celebrations in 1806 with the end of the state procession and levee on William's birthday (4 November) in 1806, and though he continued to make no public appearance on St Patrick's Day he did on occasions wear the shamrock ostentatiously and promote the tune 'St Patrick's Day' as the national air.[80] Such recognition must have eased and possibly urged the regimental adoption of Patrician symbols and observances. These suited Irish regiments because they were distinctively Irish in an army which more and more was playing up the idea of British 'nations' united under the British crown. One of the strongest, and certainly one of the earliest places where the Patrician tradition came to reside in the nineteenth century was among the Irish military.

Did the Irishness produced out of military service, then, make Ireland like Scotland? Not really. Army and society in Scotland forged a closer and closer relationship in view of the importance of the Scottish regiments as an expression of national identity. Though the wars of the Napoleonic period ended the flight of the 'wild geese' between Ireland and Continental armies and therefore concentrated Irish military service and an Irish military tradition within the British army, that tradition was largely left to the Irish regiments to use for themselves. Catholic nationalism did not invoke Irish militarism because it argued for political and constitutional reform to make amends for a past of conquest and subjugation; certainly not separatist, it had no use for myths of national resistance, with the 'wild geese' positively an embarrassment from their association with France. It sought concessions from the British crown and its accent therefore was on loyalty to Britain and an Irish identity based on culture rather than warriordom. Protestant nationalism in Ireland similarly came to embrace Union because British power was accepted as the ultimate security of the Ascendancy. Any celebration of Irish military achievement within the British army ran the risk of pointing to increasing Catholic participation and the threat this posed in the light of Ireland's history of Catholic perfidy and rebellion. Neither of these nationalisms could make much of an Irish military tradition, the Catholics not wanting to draw attention to national

---

[79] Cunliffe, *Royal Irish Fusiliers*, 453; *Faulkner's Dublin Journal*, 4 Dec. 1813.
[80] Hill, 'National Festivals', 30–51.

defeat and humiliation or to rebellion, the Protestants fearful of fuelling Catholic pretensions. Significantly, where Scotland's greatest monument of the war, the National Monument, was intended to commemorate the country's military service, Ireland's carried only the name of Wellington and, situated in Phoenix Park, was nearer to the viceregal lodge than to the heart of Dublin. In vain was it argued that the obelisk ought to be regarded as the 'offering of Irishmen to an Irishman', that Wellesley's title was 'not Irish' and was 'accidental'.[81]

Scotland was able to strike a more confident pose within the Union as a result of its war contribution. Ireland's contribution was on a much larger scale but the war can easily be represented as deepening its subordination with the loss of parliamentary independence in 1801, acute feelings of insecurity on the part of the Protestant minority, and the development of viceregal magnificence at Dublin. If, too, Scotland was a Celtic kingdom re-armed when local forces largely took over from regular garrisons, Ireland was not such an obvious case. The Irish volunteers of 1778–83 had made the British state extremely wary of what local forces in Ireland might portend. Especially after the rebellion of 1798, the trend was for the Irish militia as a proportion of the Irish garrison to be reduced while the Irish yeomanry was constantly subjected to the crown's attempts at closer control. Neither Catholic militia nor Protestant yeomanry inspired confidence as sectarian feelings intensified; they were potentially dangerous armed particularisms—'individual armies' in Lord Westmorland's words[82]—which might repeat the earlier crisis over the volunteers. In the end authoritarian views of Ireland and armed populations prevailed over more liberal views. Pitt and Dundas wanted to integrate Catholic Ireland into the British imperial state by conceding political and civil rights and offering military careers, yet another instance of an imperial policy which sought to reconcile local diversity with imperial requirements. In contrast, the Addingtonians were primarily interested in Catholic Ireland as a source of manpower for the British army overseas. They can easily be identified with Protestant Ascendancy, British and Protestant armed supremacy in Ireland, and opposition to Catholic possession of military office, and possibly also with the efforts made from about the turn of the century to Anglicize and Protestantize the Irish population.

All in all, the war does not seem to have created the more equal relationship between Ireland and England that it did for Scotland and England. Ireland was not nearly as successful as Scotland in advancing its national identity within the United

---

[81] *Dublin Evening Post*, 22 Sept. 1814. Scorn was also poured on the committee's preoccupation with the 'antient testimonials of Rome' and therefore probably the British imperial connotations of the monument, ibid. 13 Sept. 1814. For support for a site in Dublin see ibid. 13 Dec. 1814; J. Warburton, J. Whitelaw, and R. Walsh, *History of the City of Dublin* (2 vols., Dublin, 1818), ii. 1103–6. The monument originally was to include an equestrian statue of Wellington.

[82] McAnally, *Irish Militia*, 10.

Kingdom or in advertising its contribution to British imperial power. If the state was served by more Irish soldiers than ever before, Irish military pride mostly existed within the army and Irishmen had in no sense ended the English occupation of their country by taking over its defence themselves. Even so, this, in the last analysis, gives too much play in history to identity and consciousness and insufficient to military events. The fact was that once European warfare achieved a new magnitude in which whole national populations might have to be mobilized England's old military suzerainty over the British archipelago was gone for ever. The new strategic vulnerability of Britain as the age of the mass army was entered was not something that was going to pass quickly, and, consequently, England's dependence on Scottish and Irish arms for her own security and for defending her international position profoundly affected the balance of the Unions. Because of these changed conditions of war, Irish opposition and disaffection, Catholic particularism, became more, not less, serious matters for Britain despite the political dominance the Union conferred. Whatever comfort the Protestant Ascendancy drew from the Union of 1801, it had no defence against the logic of a British state dependent on Irish military resources unable to risk alienating the Catholic population indefinitely. When the first real test of Britain's will to resist a powerful Irish opposition came in the crisis of 1828, the government in London soon capitulated; and, appositely, a general, one with Irish experience moreover, was the prime minister. The fundamental issue of the Anglo-Irish relationship was how to secure Ireland as a strategic asset rather than as a strategic liability:

where [wrote Edward Wakefield] exertions of a whole people are become necessary, governments yield to expediency . . . or to speak plainly, a knowledge of their weakness induces them to court assistance, by making those concessions and yielding those natural rights which they withheld in violation of the principles of justice. When the present situation of the United Empire is considered, it will be admitted that the active co-operation of the Irish Catholics would add greatly to its strength and lessen in no small degree the danger with which it is threatened. To attain this co-operation so desirable in every point of view, nothing more is necessary than to afford them a participation in the blessings of the constitution.[83]

---

[83] Colley, *Britons*, 326–8; Wakefield, *Account of Ireland*, ii. 636.

7
The Problem of Order

ONE most interesting aspect of the problem of order in Britain during the Age of Revolution is the enormous gap between the threat of revolution as imagined by government and ruling groups and the innocuousness of physical force protest in the actual event. Violent disorder, for the most part, remained localized, limited in its aims, and easily subdued, if necessary, by a reliable military. Outside Ireland insurrectionary activity was carried on by small, highly vulnerable groups who were mainly protected from government counter-action by their own very limited organization and by the tenuousness of the links they maintained across the country. Even the Luddite outbreaks, famously dubbed 'quasi-insurrectionary' by E. P. Thompson, drew on military reserves less than the figure of 12,000 troops stationed in the 'disturbed districts' has been made to imply; for the normal wartime garrison of the area covering Yorkshire, Lancashire, and the Midlands was around 7,000 troops, in fact was 7,421 men on the eve of the troubles in March 1811 and had been as high as 8,437 men in February 1810.[1] Yet conservatives and the authorities remained transfixed by the French revolution and the apparent ease with which the old order had been overthrown. They were unable to free themselves from the belief that behind any popular opposition there lurked a dangerously subversive, secret radicalism whose fanaticism was matched only by the volatility of the materials it was dealing with. The main instrument of revolution was seen to be the crowd, created by clever manipulation of popular discontents and the means of proliferating protest and violence. Worse, the French revolution produced the spectre of the armed populace joined and strengthened by a suborned soldiery. It is not emphasized nearly enough that governments felt increasingly anxious about the arms and military skill which popular oppositions might command. The conservative reaction to the revolution needs to be understood not least as a response to the fact that the loyalty of the army could no longer be taken for granted and that the armed crowd was the all too likely concomitant of the armed nation.

[1] In Jan. 1807, for example, 1,789 cavalry and 5,370 infantry were stationed in the North-West, Yorkshire, and Inland military districts. Distribution of troops in districts, 1 Jan. 1807, Dropmore MSS, BL Add. MS 59287, fos. 93–6. F. O. Darvall, *Popular Disturbances and Public Order in Regency England* (London, 1934), 1, 258–60, originated the statement that the army needed to put down the Luddites was larger than that sent to Portugal under Wellesley in 1809.

The failure of the royal army of France to restore control in 1789 was the negative explanation for the revolution's success and it sent shock waves around the political and military establishments of Europe. Never before, in modern times, had a professional regular force collapsed in the face of civilian unrest. The armed hegemony of the state over the population suddenly appeared much less secure than it had been. During the high tide of the anti-radical reaction in Britain in 1792–3 it is interesting that this anxiety was shared by propertied opinion generally, the middle-class correspondents of the loyalist associations showing serious concern about pay and conditions in the armed forces.[2] Britain's rulers and generals must have felt the impact of these events the more because of the naval mutinies of 1797 when most of the home navy was rendered unserviceable by massive insubordination and suspected sedition, with the army affected as well. On this occasion the government acknowledged the critical importance of keeping military and civilian grievances separate by making incitement of mutiny a capital felony.[3] But already, from 1792 in fact, it had become concerned to meet the soldiers' complaints about their declining living standards in order to prevent the politicization of their discontent. In that year a pay increase was awarded, and another in 1795, both at times of mounting disorder and resurgent radical activity and even less coincidental in view of the long period of neglect preceding these concessions.[4] The swiftness with which the question of army pay was dealt with in May 1797 further suggests that the loyalty of the soldiery was now taken very seriously, with the possible connection between indiscipline and political disaffection fully acknowledged.[5]

Mutiny and insubordination in the army and navy as a worrying political threat diminished quite rapidly after 1798, which indicates how shallow the radical penetration always was, with the exception of the United Irishmen in the navy whom the authorities themselves had largely placed there as conscripted suspects and rebels.[6] Within the army rank and file protest was again dealt with in traditional ways, by transferring troublemakers away from the regiment or by making a severe example of a few ringleaders, perhaps by the more drastic measure of shifting an

---

[2] Philp, 'Vulgar Conservatism', 49.

[3] By 37 Geo. III, c. 70 and 37 Geo. III, c. 40 (Ireland), which were renewed on various occasions during the remainder of the war until 1817 when they were made permanent (57 Geo. III, c. 7).

[4] Fawcett, the adjutant-general, in a revealing letter to Lord Cornwallis in India, 3 Mar. 1792, wrote of his long struggle to increase the pay of soldiers before the ministers conceded. Cornwallis MSS, PRO30/11/270, fo. 85. For the concern that brought about the 1795 increase see Brownrigg to Duke of York, 20 July 1795, Brownrigg MSS, WO133/1. Neither pay increase coincided with the strong drive for recruits which occurred at the outset of the war from late in 1792 until the end of 1794.

[5] Disaffection in the armed forces, 1792–8, is covered, but not exhaustively, in C. Emsley, 'Political Disaffection and the British Army in 1792,' *Bull. Inst. Hist. Res.* 48 (1975), 230–45; R. Wells, *Insurrection: The British Experience 1795–1803* (Gloucester, 1986), 79–109, 145–51; Elliott, *Partners in Revolution*, 133–44.
[6] McDowell, *Ireland*, 494–6; Wells, *Insurrection*, 166–7.

entire regiment to a new station. The abatement of soldier discontent generally reflected the improvement of the soldier's lot achieved through higher standards of military administration and the improved professionalism of the officer corps. A long war also produced a long service army and stronger regimental communities, the latter fostered by the concentration of troops in large barracks and garrisons which reduced the amount of contact with civilians. There was in Britain sufficient barrack accommodation for 18,000 men in 1794 and 125,000 in 1806; by the latter date there were forty-eight places which could hold more than a thousand troops.[7] If disloyalty existed anywhere in the army after the radicalism of the 1790s had spent its strength, it was expected to be found in predominantly Irish regiments or, ironically, the Foot Guards. The Irish, kept away from Ireland, turned out to be much like the rest of the British soldiery, drunken frequently but rarely insubordinate and almost never mutinous.[8] The Guards were a different proposition because they mostly remained in and around the capital, inevitably fitting themselves into the civilian society and economy, forming, it has been said, an extension of London's proletariat. They proved restless at the time of the naval mutinies and were implicated in the Despard conspiracy of 1802.[9] But in the course of the war the Guards came to be treated little differently from the line regiments, as the army struggled to find sufficient men for its force in the field. The king's resistance to their deployment abroad rapidly collapsed after 1798, and even the home battalions were not necessarily stationed in London. At the height of the Peninsular War nearly two-thirds of the Guards were in Spain. Under these conditions the particular danger their local associations presented moderated into insignificance until the return of peace.[10]

There was, then, growing confidence in the political reliability of the army. Yet

[7] Statement of barracks in Britain, 30 Dec. 1794, Windham MSS, BL Add. MS 37891, fos. 15–16; account of all barracks, 6 Mar. 1806, Dropmore MSS, ibid. 59286, fos. 32–4. I exclude the Channel Islands from the calculation. F. C. Mather, *Public Order in the Age of the Chartists* (Manchester, 1959), 164, says that by 1815 there were 159 barracks able to accommodate 16,854 cavalry and 138,410 infantry.   [8] Karsten, 'Irish Soldiers in the British Army', 41–4.

[9] Wells, *Insurrection*, 80, 105; M. Elliott, 'The "Despard Conspiracy" Reconsidered', *Past and Present*, 75 (May 1977), 56. Discontent among the Guards and militia at Warley Camp in 1795 forced the government to increase the pay of the army. See above, n. 4.

[10] Dundas wanted to send a brigade of Guards to the West Indies with Abercromby in 1795, but George III vetoed the proposal. Dundas to the king, 15, 18 Aug. 1795, *George III Corresp.* ii. 380–2; Dundas to Duke of York, 5 Oct. 1795, WO6/131/80–90. Three battalions of Guards were placed in Ireland, 1798–9, and a brigade of Guards formed part of the force sent to Holland in 1799. But the real change of policy occurred in 1800 when two battalions were allocated to Abercromby's army in the Mediterranean. Thereafter, the Foot Guards regularly joined the army in the field. By January 1813 there were 4,857 Guards in the Peninsular and 2,774 at home. Almost all of the latter crossed over to Holland at the end of the year to help press home the final attack on Napoleon. See Duke of York to Lord Bathurst, 31 Jan. 1813, WO25/3225; 'Force in Holland', 4 Jan. 1814, WO1/658/25. After the war the Guards continued to cause anxiety at times of political excitement in London. For trouble in the 3rd regiment in 1820 see Cookson, *Liverpool's Administration*, 248–9.

fears that armed power might be turned against established authority would not go away because the enormous expansion of military force for home defence introduced the 'democracy' to military training and discipline. Warnings against creating an armed populace were first heard when Pitt's government proposed volunteer corps in 1794 and again with the supplementary militia, which the ministers did not disguise was a way of establishing a large reserve of trained manpower.[11] Soon afterwards the burgeoning of volunteer numbers into a mass movement intensified these anxieties by offering a huge amount of armed force loosely organized and probably beyond the means of effective control. To what degree the possession of arms had become uncustomary in eighteenth-century British society, or military service unfamiliar, is difficult to say. After the affray at Tranent in East Lothian in 1797 when the cavalry killed twelve civilians, one worried local gentleman claimed two-thirds of the 'lower order of the people' owned firearms and moreover were excellent shots from amusing themselves in summer evenings by firing at 'marks'.[12] Armed gangs of poachers and smugglers were notorious in some parts of the country. On the other hand, popular disorder usually became the difference between the unarmed or lightly armed crowd and the force a small number of troops could present. Moreover, the perception of Britain as a 'commercial' society lacking 'military spirit' was frequently articulated.[13] Becoming an armed nation was certainly taken to mean that arms might get into the wrong hands, including hands which had previously lacked them. But more worrying still was a situation where the army's advantage of military discipline and skill over the numbers of the crowd disappeared and the 'people' themselves became the ultimate guarantors of internal order as well as of the country's defence. When a weavers' protest was brewing in Glasgow in 1812, the leading magistrate explained how most of them 'have been local or regular militiamen, volunteers or disbanded soldiers, and being accustomed to the use of arms are far more formidable than the undisciplined rabble of former days'. These fears led on directly to the act against unauthorized drilling in 1819, the first and least contentious of the 'Six Acts' passed that year to curb popular radicalism.[14]

At the level of 'high' politics concern about the larger consequences of the armed nation is best represented by Addington's administration. As noted in Chapter

---

[11] e.g. J. Ross to General J. Grant, 29 Mar. 1794, Macpherson Grant of Ballindalloch MSS, Ballindalloch Castle, Banffshire, bundle 434; Marquis of Buckingham, 'Observations on the plan for raising an additional militia' [Oct.? 1796], Chatham MSS, PRO30/8/117, fos. 98–101.

[12] D. Cameron of Blainslie to Dundas, 27 Apr. 1798, Laing MSS, EUL La. ii. 501; Logue, *Popular Disturbances*, 89.

[13] Sir George Shee wrote of Britain's need 'to change our national character from a mercantile to a great warlike people, or at least to engraft the one character determinably upon the other', paper, 16 Mar. 1803, Pelham MSS, BL Add. MS 33120, fos. 104–9.

[14] J. Dunlop to Lord [Melville], 3 Feb. 1812, HO102/22, fo. 156.

3, Pelham, Hobart, and Yorke exemplified the ministers' definite preference for militia over volunteers as the more efficient and controllable species of force. Westmorland, later in Addington's Cabinet, took issue with Pitt in 1794 over 'arming people . . . when the middling rank of people are in possession of arms, and laws have not always the power of enforcing obedience, and the colonel and private change duties'.[15] Here was pointed out the great danger of creating military power in society over which the usual social and legal controls would not necessarily operate. Such views were undoubtedly reinforced by the behaviour of too many volunteer corps during the 'scarcity' of 1800–1. In a number of places the volunteers refused to turn out to face rioters and the authorities there were forced to write them off as a law and order force.[16] All the doubts about the volunteers came to a head in Addington's administration. The dissolution of the corps at the end of the Revolutionary War, with the exception of some yeomanry, was the uncompromising response. This was the more hard-headed because Dundas had conceived the volunteers as offering a permanent solution to two basic problems the British state was facing; the first was the paucity of military force immediately available to local magistrates in an age of increasing disaffection; the second was the problem of national defence posed by the large garrisons France maintained on the Channel coast and which provided her with the means of assembling an invasion army at short notice.[17]

Addington's government acted in character by immediately attempting to secure better control of volunteer arms. In many cases these had been issued to individuals who kept and maintained them at home, this because corps were paid nothing to establish armouries or for the upkeep of their weapons. Among the articles the Stirling volunteers subscribed to in 1800 was one that allowed each man to have his musket but another that he might be required to hand it back if he was away from home for a long period.[18] The authorities, understandably, had little faith in the ability of commanding officers to keep strict account as members came and went, weapons fell into disrepair, and ordnance-issued arms were mixed with arms procured by the corps or private individuals. Hobart, as the new war minister in 1801, asked for money to establish armouries and for unauthorized possession of

---

[15] Westmorland to Pitt, 8 May 1794, Chatham MSS, PRO30/8/331, fos. 237–40.

[16] Beckett, *Amateur Tradition*, 86; C. Emsley, 'The Military and Popular Disorder in England, 1790–1801', *J. Soc. for Army Hist. Res.* 61 (1983), 105–6; Wells, *Insurrection*, 255–6; Bohstedt, *Riots*, 49–51; Sir Ralph Abercromby to Duke of York, 8 Apr. 1800, WO1/621/307–8. An incident at Macduff, Banffshire, involving the volunteers, is fully described in G. Forbes to Lord Fife, 3 Apr. 1800, HO102/17, fos. 197–200.

[17] For Dundas's opposition to the disbandment of the volunteers see his letter to Sir James Pulteney, 6 Apr. 1803, Melville MSS, SRO GD51/1/979 and Dundas to Addington, 29 July 1803, Sidmouth MSS, Devon RO, 152M/C1803/O2323. Dundas wrote to Addington on the same subject in Sept. 1802.

[18] Minute book of Loyal Stirling Volunteers, 5 Mar. 1800, Central Region (Scotland) Archives, SC8/2/46.

arms by ex-volunteers to be made a punishable offence at the hands of the magistrate. The latter provision, included as it was in the Volunteer Act of 1802, was important because it made the point that among voluntary associations serving public purposes armed associations ought to be the first to be treated as public bodies by the state.[19] But after Hobart's reforms, there was little else that could be practically achieved to reduce the danger of volunteer arms getting into the wrong hands. The clerk of the ordnance referred in 1804 to the ammunition depots for the volunteers 'which are now scattered all over the kingdom in hired warehouses'; and there would have been an even greater dispersal of arms as the enormous quantity distributed after 1803 found its way into literally hundreds of armouries, many undoubtedly small and improvised—like the ironmonger's store used by the Mortlake volunteers—and scarcely very secure. While the advent of the local militia may have helped a bit by reducing the number of units, the fact was that at this time an armed population could not be had without placing arms within reach of the populace. In turbulent, teeming Glasgow in 1812, where the best precautions were surely taken, the arms of the local militias of Lanarkshire and Renfrewshire lay in 'detached warehouses' and the magistrates did not know how they could keep them from ten or twelve thousand protesting weavers.[20]

Pitt, however, in pressing a mass levy on Addington's government, mercilessly flouted the ministers' view that domestic military force should be kept in carefully selected hands and formally regulated as far as possible. Typically, he opposed 'the right of possessing arms inherent to every British subject' to their anxieties about whither the armed nation might lead.[21] Where the Addingtonians wanted greater protection from dangerous social divisions, Pitt (and Dundas) saw military service as a way of reducing social tensions. They believed that all parts of society, even including Catholic Ireland, could be mobilized in resistance to a French attack and that the experience would have a salutary, because powerfully unifying, effect. National defence patriotism gave the gentry and local élites opportunities of asserting and restoring their social leadership. All classes would discover the power of the national bond under the threat of foreign conquest; radicalism would be marginalized by military participation as the lower orders were brought into closer

---

[19] See above, 76; memorandum on volunteer corps, May 1801, WO1/407/549–61. See also J. Atkinson to J. Fordyce, 3 May 1798, Sir J. Mitford to Dundas, 4 June 1799, Melville MSS, SRO GD51/1/934, 964.

[20] W. W. Pole to Lord Chatham, 30 June 1804, SPOI CSO OP174/6; J. E. Anderson, *A Short Account of the Mortlake Company of the Royal Putney, Roehampton and Mortlake Volunteer Corps 1803–6* (Richmond, 1893), 13–15; J. Dunlop to Lord [Melville], 3 Feb. 1812, HO102/22, fo. 156. Mortlake volunteers of 1803 who promised to take good care of their muskets were permitted to take them home. According to a memorandum of 23 Jan. 1805, this practice continued and corps had been paid the arms allowance without having proper armouries. Liverpool MSS, BL Add. MS 38358, fos. 244–50.

[21] Pitt, 'Further considerations on the plan for a general enrolment and array of the people', 2 July 1803, Sidmouth MSS, Devon RO, 152M/C1803/OM15.

contact with and acquired greater confidence in their superiors. The breadth and boldness of Pitt's conception of the armed nation were fully discovered with his proposal of a *levée en masse* in 1803. But the idea also needs to be understood as extending beyond preparations to defeat invasion to ideas, admittedly never very clearly articulated, of national and social restoration in an age of crisis.

The accommodation of the conservative, cautionary views of the Addingtonians to Pitt's had to wait until Castlereagh became war minister and the local militia came into existence. Windham's training scheme was another version of the mass levy, and Castlereagh himself, for a time, pondered ways of saving it. The local militia, on the other hand, was carefully conceived enough to satisfy those who wanted an armed nation based on the principle of universal service and those who wanted adequate securities against an armed populace. Dundas in retirement, who previewed Castlereagh's plan, repeated his support for 'general training' and merely disapproved of the obligation falling on older men with families and settled occupations.[22] Anxious conservatives were reassured on three main counts: local militia battalions were county-organized under the lieutenancies, and therefore command could be expected to reside in the safe hands of the established social leadership; they were fully fledged military formations in which the authority of the officers was at all times upheld by the Mutiny Act; their arms would mostly be held in the same, relatively secure county depots used by the 'old' militia, instead of being more widely distributed without a permanent guard, as was often the case with the arms of the volunteers. Of course, the local militia also put local armed power into larger, more efficiently trained units which, if they did mutiny, presented a considerable threat. Great alarm occurred when disturbances broke out in several regiments in 1809–10.[23] But the employment of troops of the King's German Legion against the Ely battalion—which infuriated the radical press and landed Cobbett in prison for seditious libel—made the point that the local militia could be treated like soldiers in a way the volunteers could never have been.

A radical hand in the local militia disorders was immediately suspected or detected. The fear would not go away that sinister attempts were forever being made to corrupt the military in spite of their generally good record, even of local forces acting in their own localities. It was inevitable that soldiers would be exposed to a radicalism increasing its social influence, and armed civilians in the auxiliaries more so. But evidence is lacking that radicals or radical ideas were significant in any of the major disorders affecting the non-regular forces in Britain. The Scottish

---

[22] Lord Melville to Castlereagh, 9 Apr. 1808, Melville MSS, NLS MS 3835, fos. 58–61.
[23] Eight troops of yeomanry were called into Devizes when trouble occurred in the local militia battalion. W. Hughes to R. Ryder, 11 June 1810, HO42/107, fos. 276–7. A full regiment of militia and regular cavalry were sent to Bath in May 1810 to deal with insubordination in the West Mendip (Somerset) battalion. Smith, 'Local Militia', 244–6.

fencible mutinies in 1794–5, when the troops resisted leaving the country or released comrades whom they believed to have been unjustly sentenced for punishment, were typical regimental protests. At no stage did the mutineers receive outside help or claim that outsiders had incited them to act as they did, though it was an obvious defence in the circumstances. The trouble in the local militia was similarly focused on the men's grievances against their officers. A crowd in Bath supporting the men of the West Mendip battalion and shouting radical slogans was the only overt sign of radical interference in all the disturbances. Again, no soldier threatened with punishment pleaded that others had coerced or manipulated him.[24]

In the food disorders of 1795 and 1800–1 there clearly was considerable inter-action between popular protest and feeling among the militia and volunteers. During 1795 the militia stationed in southern England were particularly to the fore in demanding supplies at a fair price, acting to all intents and purposes like any other crowd, albeit armed. In the second scarcity the volunteers in places as far apart as Devon and eastern Scotland disgraced themselves in the eyes of the authorities either by joining crowds or refusing to act against them. Following E. P. Thompson and Eric Hobsbawm, historians have long been satisfied that the eighteenth-century food riot rested primarily on popular conceptions of social justice, specifically the right of the poor to necessities at prices they could afford and retention of local supplies for local use when shortages arose. The major outbreak in 1795—the occu-pation of Newhaven by the Oxfordshire militiamen—reveals 'no concrete evidence of democrats' activities and the Court Martial also failed to elicit any'. Military comradeship undoubtedly contributed to the solidarity of the protests, but if demo-cratic radicals did attempt to tamper with the loyalty of the men the effect was insignificant alongside the soldiers' resort to popular custom.[25]

The strength of popular attitudes in the volunteers is hardly surprising since they were and remained civilians. On the other hand, the 'regular' militia, what-ever its unreliability in 1795, rapidly improved its reputation to the point where it was entirely trusted and trustworthy in the disorders of 1800–1. Its poor showing at first can be put down to the fact that the regiments were young, the officers inexperienced, and discipline affected by inadequate accommodation until a suffi-cient number of infantry barracks existed in southern England. An immediate cause of the trouble was that soldiers in billets bought their own meat and bread, and therefore were exposed to price fluctuations, more so than many workers, who were protected to a degree by charitable subscriptions and the Poor Law. Once the troops were guaranteed their rations whatever the market price, a change intro-duced in 1795 and confirmed in 1797, they were no longer hurt by inflation and

---

[24] Prebble, *Mutiny*, 263–391; Smith, 'Local Militia', 232–57.

[25] R. Wells, 'The Militia Mutinies of 1795', in J. Rule (ed.), *Outside the Law: Studies in Crime and Order 1650–1850* (Exeter, 1982), 35–64; Bohstedt, *Riots*, 27–68; Beckett, *Amateur Military Tradition*, 86.

their participation in food disorders became a thing of the past.[26] As the Gordon Highlanders were reminded by their lieutenant-colonel in the dearth of 1800, they could not in the circumstances expect meat of the quality they were used to but they should also 'look about them and compare their own comfortable position with that of the labouring class of people, the produce of whose labour does not admit of their buying meat at all'. This divided soldiers from civilians in a most important way, and anything which promoted that separateness helped to provide the basic conditions for ensuring the loyalty of the soldiery. Even the local militia, enjoying soldiers' comforts for only a short period of the year, seem to have considered themselves fortunate, especially when times were hard for the rest of the population.[27]

Most trouble within the army and 'permanent' auxiliaries assumed the form of 'trade disputes' in which pay and conditions were the chief issues and the rank and file took collective action, usually by peaceful representation through the NCOs, against their officers. Soldiers, regarded as little better off than slaves by civilians, still maintained a firm sense of their 'rights' in terms of army regulations, parliamentary legislation pertaining to them, their original agreement to enlist, and their general entitlement to fair treatment. During the wars the worst insubordination occurred in 1794–5 when fencibles were ordered to Ireland and most of the new line regiments were broken up and drafted as the army tried desperately to assemble a West Indies expedition after the losses in the Low Countries, sometimes in clear violation of the men's terms of service. 'We [enlisted],' the men of the 105th and 113th complained in a printed handbill, 'on condition of returning to our homes at the approach of peace; but what is now the case? All faith is broken with us. We are led to be incorporated with Regiments that will never be reduced, except by a formidable enemy and the more formidable climate of the WEST INDIES.'[28] In later cases the generals proceeded more circumspectly; for example,

---

[26] R. Wells, 'The Militia Mutinies of 1795', in J. Rule (ed.), *Outside the Law: Studies in Crime and Order 1650–1850* (Exeter, 1982), 72–3; Duke of York to Sir Charles Grey, 6 May 1797, Univ. of Durham, 1st Earl Grey MS 1086. In 1795 the soldier was given 1*d.* extra per day for bread and another for meat, based on calculations that this would be sufficient for him to buy 1½ lb. of 'ammunition' bread and ¾ lb. of meat for his daily rations. Most soldiers preferred a lesser ration of higher quality 'household' bread, and in 1797 the government agreed to meet the cost of providing 1lb. of bread and ¾ lb. of meat per day if bread exceeded 1½*d.* per lb. and meat 6*d.* per lb. For 1795 see Brownrigg to Duke of York, 20 July 1795, Brownrigg MSS, WO133/1. For 1797 see J. W. Fortescue, *History of the British Army* (13 vols., repr. New York, 1970), iv. 935.

[27] Regimental orders, 15 May 1800, Gardyne, *Gordon Highlanders*, 76; Smith, 'Local Militia', 264–5. For a militiaman's expenditure see Wakefield, *Account of Ireland*, ii. 826 n.

[28] Prebble, *Mutiny*; M. Duffy, *Soldiers, Sugar and Seapower: The British Expeditions to the West Indies and the War Against Revolutionary France* (Oxford, 1987), 173–4; T. H. McGuffie, 'The Short Life and Sudden Death of an English Regiment of Foot', *J. Soc. for Army Hist. Res.* 33 (1955), 16–25, 48–56. Emsley, 'Military and Popular Disorder', 103, mentions mutinies in 104th (Manchester), 105th (Leeds), 111th, and 113th (both raised in Birmingham), and in two Irish regiments.

the militia who went urgently to Ireland in 1798 were all strictly volunteers, with the march of some regiments countermanded because half or more of the men refused to go.[29] As with civil disturbances, the resort to violence occurred when other methods had failed or were considered as unlikely to succeed in the circumstances. Outside interference in these protests was rare, and probably became rarer as troops withdrew into barracks and regiments were regularly shifted from summer to winter quarters and from one place to another. Soldiers and civilians rather continued their age-old relationship of preying on each other. A long-serving militia became almost as distant from civilian society as the regulars, further reducing the probability of a conjunction of military and civil disorder. A core of veteran militiamen in the regiments ensured the rapid assimilation of recruits, who anyway came to be drawn less frequently from the county of the regiment and who often enlisted to embark on a soldier's career.

Obviously, then, the problem of order in the armed nation came to centre on the infantry volunteers, who were numerous and, it seemed, incorrigibly resistant to professional military standards and behaviour. Much greater confidence was placed in the local militia, in spite of the inauspicious start the mutinies of 1809–10 gave it. These, at least, remained soldiers' protests settled by soldiers' methods, whatever the enticements of the populace in some instances; and they could also be taken as showing the advantages of a reduced localism and civilianism in the main auxiliary force. Thus at the height of the Luddite disturbances in 1812 the local militia, admittedly with some reservations on the part of the magistracy, were called out in the affected counties to occupy the large towns and release the regular cavalry for patrol work in the countryside.[30] The reliability of the volunteers, after the disgraces of 1800–1, was never tested to this extent, if we except some small embodiments during the weavers' strike in Lancashire in 1808 and the employment of the socially superior London corps in the Burdett disorders of 1810.[31] Cavalry, anyway, were always deemed more effective than infantry against crowds and could patrol a wider area. Though there was no official policy, with local rulers having first responsibility for law and order, it does seem that the volunteers were deliberately kept out of harm's way, not even used sparingly to put down civil unrest, so suspicious were the authorities of the plebeian movement that came into existence in 1803.

The yeomanry as police were everything the volunteer infantry were not. They were organized under officers whose social influence provided effective control

---

[29] Duke of York to the king, 12 Sept. 1798, *George III Corresp.* iii. 123; Colley, *Britons*, 257; Cripps, *Royal North Gloucester*, 70.

[30] Smith, 'Local Militia', 258–84; Darvall, *Popular Disturbances*, 256–7 (though the distinction between militia and local militia is not clear here).

[31] Lord Hawkesbury to Earl of Derby, 9 July 1808, Hawkesbury to Earl Fitzwilliam, 13 Aug. 1808, HO51/87, fos. 129, 149; R. Brownrigg to Colonel Herries, 10 Apr. 1810, PRO30/3/1. I am indebted to Dr Austin Gee for these references.

in lieu of the Mutiny Act and the articles of war; and, as well as putting military leadership into proper hands, they coalesced around the strong neighbourhood of farmers and other 'middling sort' in the localities.[32] By the end of the Revolutionary War, if not sooner, these corps were being hailed as the success story of the civilian mobilization, and many were saved from the general dissolution of the volunteer movement in 1802 for permanent establishment.[33] In contrast, the infantry volunteers too often seemed to lack any coherence. The incompetence of many officers was accentuated by their low status and inadequate informal authority. Where the ranks were filled from a mobile proletariat, the turnover of men greatly impeded the development of properly communal corps. More frequently, service in the volunteers could lump respectable artisans and rough labourers indiscriminately together, ignoring potent social differences which were observed in the charities and other voluntary organizations.[34] Such problems were multiplied by the huge mobilization at the start of the Napoleonic War. The number of corps reached nearly 1,600 in 1803–4 which simply added to the amount of officer inefficiency and rank and file insubordination; Charles Yorke as home secretary in 1803 was overwhelmed by the tide of paper that came into him from disputing volunteers.[35] Furthermore, the movement was plebeianized by the expansion, so that popular contempt for military authority and military ways was fully expressed and the reciprocities between the poor and their superiors were expected to be continued by the officers. The Iver Volunteers near Uxbridge refused to take the oath of allegiance almost certainly because they understood it as a form of enlistment. The incident which destroyed the Sutton company of the Ely battalion originated out of the men's insistence that they be allowed to combine drink and drill; the issue for them was the right to drink while doing hard work which any employer respected. Forming larger units, which the government promoted, tended to exacerbate these ill effects because it could place strangers in command and weakened the communal and social basis of corps.[36]

[32] Beckett, *Amateur Military Tradition*, 76.

[33] Duke of York to [Dundas], 8 Apr. 1798, WO1/619/165–6; memorandum on volunteer corps, May 1801, WO1/407/549–61.

[34] For the high turnover of men through some corps see below, 233–4. Charles Yorke, as home secretary criticizing the volunteer system, thought a 'particular difficulty' was the 'assembling indiscriminately the Gentlemen Volunteers with those of the lower classes of life'. He also commented that the 'necessary qualifications' for volunteer officers were 'knowledge of actual service, intellect, vigour, good manners and temper . . . your *Old Soldier* is the last man I would pitch upon'. 'Communication received from Mr Secretary Yorke concerning the volunteers' [1803], Hope of Lufness MSS, SRO GD364/1/1139/5. Lord Sheffield in his North Pevensey Legion tried to keep farmers and 'unsightly men' in separate companies. Sebag-Montefiore, *History of the Volunteer Forces*, 264.

[35] N. Jekyll to G. Rose, 26 Feb. 1804, Chatham MSS, PRO30/8/241, fos. 194–201.

[36] For the Iver Volunteers see C. Yorke to Lord Grenville, 12 Oct. 1803, HO51/74, fos. 206–7 (reference from Dr Austin Gee). An officer of the Berwickshire yeomanry considered it counterproductive to have volunteers take oaths of allegiance because they would be mistaken for the attestations sworn by soldiers on enlistment. 'Plan for rendering more effectual the services of the yeomanry

The doubts, then, surrounding the volunteers were not that they were a civilian force—in the new circumstances of war this was a necessary evil—but that they could not be adequately controlled by established authority. The option of an 'armed peasantry', who would be organized in military formations only when invasion was imminent, was open to similar (and greater) objections that local leaders would neither command them for training nor for actual service. Parochial training carried on by itinerant NCOs and raw levies hastily assembled into battalions under officers who did not know the men magnified the dangers of creating armed force that all too easily could metamorphose into the armed crowd. Not surprisingly, universal training as an alternative to the more formally organized volunteers never materialized. But it is worth repeating that the 'volunteer system' had a more tenuous existence than is usually understood; abandoned in 1802, revived with some reluctance in 1803, only maintained after 1806 until a replacement could be found. The problem of finding suitable officers proved insuperable, mainly because half-pay officers were not attracted and because volunteer officers mostly chose themselves by taking the initiative to raise a corps.[37] Otherwise the army and government made little headway in seeking to impose greater military order on the volunteers, defeated on the one hand by middle-class traditions of voluntary endeavour, which were, to a significant degree, localist and democratic, and on the other by a more general resistance to 'military servitude'.[38]

Yet if the localism and populism of the volunteers made them unemployable as police, their officers and, more important, the generals and politicians had every faith that they would march against the French if ever they invaded. The great Francophobic display of 1803-4 seems to have removed any lingering doubts on this score. The Duke of York's plan for arming volunteers throughout the country in order to have a huge reserve on hand to meet any attack was immediately endorsed by his minister, Hobart, who said he was 'fully persuaded' the corps would march where ordered in the event of invasion whatever restrictions they had placed on their service.[39] Pitt and Dundas were ecstatic about the popularity of volunteering, wanting no limitation of numbers, no offer refused, nothing to lower the intensity of the public's patriotism: 'I hope to God therefore that the zeal and spirit which is rising on the coast and through the country will not be damped by any of the trivial difficulties which arise in Downing Street.'[40] Downing Street, in

---

cavalry', 1803, Hope of Lufness MSS, SRO GD364/1/1136/4. A case study of volunteer attitudes and insubordination is found in my article, 'Sutton Volunteers'. Fortescue, *County Lieutenancies*, 104-10, 199-200, gives numerous examples of 'volunteer indiscipline'.

[37] Ibid. 112-14. Some lieutenancies tried to control the selection of officers. Cookson, 'Volunteer Movement', 877-8.   [38] Ibid. 870-1, 889; Beckett, *Amateur Military Tradition*, 82-3.

[39] York to Lord Hobart, 30 June, Hobart to York, 6 July 1803, WO1/625/333-6, 377-9.

[40] Pitt to A. Hope, 29 July 1803, Melville to General Vyse, 14 July 1803, to Addington, 29 July 1803, Hope of Lufness MSS, SRO GD364/1/1137/16, 1136/2, 6.

fact, went with the tide. Addington's government, it is worth remembering, in spite of its dislike of an armed populace, prepared over 350,000 civilians for armed service. The army, moreover, denoted four-fifths of the volunteers as a 'moveable force' to march against the invader, except in the manufacturing and metropolitan counties (where it was reduced to three-quarters) and Scotland.[41] These may have been the numbers the situation was deemed to require, but they also indicate the government assumed the loyalty of plebeian volunteers in any confrontation with the French, if not the loyalty of the masses who would have been left lightly policed with such a heavy concentration of force against the enemy. One minister wrote of the 'unexampled' and 'unexpected' 'zeal and spirit of the country',[42] and it may be that the heady experience of 'national unanimity' in 1803–4 finally convinced the political class that the menace of 'sedition' had greatly dissipated. Certainly, the Luddite disorders were handled with some aplomb, the government insisting on the employment of local militia.

Too much can be read into the government's refusal to train the volunteers as light infantry, able to fight in loose order over different terrain and move equally quickly to attack or retire from enemy concentrations. A cult of light infantry there surely was, particularly served at this time by the *tirailleurs* of the French revolutionary armies.[43] But in Britain the argument that this was the sort of military force most appropriate for an armed citizenry defending the *patrie* found little favour in the highest circles. The fact was that the Duke of York and his 'Prussians' regarded the use of light troops as a highly specialized craft, for which the men themselves had to be specially selected. If the authorities were afraid of creating an irregular force that might be turned against them, the greater consideration by far was that civilians in arms had neither the officers nor the training opportunities to master this kind of warfare. Much better that these auxiliaries were drilled for the line where their brigades would be commanded by professionals and they could get by with a few basic movements.

On the other hand, civilian possession of artillery was taken extremely seriously, as shown when the Irish government in 1792 worried about the cannon that the United Irishmen might manufacture or repossess from the old volunteers.[44] At the beginning of the war it was established practice for infantry to have their own 'battalion guns', and a few of the early volunteer corps were so equipped; for

---

[41] 'Distribution of the volunteers in Great Britain shewing the moveable force' [23 July 1804], ibid. 1147/1.   [42] Lord Camden to the Duke of York, 26 May 1804, WO1/628/18–19.
[43] Houlding, *Fit for Service*, 240, 251–2, 374–6; N. Jekyll to G. Rose, 26 Feb. 1804, Chatham MSS, PRO30/8/241, fos. 194–201; Beckett, *Amateur Military Tradition*, 105–6; W. K. Fane, 'The Orderly Book of Captain Daniel Hebb's Company in the Loveden Volunteers (Lincolnshire) 1803–8', *J. Soc. for Army Hist. Res.* 4 (1925), 154.
[44] Lord Westmorland to Dundas, 5 Dec. 1792; 'Volunteer cannon as far as have yet been ascertained by returns', 12 Dec. 1792, SPOI Westmorland MSS 78, 83.

example, at Halifax, Bradford, and Edinburgh.[45] But by 1803 the artillery volunteers consisted only of men called out to man the 'great guns' of harbour batteries. What had far greater significance for civil and military order in the future was the addition of a horse brigade to the army's field artillery and which, kept on the home establishment after 1815, formed perhaps the last line of defence against the insurrectionary crowd.[46]

It is hard to avoid the conclusion that Britain's Irish experience mainly formed the anxieties induced by an armed populace, which the volunteers could be conceived to be. The Irish volunteers of the American War showed only too well how the power of the state could be emasculated if an independent military power was allowed to exist. The scars of that episode remained raw and unhealed in 1792–3 as London and Dublin struggled to head off a revival of the movement. Thereafter Irish disorder and disaffection was armed to an extent that dismayed Britain's rulers, whether one took account of actual incidents or French-backed insurrectionary plans or the suspicion surrounding Catholic militiamen. A major point of the army's operations in 1797–8 was to disarm the population by seizing all weapons not held by acknowledged loyalists—with careful accounts kept of the haul. Beginning with the Insurrection Act of 1796, a series of arms acts stretching beyond the peace empowered the magistracy to search for arms and license their possession. The arms raid became a constant feature of Irish disorder, exceptionally difficult to deal with during the war when the yeomanry kept their weapons at home in self-defence.[47] Eighteenth-century Ireland was already a society where the number of firearms in private hands was very large, and from the late 1780s increasing social and sectarian tensions easily turned into armed conflict. The government's attempts to impose order by armed force only added to the violence and therefore the amount of armed protection people sought for themselves. Such a breakdown of social relations provided Britain's rulers with another worst case scenario besides revolutionary France of the possible consequences of an armed population.

Ireland was food for thought: the Addingtonians who felt most strongly the

---

[45] R. P. Berry, *A History of the Formation and Development of the Volunteer Infantry* (London, 1903), 314–16; *Edinburgh Evening Courant*, 8 May 1797.

[46] For the strength of the home force of artillery, including the horse brigade, 1801–19 see *SP* 1806, x. 7–9; 1813–14, xi. 335; 1817, xiii. 201; 1818, xiii. 191; 1819, xv. 161. For the relative weakness of the artillery before 1793 see ibid. 1813–14, xi. 342. A detachment of horse artillery (two guns) was present at Peterloo. See Palmer, *Police and Protest*, 283, 436–7; Mather, *Public Order*, 159, 162–3 for the deployment of horse artillery to combat public disorder.

[47] McDowell, *Ireland*, 574–81. Registration of arms began in 1798. Up to 1820 the act was renewed by 47 Geo. III, sess. 2, c. 54, 50 Geo. III, c. 109, 53 Geo. III, c. 78, 57 Geo. III, c. 21, 1 Geo. IV, c. 47. Legislation (36 Geo. III, c. 42 (I), 39 Geo. III, c. 37 (I), 40 Geo. III, c. 96 (I), 47 Geo. III, c. 8) also controlled the manufacture and sale of gunpowder, arms, and ammunition. For yeomanry arms see two returns of the corps of Co. Limerick in 1807, where numerous thefts are reported. SPOI CSO OP232/5/1, 15.

dangers inherent in mass arming often had served in Ireland. Westmorland, when
lord lieutenant, warned Pitt that Ireland had shown 'arming people' to be 'a rather
dangerous experiment'. With Hobart as his chief secretary in 1792, he had contended with the incipient volunteer movement in Dublin and Belfast, only too
aware of the earlier movement during the American War which set an example of
arming by private initiative in the name of the national interest. To some extent,
the very threat of volunteers had forced the Castle's hand; the alternative of a
militia had been required to prevent the revival of fears that Ireland would be left
without adequate military force.[48] Pelham was another who had struggled to govern Ireland in the face of increasing armed violence. As chief secretary in the
period leading up to the rebellion, he was deeply involved in the Castle's counter-
insurgency policy and in a situation where the authority of the law steadily gave
way to military force. After 1798 attention focused on the Irish militia as inefficient, and in its Catholic parts, possibly disloyal.[49] Addington's government again
showed its sensitivity over control of the armed force the war had created by pressing for an 'interchange' of militia between Ireland and England in order to reduce
Catholic numbers in the Irish garrison.[50] At one stage, Addington and his ministers, supported by the views of Portland and Windham, may even have contemplated the abolition of the Irish militia; certainly, the question was referred to the
generals on the Irish establishment, who could say nothing in the militia's favour.[51]

   In Ireland there was always acute tension between the armed nation and social
order because Catholic–Protestant differences were too powerful for any patriotic
consensus to form. The war created Catholic armed force in Ireland on a scale not
seen since the Jacobite–Williamite conflict of the 1690s, and this at a time when
for other reasons the relationship between the two communities became critical—
Britain's rulers, in comparison, felt increasingly confident about the unity of the
British wartime society and its anti-Gallican patriotism. As already mentioned,
Catholic recruitment into the regular army presented few problems. Irish regiments
were quickly sent out of the country, if only to check desertion, and they returned

---

[48] Westmorland to Pitt, 8 May 1794, Chatham MSS, PRO30/8/331, fos. 237–41; McAnally, *Irish Militia*, 9–13; Westmorland to Dundas, 5 Dec. 1792, SPOI Westmorland MS 78; R. Hobart to E. Nepean,
30 Nov. 1792, 28 Jan., 19 Mar. 1793, SPOI CSO VIIIA/1/3.

[49] e.g. Captain H. Taylor to R. Brownrigg, 14 Sept. 1798, Melville MSS, NLI MS 54A/153;
Cornwallis to Dundas, 19 July 1799, WO1/612/85–6; Wickham to Castlereagh, 14 Aug. 1803, Wickham
MSS, Hampshire RO, 38M49/1/7/17.

[50] A circular was sent to the regiments in July 1801 inviting them to volunteer for service in England in case of invasion. Abbot to the militia colonels, 30 July 1801, Colchester MSS, PRO30/9/105,
fo. 6; Abbot to Addington, 30 July, 19 Sept. 1801, Sidmouth MSS, Devon RO, 152M/C1801/OI61–2.
Abbot hailed the proposal as a step towards 'the interchangeableness of militia throughout the United
Kingdom'.

[51] Abbot to Lord Pelham, Jan. 1802, Colchester MSS, PRO30/9/122, fos. 54–6. For Portland and
Windham see McAnally, *Irish Militia*, 164, 178.

during the war only when there was no alternative. For example, in 1807 the government, with ample apology, dispatched the second battalion of the 83rd to Ireland; its stay was relatively short—eighteen months. The 89th, twice reduced to half-strength after going to the Continent in 1794 and to Egypt in 1801, also was allowed to recuperate in Ireland.[52] But these were the exceptions that proved the rule. Of twenty-one line regiments in Ireland at the outbreak of war in 1793, only three, all very weak, returned before the end of the Revolutionary War.[53] When rebellion broke out in 1798, three Guards battalions went to Ireland because most of the available line infantry were ruled out by their Irishness.[54] During the Napoleonic War two out of fifteen line battalions that were emphatically (60 per cent or more) Irish on the inspection returns of 1813 served as part of the Irish garrison, one of which (the second battalion of the Connaught Rangers) was there primarily to receive militia recruits. Not Irish regiments in the army but Irish militia in Ireland posed the issue of how safe it was to create Catholic armed force.

It is tempting to see the largely Protestant yeomanry as a deliberate counter to a largely Catholic militia. But at the time Protestants of the Ascendancy agreed that the security of Protestant Ireland rather depended on the size of the British garrison kept in Ireland against the militia; or, better still, against no militia at all. The Ascendancy never was reconciled to Catholic participation in home defence, not even after the Union strengthened the British hand in Irish military affairs. Manners, the Irish lord chancellor, as late as 1807, spoke of dissolving 'all the southern regiments': 'when the mass of the people are supposed to be disaffected to the government of the country a militia is not the mode of defence or safeguard to be resorted to.' Castlereagh, for the same reason, could not see how the local militia could be extended to Ireland.[55] The militia was in most serious danger of abolition soon after the rebellion when, in the heightened state of Protestant feeling, it became more suspect than ever. Worse, Cornwallis as military commander in Ireland constantly complained of its indiscipline and inefficiency, including very few militia in his field force.[56] He sought a solution in the exchange

---

[52] C. Long to Duke of Richmond, 25 Aug. [1807], Richmond MSS, NLI MS 59/195; Cunliffe, *Royal Irish Fusiliers*, 6–22.

[53] Similarly, of 28 battalions stationed in Ireland during the peace of 1802–3, only 4 rejoined the Irish establishment before 1814. This information is obtained from the paymaster-general's register, National Archives (Ireland), M. 464.

[54] Duke of York to Dundas, 2 June 1798, HO30/2, fos. 34–6.

[55] Lord Manners to Duke of Richmond, 3, 7 Sept. 1807, Richmond MSS, NLI MS 61/350–1; Castlereagh to Sir A. Wellesley, 2 Dec. 1807, WO1/612/305–22.

[56] Cornwallis to Dundas, 14 Mar. 1799, Melville MSS, BL Add. MS 40100, fo. 212; Cornwallis to Dundas, 19 July 1799, WO1/612/85–6; Cornwallis to Dundas, 7 Sept. 1799, HO50/29; Cornwallis to Portland, 1 Nov. 1800, WO1/771/505–9. For Cornwallis's troop dispositions see 'Sketch of the forces proposed to be first moved . . .', 25 Mar. 1799, Chatham MSS, PRO30/8/323, fos. 61–2; 24 Oct. 1800, Morrison MSS, NLI MS 5006/48; 8 May 1801, Kilmainham MSS, NLI MS 1330/209–10.

of regiments with Britain, which would have appealed to the Ascendancy by adding British and subtracting Irish troops from the garrison. The proposal was put to
London, only to discover that the king's opposition to Irish militia on British soil
was adamantine.[57]

What saved the militia against the advice of the generals was the powerful
interests arrayed in it which in the delicate days of the Union no government
wished to offend.[58] Addington's ministers were soon pressing ahead with a 'general' militia bill for Ireland, as they had already done for Britain. When the peace
seemed unlikely to last, this project was put aside as they sought ways of quickly
reconstituting the force without the long and involved, and unpopular, process of
a ballot.[59] However, in the Napoleonic War the balance of British and Irish force
comprising the garrison of Ireland was weighted strongly in favour of the former,
around 60 per cent increasing to around 70 per cent once the 'interchange' of
militias began in 1811. These were similar to post-rebellion figures—before 1798
the British component made up under half of the total strength.[60] That Dublin and
London kept a close eye on the proportion of militia is perfectly clear. Fitzwilliam
spoke of having 20,000 militia and an equal number of regulars; Hardwicke, dis-
cussing a large augmentation of the militia, wanted to know the 'principle of policy' concerning 'the proportion to be maintained in Ireland between his majesty's
regular and militia forces'.[61] The vital point commending the exchange of militias
in 1811 was that at one and the same time it released regulars in Ireland for overseas service and reduced the number of Irish militia stationed there.

The placement of militia regiments within Ireland was also given careful consideration. The general rule applied that, once embodied, they should serve outside
their native counties. But, in addition, 'Catholic' regiments were known and identified as such. On the evidence of Edward Wakefield, who made extensive inquiries
on the subject in 1808–11, the militias of at least twelve counties were strongly
Catholic: Kilkenny, Tipperary, Waterford, Cork, Kerry, Limerick, Clare, Galway,

[57] Cornwallis to Dundas, 14 Mar. 1799, Dundas to Cornwallis, Mar. 1799, king to [Dundas], [March 1799], Melville MSS, BL Add. MSS 40100, fos. 212, 214–18, 220.

[58] C. Abbot to Lord Pelham, Jan. 180[2], Colchester MSS, PRO30/9/122, fos. 54–6. See also Lord Cornwallis to Dundas, 7 Sept. 1799, HO50/29: 'any step that would raise a clamour and disgust the colonels of militia might prove fatal to the Union'.

[59] Lord Hardwicke to Wickham, 12 Nov. 1802, Wickham to Castlereagh, 14, 21 Nov. 1802, I. Corry to Wickham, 24 Nov. 1802, Castlereagh to Wickham, 27 Nov. 1802, Wickham MSS, Hampshire RO, 38M49/5/10/87, 1/7/10, 13, 5/9/71, 1/6/20; Hardwicke to Lord Pelham, 14, 28 Nov. 1802, Hardwicke MSS, BL Add. MS 45031, fos. 77–80.

[60] Return of the effectives in the British army 1793–1806, *CJ* lxi. 637. In Dec. 1813 there were in Ireland 14,000 regulars, 11,000 British militia, and 11,000 Irish militia. Palmer, *Police and Protest*, 161.

[61] Fitzwilliam to Portland, 29 Jan. 1795, Fitzwilliam MSS, Sheffield Library, F5/30–3; Hardwicke to C. Yorke, Feb. 1804, Hardwicke MSS, BL Add. MS 35705, fos. 139–41. See also Castlereagh to W. Wickham, 18 Nov. 1802, *Castlereagh Corresp.* iv. 242–3; Wickham to Castlereagh, 14 Aug. 1803, Wickham MSS, Hampshire RO, 38M49/1/7/17.

Roscommon, Westmeath, King's, and Dublin. We can surely add Mayo, and a return of light companies made in 1802 suggests Longford, Meath, Kildare, and Carlow as well.[62] From the same sources the regiments with a substantial (but not necessarily majority) Protestant contingent appear to have been those of the Ulster counties, Sligo, Leitrim, Louth, Wicklow, and Queen's. Cornwallis, after the rebellion, kept the great majority of the Catholic regiments in the southern and central military districts where they were overlooked by powerful concentrations around Cork, Athlone, and Dublin. A careful mix of Catholic and Protestant corps was also maintained. In 1800, for example, the Belfast garrison consisted of the South Mayo and Londonderry regiments while Wexford had the Kilkenny and Sligo regiments and Killala the Limerick city militia and the Leicester fencibles.[63] Throughout the war Protestant regiments seem to have been stationed more frequently in Dublin with its large garrison than Catholic, which gave them the best opportunities of perfecting battalion drill and discipline and brigade movements alongside the regulars. All militia in Ireland spent periods when they were broken up into detachments for police duties—a division of his regiment that every commanding officer cursed; but the rotation through Dublin suggests that the Protestant corps were more favourably treated in this respect and therefore likely to be better trained and generally more proficient.[64] Certainly, when the interchange with England began in 1811, some discrimination was practised, with relatively few Protestant regiments permitted to leave the country. In the first interchange twelve Catholic and three Protestant (Louth, Leitrim, and Sligo) regiments went to England; in the second in 1813 eight Catholic and six Protestant. Six (Armagh, Tyrone, Cavan, Donegal, Wicklow, and Queen's) out of fifteen Protestant regiments were never included in these exchanges. Moreover, the three Catholic regiments (Limerick City, Cork City, and Co. Dublin) that stayed in Ireland throughout all belonged to urban centres, their officers probably reluctant to leave the country because of their business concerns.[65]

[62] Wakefield, *Account of Ireland*, ii. 597–631; Brigadier-General W. Scott to Lord Hardwicke, 18 Jan. 1802, Hardwicke MSS, BL Add. MS 35675, fos. 1–4.

[63] The distribution of troops, 1798–1800, can be followed in 'Stations and strengths of the regiments', 1 Oct. 1798, Hardwicke MSS, BL Add. MS 35919, fo. 88, cited Ferguson, 'Army in Ireland', 181; 'Sketch of the forces', 25 Mar. 1799, Chatham MSS, PRO30/8/323, fos. 61–2; 'Sketch of the forces', 24 Oct. 1800, Morrison MSS, NLI MS 5006/48.

[64] While the English militia were in Ireland, 1798–1800, no Irish militia appear to have served in the Dublin garrison. Thereafter, Ulster units were regularly stationed there. In June 1801 the South Down and Tyrone militias were in Dublin; in May 1804 Londonderry, Antrim, and Roscommon; in July 1806 Cavan, Monaghan, and Wexford; in Nov. 1807 Monaghan, North Down (at Chapelizod), King's, and Tipperary. See 'Sketch of the forces . . .', 27 June 1801, Kilmainham MSS, NLI MS 1331; 'Spring half-yearly inspection of the infantry' [May 1804], Stations [July 1806], ibid. 1332, 82–3, 526–9; Stations [Nov. 1807], WO1/612/301–4.

[65] The movements of Irish militia to and from England are traceable in the paymaster-general's register, National Archives (Ireland), M. 464.

Interchange became the key policy to avert the danger of a Catholic militia in Ireland. As a security for Protestant Ireland, the idea was first taken up by Cornwallis and Castlereagh when they were attempting to build support for the Union; the Irish parliament in April 1799 passed legislation authorizing up to 5,000 militia to serve away, which nicely made the point that the Anglo-Irish connection was now more valuable than ever for the country's defence.[66] In the event, just two regiments out of many which volunteered were sent away, the Wexford and King's, spending a year in garrison in the Channel Islands. Cornwallis's and Castlereagh's promotion of interchange perhaps makes surprising the subsequent enthusiasm of Addingtonians and other anti-emancipationists for it, but the truth is that the issue became closely tied up with the defence of the Protestant state. Within a few months of arriving in Dublin, Lord Hardwicke, with Charles Abbot his chief secretary, was collecting offers from the militia to reinforce the British defences if invasion occurred, which underlined the military advantages if the different militias were available anywhere in the British Isles. A firm recommendation to Addington's Cabinet in favour of interchange followed, repeated in 1803 and 1804.[67] Yet further attention was paid to the subject in 1807 by Lord Hawkesbury as home secretary and the Dublin government under the Duke of Richmond and Sir Arthur Wellesley.[68] There was, therefore, a consistent 'Protestant' interest in the proposal, one mindful of the military arguments but emphasizing, as Abbot put it, that the 'political benefits . . . ought to outweigh all other considerations'.

Why, then, was interchange delayed until 1811? Most accounts blame the king for his opposition, and the English militia colonels who were often MPs or peers with access to the highest levels of government. While both parties were important factors in the situation, it has never been sufficiently appreciated that there was also a Pittite or 'Catholic' view of the question. In 1799 Dundas responded to Cornwallis by telling him, in effect, that there was no basis for an interchange: Britain had no need of additional militia for home defence and Ireland ought to be made 'independent' of the English militia, service there being so unpopular. The two regiments sent to the offshore garrisons of Jersey and Guernsey may be said to have gratified Irish feelings without in any way appearing as an exchange for the

---

[66] McAnally, *Irish Militia* 145–7; Lord Cornwallis to Dundas, 14 Mar. 1799, Melville MSS, BL Add. MS 40100, fo. 212.

[67] McAnally, *Irish Militia*, 162–3, 165–6, 182–4; Abbot to Addington, 30 July 1801, Sidmouth MSS, Devon RO, 152M/C1801/OI62; Abbot to militia colonels, 30 July 1801, 'List of militia regiments who have volunteered their services', Abbot to Lord Pelham, Jan. 180[2], PRO30/9/105, fos. 6, 54–6, 122, 132; W. Wickham to Castlereagh, 19 Nov. 1802, *Castlereagh Corresp.* iv. 246; Lord Hardwicke to Wickham, [Nov. 1802], Wickham to Castlereagh, 21 Nov. 1802, Wickham MSS, Hampshire RO, 38M49/5/10/100, 1/7/13; Hardwicke to C. Yorke, 17 Sept. 1803, Feb. 1804, Hardwicke MSS, BL Add. MSS 35775, fo. 16, 35705, fos. 139–41.

[68] Wellesley to Richmond, 13 July 1807, Hawkesbury to Richmond, 18 Aug., 16 Sept., 1 Oct. 1807, Richmond MSS, NLI MSS 58/41, 70/1338, 1341, 1344.

English regiments that had gone to Ireland. Further, the refusal to accept the Irish offers ignored the advice of the foremost general of the day.[69] All this needs to be understood in the context of the emancipation debate. That debate was mainly about Catholic loyalty to the British state, and one of the most important considerations the emancipationists could bring to bear was Catholic military service, particularly in defence of Ireland itself. To implement the interchange would be to occupy Ireland with an overwhelmingly Protestant force, feeding the view that the Union was designed to marginalize the Catholic Irish in a larger United Kingdom. The failure to carry emancipation in 1801 merely made it more necessary than ever to keep the Irish militia in Ireland.

This was not an easy position to defend. The military saw obvious advantages in being able to move the national militias freely within the British Isles, and it was a commonplace that Paddy was a better soldier out of Ireland than in, while he was also more to be trusted. Moreover, interchange enabled anti-emancipationists to take over the argument of their opponents about the incompleteness of the Union and the need for closer integration of Britain and Ireland. When Irish and English were ready to defend each other's country, the political bond would be indissoluble. Once they were thrust into each other's company in this way, the 'connections and friendships' making them one people, lower orders as well as gentry, would begin to be formed. Usually the process was put in assimilationist terms. As Irish militia officers told an English visitor: 'the intercourse would have a strong tendency to attach the Irish to [England] and to civilise Ireland by a conformation of habits.'[70] Irish MPs who supported emancipation found it particularly difficult to resist the military and 'moral' arguments in favour of interchange. Castlereagh's parliamentary record on this issue, especially when he was a minister in an Addington administration crumbling under Pitt's assaults, was a tissue of evasions thinly disguising his real opinion that the national militias 'ought to be an imperial force for the defence of the empire at home'.[71]

Interchange first came into parliamentary discussion in 1804 when Addington's government included a proposal to bring 10,000 Irish militia to England among other military measures, mainly designed to give the army an offensive capability. The militia proposal stood on its own. As a reinforcement it was not needed; neither was it intended to prepare the way for volunteering into the line. Rather,

---

[69] McAnally, *Irish Militia*, 147–8; Dundas to Cornwallis, Mar. 1799, Melville MSS, BL Add. MS 40100, fos. 214–18. Thirteen English militia regiments served in Ireland, 1798–9, and two (Carmarthen and 2nd West York) in 1799–1800.

[70] McAnally, *Irish Militia*, 242, quoting John Carr, *The Stranger in Ireland, or a Tour in the South and West Parts of That Country in the Year 1805* (London, 1806), 523. See also Richard Ryder, the home secretary, on the interchange bill in 1811, *PD* 1st ser. xx. 131.

[71] McAnally, *Irish Militia*, 145–6; *PD* 1st ser. i. 1088–90, ii. 63–5, xx. 133. For Irish whig support of interchange in 1804 see ibid. ii. 50–6 (H. C. Hutchinson), 81–2, 134–5 (Sir John Newport).

it was the outcome of Addingtonian sensitivities over the reliability of the Irish militia, sensitivities strung to a high pitch after Emmet's rebellion in July 1803. Yorke told Hardwicke he wanted the transfer 'so as to enable us to bring away 6,000 or 7,000 of those which are the least to be depended upon'. Interestingly, Castlereagh, against Yorke's opposition, persuaded the Cabinet to raise additional militia to replace the number sent away. His priorities, clearly, were to keep the Irish militia in Ireland at strength and to challenge the notion that they were 'very bad and unsound'.[72] But all ministers surely appreciated that without adequate 'necessity' for the transfer, they could be accused of promoting an interchange; and so it proved. The English militia MPs met to pass resolutions against interchange, while the emancipationists led by Canning and Fox attacked in parliament. Both sides refused to make the issue the loyalty of Irish Catholics, an unmentionable parliamentary subject. The most explicit statement came from the Irish lord chancellor, the rabidly 'Protestant' Redesdale, who in public letters to the Catholic Lord Fingall assailed the allegiance to Rome as ultimately traitorous.[73]

When interchange was at last introduced in 1811, long years of full-scale war made the difference. George III's views were the least problem; the king in 1804 and again in 1807 had been prepared to accept, albeit very reluctantly, Irish militia in England,[74] so that the Prince Regent in 1811 was not required to put up his usual conscientious opposition on his father's behalf. Of course, the Irish situation was inevitably part of the issue. Under the Duke of Richmond, lord lieutenant 1807–12, the 'Protestantism' of the Irish government intensified as it came under pressure from a powerful alliance of Catholic gentry and middle classes. No doubt it also mattered that the issue of interchange in 1811 was handled by 'Protestant' ministers, Richard Ryder at the home office and Lord Liverpool as secretary for war. But the key factor in breaking down opposition was the war situation and the priority given to the war over the Catholic question and over militia 'principles'. With an interchange it became possible to increase the British proportion of the Irish garrison while releasing the regulars there for overseas service. It also facilitated a redistribution of force within the British Isles, something desirable in 1811 as France turned towards Russia and the threat of invasion was lifted. Interchange

---

[72] Yorke to Lord Hardwicke, 11, 24 Feb., 26 Mar. 1804, Hardwicke MSS, BL Add. MS 35705, fos. 95–8, 131–2, 208–9.

[73] Lord Redesdale, *The Catholic Question: Correspondence Between Lord Redesdale and the Earl of Fingall* (Dublin, 1804). The debates on the Irish militia offer bill are in *PD* 1st ser. i. 1053–8, 1072–98, ii. 25–6, 40–67, 131–41, 149–65, 169–71, 251–3. The meeting of lord lieutenants and militia colonels is reported in ibid. 152. See also Lord Hardwicke to Yorke, 11 Apr. 1804, Hardwicke MSS, BL Add. MS 35705, fos. 226–9: 'I hope the militia volunteering will not produce much opposition in parliament. You cannot there state the advantage changing Irish militia regiments for others of a different description, but the argument of bringing the people of the two countries better acquainted with each other and thereby improving and completing the Union may fairly be urged.'

[74] Lord Hawkesbury to the Duke of Richmond, 1 Oct. 1807, Richmond MSS, NLI MS 70/1344.

was thus immensely valuable to Britain's strategic purpose at a stage of the war when Napoleon's growing involvement in eastern Europe directed increasing pressure against him in southern Europe.

At least two English militia colonels declared in the House of Commons that they would not let their personal convenience interfere with public benefit. Indeed, the interchange bill was preceded in the same session by legislation authorizing the army to take annual drafts from the militia, and the two measures together finally determined that the militia would exist primarily, in all but name, as an army reserve. While a meeting of colonels again made representations to the government, theirs was a much diminished opposition compared with 1804, signifying how much the concept of a militia had changed. The same priorities of national interest made it impossible for emancipationists to oppose interchange as a war measure. They were left to defend their cause by focusing on the issue of Catholic worship by Irish troops on British soil. This might have been expected to catch fire since the interchange bill coincided with the presentation of an impressive Catholic petition and a full-scale debate on emancipation. In the event, the ministers took safe refuge in the army's common sense; for years the commander-in-chief had required regiments in Ireland to allow soldiers to attend mass, and he now proposed to give the same general order in Britain. An order for the good discipline of the army issued annually under the authority of the commander-in-chief was a very different proposition from the clause that the emancipationists wanted in the act, which would have upheld the right of Catholics to exercise their religion under parliamentary guarantee. Appropriately, the debate over the militia interchange, an unobserved chapter in the history of the Catholic question, ended on the religious, not the military, aspect.[75]

The transfer of regiments both ways across the Irish Sea began almost immediately. In August 1811 orders went out to twenty-five British and fourteen Irish units; these comprised 11,202 and 8,956 rank and file.[76] In Ireland care was taken to avoid breaking up the British regiments into small detachments.[77] In England, where the presence of Irish soldiery would once have been unthinkable, the arrival of the Irish militia appears to have provoked little or no disorder in the areas where they were stationed. Their peaceableness at this late stage of the war, and perhaps

---

[75] For the debates on the interchange bill see *PD* 1st ser. xx. 130–4, 200–2, 292–6, 329–33, 365–7, 455–9, 643–5. The meeting of colonels on 27 May is mentioned ibid. 29. McAnally, *Irish Militia*, 245, cites *Freeman's Journal* for an account of a Catholic meeting in Dublin, 28 May, at which O'Connell called the bill a conspiracy 'to take away our native army from us'.

[76] Memorandum for the war office, 15 Aug. 1811, WO3/157/392–3; 'British militia regiments proceeding to Ireland', 'Proposed stations of militia regiments arriving from Ireland', Hope of Lufness MSS, SRO GD364/1/1214/15. Two further British regiments were sent before the year was out, and one Irish, bringing the totals up to about 13,500 and 9,300.

[77] 'Quarters of the army in Ireland', 25 Oct. 1811, Clinton MSS, NLI MS 10215.

the absence of civilian provocation, contrasts with the reputation of Irish troops in the 1790s when they were often blamed for unruly behaviour.[78] No doubt the difference owed much to the higher standards of discipline that a long war had inculcated in both officers and men, and to the ample provision of barracks within which those standards could be more effectively applied; Sir John Hope, on assuming the command in Ireland in 1812, found the militia 'considerably improved within these few years'.[79] What mattered even more was the judicious distribution of Irish militia among the large garrisons along the south coast of England and in East Anglia, places which by this time had literally become garrison towns. The stations of the fourteen regiments in 1811 make this quite clear—Ipswich, Colchester, Chelmsford, Chatham, Canterbury, Dover, Chichester, Portsmouth, Plymouth. The south and east remained the usual posts of the Irish militia. Two interesting exceptions occurred in 1812 when the Louth and Carlow regiments, the latter strongly Catholic, were in the manufacturing districts at the time of the Luddite disturbances. Along with the local militia employed in the same area, they showed the government's increasing confidence in the good order and discipline of the long-serving auxiliaries.[80]

The convolutions of the interchange issue serve to remind us that military service could be a politically charged subject, ranging far beyond patriotic platitudes. Whom it was safe to arm, and under what conditions, were questions which rarely permitted easy answers, whether they referred to a trained population, volunteer forces, or militias. Given thus, this was the reverse order of preference that took shape during the French wars. Compulsory training did not commend itself because armed force not formed into properly constituted corps was potentially uncontrollable. Volunteers, particularly under the hectic conditions of 1803–4, revealed the limited control possible if martial law was not applied, a problem magnified if officers also lacked social status and influence. Militia, in contrast, were under military discipline and further decivilianized by service away from their counties and long embodiments. They were also commanded by county grandees and gentry. Even the local militia was considered a great improvement on the volunteers as more recognizably a *military* and a *county* force. This preference for militia kept being asserted, as early as the formation of the Irish militia in 1793 and as late as the final dissolution of the infantry volunteers in March 1813 in order to provide arms for the Prussian uprising against the French.

[78] McAnally, *Irish Militia*, 247–8; Emsley, 'Military and Popular Disorder', 111.
[79] Hope to Alexander Hope, 16 Mar. 1812, Hope of Lufness MSS, SRO GD364/1/1222/5.
[80] For stations in 1811 see 'Proposed stations of militia regiments arriving from Ireland', ibid. 1214/15. Stations from Jan. 1812 are given in 'Statement of the different changes of quarters', 27 Apr. 1814, *CJ* lxix. 645–7.

The only full-length study of the local militia depicts it as a loyalist force established to counter growing opposition to the war and more fundamental sources of social unrest in the radicalism and urban disorder of the age. Unlike the volunteers, the authority of officers was now upheld by martial law. Loyalty was inculcated by means of oaths, sermons, and military ceremonies, and by upholding a code of proper conduct to the extent that the regiments were used as 'moral reformatories for the lower classes, a government-sponsored equivalent of the Society for Suppression of Vice and the Bible Society'.[81] However, while the local militia as superior to the volunteers in efficiency and discipline can be accepted, it is difficult to believe that it was such a specific response to ruling class concerns about popular opposition and increasing social conflict. If this were the case, the economies the government forced on the local militia from as early as 1810 become hard to understand. First, the number of permanent NCOs and training days were reduced, indicating the priority of retrenchment over efficiency; then in 1812 the establishment was cut by over a third and some other savings adopted; in 1814 training was suspended altogether. Nor was the local militia the particular object of pro-war, anti-radical endeavours. The volunteers bathed in the same culture of patriotism and likewise were exposed to the moral paternalism of their officers which, often through the rules and regulations of corps, emphasized the values of sobriety, regularity, civility, and obedience to authority. *Hints for the Economical and Internal Regulation of Volunteer Companies in Scotland* (1797), published by a volunteer colonel, wanted 'any act of IMPIETY, IMMORALITY, or DISLOYALTY' and 'any degree of TURBULENCE or DISOBEDIENCE' punished by the discharge of the offender.[82] The Birmingham volunteers on one famous local occasion acted to prevent a revival of the 'barbarous sport' of bull-baiting, marching out against the crowd and seizing the animal.[83]

In the last analysis, the local militia, like the volunteers, existed primarily as a home defence force, savaged therefore by the government once the French were diverted into eastern Europe and when the regiments turned out to be a disappointing source of recruits for the army. The view persisted after the 1790s that law and order were inadequately defended, but among the auxiliaries it was the yeomanry who had long commended themselves as additional police and whose continuation after the war was taken for granted. They, not the local militia, became

---

[81] Smith, 'Local Militia', 208–11.

[82] The author, Patrick Crichton, commanded a battalion of the 2nd regiment of Royal Edinburgh Volunteers. The Stirling volunteers included the quoted provision in their articles. Minute book of Loyal Stirling Volunteers, 1800–4, Central Region (Scotland) Archives, SC8/2/46. See also *A Friendly Address to the Volunteers of Great Britain* (Hitchin, 1803), Hitchin Volunteers MSS, Hertford RO. At Chelmsford fines were ordered for non-attendance at monthly church parades. A. B. Bamford, 'The Loyal Chelmsford Volunteers', *Essex Rev.* 36 (1927), 95–6.   [83] Hart, *Royal Warwickshire*, 32–3.

guardians of domestic order, the crown's choice made obvious in 1813 when they were offered peacetime subsidies while the local militia passed rapidly out of existence. And though most of the armed policing in the early nineteenth-century society was still done by regulars, the amount of service required of the yeomanry was not insignificant; in the year of greatest activity, 1842, eighty-four troops from eighteen different corps went on duty in fifteen counties for a total of 338 days.[84] This demand from the civil power reflected, in part, the smallness of the cavalry force the army kept in Britain—5,100 on average between 1817 and 1832[85]—but it also served to sustain the strength and efficiency of the yeomanry beyond what the patronage of county magnates would have accomplished by itself. Of all the civilian-based forces up to this time, the yeomanry was the first to maintain its vitality during a long period of peace. From the beginning Dundas worked towards this end, and Addington's government in 1802 and Liverpool's in 1815 made equally important decisions to carry an 'efficient' yeomanry establishment into the peace. 'Suppose,' wrote Dundas in 1797, 'we shall be able at all times to preserve in Great Britain a cavalry force . . . formed from men of property and substance living in the country and not infected with the poison of large towns, and this to an amount of not less than 20,000 men, I ask you if it is possible to figure such a bulwark of strength to the safety of the constitution of the country as would arise from such a circumstance.'[86]

So panegyrized, the yeomanry reminds us that the great mobilizations of the French wars occurred at the same time as a crisis of order affected British society in which authority grappled with political, religious, and Irish oppositions as well as with increasing crime and protest generated by distress. During the wars military force was freely available to augment other police resources, and, on the whole, even the non-regulars proved equal to the task if and when they were called upon. The comment is sometimes made that the early nineteenth-century society was policed much as the eighteenth-century society had been with law and order depending on a small number of local officials backed up occasionally by the intervention of the army. Yet such a view sits oddly with contemporary perceptions of rising disorder and with the decision to perpetuate the yeomanry. Perhaps Ireland sharpens our understanding of the British situation, for in Ireland the threat of social violence was deemed serious enough to require a yeomanry force of about 40,000, or half the wartime strength. An armed constabulary, which by the 1830s

---

[84] Beckett, *Amateur Military Tradition*, 141.

[85] Return of establishments and effectives, 1817–32, *SP* 1831–2, xxvii. 117–21. Though the cavalry force kept in Britain after 1815 was twice what it had been before the wars. See also Duke of York, 'Memorandum respecting the cavalry', 16 May 1814, WO25/3225.

[86] Dundas to the Duke of Buccleuch, 10 June 1797, Melville MSS, SRO GD51/1/887/1. See also his circular to the Scottish lord lieutenants, 14 May 1794, HO102/11, fos. 26–34, in which he refers to yeomanry cavalry as laying 'the foundation for some permanent system' of defence and police.

was over 7,000 strong, was also raised.[87] Britain differed only in degree. In both countries the government was prepared to increase its police resources as far as seemed necessary by retaining part of the wartime auxiliaries and by making use of ex-soldiers either to form bodies of armed police or to release regulars for police service. The up to 20,000 men of the British yeomanry were a formidable addition to the forces of law and order, bearing in mind that about 2,500 regular cavalry were all that had been previously available.[88] The militia staff, usually old army men like the Irish constabulary, were regarded as another resource.[89] The militia itself was called out for training on four occasions between 1820 and 1831 whenever there was a serious threat of popular disturbances. To these were added in times of emergency other bodies derived from the military; for example, in the Peterloo years veterans battalions, in 1843 corps of pensioners. Britain moved only slowly towards a large and coherent police organization, but during that time soldier-civilians, in continuation of what had happened during the French wars, were key defenders of public order.[90]

All this means that the sort of apprehensions the Addingtonians had of armed power getting into the wrong hands were, generally speaking, never justified. Military service more obviously produced civil officers and 'magistrates' men' than it did insurrectionists, again borne out in the number of ex-soldiers who joined the new constabularies.[91] Military pensions, as these were regularized during the war, required the holder to be at the government's disposal, exemplifying this idea of the soldier as public servitor. Dundas's consistent interest in compulsory training, taken up by Pitt as the *levée en masse* in 1803, showed a similar belief in the 'military spirit'. These two understood how national defence could channel powerful patriotic instincts and Francophobic passions, and they envisaged the organization of national defence under the 'natural leaders of society' breathing new life into the old hierarchical order. In the same way they saw military service as a prime means by which the marginalized élite and population of Catholic Ireland could be incorporated into a larger British system. At the time plenty were willing to believe that volunteering had effectively blocked the progress of 'Jacobinism', and it is true that the anti-invasion mobilizations of 1798–1805 were experienced as a massive show of national unity and strength, leaving no part of society

---

[87] Broeker, *Rural Disorder*, 215, for number of constables. For yeomanry strength see *SP* 1817, viii. 467; 1821, xix. 177–86; 1847–8, lvii. 547.

[88] In Jan. 1793 there were 2,644 cavalry in Great Britain. Return of effectives of British army 1793–1806, 17 Dec. 1806, WO1/903/33. For yeomanry strength see *SP* 1817, xiii. 225–7; 1847–8, xli. 87; 1850, xxxv. 127–39.

[89] For example, they were employed to enforce evictions at Culrain in Ross-shire in 1820. *Edinburgh Magazine*, vi (1820), 282–3.   [90] Mather, *Public Order*, chs. 4–5.

[91] C. Emsley, *Policing and its Context 1750–1870* (London, 1983), 64–5; Palmer, *Police and Protest*, 225–7, 253, 300, 302.

unaffected. National defence existed above political and religious differences, above Scottish self-consciousness, above radical opposition. It existed too in spite of significant localisms. The armed nation did create new anxieties about order, but it also strengthened the military contribution to order before a civil police was properly established and, even more important, at least at the level of 'high' politics, restored confidence in the means available to contain popular revolution.

8

Armed Nationalism

WAR and nationalism converged, it has often been said, in the era of the French revolution when first France and then France's adversaries discovered that organized mass resistance was the price of state survival. In the process both were transformed. Wars became struggles between peoples whose fighting spirit depended on appeals to save the *patrie* and the ideals and values it was said to enshrine. The idea of the nation was lifted out of the salons and universities and calculatedly refashioned into a popular creed. In Sir Michael Howard's schema for the history of European warfare, the 'wars of the nations' lasted until about 1870 by which time, with the increasing pace of industrial and technological development, manpower alone was no longer the basic military resource. The association of nationalism and war, however, only intensified as war economies were created and home populations remote from the front line were exposed to attack. Participation appeared to be a key factor in understanding the relationship between war and society. Only make the 'addition of mass' to war and governments and ruling groups would place a premium on obtaining the coherence and co-operation of the wartime society. Nationalism was the original answer to this problem, first posed during the wars of the revolutionary era for revolutionary and *ancien régimes* alike.[1]

Nationalism, according to this conventional overview, was an official ideology whose success was usually taken to need little further explanation. Such doctrines conformed to a Europe of fiercely competitive and frequently warring states. Revolutionary France showed the rest of Europe the power of such an ideology when the republic was carried to victory in 1793–4 against a formidable coalition of powers. Britain's volunteers evinced the same 'warlike spirit' and 'patriotic unanimity' when their country was threatened with attack. The revolts of Spain and Germany against Napoleon showed how nationalistic impulses lurked in even unprogressive societies and fragmented states. Nationalistic appeals simply manipulated the xenophobic passions and defensive instincts of populaces and directed these feelings into more effective national defence and military service that the state required.

Britain has never been understood as exceptional in this respect. Indeed, in her

---

[1] M. Howard, *War in European History* (London, 1976), 79–80, 86–7; Best, *War and Society in Revolutionary Europe*, 52–66. On the importance of participation see M. Howard, 'Total War in the Twentieth Century: Participation and Consensus in the Second World War', in B. Bond and I. Roy (eds.), *War and Society* (London, 1975), 216–25.

authoritative treatment of British national consciousness, Linda Colley sees the wars against the French republic and Napoleon as a key experience in the 'forging' of a British nation. Popular Francophobia, originally founded on Protestant and libertarian obsessions, and extended and deepened by a century of struggle with Bourbon France, now reached an unsurpassed intensity on several occasions of threatened invasion, most notably in 1803–5. During these crises the country, all classes, soaked in patriotic rhetoric. The wars as a whole produced public monuments, public ceremonial, military glamour—difference, spectacle, entertainment in a society where these were still largely limited to what people could provide for themselves. Colley's emphasis, however, is on actual participation in national defence by the huge numbers who responded to calls for voluntary service, whether armed or unarmed. When the parish returns were collated as county totals, no part of the country was shown to be reluctant or indifferent. In the return submitted to parliament in 1804, some 532,000 men were reported as already serving or offering service, with not all counties responding or sending complete information. Colley regards these war mobilizations as a momentous nation-forming experience, because so many were brought into actual *national* service. Where she most differs from the standard account of war and nationalism is in pointing to the meagreness of official patriotism alongside the contribution of the middle classes. But Colley's explanation still fits neatly into the general hypothesis that war became armed nationalism. War which engaged all parts of society, she may be paraphrased as saying, created a climate of national involvement never more favourable for the growth of national consciousness. Nationalism, in the sense of the exploitation and promotion of national consciousness for specific ends, also was the consequence of mass mobilization; for national defence that depended on the populace inevitably induced anxieties among the possessing classes, who just as inevitably produced the rhetoric of a whole society under attack.

However, such a generalized and uncomplicated account of war, national consciousness, and nationalism is a little too pat, if studies of revolutionary and Napoleonic France are any indication. For example, the revolutionary patriotism of 1793–4 has to be set against the great variation in the response of even loyal departments to the conscription decrees of the Paris government. And if the Jacobins at that time led a war of national defence to create an armed nationalism, it had precious little effect in containing resistance to conscription later on or in raising the country against invasion in 1814. Peasant France, in the poorer south at any rate, remained outside national politics until the 1840s, or so it has been claimed.[2]

In the case of Britain, recent work on the loyalism of the 1790s casts most doubt

---

[2] M. Bouloiseau, *The Jacobin Republic 1792–4* (Cambridge, 1983), 129; J.-P. Bertaud, *The Army of the French Revolution* (Princeton, 1988), 111–17; A. Forrest, *Conscripts and Deserters: The Army and French Society during the Revolution and Empire* (Oxford, 1989); R. Price, *A Social History of Nineteenth-Century France* (London, 1987), 182–6.

on the propositions that national threats produced a unitary response and that there was a regular chronological progression towards the 'made' nation. In 1792–3 loyalism was composite in the sense that it could incorporate Foxite opinion, moral reformers who were seeking an orderly and God-fearing society, and the middling and lower orders as well as the established leaders of local communities.[3] The intensity of the attack on radicals and radicalism also varied enormously across the country. By the spring of 1793, after barely six months, loyalism as a nation-wide mobilization of communities had faded out of existence. Moreover, the ubiquity of the public response while it lasted needs to be compared with the very limited spread of military volunteering before 1797.[4] Scottish loyalism and volunteering appear to have had a different relationship again, the latter expanding so strongly from 1794. The wave of loyalism that swept over the country in 1792–3 was succeeded by waves of national defence patriotism in 1798, 1801, and 1803–5. The episodic character of these mobilizations raises the question of whether there was any chronological development of the nationalism associated with them and its social impact or whether they remained essentially short-lived crises with no profound effects. One continuity that is accepted is the middle-class hand apparent in virtually all activity embracing loyalism, national defence, and monarchism, in which respect Britain differed strongly from France where the state from the time of the Revolution was foremost in instigating public events and conducting propaganda. Perhaps, though, the British state is worth a second look, for there are signs that Pitt's government wanted to go the French way in 1798–9.

Loyalism, now receiving increasing attention, threatens to obscure the importance of national defence patriotism.[5] Yet this patriotism was distinctive and, in many respects, far exceeded loyalism. The loyalism of Pitt's government was generally low-key, especially after the massive demonstration of loyalist opinion in 1792–3—repeated, it is often forgotten, at the end of 1795 when the king received over five hundred addresses congratulating him on his escape from assassination.[6] Pitt decided against censorship, did nothing towards creating a centralized police force, and took the chance of prosecuting radical leaders in the ordinary courts. Loyalists, however numerous, for most of the time in most places were unorganized, loyalism, at ground level, little more than a set of attitudes standing against the supposed miasma of radical ideas. This was nothing like the later war patriotism. National defence patriots had a visible adversary and an obvious threat to prepare against in the armed power of France. Commitment and service to the nation was

---

[3] Ginter, 'Loyalist Association Movement', was the first to indicate this pluralism.
[4] See above, 26.
[5] For example, Dickinson, 'Popular Loyalism', 524 simply fuses volunteering with loyalism.
[6] Cookson, *Friends of Peace*, 152. M. Philp (ed.), *The French Revolution and British Popular Politics* (Cambridge, 1991), 48, 64 n. 42, mentions only the public opinion mustered against anti-radical legislation also at the end of 1795. H. T. Dickinson points out that from 1789 there was a series of occasions which prompted a large number of addresses to the king, 'Popular Loyalism', 528–9.

personalized to a high degree through the oaths required of volunteers or the pledges given under the Defence Acts or the names attached to subscription and committee lists. And such patriotism possessed organizational strength, most obviously in the vast and much ramified system of national defence that was developed but also in numerous local committees often linked to volunteer corps or to a national fund. The Patriotic Fund, set up in 1802 and lasting for the duration of the war, was a powerful example of central direction combining with local effort.

Loyalism, essentially, had always been something projected onto the populace from above. National defence patriotism, particularly in the form of a mass volunteer movement, was clearly different, more popular and more dangerous in the wrong hands. For the sake of order and national defence, armed and organized civilians had to be made subservient to the authority of the crown and parliament and to act under the eye of the army and the county lieutenancies. More than this, national defence patriotism emphasized service (as patriotism in the age of total war would come to emphasize sacrifice as well). 'It is of much importance', said Dundas in an official circular, 'to extend, as widely as possible, that feeling of confidence that will naturally result from men of every description being placed in a situation to take, in their respective stations, an active part in the defence of the country.'[7] In 1798 Dundas's plan for national mobilization, the extension of volunteer service beyond the locality, and the collection of pennies from the poor in aid of the 'voluntary contribution' signified the impositions that the times demanded, even from the king's humblest subjects. Loyalism, in its appeal beyond the propertied classes towards the formation of a 'vulgar conservatism', had sought to persuade the lower orders; it had never sought to extract from them. It may be that the aim and effect of loyalism was never popular consent, merely popular compliance.[8] Patriotism, on the other hand, demanded action or a preparedness to act, an instrumental, as opposed to an expressive, participation more like the active loyalism that Reeves' Association had endeavoured to promote among the élite and the middle classes.

A second difficulty with emphasizing the continuity between loyalism and national defence patriotism follows on from this difference, and that is the broadly different popular rhetorics that each produced. Loyalism on the streets posed the opposition between 'French principles' and the order and justice and other 'blessings' of British society. This kind of discourse undoubtedly appealed to the middle classes who held deep fears of the 'mob' and 'levellers' and who took very seriously the alleged French attack on religious and family (including sexual) values.[9] But its

---

[7] Dundas to the lord lieutenants, 6 Apr. 1798, Essex RO, D/DHa 01/10.
[8] Philp, *French Revolution*, 16.
[9] The sexual theme in the Revolution debate deserves more emphasis. See, for example, Windham to Burke, 17 Jan. 1796, *Windham Papers*, ii. 3; T. Newman, *The Love of Our Country: A Sermon Preached Before the Volunteer Tendring Troop of Cavalry* (Colchester, 1799), 14; *PH* xxxiii. 1306–8.

influence on the lower classes was probably limited, mainly because it failed to address the realities of their existence—there were few, if any, 'blessings' in their insecurity, powerlessness, and economic deprivation.[10] Patriotic rhetoric, in contrast, was able to portray the threat of foreign invasion and conquest not only in highly graphic terms but also as a *personal* danger. We still await a study of the theme of atrocity in both the literature and propaganda of the war period. Reportage of the Revolution began the dehumanization of the French, while the crisis of 1798 saw these representations transferred onto the French soldiery, who hereafter were depicted as 'banditti', as a raping, murdering, plundering horde.[11] From 1801, after accounts of his alleged atrocities in the East were published, demonization of the enemy concentrated on the figure of Napoleon, which reached the level of almost hysterical invective during the 'great terror' of 1803–5.[12] Patriotic propaganda, therefore, intended to inspire national resistance against the invader, had no difficulty in linking national and personal survival. The importance it placed on national unity and the obligation of all to serve or assist their country is further seen in the broadsides, songs, and pamphlets addressed to groups perceived to be outside the main structures of society—Irish migrants, women, soldiers and sailors.[13] The sheer volume of published material in 1803 or 1804, far exceeding the production of loyalism in any year and which, it is fair to say, paid much greater attention to the lower classes, in itself indicates the strength of the drive for mass participation.[14]

[10] Philp, 'Vulgar Conservatism', 62–3.

[11] e.g. H. Goudemetz, *Historical Epochs of the French Revolution* (trans. F. Randolph, Bath, 1796); A. Aufrere, *A Warning to Britons Against French Perfidy and Cruelty* (London, 1798); Sir J. Dalrymple (and J. Gillray), *Consequences of the French Invasion* (London, 1798); Sir Sidney Smith, *Narrative of the Treachery and Inhumanity of the Renegade Bonaparte and the Defeat of His Army at Acre* (Bristol, 1800?).

[12] Sir Robert Wilson's exposures were particularly influential. See his *History of the British Expedition to Egypt* (London, 1802). Sir Sidney Smith also provided an account in his *Siege of Acre* (1801), as did J. P. Morier, *Memoir of a Campaign with the Ottoman Army in Egypt from February to July 1800* (London, 1801) and William Wittman, *Travels in Turkey, Asia Minor, Syria and Across the Desert into Egypt During the Years 1799, 1800 and 1801, in Company with the Turkish Army and the British Military Mission* (London, 1803). The most accessible collections of the anti-invasion propaganda of 1803–5 are Wheeler and Broadley, *Napoleon and the Invasion of England*, and F. J. Klingberg and S. B. Hustvedt *The Warning Drum: The British Home Front Faces Napoleon: Broadsides of 1803* (Berkeley, 1944). S. Cottrell's work offers the best analysis of this material.

[13] *Address to Irishmen Residing in England*; *Old England to Her Daughters: Address to the Females of Great Britain*; *The Sailor to His Messmates*; *Navy of Britain, Terror of Your Foes and Wonder of the World! Brave, Magnanimous Sailors!*; *A Dialogue Between a British Tar Just Landed at Portsmouth and a Brave Soldier Lately Returned From Egypt*; *Brave Soldiers, Defenders of Your Country!* in Klingberg and Hustvedt, *Warning Drum*, 76–9, 106–7, 115–17, 155–6, 160–2, 166–9. *An Address to the British Navy*; *To the Women of England* in Wheeler and Broadley, *Napoleon and the Invasion of England*, 275, 277.

[14] Philp, *French Revolution*, 8 n. 20 (counting printed songs). For the number of loyalist pamphlets see G. Claeys, 'The French Revolution Debate and British Political Thought', *Hist. of Polit. Thought*, 11 (1990), 59–80; G. T. Pendleton, 'Towards a Bibliography of the *Reflections* and *Rights of Man* Controversy', *Bull. Res. in Humanities*, 85 (1982), 65–103.

The government initiated the creation of a serving public in 1797 as it faced up to the possibility of a massive French attack with the end of the Franco-Austrian war. Cornwallis had already cited the examples of the Americans and the French to show the advantages of local civilian forces, and a plan for associations of householders in urban parishes was sent out in May. Such associations went well beyond the mainly expressive actions that had characterized the earlier loyalist movement; they were to be maintained as an armed force the magistrates could call upon, preferably properly trained and backed by a wider body of subscribers, including all or most householders. Too much can be read into the 'right' given women householders to recommend members—they were given it as householders, not women—but the provision did emphasize the point that communities were being mobilized and that within communities comprehensive alliances of the propertied were what was required.[15] For the moment, however, a patriotic public did not manifest itself; the proliferation of local corps and associations, outside Scotland anyway, remained only modest in 1797, mainly because the government continued to regard them as having only an indirect role in national defence. As we have seen, Dundas, early in 1798, decided to formulate a plan of national defence based on armed volunteers acting in any part of their military district under the command of the army and on unarmed civilians organized in their parishes to drive the country and assist the field forces. Here the focus was on the public service large numbers could render in resistance to foreign invasion, if necessary going outside their localities. Dundas's conception of national defence refuted the localized, élitist, and divisive character of the older loyalism. Even so, the government had to struggle hard for a time against the local service priorities of the volunteers, and in some places volunteering proved unable to mitigate the political animosities loyalism had engendered.[16] But, in general, national defence patriotism quickly superseded loyalism, plunging much deeper roots into civic and bourgeois cultures and blossoming into a popular consensus, temporary though it may have been, that embraced all classes. Loyalism from 1798 existed primarily within the party politics of the élite, directed against the whigs and their supporters in the spirit of the *Anti-Jacobin* and its successor, the *Anti-Jacobin Review*, started in July 1798.[17]

The national service Dundas devised took on patriotic values and ideas the more easily because it was preceded by a period of some months in which Pitt's government had tried, more openly and vigorously than ever before, to create a public

[15] *Annual Register*, 39 (1797), Chronicle, 237–8.

[16] e.g. Extract of letter from T. Bancroft of Bolton to the Duke of Portland, 3 May 1798, WO1/769/471–2. For the participation of anti-Pitt oppositions in volunteering see Cookson, *Friends of Peace*, 168–9.

[17] Ibid. 90, 100–2, 167–8. Pitt in Jan. 1798, uncharacteristically, wrote an anonymous article for the *Anti-Jacobin*. A. D. Harvey, *Collision of Empires: Britain in Three World Wars 1793–1945* (London, 1992), 16.

opinion in favour of the war. The collapse of peace negotiations in September 1797, the end of the Franco-Austrian war in October, and the decision to seek an enormous increase in war taxation perpetuated a 'cave' of opposition within the government's parliamentary ranks and produced ominous stirrings of popular dissatisfaction. Pitt's aim was to depoliticize the war, partly by pushing the Foxite whigs further into the isolation they had imposed on themselves by secession from parliament—hence the dismissals and prosecutions of 1798—but also by presenting the war as unavoidable, with the nation's greatness, and, if the French attempted invasion, its very survival, at stake.[18]

The public's responsiveness to this sort of appeal was first shown in the national thanksgiving for Camperdown and St Vincent in December 1797, which was a full rendition of the old navalist patriotism down to the sight of tars marching to St Pauls with their battle trophies; perhaps 200,000 people watched the spectacle.[19] Colley is mistaken in saying that the king instigated the event, though it is true that he had already proposed to visit the fleet at the Nore to lay the ghost of the mutinies.[20] On hearing the news of Camperdown, Grenville immediately wanted to exploit the victory by some public extravaganza, and he does not seem to have been the only minister who saw an opportunity to emulate the organized patriotism of the French state: 'if we had done in this war half that our enemies have done to raise the courage and zeal of their people, we should not now be where we are.'[21] Pitt went straight on to the 'voluntary contribution', his scheme though the idea in this instance originated outside the Cabinet. Originally intended to allow individuals to avoid assessment for certain taxes, the proposal was steered by Pitt towards public meetings at which the propertied would find it difficult to hold back from patriotic generosity; opposition to increased taxation was to be quelled by proving the existence of a large patriotic public prepared to accept the financial sacrifices that the war required. Pitt aimed to appeal to the wealthy classes particularly through county meetings; but it is interesting that he looked to the king and the City to give a lead, when their participation in the naval thanksgiving had been equally important.[22]

---

[18] For the manœuvrings of dissident Pittite MPs see *George III Corresp.* ii, pp. xxi–xxix; R. Mitchison, *Agricultural Sir John, the Life of Sir John Sinclair* (London, 1962), 167–76.

[19] Portland to the King, 24 Nov. 1797, *George III Corresp.* ii. 642, for the government's wish 'to have the business *well* done'. *The Times*, 20 Dec. 1797 has an account. For the sermon preached at St Paul's see Bishop of Lincoln, *A Sermon Preached at the Cathedral Church of St Paul, London, Before His Majesty and Both Houses of Parliament on Tuesday, December 19th 1797* (London, 1798).

[20] Col. Brownrigg to Sir Charles Grey, 24, 26 Oct., 1 Nov. 1797, Univ. of Durham Library, 1st Earl Grey MSS 1218–19, 1225.

[21] Grenville to Lord Spencer, 13 Oct. 1797, *Private Papers of George, 2nd Earl Spencer*, ed. J. S. Corbett (4 vols., London, 1913–24), ii. 196.

[22] Pitt to Lord Mornington, 26 Jan. 1798, Rosebery, *Life of Pitt*, 206–7; Pitt to Lord Camden, 8 Feb. 1798, Chatham MSS, PRO30/8/325, fos. 3–4.

Collected from February to May 1798, the 'voluntary contribution' dovetailed neatly with the huge expansion of volunteering and with the defence preparations that began in earnest after Dundas's Defence Act had passed in April. Though little noticed by historians, its importance for the development of national defence patriotism can scarcely be exaggerated; for it both laid down a rhetorical base and established the national subscription as a means of social mobilization and consensus-building extending to the lower orders. Pitt's conception of the 'contribution', therefore, was at once transcended; national defence patriotism in 1798 took over from loyalism the attempt to suppress popular politics by finding and displaying 'national unanimity'. 'Patriotism' in the sense of disinterested and even sacrificial service on behalf of the nation at war acquired this straightforward meaning and came into common usage mainly under the impetus of this movement. Most of the dominant themes associated with this kind of patriotism were quickly present: the suspension of party animosities; national unity; universal service; national survival; the demonization of the foreign enemy.[23] Such ideas were easily transferred into volunteering and the organization of national defence, which in activating local communities similarly came to depend on inclusiveness and solidarity. County meetings drove the 'contribution' down into the parishes and the unassessed lower orders, it apparently occurring to the gentry that numbers of subscribers could be made into an important statement of national resolve.[24] Of course, examples of the self-sacrifice of the poor were then suitably publicized. Chelmsford also made a point of distinguishing 'female contributions' when publishing its list. In Staffordshire the proprietor of the county paper collated all the parish lists into a book which recorded about 7,500 separate contributions.[25]

Important to remember is the subscriptions that followed the 'voluntary contribution' in quick succession: numerous local ones in support of the new volunteer corps; that launched in October after the Nile victory on behalf of the wounded and the dependants of the dead; and the 'naval pillar' subscription started in July 1799 to commemorate the naval triumphs of the war. Hereafter national subscriptions

[23] Good specimens of the rhetoric induced by the 'voluntary contribution' are found in R. Askew, 'Shropshire Patriotism in 1798', *Trans. Salop Arch. and Natural Hist. Soc.* 1 (1878), 260 n. 1; resolutions of Royston vestry meeting, *Cambridge Chronicle*, 17 Mar. 1798.

[24] Askew, 'Shropshire Patriotism', 260 n. 1; *Cambridge Chronicle*, 17 Feb. (lord lieutenant's address), 3 Mar. 1798 (Huntingdon meeting); D. G. Vaisey, 'The Pledge of Patriotism: Staffordshire and the Voluntary Contribution, 1798', in M. W. Greenslade (ed.), *Essays in Staffordshire History* (Stafford, 1970), 214–15. It must be said the meeting of London merchants and bankers on 9 Feb. commended the plan to 'all Bodies corporate', 'all the principal Cities and Towns', and to the 'Ministers and Church-wardens of every Parish'. *The Times*, 10 Feb. 1798. In 1794 the county gentry had shown interest in collecting defence subscriptions from a broader public. Eastwood, 'Patriotism', 158.

[25] 'Voluntary contributions in aid of government by the inhabitants of Chelmsford' (broadsheet), Essex RO, Library folder (military); Vaisey, 'Pledge of Patriotism', 216–17.

were definitely modelled on the 'voluntary contribution', going below the county to the individual parishes and collected as contributions to a national fund, well publicized as coming from every part of the country. In its inaugural declaration in July 1803 the Patriotic Fund wanted to join 'the mite of the labourer . . . with the munificent donation of the noble and wealthy' as 'the best pledge of our unanimity'.[26] The centrally organized, parochial-collected patriotic subscription has a virtually continuous history from 1798 until the famous 'Waterloo Fund' at the end of the war. Apart from producing the symbolic accord of communities and nation, the subscriptions were perhaps most effective in inducing a sense of patriotic participation among groups excluded from military service—like women, those too old, or those who could not be suitably accommodated according to their social status in the volunteers. The Waterloo Fund, the most successful of them all, raised nearly £500,000.[27]

The naval thanksgiving and Pitt's 'voluntary contribution' look even more like the beginning of state-initiated patriotic activity because Nelson's great victory at the Nile later the same year ushered in a period of celebration and thanksgiving in which the project for a naval monument stands out as obviously government-promoted; the subscribers were headed by royal dukes, the peerage, and the Cabinet, a veritable give-away of official interest. It was 'the first major attempt in Britain to raise a public monument commemorating national heroism by public subscription'. In the event, sufficient funds were never collected, though this did not deter proposals far more grandiose than the gigantic column originally contemplated—Major Cartwright's 'Hieronauticon' was designed as a massive 'temple', worthy, said its author, of being regarded as the eighth wonder of the world.[28] Failure ended any further semi-official enterprise of this kind until after the war; war monuments erected during the war belong in the provinces, where they were closely associated with the civic identities of new cities like Birmingham and Liverpool or with Scottish and Irish self-consciousness. Perhaps the 'naval pillar' fell victim to the unpopularity of Pitt's income tax, recently introduced. A deeper explanation is that it was compromised by its origins since patriotism had established itself, better than loyalism had ever done, as a creed above party. Certainly, its fate contrasts with the huge success of the City's subscription

---

[26] *The Times*, 21 July 1803. See also the resolution 'that all Sums, however small, which shall be offered by the Patriotism of the poorer Classes of our Fellow Subjects shall be accepted'.

[27] *Edinburgh Magazine*, iii (1818), 86–7.

[28] Very little is known about this project. See A. Yarrington, *The Commemoration of the Hero 1800–64: Monuments to the British Victors of the Napoleonic Wars* (New York, 1988), 57 n. 2, 338–45. There is an advertisement in *The Times*, 19 July 1799. In 1799 a play called *The Naval Pillar* was performed. Wilkie, 'The Set Scene', 18.

marking the battle of the Nile which preceded it by a few months, and which, no doubt, persuaded the ministers to try their own.

Furthermore, the end of the 'naval pillar' seems to have roughly coincided with the government's withdrawal from state-sponsored, public patriotic activity. Not only was London's adornment as an imperial capital postponed but the majority of important patriotic occasions—the great volunteer reviews of 1799, 1800, and 1803, peace and victory celebrations, the royal jubilee of 1809—continued to be set up by other hands. Indeed, the Garter ceremony in June 1805 and Nelson's funeral in January 1806 were the last great state occasions before the centennial of the Hanoverian succession and the visit of the victorious sovereigns in 1814. This inactivity is the more surprising in view of British awareness of the French state's use of architectural and ceremonial display which reached new heights of opulent splendour under Napoleon.

Any explanation of why this happened must take close account of the roles of the monarchy and the City, both of which can be said to have become major forces in patriotic image-making and mobilization from 1798. National subscriptions were invariably City-organized, institutionalized, we might say, during the Napoleonic War by the Patriotic Fund at Lloyd's which operated through a well-formed network of country members and local notables to activate the parishes. The 'voluntary contribution' effectively commenced in the City; and the Nile subscription under the leadership of J. J. Angerstein, the financier who began the Patriotic Fund in 1803, determined that the City would initiate and control all such efforts in the future.[29] Along with the monarchy, the City succeeded in attracting the attention of the nation and lifted patriotic display and endeavour out of a purely local context. The largest shows were in London and the most lavish, apparently drawing in people from some distance away.[30] As Colley has noted, the City's government after 1797 did not balk at producing and paying for increasingly elaborate 'festivals', which greatly relieved the pressure on the state to go 'the French way' and which may underlie its total disengagement from patriotic occasions after 1805.[31]

The king, for his part (and the royal family), took readily to public show and increased his participation as an important part of the process whereby the monarchy developed into the most potent symbol of national unity. Again the timing is suggestive. The king attended fifty-five command performances in London's

---

[29] *Cambridge Chronicle*, 13 Oct. 1798; Colley, 'Whose nation?' 110. Angerstein's patriotic activities receive no mention in his *DNB* entry.

[30] Colley, 'George III', 119 for John Carrington of Bramfield who journeyed all the way from Hertfordshire to see the volunteer review of October 1803. J. C. D. Clark, 'England's Ancien Regime as a Confessional State', *Albion*, 21 (1989), 457, cites the diary entry of a Yorkshire manufacturer on the thanksgiving day of 1797 which notes the celebrations in London.

[31] Colley, 'George III', 108–9.

theatres in 1797–1800, compared with twenty-two in the previous three years.[32] Royalty and the patriotic crowd never came together more frequently than in 1799 when George III attended four reviews of volunteers in and around London over eight weeks of the summer. The summer of the following year he reviewed the Hertfordshire corps at Hatfield and again met thousands of volunteers in Hyde Park on the occasion of his birthday.[33] It needs to be appreciated that this association with national defence served to separate the king from politics at a time of renewed contentions as Pitt's ascendancy faltered. Britain's military and diplomatic isolation from 1797—only temporarily relieved by the Second Coalition in 1799—was the first wound the administration could not manage to stanch. A second was the income tax which, for good reasons, was interpreted as favouring landed over commercial property, and around which a popular opposition to Pitt soon formed in the City. A third was a widely held and ever growing suspicion that Pitt was soft on Catholic emancipation which, with the horrors of the Irish rebellion, reawakened all the old Protestant prejudices of British society.[34] The propertied consensus that loyalism had provided could not be sustained in these conditions.

It also made sense to consider the common people as more disposed to royalism than loyalism because the latter required them to accept that they were beneficiaries of the existing order while the former rested on simple verities that the king was the traditional centre of government and the wielder of hallowed authority.[35] Both politicians and George III appear to have promoted the monarchy as the preeminent national symbol, the politicians, for example, countenancing heavy expenditure on the palaces and the king increasingly acting as the patron of national valour and achievement.[36] George III's 'apotheosis' is rightly dated back to the 1780s; but there are reasons for believing that the crises of war and political conflict after 1797 gave renewed impetus to royal image-building. Moreover, when this amount of exposure was reduced with the king's increasing infirmity, the large-scale renovation of Windsor Castle commenced, and Windsor became not only a magnificent royal residence but the place where the public now came to the king.[37]

Of course, whatever royal image-making there was, it mattered less than the

---

[32] K. B. Pry, *'Dread the Boist'rous Gale': Theatre in Wartime Britain 1793–1802* (Ann Arbor, n.d.), 69–71. George III also seems to have made a point in 1799 when he broke a three-year boycott of Drury Lane by going to see Sheridan's patriotic play *Pizarro*. By 1799 'God Save the King' was played before every theatrical performance. Pry 199.

[33] *Annual Register*, 41 (1799), Chronicle, 22–3, 24 (4 June, Hyde Park; 21 June, London; 4 July, Wimbledon Common; 1 Aug., Lord Romney's); 42 (1800), Chronicle, 17–18, 23, 25.

[34] Probably Pitt's anti-whig vehemence in 1798 also lost him more support than he gained.

[35] As a correspondent of Reeves' society pointed out. Philp, 'Vulgar Conservatism', 54. Pitt in 1795 told parliament that monarchical splendour counteracted radicalism. Colley, 'George III', 111.

[36] Ibid. 99–100, 108.

[37] Office of Works expenditure on Windsor totalled £13,500 in 1796–9, £20,900 in 1800–3, and £94,300 in 1804–7. H. M. Colvin, *The History of the King's Works* (6 vols., London, 1963–82), vi.

perceptions of the monarchy that George III's subjects entertained. Though there is no fully convincing explanation of how it happened, the king did become the primary symbol of an ancient, unified, glorious British nation, and such a symbol became particularly potent amid the stresses and uncertainties of war on top of the revival of popular politics and the challenge to the confessional state. Loyalism's 'king and constitution' patriotism was outdated after 1798 because the constitution now was subject to debate, especially where Anglican privilege was concerned. 'King and country', on the other hand, indicated the source of and was a declaration of unity, one which was to serve into the era of democracy and total war. 'God save the king', consecrated as the 'national anthem' in the 1800s, and the Union flag of 1801 emerged almost simultaneously as the chief emblematical references.[38]

The political control of 'king and country' patriotism, therefore, proved to be highly elusive. The City was better organized to run national subscriptions, and any the ministers initiated were either condemned as unconstitutional taxation (which had happened in 1794) or were compromised by their political origins; in 1798 some whigs publicly objected to the 'voluntary contribution' as blatant manipulation of the country's anxiety.[39] In the same way the naval thanksgiving of 1797 was condemned by an opposition paper, the *Morning Chronicle*, as a 'Frenchified farce' and Pitt on the day was reported to have been burnt in effigy at several places in London.[40] Even after Napoleon's aggressiveness in 1803 had largely depoliticized the war, there was no concerted attempt by ministers to turn patriotic feeling to their advantage. The crisis of 1803–5, when compared with events in France ten years before, was remarkable for how little the state did to bolster public morale outside actual preparation of the country's defences. Once again, it was the City through its Patriotic Fund that launched a national subscription. The City also issued the 'declaration of the merchants and bankers' which, adopted as a popular manifesto, was the nearest the British had to the famous revolutionary decree of the *patrie* in danger and the *levée en masse*.[41] As a spectacle Pitt's funeral in January 1806 was far outmatched by Nelson's, held the same month, so that the two events can be made to stand for the separation of politics from patriotism, at least in a public view.

658–9. J. J. Sack, *From Jacobite to Conservative: Reaction and Orthodoxy in Britain c. 1760–1832* (Cambridge, 1983), 112–45, thinks the cult of monarchy in late Hanoverian Britain was less significant or sustained than Colley has claimed, though he admits the strength of middle-class royalism during the war. See Harvey, *Collision of Empires*, 181–5 for some useful remarks.

[38] Colley, *Britons*, 209. See *Annual Register*, 43 (1801), Chronicle, 1–2 for the ceremonies surrounding the inauguration of the Union with Ireland on 1 Jan. 1801 in which the new Union flag was the most prominent symbol. [39] *PH* xxxi. 83–9; Cookson, *Friends of Peace*, 167–8.

[40] Colley, 'George III', 109–10, 126.

[41] *The Times*, 21 July 1803. For the merchants and bankers' declaration printed as a broadsheet see Klingberg and Hustvedt, *Warning Drum*, 126–8.

Whether the politicians dealt with the City on these matters, as Pitt surely did with the 'voluntary contribution' in 1798, would be interesting to know. Most probably the City acted alone.[42] In the 1800s there was ongoing conflict between the aldermen and a radical party in the livery, and later in the Common Council, differences which often revolved around national issues and loyalty to king and country. In claiming to be 'patriots', City radicals revived the old association of patriotism with opposition politics, in this case particularly criticism of the war and oligarchy. The patriotism of the aldermen, on the other hand, emphasized civic display, support of the war, and veneration of the monarchy.[43] At the time of the royal jubilee in October 1809, the issue between the two was over *how*, not whether, it should be observed, and London once more acted ahead of the rest of the country. In this instance, the government was scarcely in a position to give directions even if it had wanted to, torn apart as it was in September by Canning and Castlereagh's rivalry.[44]

If the state did little directly to develop a patriotic public, indirectly it did much to establish service as a pre-eminent patriotic value. Service, of course, in this context above all meant armed service. From this period dates the real beginning of enormous public interest in the armed forces; the army and navy's own achievements, together with the intense nationalism that the war generated, made them leading symbols of national power and success, and they came to epitomize loyalty and service in the special relationship they had with the monarchy, the source of authority and the fount of honour. These are difficult processes to trace, but one way of understanding them is to consider the system of rewards and honours that the crown operated with respect to the armed forces. The major change that occurred during the war was the recognition of meritorious service extended to lower ranking officers and even the rank and file, complementing the improvements made to their pay and pensions and to their status generally. In the navy, after Howe's victory in 1794, the practice was established of awarding gold medals

[42] Robert Wigram organized the merchants' declaration of loyalty to Pitt in 1795. Thorne, *House of Commons*, v. 554–6.

[43] e.g. a meeting of the livery on 29 June 1803 when resolutions against the income tax were carried but also at the close of business a resolution affirming support for the war. *Annual Register*, 45 (1803), 402. For City politics at this time see J. A. Hone, *For the Cause of Truth: Radicalism in London 1796–1821* (Oxford, 1982), 130–3, 150, 168, 179; J. R. Dinwiddy, '"The Patriotic Linen Draper": Robert Waithman and the Revival of Radicalism in the City of London 1795–1818', *Bull. Inst. Hist. Res.* 46 (1973), 72–94; H. T. Dickinson, 'Radical Culture', in C. Fox (ed.), *London—World City 1800–40* (New Haven, 1992), 209–24.

[44] Colley, 'George III', 112, says the Committee of Merchants and Bankers originated the idea of a jubilee celebration. *Examiner*, 1, 8 Oct. 1809, reports meetings of the Common Council on the matter. A Guildhall illumination and public dinner were voted at the first of these, but this decision was overturned subsequently in favour of a donation for the relief of debtors, such as the king himself made.

to the flag officers and captains involved in victorious fleet actions, while the masters, commanders, and first lieutenants were all promoted. Similar medals were awarded to field officers in the army from 1806. The Waterloo Medal, however, was the first official campaign medal, issued to all present at the battles of 16–18 June 1815, regardless of rank.[45]

The medals presented for the victory of Maida in 1806 and continued during the Peninsular War replaced a proposal of Pitt's government in 1805 for an entirely new order for the armed forces. This Naval and Military Order of Merit, as it was to be called, makes even clearer the interest being taken at the time in greatly increasing the number honoured for service by the crown, therefore to emphasize the crown's leadership of the armed forces; unlike the Order of the Bath, the number of knights was unlimited; officers of any rank could be admitted; medals were to be awarded to any below commissioned rank. By the time of Pitt's death in January 1806 and a change of administration, royal approval of the order had been obtained, the statutes had been drafted, its colour decided, and its insignia designed.[46]

It was, by its provenance, obviously a response to Trafalgar and also over-crowding of the Order of the Bath. But even more obviously it was a response to Napoleon's Legion of Honour which was similarly aimed at the armed forces and open in its membership and which had received much publicity when the first investiture was held with great ceremony at the Invalides in July 1804. Why the Order of Merit was never instituted, then, is a question of some consequence. Though there is no direct evidence, it would seem from views about such honours that were aired later in the century that the existing system of awarding naval medals was preferred as making the honour more exclusive and therefore more prized.[47] Perhaps the problem on reflection was that the proposed order was too imitative of the Legion of Honour in including *all ranks*, even if unlike the Legion the different grades of the order were reserved according to the naval or military rank of the recipient. Napoleon as warlord had to create a loyalty to himself in the army, and he therefore operated a system of reward which was generous and open to all and as personalized as possible.[48] In the British army loyalty to the crown was

---

[45] Lord Spencer to Jervis, 7 Mar. 1797, *Spencer Papers*, ii. 95; Spencer to the king, 4 Oct. 1798, *George III Corresp.* iii. 134–5; W. B. Rowbotham, 'The Flag Officer's and Captain's Gold Medal 1794–1815', *Mariner's Mirror*, 37 (1951), 260–81; L. Smurthwaite, 'Glory is Priceless! Awards to the British Army During the French Revolutionary and Napoleonic Wars', in A. Guy (ed.), *The Road to Waterloo*, 168–70, 171–2.

[46] Sir Isaac Heard to Pitt, 21 Nov. 1805, Chatham MSS, PRO30/8/144, fos. 7–8; Lord Hawkesbury to Pitt, 12, 14 Dec. 1805, ibid. 143, fos. 84–93; Heard to Lord Spencer, 9 June 1806, Liverpool MSS, BL Add. MS 38378, fos. 19–47. A proposal in 1797 for a 'Naval Order of Merit' is to be found in *Spencer Papers*, ii. 205–7.   [47] Guy, *Road to Waterloo*, 177; Strachan, *Wellington's Legacy*, 102.

[48] For Napoleon's honours system see J. A. Lynn, 'Toward an Army of Honour: The Moral Evolution of the French Army, 1789–1815', *French Historical Studies*, 16 (1989), 152–73.

expressed through the regiment, and, in return, the crown honoured regiments rather than individuals—the practice of granting battle honours began in 1802 after the Egyptian campaign.[49] In the last analysis, the failure to institute the Order of Merit seems to have accorded with the Duke of York's priorities—a dazzling officer class in the Continental style mattered less to him than having proud officers in proud regiments.

Even so, an honours system was established during the French wars which for the first time took in ship commanders and battalion officers. There were 124 recipients of the naval medal and 681 of the army medal, and these numbers exceeded by twelve times the number made Knights of the Bath, the crown's older mode of recognizing valour and success.[50] Furthermore, the traditional rewards themselves were distributed with increasing profligacy. Membership of the Order of the Bath, limited to thirty-five by the original statutes, rose to seventy-two with the removal of the limitation in 1812, and, as reorganized in 1815, the Third Class (Companions) at least, was open to as many as qualified. Set up thus, the Order continued to provide for the lower ranking officers as the war medals had done. By 1845 membership had climbed to 685.[51] Meanwhile, a significant number of generals and admirals were added to the peerage, part of a trend, increasingly under ministerial rather than royal control, by which the British nobility assumed more of the character of a service class. Half the peers created after 1801 went to the House of Lords as victorious military commanders or as distinguished diplomats, judges, and administrators, and, as has been well observed, most of them continued in their careers to remain prominent and influential. They were displayed to the rest of society as individuals who received the highest honours in the gift of the crown as a reward for outstanding achievement in public life.[52]

Not only, then, were honours for service spread more widely but the value of service was emphasized by the kind of honour that service could earn—here Wellington's dukedom said all. Service, in the late eighteenth-century application of the word to office-holding, gave an individual a 'public character' or, much the same thing, placed him in 'public life', which was usually made to imply some sacrifice of private pleasures and interests.[53] Furthermore, service in this sense was a gentleman's occupation, as parliament's thanks to the volunteers in 1814 made

[49] S. N. Milne, *The Standards and Colours of the Army from the Restoration* (Leeds, 1893), 140, 195.
[50] Rowbotham, 'Gold Medal', 280–1; Guy, *Road to Waterloo*, 169. There were 67 KBs created from 1793 to 1814. W. A. Shaw, *The Knights of England* (2 vols., London, 1906), i. 167–79.
[51] Guy, *Road to Waterloo*, 167–8, 170–1; J. C. Risk, *The History of the Order of the Bath* (London, 1972), 61. In 1845 there were 75 GCBs, 96 KCBs, and 514 CBs.
[52] M. W. McCahill, 'Peerage Creations and the Changing Character of the British Nobility, 1750–1830', *Eng. Hist. Rev.* 96 (1981), 259–84.
[53] See e.g. the obituary of Matthew Brackenbury, the commanding officer of the Ely Volunteers, *Cambridge Chronicle*, 11 Oct. 1806.

very clear; the officers were thanked for services to 'their King and Country' while
the rank and file in a separate resolution were thanked for 'their meritorious
conduct'.[54] It was equally clear that military service, as national service *par excellence*, ranked higher than other kinds since the highest levels of the state gave it
recognition and reward, up to the most lavish scale imaginable. At the same time,
the British state, until later in the nineteenth century, remained averse to the cult
of the hero.[55] Whatever the popular adulation of Nelson during the war or afterwards, a generation or more separates the great column in London's busiest thor-
oughfare from the comparatively obscure monument placed in the interior of St
Paul's not long after his burial. Indeed, the monuments to Nelson and other war
heroes in St Paul's were part of a considered attempt not to glorify individuals so
much as create a shrine dedicated to the state for the encouragement of patriotism
based on service. Public funds for this British pantheon were first voted in 1795,
but as the scheme developed over the next twenty years the emphasis came to be
placed on the recording of fame rather than on the artistic expression of fame
through magnificent individual monuments; eventually there were complaints that
two or three heroes were being commemorated by a single work.[56] As with the
honours system that arose out of the war, the St Paul's monuments look more
towards a service class than a nationalistic public.

All this needs to be set in the context of the numbers who accepted military or
naval office under the crown during a period of prolonged war. Patrick Colquhoun,
at the end of the war, estimated that there were almost 30,000 officers in the armed
forces if the militia were included—which does not seem wide of the mark.[57]
We could add to this total 16,000–18,000 volunteer officers or 8,000 local militia
officers, and also officers of the Irish yeomanry.[58] The peacetime strength of the
late eighteenth-century armed forces included about 6,000 army and navy officers.[59]
Such was the scale of military expansion after 1793 that Britain could be said to

---

[54] *CJ* lxix. 438.   [55] Colley, 'Whose Nation?', 105.

[56] Yarrington, *Commemoration of the Hero*, 61–7.

[57] P. Colquhoun, *A Treatise on the Wealth, Power and Resources of the British Empire* (repr. New
York, 1965), 127. A return dated 11 May 1814 gave 15,424 army officers, including those on half-pay.
To these would have to be added officers of the engineers and artillery, *CJ* lxix. 643–4. There were
3,908 British and Irish militia officers in 1808, ibid. lxiii. 623–4, 625. W. James, *The Naval History of
Great Britain* (6 vols., London, 1886), vi. 116 gives the number of naval officers, including masters, as
5,710 in 1814. But this figure, unlike Colquhoun's, excludes officers of the marines and ship's doctors
and pursers who also held the king's warrant.

[58] For the number of volunteer officers, 1804–8, see *CJ* lxiii. 617–18. For the local militia see Smith,
'Local Militia', 84. In 1817 the Irish yeomanry had 1,538 officers and 40,458 rank and file, so that its
complement of officers in wartime must have been around 2,500. *CJ* lxxii. 609.

[59] McGuffie, 'Significance of Military Rank', 214, counts 3,328 'regimental' officers on the Army
List of 1790. James, *Naval History*, i. 53, notes 2,442 naval officers in 1793.

have acquired an officer class similar in size and importance to those found in the more militarized societies of Continental Europe.

To regard volunteer officers as members of an officer class exaggerates, of course, the extent to which they divested themselves of their civilian origins. Yet it must be equally wrong to suggest that they were untouched by ideals of service and loyalty to the crown strongly upheld by the military. They were part of a military organization; they held the king's commission and wore the king's uniform; the army looked to them to make their units 'fit to serve in the line'; they exhibited military glamour in places that rarely, if ever, saw the sight of soldiers. All volunteers in 1803 were required to take an oath of allegiance to the king, and it is interesting how, in many cases, their officers arranged for this to be done with particular ceremony.[60] The royal reviews of the volunteers in London in 1799 and 1800 took place on the king's birthday; those of 1803 on or close to the anniversary of his accession. Almost everywhere corps paraded in public on one or other of these occasions. They also marched out to celebrate victories in the traditional military way, firing the spectacular rolling volleys of the *feu de joie*. Their service was ended in 1802, revived in 1803, and again ended in 1814 with parliament's vote of thanks, the same formal recognition and ultimate accolade bestowed by the state on victorious generals and their armies.[61] Volunteering may have begun at the level of mainly local concerns, but it soon was being built around national defence and the idea of public service.

National defence gave a public role and public authority to so many we have to accept it as making a major contribution towards that broad and broadening participation in public life that Paul Langford has described.[62] His eighteenth century disconcertingly ends in 1798, on the very eve of the great volunteer mobilization; but the overall picture is clear, one of increasing public enterprise, sometimes authorized by statute, sometimes not, which produced numerous public bodies which engaged a vast number of the propertied well below the status of the gentry who directed county affairs. Volunteer corps were similar to other voluntary bodies in that they were formed and conducted at the local level under the auspices of and usually by general accord of the propertied families. The yeomanry cavalry were officered by the county gentry and their associates. In the infantry the larger corps were commanded by hardly less respectable individuals, but the far more numerous small corps gave commissions to plenty below the rank of the minor

[60] On the fast day, 19 Oct. 1803, many London volunteer corps attended church and then paraded to have the oath of allegiance administered. See *Annual Register*, 45 (1803), 442–6. For a 'country' corps see H. J. Wilkins, *History of the Loyal Westbury Volunteer Corps 1803–14* (Bristol, 1918), 24–5.

[61] Wellington resisted the award of a Peninsular medal on the grounds that the army had been sufficiently rewarded through the thanks of parliament. Guy, *Road to Waterloo*, 177.

[62] See above, 50.

gentry down to the middling level of yeomen and tenant farmers in the country-side and the small tradesmen or shopkeepers in the towns. These belonged to the class which provided the petty officials of town and parish. To their betters in the volunteers they were 'plebeians' who frightened away the 'men of rank and property' who should have taken commissions.[63] The local militia, and even the 'old' militia, also frequently made officers of those who scarcely qualified as 'gentlemen'. At least two-thirds of the local militia officers transferred from the volunteers, so that the gentrification of the new force was very limited in spite of property qualifications and the best efforts of lord lieutenants and commanding officers.[64] Long embodiments and service away from their counties drove the gentry out of the other militia except for the field ranks. The lower commissions were increasingly taken by old army men or youngsters from 'middling' families seeking a way into the army.[65] The pattern is clear. Military expansion consigned large tracts of military office-holding into the hands of the classic components of the middle class—the non-landed, the modestly wealthy, those of uncertain gentility. 'Commissions', a memorandum on the volunteers intoned, 'have very generally been obtained by persons whose situation in life is not likely to secure the consideration and respect of those associated with them, and with whom men of rank and property are unwilling to be mixed.'[66] And this was in March 1803, before the gigantic and even more egalitarian volunteer movement of the Napoleonic War.

Military service was valued as a means of fixing status in a society where social distinctions were increasingly confused by urbanization and growing affluence.[67] The holder of military office held an appointment from the crown, wore the king's uniform to distinguish his position, and, as an officer, could lay claim to the title of gentleman. Even the urban gentry, rulers of their local universe, found satisfaction in the colonelcy or majority that might put them on the same level as the county

[63] For a description of the officers of various corps see Cookson, 'Sutton Volunteers', 47–8; Cookson, 'Ely Volunteers', 167–8; Berry, *Volunteer Infantry* 306–10 (Huddersfield); List of inhabitants, 'List of those Chelmsford Volunteers who marched to Braintree', Essex RO, L/U 3/8; Loyal Stirling Volunteers minute book, 5 Mar. 1800 and list of proposed officers in 1803, Central Region (Scotland) Archives, SC8/2/46. For plebeian officers see Smith, 'Local Militia', 52; H. C. Cardew-Rendle, 'Commissioned Officers of the Surrey Volunteers', *Notes & Queries*, 194 (1949), 544; 195 (1950), 101; Colley, 'Whose Nation?', 114.

[64] Smith, 'Local Militia', 51–126. By April 1810 6,587 volunteer officers, equal to two-thirds of the total establishment of 9,562, had transferred. *SP* 1810, xiii. 399–405.

[65] Charles Michell, *Principles of Legislation*, pp. 447–8, cited by Langford, *Public Life*, 300. Michell in 1796 said that the field officers of the militia 'often belong to the lowest class of independent gentry', that the captains were 'men of small fortunes, or relations and dependents of the colonel', and that the subalterns were 'sons of farmers and tradesmen, who are tempted by a red coat . . . and apparent equality with gentlemen'. Also Western, *English Militia*, 311 ff.; Smith, 'Local Militia', 65.

[66] Memorandum on volunteers, 18 Mar. 1803, WO1/407/541–2.

[67] P. J. Corfield, 'Class by Name and Number in Eighteenth-Century Britain', *History*, 72 (1987), 38–61.

gentry while confirming the consequence of their town in the wider world. The tremendous growth of the home forces and also the regular army during the wars opened opportunities to many in the burgeoning middle classes to whom military service offered a career or an avocation, patrons possibly, and social credentials. It was then, surely, rather than later, that they became the numerically dominant element in the officer corps of the army.

Middle-class interest in the military probably ought to be compared with the civilianism of the gentry. In England, though much less so in Scotland and Ireland, the gentry's pursuit of military patronage had always been checked by the smallness of the army, and in the late eighteenth century this effect may have been reinforced by rising land incomes which the wartime economy took to record levels. Few can have been deceived about the urban base of the volunteer movement of the 1790s when the town corps were generally the largest infantry corps and the most efficient and when the county lieutenancies had very limited practical control over any volunteers. In the crisis of 1803 the initial surge in volunteering outside Scotland was geographically specific, concentrated in the south and southeast; and the county élites became seriously involved only when threatened with a compulsory levy. Likewise, the agricultural counties had most trouble in finding officers for the local militia after 1808.[68] We need to know more about the English gentry's attitude to military service and military careers. Our present knowledge suggests that their relative unenthusiasm for either made it possible for the middle classes to be the main beneficiaries of the proliferation of military office during the war. And middle-class men, having won more like their fair share of army commissions, the 'officer and gentleman' of middle-class origins typified the officer class of the post-Waterloo period.[69]

The appetite of the middle classes for military office—one volunteer commander wrote of 'plebeians who look up to volunteer rank with as much eagerness as I look down upon it'[70]—presents the armed nation as the product of social forces that go well beyond what the state by itself could contrive. Linda Colley has rightly insisted on the amount of patriotic initiative that existed outside the ruling élite, especially among '*nouveau riche* and bourgeois elements' who used patriotism to advance and secure their status by acting as public servitors and social leaders.[71] Such activity was not confined to military participation but extended to public celebrations, charities for soldiers and seamen, patronage of the arts, monument

---

[68] According to the return of volunteer corps dated 9 Dec. 1803, *SP* 1803, xi, about 75 per cent of the English infantry raised under the 'June allowances' (i.e. before Aug. 1803) were drawn from the coastal counties from Cornwall to Essex and the metropolis. The cavalry were more evenly spread, with about one-third of the total strength coming from these areas. For the local militia see Smith, 'Local Militia', 75–91.   [69] Strachan, *Wellington's Legacy*, 110.
[70] Cardew-Rendle, 'Commissioned Officers', 101.   [71] Colley, 'Whose Nation?', 109–11.

building, and the issue of medals. If the commercial exploitation of patriotism had received the attention it deserves, we should no doubt have an even stronger impression of patriotism as something that largely occurred regardless of Britain's rulers. The latest work on the loyalist movement of 1792–3 subordinates it to middle-class concerns to a surprising degree. What at John Reeves' initiative started out as an attempt to invigorate the local magistracies against popular radicalism found more of a response among those immediately below local rulers in the social structure—lesser clergymen, tradesmen and merchants, small rentiers. Such people in corresponding with Reeves' Association wished to be identified as propertied, intelligent, and responsible members of the community worthy of acting alongside persons of rank and quality, and they therefore separated themselves from the lower orders whose gullibility and envy of their betters, they said, made them the part of society most vulnerable to radical ideas. Under this influence the Association came to develop an impressive propaganda effort which carefully distinguished between the two different audiences being addressed; on the one hand, the 'middling, responsible and reasoning orders'; on the other, the 'vulgar'.[72]

Volunteer patriotism could be similarly assertive of status against the élite and yet conservative about social order. Many corps remained fiercely independent of the county lieutenancies, resisting amalgamation, ceding only a *pro forma* control of appointments and promotions, and generally managing their own affairs by dealing directly with the home secretary and the secretary at war. These attitudes tended to be most pronounced among urban corps, which even in quite small towns became important items of urban identity and equally important vehicles for middle-class pretensions; the West Riding towns, for example, organized their own 'military festivals' in 1795–6; Chichester and Lewes fought strenuously and successfully against the Duke of Richmond's desire to have all Sussex units in 'ordinary soldier's cloth'. While the local militia restored much of the control over county forces the lord lieutenant had lost to the volunteers, it proved impossible to exclude non-gentry officers with any rigour, initially because the transfer of volunteers was a way of filling the county quota with already trained men and experienced officers, later because sufficient officers could be found, especially for the lower commissions, only by broadening or ignoring the property qualifications.[73]

On the other hand, volunteer officers faced their rank and file with only the authority their social position and personal qualities gave them, little enough at times. There was a vast problem of military order in the volunteers because officers could not automatically expect respect for their rank but had to build it themselves.

---

[72] Philp, 'Vulgar Conservatism', 51–5.
[73] Cookson, 'Volunteer Movement', 872–8; Smith, 'Local Militia', 43–91. For the Sussex example see A. Hudson, 'Volunteer Soldiers in Sussex During the Revolutionary and Napoleonic Wars, 1793–1815', *Sussex Arch. Coll.* 122 (1984), 179.

One reason for the oath to the king in 1803 was that it bound men in the most solemn way possible and took advantage of the monarchism of the lower orders; in swearing to serve the king, volunteers were reminded that those who commanded them held the king's commission and that obedience to them represented more than deference to social superiors or the loyalty of members to the associated body.[74] In 1803, too, the king's medal was to be offered to the best marksman in each volunteer company.[75] But officers mostly tried, if they tried at all, to create a loyalty to themselves by posing as the leaders of a fraternity of arms; this allowed them the advantages of rank and authority but also required them to benefit those over whom these were exercised. Much of the expense of corps was borne by officers who, if they did not put their pay to the common fund, usually laid out considerably more for the sake of the 'comfort' and 'respectable' appearance of their corps. The Edinburgh artillery volunteers formed a 'stock purse' for the purpose of 'obtaining better, handsomer and more comfortable clothing' and for supporting the privates' families in the event of hardship.[76] Quite small corps were capable of expressing their comradeship of arms by a distribution of tokens or medals.[77] 'The ruling principle' of volunteering, said Patrick Crichton, a former army officer turned Edinburgh merchant and volunteer, was 'to extend every act of brotherly affection to one another, and to render their present association a bond of future amity':

Another advantage, which it is impossible to define or appreciate, will certainly result from such associations formed on the principles of loyalty and patriotism; a greater degree of intercourse among the various ranks of life; confidence, esteem and friendship among all who are cordially engaged in one common cause and who are brethren in arms, how different soever their possessions or stations in life may be. Such sentiments and such

---

[74] The Defence Act of 1803 introduced the oath of allegiance (43 Geo. III, c. 96, s. 58). Previously, volunteers had assented to articles of enrolment, accepting the rules of the corps and the authority given to officers. On oath-taking in the 18th cent. see Langford, *Public Life*, 99–114; Eastwood, 'Patriotism', 161.

[75] 'Memorandum in regard to arming, training and other measures', 25 July 1803, WO1/625/547–51.

[76] *Edinburgh Evening Courant*, 8 May 1797. In nine months (June 1803–Mar. 1804) the two Walmer companies were over £200 in debt, which the captains agreed to clear. They had already subscribed their pay. For these accounts see Liverpool MSS, BL Add. MS 38358, fos. 85–97. The Edinburgh and Midlothian volunteers all seem to have pooled the officers' pay. See Duke of Buccleuch to Duke of Portland, 4 Feb. 1798, Melville MSS, SRO GD51/1/905/2. The commanding officer of a Cambridge-shire battalion sought funds for the 'furnishing of music and other necessary accoutrements', explaining that his was a corps of labourers, with farmers as officers, and that therefore he alone had met expenses beyond the government grants. John Wylde to Lord Hardwicke, 6 Jan. 1807, Hardwicke MSS, BL Add. MS 35676, fos. 1–2.

[77] R. J. Wyatt, 'Suffolk Volunteers at Worlingworth 1798–1802', *J. Soc for Army Hist. Res.* 61 (1983), 94–5. Wheeler and Broadley, *Napoleon and the Invasion of England*, ii. 327–36, also provide information.

connections must be gratifying as well as useful even to the rich and great, while to the less affluent and happy they will ensure comforts the most solid and permanent.[78]

Crichton was addressing officers or prospective officers. Songs specially composed for volunteer corps (at the behest and according to the taste of officers) were similarly emphatic about the fraternity of volunteers and their united resolution to defend king and country:

> From high Dunedin's towers we come,
> A band of brothers true.
>
> May we prove in valour *equals*
> Whatsoever our degree,
> *We will* shew the Gallic tyrant
> That we're 'Loyal, Brave and Free.'
>
> Tho' not alike in shape or size, our sentiments
> agree, Sirs,
> And should Frenchmen doubt our patriot zeal, e'en
> let them come and see, Sirs.[79]

There is irony in the close correspondence between *fraternité* in revolutionary France and patriotism in old regime Britain. Though British volunteers rarely called themselves 'citizens', they were, as songs show, readily comprehended as 'men', 'freemen', 'Britons', or 'Christians'—'men' defending hearth and home, 'freemen' defending their liberties, 'Britons' defending their native land, 'Christians' defending religion. These, like 'citizens' in the French revolutionary context, were all-inclusive categories. Pamphlets, sermons, and broadsides would multiply these examples many times.[80]

In presenting their corps as 'patriot bands', officers were no doubt most conscious of the need to avoid disputes of precedence and authority among themselves, easy to spark off in a situation where voluntary association was combined with military subordination.[81] Patriotic fraternity, however, could also be made to have democratic implications in that it stressed the universal obligation and common

---

[78] *Hints for the Economical and Internal Regulation of Volunteer Companies in Scotland* (Edinburgh, 1797). For Crichton see officers of Royal Edinburgh Volunteers to lord provost of Edinburgh, 9 Dec. 1795, Melville MSS, NLS MS 1049, fos. 58–9.

[79] Wheeler and Broadley, *Napoleon and the Invasion of England*, ii. 246, 299–300; 'Pro Rege, Lege, Grege' for the St Martin's Volunteers, London, *Cambridge Chronicle*, 25 Aug. 1798.

[80] Another good example of volunteer fraternity is Sir George Cayley's farewell address to the Pickering Lyth infantry in 1808. M. Ashcroft, *To Escape the Monster's Clutches: Notes and Documents Illustrating the Preparations in North Yorkshire to Repel Invasion* (Northallerton, 1977), 92–3.

[81] *A Friendly Address to the Volunteers of Great Britain*, 10, declaimed that 'the *genuine British Volunteer* . . . will never endeavour to raise discontents, or to excite cabals concerning the unimportant and trifling detail of his cloathing and accoutrements, or his personal situation in the corps. He will rely on the judgment and impartiality of those who have been appointed to the arduous task of commanding.'

interests inherent in national defence. Some radicals, most consistently Major Cartwright, were very ready to draw the connection between military citizenship and political rights; freemen called on to fight for their country were the more effective national defenders if their representation was also at stake—what Cartwright called the coincidence of the 'military and political energies of the constitution'.[82] But no volunteers took up this argument in an attempt to extract political concessions by using the threat of their military power. The fact was that insurrectionary radicals, when they tried to subvert the armed forces, preferred to turn to the army; while the constitutionalists concluded that, if the choice had to be made, military order and defence of the nation mattered more than their politics—'the national independence must be supported', said Wyvill.[83] It was Roman Catholics wanting to hold military office and Catholic religious observance in the army who did most to advance civil rights out of the military exigencies of the state. Catholics came to make much of the military service they rendered; radicals did not.[84] Volunteering's social doctrine remained a generalized appeal to British freemen to act in defence of king and country under established social leaders without regard for political or religious differences. Volunteer fraternity, moreover, was superficially egalitarian, as shown by the interest excited when a gentleman served in the ranks; it really meant respect in the military situation for the same reciprocities that eased tensions in the social hierarchy, the subordination of the lower orders being returned by paternalistic concern and protection on the part of their superiors. Fraternity in its British context, it is worth adding, sought co-operation across the social structure rather than across territories, signifying the lesser intensity of regional particularisms in the British state.

Apart from this social conservatism, the insecurity about rank and authority also articulated by volunteer patriotism gives it a middle-class feel. The *parvenu* volunteer officer coping ineffectually with a bumbling rank and file was made into a common figure of fun, but, like all good satire, the humour related to concerns and issues of the time and invited the audience to recognize themselves.[85] Warnings against ostentation in place of efficiency also featured in the pamphlets of advice

[82] N. Churgin, *Major John Cartwright: A Study in Radical Parliamentary Reform, 1774–1824* (New York, 1963), 242–9; Cartwright's requisition for meeting of Middlesex freeholders, 25 Jan. 1806, Holland House MSS, BL, Add. MS 51468, fo. 93. His most involved work on military reform in relation to political reform was *England's Aegis; or the Military Energies of the Constitution*, published in 1804 and again in 1806.

[83] Wyvill to General Hale, 10 Apr. 1798, Wyvill MSS, North Yorkshire RO, 7/2/119/13. The most famous radical discussion of this issue, interrupted by the arrival of arresting officers, took place in the London Corresponding Society in April 1798. See *Selections from the Papers of the London Corresponding Society 1792–1799*, ed. M. Thale (Cambridge, 1983), 429–35.

[84] See above, 175. Ashcroft, *To Escape the Monster's Clutches*, 52, mentions the concerns of Catholic gentry in the North Riding in 1796 and 1798.

[85] Colley, *Britons*, 283–4; [T. Harris], *The Coggeshall Volunteers* (1803).

addressed to officers. *A Letter to the Volunteers* (1803), almost certainly written by an army officer, followed this theme, and ventured into another area of middle-class sensitivity by pointing out how socially exclusive corps, privileged with respect to militia ballots, would alienate the 'poorer class'.[86] As we have seen, volunteering was envisaged as an instrument of social order because it was believed that the comradeship of corps offered opportunities of strengthening relations between the classes. This comradely ideal, together with the amounts raised in support of volunteers and, in some cases, the charity promised to volunteers and their families, is suggestive of the anxiety felt by the middling ranks as urbanization and other social changes threatened to produce ungovernable communities. This is further suggested by the rules drawn up for volunteer corps that extended to behaviour away from the corps, commending sobriety, piety, and other virtues. A soldierlike obedience to authority, sense of duty, neatness of person, and loyalty beyond self were implicitly upheld for civilian life because the volunteer was seen as belonging to both worlds. One tract, printed at Hitchin in 1803 and presumably circulated to the Hitchin volunteers, presented the 'patriot soldier' virtually as a moral exemplar; the articles of the same corps required proceedings to be taken against any member 'whether on duty or not . . . guilty of any misconduct affecting his character or reputation'.[87] What was transferred into the volunteers, especially in the more proletarianized movement of the 1800s, was gnawing apprehensions about social order held by middling people, but different from 1792–3 in that the problem of control was more directly theirs and more of a test, therefore, of their social authority.

In the event, volunteer casualness and irregularity were never suppressed to anyone's satisfaction, a major reason why a local militia acting under army discipline became an attractive alternative. The failure of the volunteer system was complex, comprising high politics as well as local circumstances; but it does include rank and file attitudes to service which can be depicted as self-interested yet patriotic, much as their officers were conscious of the status rewards of service while wishing to show their loyalty and contribute to the nation's defence. If we believed the counter-invasion propaganda directed at the lower orders, we could imagine a populace fired up by nationalistic and Francophobic emotions, the latter rather more than the former. Unfortunately the documentary record yields few comments on the war made directly by people of this status; of those who are given voice, those who cursed the king and the war are more likely to be there, the very

---

[86] Klingberg and Hustvedt, *Warning Drum*, 38–47.

[87] See above, 205; *A Friendly Address to the Volunteers of Great Britain* (1803), Herts RO, Hitchen Volunteers, Box 4. The articles of enrolment are found in Box 1 of the same collection. See also the rules of the Frampton Volunteers, Whiting, 17–18.

act bringing them into notice.[88] Still, at times of threatened invasion no serious opposition to the organization of national defence was reported; and the numbers joining the volunteers or crowds on patriotic occasions make it fair to assume that the common people were seized by the same spirit of national resistance as the propertied classes.

What was different about the national defence patriotism of the lower orders was the calculative, opportunistic attitude that was taken towards service by individuals and the collective opposition offered when service was believed to threaten general interests. Service, in other words, was overtly conditional. Volunteer commanders, especially in Scotland where wage levels were significantly lower, maintained that it was the pay that kept working men in their corps. In many cases this counted as additional income thanks to the co-operation of employers or careful fixing of the hours of drill.[89] The rank and file seem to have been very successful in propagating the view that they would not serve unless they were adequately compensated. At Whitby men were paid for parades cancelled because of the weather. At Mortlake in Surrey:

Captain King produced to the Committee an account for 12 1s. 1d., sums claimed by some members of the Corps for loss of time from their occupations through attending drills from 6th October to the 25th November then last, which sums were ordered to be paid, although exceeding the rate of charge originally intended to be given or allowed, and he was requested to inform those who demanded allowances that if drill did not begin until after seven p.m. nothing would be allowed, but when drill on field days interfered with working hours remuneration, if demanded, would be given for one hour more than the time they were actually detained on service.[90]

Nor was volunteering allowed to interfere with the mobility of labour as men searched for employment according to their needs. The Duke of Buccleuch described the corps of Edinburgh and the surrounding area as in 'constant change', which, he explained, 'must always be the case in corps formed as they are, of apprentices, masons, carpenters and other young artificers who come to Edinburgh to improve themselves, and after a time return to the country or go south for further improvement in their trades'. In 1806 these units were said to lose at least 15 per cent of their strength each year. A comparable attrition rate occurred in the Isle of Ely, where there was a highly mobile rural proletariat. Fyvie in Aberdeenshire, with a population of 'farm servants who are so very fluctuating that the half

---

[88] *Leeds Mercury*, 7 Oct. 1809; Colley, *Britons*, 308; R. Glen, *Urban Workers in the Early Industrial Revolution* (London, 1984), 136. [89] For Scotland see above, 142–3.

[90] Ashcroft, *To Escape the Monster's Clutches*, 158; Anderson, *Mortlake Volunteers*, 14. See also Ralph Creyke's comment in Ashcroft, 73: 'the price of labour in this thinly inhabited district is so very high that a moderate subscription will not induce men to give up their time and prepare themselves for service.'

of the corps might happen to leave the parish at the first term' existed alongside Monquhitter 'where they can easily get a company of tradesmen residing within the village who are perfectly stationary'.[91] Once exemption from the militia was granted to volunteers in 1799, it was soon apparent how a ballot produced an inflow and then an outflow of men. Much of the volunteer expansion in 1803 must have been built on the fears that three ballots in quick succession induced, and the figures clearly show that the subsequent decline was arrested only when another general ballot occurred in 1807.[92] Volunteering in these terms was something lightly superimposed on the world of the poor, accepted for the material benefits it provided but disposable whenever service offered lower returns—as when a ballot was not in prospect—or interfered with the means of securing a livelihood and other important concerns.

The refuge from ballots that the volunteers provided helped to ensure that the Napoleonic War, though the period of greatest mobilization, was remarkably free of militia disorders. However, on plenty of occasions the volunteer service itself was found irksome and exploitive, and the rank and file mutinied or made representations in collective defence of their interests and 'rights'. Most of these conflicts boiled down to differences between the military values and behaviour volunteering upheld and a popular culture that included deep apprehensions of the army: the army, according to these folk beliefs, took men away for ever, made slaves of them, and left them to rot and die in far-off places. Volunteers at Iver in Buckinghamshire would not take the oath because they feared that it was the same oath taken by recruits on enlistment. Likewise, men refused to sign anything in one Cambridgeshire parish, this being associated with the attestations that recruits signed; the 'form of articles' of enrolment recommended for volunteers in 1803 and sent around the county specifically promised that the men would never be drafted into the army or militia.[93] When volunteer corps began short periods of

---

[91] Duke of Buccleuch to Duke of Portland, 4 Feb. 1798, Melville MSS, SRO GD51/1/905/2; C. Hope to Lord Cathcart, 27 Sept. 1806, Melville MSS, SRO GD51/1/986; Cookson, 'Ely Volunteers', 173–4; J. Hay to J. Forbes, 16 Oct. 1803, Gordon MSS, SRO GD44/47/36.

[92] Memorandum on volunteers, Jan. 1801, WO1/407/609–12; Fortescue, *County Lieutenancies*, 198. In 1803 an act passed on 11 Aug. clarified the point that volunteers were exempt from militia ballots and Army of Reserve ballots. 'Progress of measures respecting volunteers', n.d., WO1/407/521–31. Volunteer numbers stabilized at around 295,000 in 1807–8, having been 342,000 in Jan. 1804. *CJ* lxiii. 617–18. Perhaps the numbers present at inspections and absent without leave show the effect of the militia ballot to better advantage. In the Western district from July to Nov. 1807 numbers present increased from 21,128 to 23,870 and the total absent without leave almost halved, down to 2,248 from 4,008. General returns, Nugent MSS, National Army Museum, 6807/178.

[93] Beckett, *Amateur Military Tradition*, 102; J. Harvey to Lord Hardwicke, 14 May 1798, Hardwicke MSS, BL Add. MS 35670, fos. 53–5; 'Form of articles to be entered by all those who enroll themselves as volunteers', Cambridge RO, Ely and South Witchford Subdivision MSS, Box 2. Cambridgeshire doubted that it could fill its quota of volunteers 'unless they are *publickly* assured that they will not belong to any regiment'. B. Keene to Charles Yorke, 11 Sept. [1803], HO50/62.

'permanent duty' for training purposes, there was an equal suspicion of service outside the locality. Two 'village companies' near Cambridge refused to march in May 1804 and had to be disbanded.[94] Opposition occurred either because men feared that they were being enticed into the army or because they feared loss of earnings and employment. In these collective protests volunteering linked up with popular conceptions of social justice and acceptable practice, including the obligations of the rich and powerful towards the lower orders.

An incident involving the Sutton company of the Ely battalion can be made into a classic example of the tension between the military citizenship upheld by volunteer officers and popular attitudes and values. When the commanding officer detected drinking in the ranks and collared an offender, he was defied by about twenty men who left the line, jeering him and firing their muskets in the air. Later at a court of inquiry the ringleader claimed that the provision of drink was 'customary' on field days and the other culprits said that they did not know that the lieutenant-colonel could give them orders over the head of their company officers. By their indiscipline the men had offended the patriotic sensibilities and service ideals, and status concerns, of a local notable turned volunteer commander. The men, for their part, had been offended by the refusal to allow them to drink while doing hard work and by the dictatorial and high-handed behaviour of one of the 'quality'.[95] In any number of lesser and less publicized episodes, the same conflicts must have been imminent. The resistance of the lower orders to their militarization is further borne out in the poor contribution of the volunteers to the recruitment of the army; the pay lists of the Ely regiment, 1803–8, record a mere thirty-five out of 1,142 men joining the army or militia; perhaps no more than six enlisted from the Leeds volunteers.[96] The volunteer movement surely represented an armed populace, but its character and ethos, thanks mainly to the rank and file, remained definitely, and often defiantly, civilian.

During the war the belief persisted that volunteering had converted the populace from 'sedition' to 'loyalty' until they 'actually fancied themselves the great supporters of government and the constitution'.[97] Colley takes up this view in presenting

---

[94] J. Barker to [B. Keene], 10 May 1804, Captain Hall to [Keene], 19 May 1804 HO50/97. Fortescue, *County Lieutenancies*, 109–10 has further examples.

[95] Cookson, 'Sutton Volunteers'. For the poor's sense of personal worth and dignity see also J. A. Phillips, 'The Social Calculus: Deference and Defiance in Later Georgian England', *Albion*, 21 (1989), 446–7 and Glen, *Urban Workers*, 123, citing an anonymous pamphlet of 1792, *A Rod For the Burkeites*.

[96] The Ely pay lists are in WO13/4207, pts. 3–5. The number enlisting in the army and militia increased as time went on: nil in 1804, 2 in 1805, 3 in 1806, 11 in 1807, 19 in 1808. For Leeds see N. J. Arch, '"A Mark of Esteem for their Beloved Commander": Thomas Lloyd and the Leeds Volunteers', *J. Soc. for Army Hist. Res.* 59 (1981), 204–5.

[97] W. McDowall to [Duke of Portland], 26 Jan. 1798, HO102/16, fo. 61; Earl of Fife to Duke of Gordon, 15 Jan. 1800, Gordon MSS, SRO GD44/47/35; memorandum relative to volunteer corps, May 1810, HO42/107, fos. 229–30.

the preparations for home defence as an intense nation-building experience: huge numbers made a voluntary tender of their services, were obligated to fight anywhere in Great Britain, and were subjected to propaganda which presented them as freemen defending a free state against military tyranny. 'The scale and duration of mass arming had a transforming effect upon British society that has hardly begun to be explored.'[98] What evidence there is from the volunteer movement does not entitle us to be so sure that a nationalistic, patriotically committed, military-interested population was its outcome. Volunteer localism, for example, could excite powerful emotions. The Sutton volunteers were never restored to obedience, and their 'town' remained so incensed at the treatment meted out to them by Ely notables that within a few weeks of the court of inquiry the corps was disbanded—all this happened in 1804 at the height of the invasion scare. If this were an exceptional case, every corps that clung to its local identity in defiance of the army, the county, and military rationalization was guilty of preferring local concerns ahead of national needs only to a lesser degree. In the most important matter of all, that of its military defence, the state continued to be faintly recognizable in its 'medieval' form, an imperfect federation of local communities. To say that Britons would have fought a war of national resistance had the French invaded is to say very little. In the Napoleonic era less unified and less homogeneous societies than Britain (France 1793–4, Spain 1808–13, Germany 1812–13) did fight such wars, which suggests that it was the immensity of the threat—extending to total defeat and foreign occupation—that even large powers now faced, not the level of political or cultural development, that primarily explains the emergence of nationalist populations.

How nationalistic is the question. The dominant and most potent theme of counter-invasion propaganda in Britain appealed, not to the public-spiritedness of the populace, but to their self-preservation if they wished to avoid slavery and conscription and whoredom for their wives and daughters.[99] This undoubtedly expressed an atavistic, high-temperature patriotism, but such patriotism was sustainable only for as long as an invasion attempt seemed imminent and was instinctive in any population rather than peculiarly British. In spite of the sheer volume of rhetoric directed at the lower classes, there is nothing yet to indicate that it did more than confirm all that they as Britons had believed about themselves in

[98] Colley, *Britons*, 308–19.
[99] Some good examples are in M. Hebditch, 'Late Eighteenth and Early Nineteenth Century Papers Relating to Organisation of the Country Against a Possible Invasion', *Yorks. Arch. J.* 36 (1944–7), 109–11. See also the broadsides in Klingberg and Hustvedt, *Warning Drum*, 48–56, 59–63, 79–83, 99–101, 148–9, 163–4, 182–3, 199–203—*Britons Beware, Bonaparte's Confession of the Massacre of Jaffa, Napoleon's Life, Bonaparte's True Character, A Peep Into Hanover, John Bull Turned Into a Galley Slave, The Consequence of Bonaparte's Succeeding, Horrors Upon Horrors*. This emphasis on personal survival through national co-operation is missed by Colley, *Britons*, 310–12.

the eighteenth century, particularly in comparison with the French.[100] Nor can national defence patriotism be said to have had a profound effect as an integrating force in society, reducing popular disorder and local particularism. As insisted above, localism and the defence of rank and file interests against officers and other authorities were congenital in the volunteers. On the only occasion when volunteers were widely used against the protesting crowd, during the food shortages of 1800–1, they frequently sided with the poor while avowing their readiness to fight the French.[101]

A case could be made out that national defence at this time accentuated the fragmentation of authority in the pre-bureaucratic state and actually added to popular grievance and disorder. Patriotic obligation was not imposed by the state. Instead—if only because every volunteer possessed the right of resignation—it was constantly negotiable with respect to the service that would be performed, the authority allowed officers, and the interests of individuals. On these loose terms patriotic commitment could happily coexist with all kinds of other loyalties. Volunteer patriotism is unrecognizable as the mass nationalism of later belligerent societies because it lacked its authoritarianism and militarism. The greatest armed challenge the British state had ever faced up to this time was met by an armed populace whose service coincided with their interests and values rather than with the needs of the state and whose attitude to soldiering was totally inconsistent with any standing the army had as an instrument of national power.

Where, then, did national defence patriotism and the associated mobilization have its greatest social effect? Certainly, it enlarged the public role of middling people, provided them with status opportunities, and introduced many of them to military careers. Patriotism as a state ideology useful to and used by an aristocratic élite against popular opposition was relatively unimportant in Britain alongside its possession by the middle classes. As a ruling device, patriotism is seen to best effect in the towns where incumbent élites, interested in developing civic cultures and often faced with the problems of controlling large, incohesive populations, readily appreciated how it could be used to unify their communities and secure their authority. National defence and their local concerns meshed perfectly. For one thing, patriotic activity mostly suppressed divisions within local élites, including the enmities usually present in corporate towns where an 'outsider' group challenged an entrenched municipal oligarchy. By arming the populace, volunteering particularly provided incentives for élite co-operation lest the élite be assailed by a monster of their making. On the other hand, the armed populace of towns, like patriotic crowds, could be presented as powerful physical manifestations of

---

[100] As Colley herself says: 'Once again the full barrage of Protestant and libertarian complacency was brought to bear against the traditional enemy across the Channel', ibid. 312.   [101] Ibid. 316–17.

communal unity and harmony; indeed, at this time there were none more power-ful. In some cases where towns did not exist as municipalities, volunteer corps, and later local militia battalions, became important communal bodies in their own right, vehicles of civic achievement and identity. For two decades of war, patriotism in its urban setting was pre-eminently a community-building force. While the growth and change taking place in urban societies often proved to be beyond the effective control of urban rulers, all kinds of patriotic endeavour were kept very much in their hands and their civic ideals never received better advertisement.

These generalizations, of course, do great violence to the complex individuality of towns. Towns, up to at least the last third of the nineteenth century, have to be understood as mostly autonomous entities pursuing their own course of development, whatever their attachment to national networks or to centralized authority. Parliament, for example, was most valued by towns because its legislative power could be used to facilitate local 'improvement' by overriding vested interests, resolving legal disputes, establishing the financial basis of public enterprises, and so on. Patriotic activity was equally prone to this localization. Small towns, the 'Banburys', the commonest sort of town, where the élite consisted of a few professional families, could only afford to raise a single volunteer corps. The most important fact about them is that virtually every one of them did, indicating how volunteering became *de rigueur* if a place was to keep any urban dignity.[102] Birmingham and Manchester, fast-growing provincial metropolises, displayed very different approaches to national defence patriotism. Birmingham organized three battalions of volunteer infantry under the overall command of the Earl of Dartmouth, one of the town's patrons. This is an excellent example of town-making by Birmingham's élite, expressing Birmingham's consequence against the rest of the county and also the cohesiveness of its society even though it was not a constituted municipality.[103] Manchester, on the other hand, in 1803 divided its volunteering effort between 'Church and King' tories, whig dissenters, and Joseph Hanson's corps of riflemen, Hanson who was to have a brief career as the weavers' advocate and as a radical leader in 1807–8.[104] Leeds was politically divided between a tory-Anglican corporation and an opposition collected around the Unitarians of the

---

[102] Local feuds seem to have caused an excessive fragmentation of volunteer corps only in Cornwall during the Revolutionary War. See C. Thomas, 'Cornish Volunteers in the Eighteenth Century', *Dev. and Corn. Notes & Queries*, 27 (1956–8), 229–36, 326–31; 28 (1959–61), 10–16.

[103] Hart, *Royal Warwickshire*, 55–82 covers the Birmingham volunteers, 1803–4. Town-making or the 'social creation' of towns is considered in R. J. Morris, 'Middle Class and British Towns', 286–306.

[104] The tories raised two large infantry regiments, the 1st and 2nd Manchester Volunteers, commanded by James Ackers and John Silvester. The whigs commanded the Manchester Light Horse (Shakespear Philips) and Manchester Independent Volunteers (George Philips). Bohstedt, *Riots*, 82–3.

Mill Hill Chapel, but put on a show of patriotic unanimity by forming a town regiment with each party commanding a battalion. In Liverpool there was serious conflict, the corporation wishing to put money into fortifications while their opponents wanted to raise volunteers.[105]

But these were local variations, of greatest importance in their local setting. Patriotism, on the whole, was a highly successful mode of presenting the town as a community under the leadership of a middle-class or pseudo-gentry élite who were willing to take responsibility for its concerns and capable of maintaining peace and good order among the inhabitants. Such élites used town-making, 'the creation of the concept of the town as a discreet, self-aware, integrated social and constitutional entity',[106] as part of the process of establishing an independent power base in a polity and society otherwise dominated by the landed classes. Middle-class and urban patriotism was always conspicuous and splendid, if only because towns could raise larger corps and produce grander spectacles. Much patriotic activity originated from town meetings, which have been recognized as important expressions of urban identity. Though they were controlled by the élite and merely purported to act in the name of the inhabitants, they were representative in a sense that other town bodies usually were not and could provide opportunities for rival groups to come together and show a united front to the rest of the world. Patriotism, rarely controversial, was particularly useful for demonstrating the essential unity of the town in this way. Indeed, it in itself promoted town meetings because subscriptions and the enrolment of men which were so often its business could be more effectively started there than anywhere else. Birmingham, in wanting to commemorate Lord Nelson with a public statue, began the appeal for funds with a public meeting from which a house-to-house canvass was organized. Liverpool, for the same purpose, opened its subscription at a town meeting where 'all classes and every shade of opinion' were represented and where William Roscoe, the leader of the anti-corporation party, was appointed to head a committee taken from both sides.[107]

Nevertheless, the town meeting as a town-making instrument was not nearly as important as the voluntary society engaged in philanthropic endeavour. In their organization these were typically based on the town, and, ideologically, they

---

[105] William Smithson and Samuel Hamer Oates were lieutenant-colonel and major of the 'Whig' battalion. Oates belonged to a leading Unitarian family. Smithson also had Unitarian connections and was active in peace petitioning in 1807–8. He later commanded the Leeds volunteers and the local militia battalion. J. Seed, 'Theologies of Power: Unitarianism and the Social Relations of Religious Discourse, 1800–50', in R. J. Morris (ed.), *Class, Power and Social Structure in British Nineteenth-Century Towns* (Leicester, 1986), 125; Cookson, *Friends of Peace*, 205. For Liverpool see J. Currie to T. Creevey, 30 Nov. 1803, Currie MSS, Liverpool RO, 920 Cur. 26.

[106] Morris, 'Middle Class and British Towns', 299.

[107] Yarrington, *Commemoration of the Hero*, 104–7, 116–19.

represented a middle-class desire to establish order and stability in the town by building paternalistic relationships with those in the urban society who were or might be outside their influence.[108] The connection between the voluntary society and patriotism is surely through the volunteers. Urban volunteer corps can be readily identified with the voluntary societies in that both kinds of organization presented themselves as public bodies originating from public meetings and both were operated as 'subscriber democracies' in that the forms of election and report were observed. Both, too, were effectively controlled by the town élite, who could exclude even aristocratic patrons, and were most vulnerable to a loss of the financial support that had started them and to intrusion by the state into their field of activity. Military volunteering, at first at any rate, was a powerful stimulant for the ideals that lay behind organized philanthropy in the towns. It was not at all that volunteers provided military force to back up the authority of the élite—this was always a dubious prospect. Rather, large numbers of townsmen might be brought directly under the influence of the élite and shown the advantages of a relationship in which their superiors provided protection and patronage and expected in return obedience, deference, and trust. The volunteer corps, in fact, offered an enticing model of what urban élites wanted urban society to be like—the well-drilled ranks of the lower orders acting under the command of high-status members of the community. Of course, the other side of the picture was a rank and file which complied and obeyed as far as suited it and a state which set its own standards and terms of service. Even so, volunteer corps could not help being self-consciously communal because they depended on local subscriptions and on good relations between officers and men in the absence of proper military authority.

Patriotism and civic philanthropy had a closer relationship than has been realized. In Birmingham the plan for a Nelson monument was contested between those who wanted to emphasize the theme of triumph and those who wanted 'use united with ornament, and Patriotism with Charity'.[109] The conjunction of the two became most explicit in the royal jubilee of 1809 when numerous towns established new charities to mark the occasion; George III himself helped to set the tone of the celebrations with a munificent donation for the relief of debtors, an example followed in a great many places.[110] So much patriotic activity was intended to convey the idea of the town not only as wealthy and powerful but—and here the inhabitants themselves were addressed—as an orderly community in which all classes were

---

[108] The best treatment is Morris, 'Voluntary Societies'. Morris has restated the importance of the voluntary societies in his *Class, Sect and Party: The Making of the British Middle Class, Leeds 1820–1850* (Manchester, 1990), especially in the concluding chapter.

[109] Yarrington, *Commemoration of the Hero*, 108–10.

[110] J. Sykes, *Local Records of Remarkable Events Which Have Occurred in Northumberland and Durham* (2 vols., repr. Stockton-on-Tees, 1973), ii. 48–9 for Newcastle and Durham; *Leeds Mercury*, 14, 21 Oct. 1809 for Leeds, York, and Liverpool; T. Preston, *The Jubilee of George III* (London, 1887).

united. Monuments to national heroes, which became a particular feature of provincial towns at this time, had a serious moral purpose beyond civic embellishment. They were sited in public space, usually close to public buildings, where they would strengthen the physical impression of the power and authority of urban rulers and where it seemed they would best induce reflections on those values of duty and service that the hero exemplified. Sir John Moore's memorial in Glasgow was considered inappropriate for the 'principal streets' where it would soon be overlooked by the rush of citizenry or cursed as a traffic hazard; and no better positioned if it was installed in the High Church where public access was limited.[111]

The local celebration of patriotic occasions similarly used public space where crowds could gather to be entertained, gratified, and, hopefully, instructed. This was part of a long process in the eighteenth century whereby civic celebration of national events was converted from semi-private, exclusive aldermanic feast into public spectacle.[112] In these celebrations the harmony and order of the community was the effect sought, the day often being preceded by appeals from the magistracy for peaceable behaviour and succeeded by congratulations that nothing untoward had occurred. Very large crowds, probably the largest seen in particular localities, were attracted to what became increasingly magnificent shows; 60,000 were said to have attended the Leeds 'military festival' in 1795; 30,000 may have crowded the small market town of Bury St Edmunds for the 'peace festival' to mark the end of the war in 1814.[113]

Patriotic display therefore exerted a powerful fascination. Orchestrated as these occasions were by urban élites, they represent another way besides philanthropy by which they attempted to define and unify their communities and secure their authority. Once loyalism had run its course—in this context mainly characterized by officially countenanced Paine-burnings—town rulers, in particular, searched for the modes of an all-inclusive patriotism. The voluntary contribution of 1798, with appeals to the poor for their pennies and bid defiance to the French, was turned in this direction. London lavishly celebrated peace in 1802; and so did many provincial towns, where special effort was often made to engage the whole community; in Bury St Edmunds, for example, the ceremonial proclamation of peace was given

---

[111] Sederunt book of the Committee of Subscribers to Sir John Moore's monument, NLS MS 2732, 71–89, 93–113. Siting monuments often caused problems. Glasgow lacked the broad streets and expansive squares of the Georgian ideal city.

[112] Borsay, 'Urban Ritual and Ceremony', 228–58.

[113] 'Extracts from the *Leeds Intelligencer*, 1791–6', *Thoresby Soc. Pub.* 44 (1956), 80; *Cambridge Chronicle*, 24 June 1814. A crowd of 50,000–60,000 came to see colours presented to the Birmingham volunteers, a ceremony held on the king's birthday in June 1798, Hart, *Royal Warwickshire*, 36–9. In 1795 20,000 saw the Glasgow Royal Volunteers reviewed on the king's birthday. C. Whatley, 'Royal Day, People's Day: The Monarch's Birthday in Scotland c. 1660–1860', in R. Mason and N. Macdougall (eds.), *People and Power in Scotland* (Edinburgh, 1992), 175.

additional meaning when the proceeds of a public subscription were distributed among 4,562 'poor persons'.[114] The use of patriotism for community-building in the early nineteenth century reached a climax with the 'peace festivals' of 1814. The treating of the populace was a particular feature of these occasions, carried as far as great open-air public feasts which exactly counterpointed the retreat of polite society into assembly rooms and other reserves.[115]

Cambridge's 'peace festival' serves as a good example of how successful urban leaders were in imposing their concerns, not to say their values and code of behaviour, on these national celebrations. The central event of the day was a dinner, free to all inhabitants of the town and held on the open ground of Parker's Piece. Nearly 6,000, it was claimed, sat down to the feast; a much larger crowd of spectators was also present. It was, therefore, in a real sense, a gathering of the whole town, something further emphasized by seating people according to their parish and arranging the tables within a great circle, intentionally symbolic, no doubt, of communal bonds. At the same time the proceedings rendered a very clear statement of where authority and power resided. The mayor had the most prominent place; the clergy and 'principal inhabitants' presided over the tables. The 'expence was defrayed by subscription', a case of the poor being treated by the rich. The tone of the occasion was good cheer, but with order and decorum, initially signified by the parochial processions to the tables. Loyal toasts and songs concluded the dinner, which was followed by another procession to 'Midsummer Green' for 'sports' and, in the evening, a bonfire. Clearly, the festival incorporated many of the features of popular holidays and recreations; but on this occasion the organizers were concerned to blend the exuberance of the 'lower sort' with their own code of self-control and respectability. The culture of patriotism was eminently useful in this respect because it directed attention away from social distinctions and possible conflict. The 'old British fare' provided—beef and plum pudding— was a universally understood symbol of national confidence and well-being. The toasts and songs rehearsed equally familiar patriotic themes—devotion to the monarchy, the country's naval pre-eminence and military success, Britain as the saviour of Europe.[116]

---

[114] Diary of James Oakes, 7, 10 May 1802, Suffolk RO (Bury St Edmunds), HA 521/6. For other celebrations in 1802 see W. Telford, *Transparencies Exhibited in Bristol and Its Vicinity on the Day of Proclaiming Peace* (Bristol, 1802); Sykes, *Local Records . . . Northumberland and Durham*, ii. 9; A. Jenkins, *The History and Description of the City of Exeter* (Exeter, 1806), 232–3; *Cambridge Chronicle*, 22 May 1802.

[115] *Leeds Mercury*, 25 June, 16, 23 July 1814; *Nottingham Review*, 10 June–22 July 1814; Soham baptismal register 1813–27, Cambridge RO, P142/1/6; J. Oakes diary, 17 June 1814, Suffolk RO, Bury St. Edmunds, HA521/9; *Cambridge Chronicle*, 24 June–5 Aug. 1814; V. Smith (ed.), *The Town Book of Lewes 1702–1837* (Lewes, 1976), 199–201.

[116] *Cambridge Chronicle*, 15 July 1814. A published account appeared immediately. See *A Narrative of the Celebrations of Peace at Cambridge* advertised in the *Cambridge Chronicle*, 15 and 29 July 1814.

The communal feasts of 1814 must count among the most evocative expressions of paternalistic ideals in the early nineteenth-century society, though it was exceptional for a place as large as Cambridge to organize one. In towns of any size the communal character of the celebrations was maintained by declaring a holiday and arranging the sort of spectacle that would bring a crowd onto the streets; Leeds in 1814 held a magnificent civic procession which wended its way to different parts of the town to read the proclamation of peace and which was brought up in the rear by those popular symbols of peace and war, the large and the small loaf.[117] In 1815 after Waterloo there were no victory celebrations of similar splendour, the end of the war in 1814 closing a period of 'unprecedented mass mobilization around patriotic events'. Over the next twenty years the patriotic crowd was to reappear with the same national ubiquity only for the coronations of 1821 and 1831.[118] This amount of patriotic activity extensive over the whole country and concentrated in a particular period might remind us of Linda Colley's remark that 'it was training in arms . . . that was the most common collective working class experience in the late eighteenth and early nineteenth centuries, not labour in a factory, or membership of a radical political organization or an illegal trade union'.[119] There can be no doubt that the authorities and the propertied classes generally looked for the signs that military service and patriotic events were producing the orderly and respectful populace they wished for, especially in wild urban places. The absence of militia rioting in Renfrewshire in 1797 was taken to show the good effects of volunteering which had converted one of the most 'democratical' counties into one of the most loyal. At the time of the royal jubilee in 1809 the *Leeds Mercury* admired a procession of factory workers for their 'regular (and contrary to the general idea of large factories) orderly and decorous appearance. Indeed the girls were neat and clean to an extreme.'[120] But Mark Harrison has told us not to mistake popular participation on patriotic occasions for popular and élite agreement on the meaning and purpose of those events;[121] and volunteering likewise provides ample evidence of the different concerns of officers and the rank and file. Patriotism as a unifying, cross-class influence in the late Georgian society is most understandable as national defence patriotism in which there was an instinctive determination to resist foreign invasion scarcely separable from long-imbibed Francophobia.

---

[117] *Leeds Mercury*, 2 July 1814. For Nottingham and Derby see *Nottingham Review*, 24 June, 1 July 1814. For Newcastle see Sykes, *Local Records . . . Northumberland and Durham*, ii. 80–1, 83. For Edinburgh see *Caledonian Mercury*, 16 Apr., 30 June 1814.

[118] M. Harrison, *Crowds and History: Mass Phenomena in English Towns, 1790–1835* (Cambridge, 1988), 234. Harrison counts thirty-six 'royal and military' crowd occasions in Bristol, 1795–1814, and twelve in 1815–35, ibid. 114.   [119] Colley, *Britons*, 312.

[120] W. McDowall to [Duke of Portland], 26 Jan. 1798, HO102/16, fo. 61; *Leeds Mercury*, 28 Oct. 1809.   [121] Harrison, *Crowds and History*, 234–67.

Such patriotism does not make sense as 'loyalty' because it did not define allegiance to anybody or anything in particular within the state, unless it were the monarch who, partly independently, partly as a consequence of national defence patriotism, was becoming a symbol above political and social contentions. Similarly, the Union flag and the national anthem and some other songs became affirmations of British identity appropriated by all and sundry; the Union flag displayed by the radicals at the Peterloo meeting and the tunes which their bands played as they marched into Manchester were equally national symbols to the yeomanry and soldiers who charged into their midst.[122] Patriotism that was merely sentiment at the popular level had most effect in breaking down the localization of home defence so that men were readier to fight anywhere on the national territory and readier to appreciate that a trained population was a necessary defence against a French armed nation. Yet this does not mean that war, years of national preparedness, deeply militarized the British populace. While the columns which marched towards Peterloo in 1819 might have been an attempt to reproduce military glamour, or reflected soldiers' understanding of the effect of organized mass, the army and soldiering remained almost an alien society and culture; late in the war men being sworn for the local militia still feared that they were being inveigled into the army.[123] War neither made the lower orders more loyal to existing institutions nor nationalistic in any firm ideological sense nor militaristic.

This contrasts with its much more profound effect on the middle classes, where it greatly extended their participation in public life and excited their paternalistic energies, if it did not in the euphoria of total victory and their country's role as 'the saviour of Europe' turn their attention from town-building to world-building. It does not seem entirely coincidental that the two greatest mobilizations of public opinion Britain had ever seen occurred in 1813–14, both of them devoted to causes which could be given a global perspective. Over eight hundred petitions in 1813 demanded the opening of India to missionaries; another eight hundred signed by three-quarters of a million people in 1814 sought the abolition of the slave trade by European powers.[124] Yet middle-class participation in war and public enterprise never produced a decisive shift in the focus of their concerns from the localities to more effective representation and power at the centre. In general, problems and issues of national defence, public order, urban growth, and economic development required more, not less, of local rulers and their propertied constituencies with the

---

[122] D. Read, *Peterloo: The Massacre and its Background* (Manchester, 1958), 131.

[123] Trial of James Asquith, blacksmith of Mirfield, *Leeds Mercury*, 7 Oct. 1809.

[124] C. H. Philips, *The East India Company 1784–1834* (Manchester, 1940), 189; S. Drescher, *Capitalism and Anti-Slavery* (London, 1986), 93–4. One might add the subscription launched in 1814 for the relief of the victims of war in Germany. According to a list appended to the Baptist Church House, London copy of the *Baptist Magazine*, 6 (1814), which I saw in 1975, 358 congregations and parishes contributed.

result that these local 'publics' continued to be deeply immersed in the affairs of their communities. When they intervened in national politics on behalf of sectional interests, as happened over the Orders-in-Council and the renewal of the East India Company's charter in 1812, the petitions were an extension of local struggles.[125] Their opposition to the corn bills of 1814–15 and the property tax in 1816 was more communal, but, typically, these great public campaigns were reactions to central decisions and depended on the very loose alliance of separate towns. All these protests were locally organized, were cast as the representations of local communities, and certainly produced no permanent confederation of urban interests in opposition to the aristocratic state.

Thus Britain in the structure of its public life remained an *ancien régime* in the sense that there was such limited development of national bureaucratic organization, whether of parliamentary politics, popular politics, or government itself. Even national defence remained heavily dependent for a long time on what local leaders could accomplish by voluntary effort. And in this situation national defence patriotism during the Napoleonic period acquires most meaning in multitudinous local contexts.

[125] Cookson, *Friends of Peace*, ch. 9.

9
The Legacy of the Armed Nation

THE Napoleonic period was the climax of the British warfare state of the eighteenth century. However we measure the national mobilization, whether by the size of the armed forces, civilian participation in home defence, the amounts raised by government borrowing and taxation, or war expenditure as a percentage of national income, all previous levels were surpassed to a degree that seems to justify regarding these wars as anticipating 'total' war.[1] Britain's military potential was especially powerfully displayed after 1809. In the last years of the war imperial successes came thick and fast—Martinique, Guadeloupe, Senegal, Mauritius, and Java captured, Sicily and the Ionian Islands occupied.[2] If in 1812 the outbreak of war with America was an accident, Britain showed every inclination to take the fight to the Americans. When war with Napoleon resumed in 1815 a large expeditionary force was immediately sent to the major theatre to bolster Britain's part in the military alliance against France. Britain's global power, together with her importance in the affairs of Europe, had never reached such heights. And these achievements were amply backed at home by the further organization of national defence through Castlereagh's local militia and the militia interchange, by basing army recruitment on the militia, by deployment of the militia overseas, and, last but not least, by continuing, in opposition to the bullionists, an expansive system of war borrowing.

These few years could easily be presented as the apogee of British power in the history of the international system, which makes the extent of the disarmament that followed, turning, it has been said, the fiscal-military state into the *laissez-faire* state, more than usually interesting.[3] Virtually nothing was left of the home forces once militia ballots ended in 1831, and even the regulars kept in Britain were depleted to the point where the generals advised an invasion could not be effectively resisted. Time and again the outbreak of trouble in one part of the empire meant the stripping of garrisons to less than safe levels elsewhere. When in 1854 Britain embarked on conflict with a major European power, its army lacked both numbers and training to fulfil its objectives.[4] Clearly, the country's armed

---

[1] C. Emsley, 'The Impact of War and Military Participation on Britain and France 1792–1815', in C. Emsley and J. Walvin (eds.), *Artisans, Peasants and Proletarians 1760–1860* (London, 1985), 58.

[2] Hall, *British Strategy in the Napoleonic War*, 184–90.

[3] Harling and Mandler, 'From "Fiscal-Military" State'.

[4] Strachan, *Wellington's Legacy*, 220–1.

establishments were reduced to a strength where any sudden large-scale intervention in Europe was out of the question and the possibility of a direct attack on the British Isles was totally discounted. There was also a widening disparity between Britain and France. Around 1790, a period of retrenchment for both countries, Britain's army was a third smaller than France's in population terms. By the 1830s and 1840s it was easily a half smaller. In 1845 Wellington went so far as to claim that France had 350,000 regular troops and national guards where Britain had no more than 5,000 'disposable men'.[5] Spending on the armed forces in France represented 30.9 per cent of total government expenditure in 1822, 35.7 per cent in 1832, and 38.4 per cent in 1842. Britain's averaged 27.8 per cent in 1821–30, 25.6 per cent in 1831–40, and 27.3 per cent in 1841–50.[6] The paradox of military reduction was that after 1815 Britain was more deeply involved in Europe than ever, attentive to commercial concerns which accounted for over 40 per cent of its exports,[7] stoutly protective of its strategic interests in the Low Countries, Iberia, and the eastern Mediterranean, perfectly ready to conclude alliances to strengthen its diplomacy, sometimes to the point of armed intervention, and always wary of a revival of French expansionism.[8]

The drive behind disarmament was certainly economic, but in a context which went much wider than the government's need to go with parliamentary and public opinion or old verities about trade being the ultimate source of Britain's power. True, Liverpool and Castlereagh talked constantly of the need to recuperate the country's finances, and Liverpool was Pitt's heir in his penchant for economic management—down to adopting a post-war policy reminiscent of the period after 1783 which provided tax relief for the propertied classes, a programme of debt reduction, and the active pursuit of trading advantages. But it needs to be appreciated, more than has been the case, that peacetime economies were able to be carried the lengths they were essentially because after the settlements of 1814–15 Britain's strategic interests in the Low Countries were secured as fully and as permanently as it was reasonable to hope for. Since Louis XIV, Britain's major concern in Europe had been to prevent any French expansion northwards and the problem had become steadily more serious as the eighteenth century advanced with the decline of Dutch power and Austria's increasing desire to withdraw from Belgium. All that happened during the Revolutionary and Napoleonic Wars confirmed the significance of the area for Britain. With France in occupation of the

---

[5] N. Gash (ed.), *Wellington: Studies in the Military and Political Career of the 1st Duke of Wellington* (Manchester, 1990), 242.

[6] P. Flora *et al.*, *State, Economy and Society in Western Europe 1815–1975* (2 vols., London, 1983), i. 382; Mitchell, *British Historical Statistics*, 396–7. [7] Evans, *Forging of the Modern State*, 395.

[8] French, *The British Way in Warfare*, 122. There were expeditionary forces to Portugal in 1826 and 1834, to Greece in 1827, to Belgium in 1831.

Netherlands, any part of the British Isles perimeter was exposed to French attack and the nation was forced to develop a system of home defence that was not only highly expensive but full of risk in a revolutionary age.

The end of war transformed this situation, indeed gave Britain a security in the Netherlands it had never possessed throughout the eighteenth century. The famous fortress barrier proposed under the Treaty of Vienna to block future French incursions into the area was the least important new development; the fortresses were still uncompleted when Belgium won its independence in 1830; besides, the French invasions of 1793–4 and 1815 rightly induced scepticism that they would only impede, not deter an attack. The large Netherlands state created in 1814 also promised more than it delivered, unable to resolve its internal divisions, militarily unimpressive, and removed from the map of Europe when Belgium separated after fifteen years. Britain's confidence that French influence and power was checked rather rested on what was the central premiss of the post-Waterloo international system. This was the clear decision of the great powers in 1814–15 that they would tolerate no further French expansionism and, accordingly, that they would act together to confine France to the frontiers fixed by the peace treaties. The Belgian crisis of 1830–2 was a case in point. Britain, unsurprisingly, took the lead in convening an international conference, the powers showed no interest in exploiting the situation for their own ends, though they might have done, and all the trouble caused by the Belgian question in ensuing years can be largely blamed on the Dutch and Belgians themselves. Because the powers quickly accepted that an independent Belgium offered the best chance of restoring stability to the area and therefore of discouraging French intervention, a major conflict was never very likely.[9]

The basic strategic conditions permitting Britain's disarmament after 1815 are revealed all the more clearly by what happened when Britain once more had to assess the possibility of a direct attack. Home defence began to engage the attention of the politicians from the mid-1840s as France increased the size of its army and began to develop a steamship navy. Further, a certain restlessness was seen to pervade French policy, severely testing relations with Britain on occasions and anticipating the more open bellicosity and revisionism of Napoleon III's regime. The reinstitution of the militia in 1852, followed by that of the volunteers in 1859—the emergence of a second British armed nation—was a response to the threat France was perceived to present in a period which saw the Concert of Europe overcome by great power rivalries. The revival of the auxiliaries was appropriate to a situation which had so many of the ingredients of the older Napoleonic invasion scares—British isolation, French military might, concern about French naval power, construction work in the French Channel ports, the suddenness with which

[9] P. W. Schroeder, *The Transformation of European Politics 1763–1848* (Oxford, 1994), 670–91.

an attack could be launched, the uncertainties surrounding a purely naval defence, the weakness of coastal fortifications, the Bonaparte factor itself.[10]

Though the 1840s were a decade of disorder and revolutionary threats in both Britain and Ireland, military, definitely not police, conceptions lay behind the restored auxiliaries. One indication of continued conservative suspicion of an armed populace is that when national defence required a larger home force a militia was chosen ahead of volunteers despite some highly vocal support for volunteering at the time.[11] Militia continued to be conceived as more under the control of constituted authority, the army, and the gentry's social influence. There was a long Addingtonian legacy, really lasting until 1863. Only then did the government of the day agree to meet most of the costs of the new volunteers, thus signalling that the movement might expand as far as enthusiasm would take it. As long as it was insisted that volunteers be self-supporting, lower-class participation in national defence was effectively diverted into the militia. The old attitudes persisted in other ways as well. The generals continued to dislike volunteers *per se* because they were inefficient and they could not see how they could be made otherwise.[12] There was also barely concealed disdain for the *parvenu* elements attracted to volunteering which broadened into an antipathy for the urban middle class who were seen as lacking military traditions and as essentially self-interested, wanting the social rewards of service without its impositions. On the other hand, the advocates of volunteering hymned all the pieties heard earlier; volunteering would arouse the 'spirit and patriotism' of the nation, 'co-mingling the classes' and 'martialising' the population so as to make the army genuinely popular.[13]

Social tensions thus continued to make the armed nation problematical, posing the incompatibility between effective national defence and public order. Order was such a central issue for early nineteenth-century Britain (as indeed it was elsewhere in Europe) that we should accept the merits of still regarding the period as an age of revolution. The British counter-revolutionary state has usually been understood in terms of its repression of popular politics and its swift and energetic reaction to any physical force threat. But it is just as important to appreciate how policy sought to avoid or contain discontent and possible violence and how well the state was prepared for the worst eventuality. On the latter point, the army stationed in the British Isles after 1815 was double the size it had been before the

[10] The debate on national defence, but not its international setting, is covered in Strachan, *Wellington's Legacy*, 196–211. For a full account of the 1859 invasion scare see M. J. Salevouris, *'Riflemen Form': The War Scare of 1859–60 in England* (New York, 1982).

[11] Strachan, *Wellington's Legacy*, 209–10.

[12] Salevouris, *Riflemen Form*, 170–1; Beckett, *Amateur Military Tradition*, 156–7; Gash, *Wellington*, 254.

[13] H. Cunningham, *The Volunteer Force: A Social and Political History 1859–1908* (London, 1975), 10–12.

Revolutionary and Napoleonic Wars with much improved means of deployment, especially between Britain and Ireland, and, with the coming of the railway, between southern and northern England. In addition, significant yeomanry forces were kept up in Ireland until the 1830s and in England throughout the period. Pensioner soldiers were a further reserve, as many as 15,000 of them organized as corps from 1848.[14] These forces were the 'guardians of order' in a way the armed nation could never be; which only emphasizes another reason, besides the relative security achieved against France, for the rapid disappearance of the armed nation on the resumption of peace. Even the yeomanry, for all their Protestantism in Ireland and property in England, showed the limitations of employing armed civilians to control social tensions, and the trend in both countries was for their replacement by professional police. The surviving remnant of the armed nation proper was the militia ballot upholding the principle of universal service. However, used as sparingly as possible during the war, always regarded as discriminatory against the poor, the ballot was soon given away by the counter-revolutionary state. Ballots for the local militia ended in 1814 and for the militia in 1831 after it had been called out for training on just four occasions. In the revival of 1852 the government asked for and contrived to obtain a purely volunteer militia.[15]

The armed nation, then, at least in its military organization, vanished as irrelevant to Britain's strategic and political circumstances. Whether its militarism and nationalism remained is another question altogether, as is the wider impact of the British population's war involvement at this time. These are important topics if only because a fundamental reordering of the state did occur from 1829 with Catholic emancipation and the Reform Act, and shorter-term explanations, however enticing, have not been able to quash interest in longer-term explanations.[16] In contrast, too, to the impressive national unity of the invasion scares, the early nineteenth-century society was a society in crisis in the sense that on many occasions a serious breakdown of public order was feared and popular oppositions kept being identified with incipient revolution.[17] Few, if any, satisfactory connections have been made between Britain's war experience and subsequent events and developments. Mass military participation has sometimes been depicted as a key factor in forcing incumbent élites to concede changes advantageous to underprivileged

[14] Return of numbers serving at home, in the colonies, and in India 1800–58, *SP* 1859, sess. 2, xvii. 8–39. On 1 Jan. 1793 there were 20,637 cavalry and infantry stationed in Britain and Ireland.
[15] Strachan, *Wellington's Legacy*, 208–9. The militia was balloted and trained in 1820, 1821, 1825, and 1831, on each occasion to meet the demands of public order. A ballot was ordered for 1829 but was later suspended.
[16] J. C. D. Clark, *English Society 1688–1832* (Cambridge, 1985), explained the carrying of emancipation and reform in terms of 'high' politics, a failure of nerve on the part of ministers. Cf. Colley, *Britons*, ch. 8, where the crisis of 1827–32 is related to slower-working processes, including the growth of national politics at the popular level. [17] Sack, *From Jacobite to Conservative*, 103.

sections of the community or, if not that, in greatly strengthening the position of such groups within the existing power structure.[18] It is true that even while the war lasted out-groups used the argument of their war contribution to advance their cause, in particular Catholic leaders in Ireland, provincial manufacturers, and popular radicals who subscribed to Major Cartwright's views of democracy going hand in hand with universal military service.[19] But the argument is one thing; assessing its importance to those who employed it and to those against whom it was directed is quite another. And if certain bodies of opinion did become more formidable because of the war, this does not have to mean that the aristocratic state had lost the political initiative and was bound, sooner or later, to succumb to its opposition. Indeed, respect has to be paid to the view that Church, monarchy, and aristocracy in the early nineteenth century remained dominant institutions upholding a hegemonic conservative ideology.[20]

In fact, the war experience added little to popular politics, whether rhetoric or substantial power. The strength or weakness of popular oppositions was mainly determined by factors other than the importance of the interests represented to the warfare state. If Catholic Irish pointed to their loyal service, larger considerations from a British perspective were that Britain had been able to draw heavily on Irish resources for over twenty years of war, in spite of withholding Catholic emancipation, and that Irish recruitment into the army continued to increase after 1815. Without a foreign threat to Britain and Ireland or the prospect of a European war, there was even less pressure to relate Irish policy to military concerns. What mainly recommended conciliation in the post-war situation was the huge cost of garrisoning Ireland, which threatened to become prohibitive once O'Connell had united Catholic opinion and had it in his power to make Ireland ungovernable. In its most important aspect, the situation in 1828 was a repeat of the situation in 1782: concession was unavoidable because coercion of a 'nation' was simply unrealistic.

The Reform Act of 1832, though even more remote than Catholic emancipation from the end of the war, can be seen as the culmination of a mass radicalism that had emerged almost immediately in the new era of peace. The chronologies of war and popular radicalism come so close to each other that we might almost be persuaded that parliamentary reform, like emancipation, went back to Britain's war experience: 'Having been compelled to draw on the armed service and incomes of unprecedented numbers of its population so as to defeat France, the men who

---

[18] S. Andreski, *Military Organisation and Society* (2nd edn., London, 1968); R. M. Titmuss, 'War and Social Policy', in Titmuss (ed.), *Essays on the Welfare State* (London, 1958), 75–87; A. Marwick, *War and Social Change in the Twentieth Century* (London, 1974).

[19] See above, 231; Cookson, *Friends of Peace*, ch. 9; Harvey, *Collision of Empires*, 195–6.

[20] As argued, most notably, in Clark, *English Society*; Sack, *From Jacobite to Conservative*; J. Cannon, *Aristocratic Century: The Peerage of Eighteenth-Century England* (Cambridge, 1984).

governed Great Britain found themselves under pressure after the peace to change the political system so that all men of property, and all working men, were given access to the vote.'[21] One difficulty with this view is that statesmen and politicians never articulated the connection between national defence and reform. As late as 1852 the Cabinet firmly rejected a proposal to enfranchise militiamen with two years' satisfactory service.[22] Even radicals in the post-war period preferred the more inclusive rhetoric of constitutional rights or that of the 'productive classes' against a parasitic aristocracy to arguments of military citizenship. Why this was so is at least partly explained by the nature of military service in the wartime society. A doctrine of military citizenship could not easily be erected around soldiers and long-serving militia because they were perceived as an out-group, selected from unstable social elements and placed under separate authority. As late as 1913 there were only 10,250 soldiers registered as voters.[23] It is true that radicals were able to make more of the issue of militia service *after* 1815 because individuals called up for training by sporadic ballots were no longer protected to the same extent by insurance, their employers, and parishes.[24] But at no time, whether during the war or later, did the militia inflict personal service on large numbers or come to be regarded as an intolerable corvée by the lower orders. Even if it had, it is well to remember that the Napoleonic conscription in France apparently did nothing to weaken a small, highly privileged electorate of *notables* before and after 1815. Neither did the volunteer mass challenge the notion of hierarchy. As a form of military obligation, volunteering was based on the leadership of élites and deployed conservative language, asking for the patriotic union of all ranks to defend the 'liberties' all Britons possessed. Indeed, the volunteer rank and file would probably have been surprised if their military service had been linked to political rights, they joining and remaining with a corps largely as suited them.

Therefore, democratic radicalism in early nineteenth-century Britain continues to be better understood in terms of a popular libertarian tradition, the politics of distress, and recognition of a 'public opinion' based on an ever-widening propertied class. It is in this last respect that the great wartime mobilization does tie up with post-war tension between 'people' and 'aristocracy' because, if the Napoleonic volunteer movement was anything, it was a movement in which lower-status members of the propertied class broadly participated and often held positions of importance. As such it forms part of that widespread and expanding participation in public affairs found in the eighteenth-century society. National defence patriotism, however, like the loyalism of the 1790s, was founded on an all-embracing alliance of property against the enemies of the state. While this propertied consensus

---

[21] Colley, *Britons*, 323.   [22] Beckett, *Amateur Military Tradition*, 148.
[23] M. Pugh, *Electoral Reform in War and Peace 1906–18* (London, 1978), 32.   [24] Ibid. 130–1.

continued to be sustained after the war by apprehensions of revolution (also by policies of cheap government), it was vulnerable to the increasing self-consciousness
of powerful urban communities and their claims of being under-represented in
national politics. But this rising urbanism would have occurred with or without the
war. Nor was there any direct relationship between the political rights conceded to
small property owners in 1832 and the military services they had rendered earlier.
The most that can be said is that national defence, from the time of the Militia Act
onwards, helped significantly to enlarge their public role and that the same public
involvement and interest continued, doubtless accelerated, during the 1820s to
lend weight to the idea of a 'rise of public opinion' operating on but outside the
formal institutions of power.[25] In this context, the Reform Act represented an
attempt to stabilize the state by hitching the broad middle class to the constitution
and revitalizing the propertied consensus, so isolating popular radicalism.

The impact of national defence participation is better gauged at the local level
where most public enterprise was concentrated anyway. National defence patriotism undoubtedly had its greatest effect in towns. In small towns it mostly served
to add to the status and dignity of leading citizens and promoted a communal
identity against the county and local magnates. In large towns it was not only an
important means by which these places could define themselves but also by which
their populations could be unified and ordered. Patriotism was probably the most
successful mode of urban paternalism in the late eighteenth and early nineteenth
century. In the volunteers and local militia larger numbers than the voluntary
societies ever dealt with were brought under the leadership and authority of the
élite.[26] The patriotic crowd was a further powerful expression of the hierarchical
relationships and community they were endeavouring to build. Loyalism, in comparison, briefly evoked a response from the lower classes, most notably in the
Paine-burnings of 1793.[27] This is not to say that hierarchs and populace attached
the same meanings to patriotic activity, only that patriotism as paternalism was
highly successful in associating the classes which was the point at which paternalist
controls could begin to take effect.[28]

National defence patriotism quickly disappeared with the end of the war and
the disbandment of the auxiliaries. Public celebration of the nation now centred on
the monarchy, but nothing occurred on the scale of the war years apart from the

---

[25] A classic statement is W. A. Mackinnon, *On the Rise, Progress and Present State of Public Opinion in Great Britain and Other Parts of the World* (London, 1828).

[26] P. H. J. Gosden, *Self-Help: Voluntary Associations in 19th Century Great Britain* (London, 1973), 12, says there were over 9,000 'friendly societies' with over 700,000 members by 1803. But these were largely self-supporting, independent, artisan bodies. [27] Philp, 'Vulgar Conservatism', 66.

[28] J. Knott, *Popular Opposition to the 1834 Poor Law* (London, 1986), 1–6, is good on popular celebrations of Victoria's coronation in 1838 countering those organized by the authorities.

observances marking the coronations of 1821 and 1831. Philanthropy, typically organized around the voluntary society, definitely became the main strategy of urban rulers for securing public order in their communities. Whatever fears of popular revolution there were, loyalism or some other variety of national salvation nationalism never re-emerged, possibly because philanthropic activity was so effective in mobilizing the propertied classes.[29] We cannot tell whether the wartime mobilization stimulated charitable effort both during the war and afterwards; the model of the voluntary society certainly had been well developed in the eighteenth century. But increasing royal patronage of public charities, something that has yet to be properly charted, may indicate an interesting connection between the extended public role that the war had encouraged the monarchy to assume and organized philanthropy. The power of royal example was shown at the time of the jubilee in 1809 when George III's donation for the relief of debtors set off a wave of like-minded projects in the towns. Some of the royal dukes particularly took up this work, Sussex, Cambridge, Gloucester, for example, and Kent, who himself around 1810 headed fifty-three different societies and charities.[30] Mainly in this way, urban élites preserved some of the patriotic monarchism that had been so prominent during the war. Undoubtedly the monarchy might have done much more for its cause, for George III, George IV, and William IV all shunned close involvement in town-making and the opportunities it offered for cultivating loyalty and popularity.

However, the post-war deflation of 'king and country' patriotism has also to be explained in terms of the waning of urban militarism. Once the local auxiliaries had gone, many places lost the armed forces which were the public bodies particularly identified with the authority and charisma of the monarchy. The army's relationship with society remained ambiguous. Soldiering was no more popular an occupation than it had ever been, as shown by annual recruiting returns which failed to rise and which included an increasing proportion of Irish.[31] Long periods spent overseas in imperial garrisons made it difficult for regiments to associate themselves with particular communities at home, a situation reinforced by the barracks

---

[29] The increase of philanthropy in the early 19th cent. is usually indexed by citing the figures in Sampson Low's directory *The Charities of London* (1861). Low counted 640 charitable bodies in London in 1860, 279 of which had been founded between 1800 and 1850, and 144 between 1850 and 1860. G. Finlayson, *Citizen, State and Social Welfare in Britain 1830–1990* (Oxford, 1994), 62. R. J. Morris lists the 'variety and profusion' of societies in Leeds in 'Clubs, Societies and Associations', *Cambridge Social History*, iii. 411–12.

[30] For the jubilee of 1809 see Preston, *Jubilee of George III*. D. Owen, *English Philanthropy 1660–1960* (Cambridge, Mass., 1965), 165–6; D. Duff, *Edward of Kent* (London, 1973), 218. George IV subscribed to seven charities in 1822, *Letters of King George IV 1812–30*, ed. A. Aspinall (3 vols., Cambridge, 1938), iii. 498. George III was not so involved, according to F. K. Brown, *Fathers of the Victorians: The Age of Wilberforce* (Cambridge, 1961), 85.

[31] For recruiting see Strachan, *Wellington's Legacy*, 56. By 1830 the Irish proportion of the army was 42.2 per cent, almost equalling the English and Welsh. Spiers, *The Army and Society*, 50.

in which they were segregated and the anti-civilianism and regimental pride they espoused in response to their isolation. Only with the Crimean War and the Indian Mutiny did the soldier's public image dramatically improve.[32] On the other hand, the army's reputation after Waterloo never stood higher. The wars had created their own literature—army and navy magazines, accounts of campaigns and famous actions, 'inside stories' of France by escaped prisoners—and this kind of writing burgeoned over the next thirty years into a large corpus of reminiscence, biography, and history.[33] A large market also existed for prints on military subjects, battle souvenirs, and public exhibitions in the form of panoramas, dioramas, and waxworks, most of this material focusing on Waterloo. Waterloo Day was celebrated annually until Wellington's death in 1852. The failure to build a Waterloo Monument after 1815 was not because of public indifference but because the artistic élites could not agree among themselves, a curious rehearsal of what was to happen to Scotland's National Monument.[34]

Few histories of Napoleonic volunteers were written before the revival of volunteering in the mid-Victorian period, which itself is evidence of the limited militarization that the wars achieved.[35] Perhaps we need to recognize volunteering as like other kinds of paternalistic activity, arising out of a particular situation or problem which the propertied classes thought it important to address but which they could easily withdraw from if circumstances changed.[36] While, then, the exploits of the army could be admired for the national greatness they conferred, military service and closer identification with the military lost their relevance or any purpose in the early nineteenth-century society. When a volunteer movement re-emerged its timing was determined by a renewed threat of foreign attack; yet within a few years the wealthy middle classes were leaving and the corps effectively became recreational clubs for artisans. No sustained interest in military service was shown by urban élites, and, indeed, whenever they acted as volunteer commanders, they showed little cordiality in their dealings with the military.[37] Middle-class civilianism flourished on notions that only the most wretched and depraved of men enlisted in the army and that military careers were more open to aristocrats than talent. Sir Henry Havelock of Cawnpore and Lucknow fame was

---

[32] O. Anderson, 'The Growth of Christian Militarism in Mid-Victorian Britain', *Eng. Hist. Rev.* 86 (1971), 46–52; Spiers, *The Army and Society*, 102–3, 116–17, 139–40; J. W. M. Hichberger, *Images of the Army: The Military in British Art 1815–1914* (Manchester, 1988), 159–65.

[33] An anthology, providing a small sample of this literature, is A. D. Harvey, *English Literature and the Great War with France* (London, 1981).

[34] See above, 150. Hichberger, *Images of the Army*, 11–12; Yarrington, *Commemoration of the Hero*, 178–201.

[35] A. S. White and E. J. Martin, 'A Bibliography of Volunteering', *J. Soc. for Army Hist. Res.* 23 (1945), 2–29; 24 (1946), 88–91 lists just four titles published between 1815 and 1850, all of them yeomanry histories.

[36] Morris, 'Clubs, Societies and Associations', in *Cambridge Social History*, iii. 410–11, 414–15.

[37] Cunningham, *The Volunteer Force*, esp. chs. 2–4.

the greater hero to the Victorian public because of his comparatively lowly origins and the middle-class rectitude and merit he appeared to represent. Perhaps as many as half of the officers in the early nineteenth-century army were drawn from outside the gentry and nobility; but this was never enough to establish a middle-class rapport with the army that went beyond admiration for its achievements in the 'Great War' with France.[38] Many reasons operated: the general lack of professional opportunity in the army after 1815 which fostered class antagonism against the aristocracy; the under-representation of the English in the officer corps; the remoteness from civilian society that imperial soldiering enforced; the aristocratic ethos that continued to be cultivated in the army.

Scottish militarism, however, was conspicuous after 1815, part of the articulation of national character that had to serve as Scotland's national identity once a 'whiggish' pre-Union history showing Scotland's independent but parallel development with England towards liberty and progress was ruled out in the eighteenth century. England was not an adversary against which an ethnonationalism could develop but a more advanced state and economy to which Scotland was beholden. The Union was a debt incurred by Scotland, repaid by Scotland's soldiers and intellectuals and later products of her 'genius'—scientists, engineers, and medical men.[39] The cult of Scottish valour was particularly important for indicating the ancientness of the Scottish nation and for providing an emotionally compelling version of Scotland's past—the struggle over many centuries of a small and poor country against more powerful foes. Wallace, Bruce, and the War of Independence excited huge public commemorations in the early nineteenth century. Scotland's military prowess during the Napoleonic Wars was explicit in the deeds of the Scottish regiments and crucially timed in the sense that it 'verified' the military tradition that was being constructed at the time. The continuation of the regiments after the wars gave the process even more contemporary meaning. Regimental history as a genre began in Scotland, and the first soldier autobiographies seem to have been produced there as well.[40] In another way Scottish society remained

---

[38] On Havelock see Anderson, 'Christian Militarism', 49–51; Spiers, *The Army and Society*, 133–4. For the social composition of the officer corps see Razzell, 'Social Origins of Officers', 253; Strachan, *Wellington's Legacy*, 110.

[39] Kidd, *Subverting Scotland's Past*; Smout, 'Problems of Nationalism', 1–21; Fry, 'Whig Interpretation of Scottish History', 72–89.

[40] The following, published before 1830, appear in the *NCSTC*: George Billanie, *Narrative of a Private Soldier in the 92nd Regiment of Foot* (Glasgow, 1819); *Journal of a Soldier of the 71st or Glasgow Regiment, Highland Light Infantry, from 1806 to 1815* (Edinburgh, 1819); Joseph Donaldson, *Recollections of an Eventful Life, Chiefly Passed in the Army* (Glasgow, 1824); John Malcolm, *Reminiscences of a Campaign in the Pyrenees and the South of France in 1814* (Edinburgh, 1826); *Eventful Life of a Soldier During the Late War in Portugal, Spain and France* (Edinburgh, 1827); *Recollections of Robert Eadie Giving a Concise Account of His Campaigns in Ireland, Denmark Walcheren and the Peninsula* (Kincardine, 1829); [T. Hamilton], *Annals of the Peninsula Campaigns 1808–14* (Edinburgh, 1829).

deeply involved with the military. About a quarter of the officers of the British army were Scottish-born in the eighteenth and early nineteenth centuries. Add at least the same proportion of Scots in the officer corps of the huge East India Company army and a great many gentry and middle-class families in Scotland could be said to have had an interest in military careers.[41]

The military exploits of Irishmen in the Napoleonic Wars, headed as they were by Wellington, were hardly less than those of the Scots. Nor were Irish soldiers backward in serving the nineteenth-century empire. Yet Irish society made little of these achievements bedevilled as it was by rival Catholic and Protestant nationalisms, each of which found Irish service in the British army difficult to accommodate. The Ascendancy, before and after emancipation, refused to admit Catholic loyalty. Catholic nationalists, increasingly alienated from the British crown, preferred to manufacture a history of resistance and rebellion against British authority.[42] An Irish military reputation was mostly contained within the army, based on the strong Irish presence that existed there from the Napoleonic period and on genuine respect for the Irish soldier as exemplifying, like the Highlander and perhaps helped by the Highlander, the primitive martial virtues of valour, endurance, and fidelity.[43] Britain, therefore, came to pay greater tribute to the Irish soldier than did Ireland. The Scottish contribution to victory in the Great War against France became a powerful ingredient in Scotland's national mythology. Ireland's contribution, which yielded nothing in its importance, was ignored by Ireland in the curious way in which different nationalisms variously select their materials.

The war, even so, profoundly affected Ireland because, if it did not begin the British military occupation of Ireland, it certainly helped the British state reach the conclusion that British military power might well have to be the bottom line of the Anglo-Irish relationship. In the eighteenth century that relationship had worked well, for the most part, on the basis of Ireland's political subordination. From the 1780s, however, Britain kept being challenged by formidable Irish oppositions which were difficult to incorporate into the political process and offered the threat of armed resistance. The extent of the breakdown of politics was shown by the 20,000–30,000 regulars stationed in Ireland throughout the nineteenth century

---

[41] See above, 127. Razzell, 'Social Origins of Officers', 250. At the time of the Mutiny there were 5,362 officers in the Company's army. J. W. Kaye, *History of the Sepoy War in India 1857–8* (3 vols., London, 1864–76), i. 626. I am indebted to Dr I. J. Catanach for this reference.

[42] Apart from writings on the rebellion of 1798, it is interesting how attention after 1840 was given to an Irish military tradition independent of the British army. See M. O'Conor, *Military History of the Irish Nation* (1845) and his *The Irish Brigades* (1855); J. C. O'Callaghan, *History of the Irish Brigades in the Service of France* (1854).

[43] E. A. Muenger, *The British Military Dilemma in Ireland: Occupation Politics 1886–1914* (Lawrence, Kan., 1991), 33–4; Womack, *Improvement and Romance*, 39–44.

compared with the 10,000 or less maintained there in the eighteenth;[44] one can wonder how the Hanoverian state with a peacetime army of 40,000–50,000 would have fared had it been asked to place in Ireland the number of troops later required. In population terms early nineteenth-century Ireland had a garrison double the size of Britain's. While this is worthy of being called an occupation, a perception also developed over the war period, mainly because of the rebellion of 1798 and continuing troubles, that occupation was what was required in Ireland. Redesdale in 1802 wrote of Ireland remaining 'for some time as a garrisoned country'. He added: 'I meant a Protestant garrison.'[45] The end of contact between Irish and French republicans, indeed the end of any serious foreign threat to Ireland after Napoleon, did not alter this situation since Ireland's rulers continued to equate public disorder, whatever its causes, with incipient rebellion. That the war contributed directly to the new policy of occupation is clear; first, it provided a strong setting by magnifying the danger of rebellion; secondly, it provided a justification for a huge increase in the peacetime garrison by exposing the limitations of the yeomanry as a law and order force and by showing that even a large army in Ireland could not prevent a disturbing amount of social unrest; thirdly, especially with the militia interchange, it established the practice of garrisoning Ireland with British troops rather than Irish-raised forces, a policy still being followed as late as the Boer War.[46] Also not to be forgotten is the infrastructure of occupation that quickly came into existence during the war; in 1831 the army in Ireland was dispersed over fifty barracks and forts with another sixty-two barracks available if the need arose.[47]

The size of the army kept in Ireland was one sign of how the military expansion of the eighteenth-century state lost nothing of its momentum in the nineteenth century, the era of cheap government notwithstanding. As David French has pointed out, if the sepoy army in the India is added to 100,000–150,000 regulars, the land forces of the British empire between Waterloo and the Crimean War more than matched those of the Continental powers with the exception of France and

---

[44] The strength of the regular army in Ireland in Jan. 1793 was 9,644 rank and file. In the early 19th cent. this was maintained at about 20,000, rising to about 30,000 in the 1860s. Returns of British army 1793–1806, 1817–32, *CJ* lxi. 637; *SP* 1831–2, xxvii. 117–21; 'Table showing the strength of the British army in Ireland 1828–44 and 1861–1910', D. N. Haire, 'The British Army in Ireland 1868–1890', M. Litt. thesis (Trinity Coll., Dublin, 1973), 333–5.

[45] R. Barry O'Brien, *Dublin Castle and the Irish People*, 43, cited Muenger, *British Military Dilemma*, 3. See also Lord Whitworth to Lord Sidmouth, 16 June 1814: '[Ireland] is not to be governed as England is, the Character and Spirit of the governed are completely different. . . . This Government must in fact be considered as a Military Government; and to be effectual must be made a very strong one . . .', cited Palmer, *Police and Protest*, 201.

[46] Muenger, *British Military Dilemma*, 123–4; Spiers, *The Army and Society*, 78–9.

[47] Return of the barracks in the UK, *SP* 1831–2, xxvii. 177–82.

Russia.[48] What has been ignored is the extent to which the armed nation of the Napoleonic period, in idea though not in substance, remained an integral part of the British military system. Its legislation, for instance, stayed in the statute book, so that the crown, among other powers, retained the authority to regulate volunteer corps and to summon the lieutenancies to organize the civilian population for home defence. The Duke of York during the war set up a 'military repository' or archive at the Horse Guards which contained the key documents describing the mass mobilization and its organization.[49] These were certainly consulted during the alarm over national defence in the 1840s and 1850s, and indeed the measures then adopted bore the heavy imprint of past experience. The fact was that a very long war had, by trial and error, produced the kind of armed force well accommodated to both the military requirements of the state and the military service society was prepared to offer.

Neither state needs nor social attitudes changed substantially in the first half of the nineteenth century, and not necessarily much later on. For defence of the British islands, particularly against the military power of France, large civilian forces, even mass mobilization, continued to be the country's ultimate security. But local muster and training, independence of the army, and low proficiency characterized the mid-Victorian as well as the Napoleonic auxiliaries because such were the terms on which it seemed the most satisfactory compromise between production and defence could be achieved. Furthermore, the limited service of the auxiliaries only reinforced the difference between civilian society and the army inherited from the eighteenth century. The regulars, disciplined, barracked, committed overseas for long periods, were the closest Britain had to a caste. During the Napoleonic Wars the militia was developed as the bridge that could span this gap when it became an important source of recruits for the army and accepted foreign service. Afterwards the generals always conceived it to be the 'reserve' force which might be re-created if the need arose. When it was revived in 1852 it was soon pressed into this role, though the irony was that the occasion was the Crimean War in which France was Britain's ally and not her enemy.

The armed nation of 1793–1815, then, ought to be considered as part of the further development of the British warfare state. It opened up access to national manpower reserves on a scale that had not been seen before. Perhaps the principle of universal service was inherent in the militia obligation as this had been restated in 1757; but militia practice fell far short of the levies that were authorized, actually raised, and paid for during the Napoleonic Wars. There was never a doubt

---

[48] French, *The British Way in Warfare*, 124.

[49] The Militia Act (1802), Volunteer Act (1804), Training Act (1806), and Local Militia Act (1808) remained unrepealed as late as the 1870s. For the 'military repository' see Duke of York to Castlereagh, 3 Aug. 1805, WO1/628/459–62. Volumes belonging to the 'repository' can be found at WO30.

that in the future the state could and would impose service on as many as national defence required, even if the numbers ran to hundreds of thousands. Of course, universal service in the nineteenth-century context was for home defence, not for the general military operations of the state. Talk of conscription by the generals at the height of the struggle with France showed how the army continued to be starved of men, something equally apparent in the numerous foreign corps taken into the army after 1809. Recruitment from the militia, however, offered the beginnings of a solution. The annual drafts begun in 1811 finally established the militia as a wartime reserve from which the army had improved (though how much improved is a good question) access to manpower resources, including in Ireland. When right at the end of the war the militia agreed to be posted outside the British Isles, the benefit for the army was the same because regulars released from garrisons were available for field operations. It could be argued that the most significant development of the war was the greater strategic flexibility with which the state could employ its forces. With militia in Scotland and Ireland as well as England, all committed to the defence of the British Isles, and with the local auxiliaries available for service throughout either Britain or Ireland, the army in 1814 was able to have over 80 per cent of its strength or 200,000 men overseas.[50]

The conscriptionist state, however, was as far away as ever. It is all very well to point to Britain's military expansion from the seventeenth century and the ever-increasing military obligations that the British state laid on its citizens, in both of which Britain can be seen to have been keeping pace with European developments. We might also acknowledge war to be an activity founded on exigency, meaning that in war governments and societies are quite capable of breaking with accustomed modes and established systems for the sake of defence and survival. But the truth is that in nineteenth-century Britain compulsory service was deemed incompatible with a commercial society whose prosperity depended on the pursuit of individual gain and with an army for the most part stationed abroad. If anything, the voluntary principle strengthened during the century with the shortening of the army's enlistment term, the revival of the militia in 1852 as a volunteer force, and the virtually uninterrupted growth of the volunteer movement from 1863.[51] Nothing could destroy the idea of a wholly enlisted regular army with separate civilian volunteers for home defence until the crisis of World War I arrived; even Haldane's territorials resisted incorporation into the Expeditionary Force that would go to France up to the last moment.[52] The British military system remained skewed towards empire and home defence, the latter based on a less than effective 'amateur tradition', with the result that whenever the army had to fight a 'large' (not to say

---

[50] Return of the British army serving in Britain and Ireland, 15 Oct. 1813, WO25/3225, gives a total of 43,706 men at a time when the army's strength was 260,797 rank and file (*CJ* lxix. 638). The force sent to Holland in Dec. 1813 further depleted the home garrison.

[51] Cunningham, *The Volunteer Force*, 105 for volunteer numbers.   [52] Ibid. 148–9.

'gigantic' in 1914) war overseas it entirely lacked the backing of a sufficient trained reserve. Such an irrational structure in military terms underlined the extent to which the British warfare state continued to be a civil rather than military creation. Society's predominance over the military had been decisively affirmed during the Napoleonic period in the way the auxiliaries had remained independent of the army, military service had been subordinated to production and social status, and compulsion had been kept to a minimum.

The Napoleonic mobilization for national defence was undoubtedly the greatest 'national project' in Britain's experience. It deserves to be called a 'national project' because it fits so exactly as a pre-bureaucratic combination of central, local, and voluntary effort for a defined, widely publicized, and accepted national purpose. Besides generating an impressive amount of legislation—on average during the war about eleven statutes per year were devoted to the militias, volunteers, and home defence[53]—national defence produced the most elaborate national planning yet seen, culminating in the army's impressively detailed counter-invasion preparations in 1803–4. This activity at the centre was accompanied by an immense volume of business transacted with the localities as instructions, commissions, and money were issued, and inspections and audits organized. Accounts, returns, and applications in equally large number went the other way. The war existed as one of those occasions in the uneven and fluctuating development of the state when central authority was heavily intrusive in the localities, in this case because national defence required co-operation on a national scale and because the crown was anxious to keep control of local military power. National defence was a state problem sufficiently important and challenging as to bring about a sustained burst of government activity when the usual pattern was for the localities to be entrusted with the enforcement of national policy with minimal supervision from outside. Not that the government's switch from passiveness in any matter made local efforts of little or no account. Only local leaders could ensure the effectiveness of government measures or provide the information the government increasingly looked for in order to identify problems and assess policies. Counties, towns, and parishes were also capable of taking initiatives of their own; in a sense every volunteer corps formed and every one not formed were independent responses to national crisis. Yet, in the last analysis, national defence showed how strong the hinge of local–central co-operation was by which British society was governed. The vast numbers enlisted alone stand as sufficient evidence. And to participation must be added publicity because the government–society relationship was further strengthened by the vigorous circulation of information and ideas from either side.

If national defence was the greatest ever 'national project', what, if anything, did

---

[53] The British, later United Kingdom, parliament passed 223 statutes on these subjects 1793–1814, but Irish legislation before 1801 (e.g. 22 militia acts) swells the total.

it contribute to state formation in Britain? The question presents itself because war still stands as the classic explanation for the emergence of the modern state with its centralized, bureaucratized authority. Clearly, the armed nation of 1793–1815 did not exist outside the existing state structure but rather expressed the loose-jointed relationship between centre and localities up to the point of the non-compliance of the latter in some instances. In anticipation of the counties' role in national defence, Dundas established county lieutenancies in Scotland, simply extending the traditional means of devolution. Everywhere, at most times, local leaders were under pressure to add to their service and add to their number. The sheer demands of the situation as the armed nation had to be organized on a greater and greater scale and then maintained produced an expansion of activity at all levels, including voluntary effort.

The importance of this was that popular disorder, counter-revolution, poverty, and associated social problems were already having the same effect. Indeed, a distinguishing feature of late eighteenth-century British society was the expansion of public enterprise, usually locally organized but often centrally supported; and the increasing amount of information available to the government and public, as cause and effect of this. As with national defence, the same general effects can be observed: of the gentry being drawn back into public life, of broadening participation in public affairs by lesser members of the propertied class, of more direct intervention into the lives of the poor by their betters. Parliamentary legislation dealing with matters of national policy is a totally inadequate measure of what was happening to Britain's political culture from about 1760 into the middle of the nineteenth century, including the extent to which central politics and government were affected by local concerns.[54] The better indices to consult for the development of public authority, together with the increasing engagement of the public which was an inseparable part of it, would be such things as the growth of government and parliamentary business, the number of voluntary societies, the size of magistracies, the increase of contested elections, and the increase of newspaper readership. Britain at the time of the Napoleonic Wars was becoming a more effective civil society in that public affairs were offering greater opportunities for participation over a greater range of issues while centre and localities were more firmly interlocked by information-collecting, publicity, and discussion than ever before.

National defence, therefore, is difficult to see as a set of emergency measures or even emergency institutions interrupting for a period longer-term trends. Instead, the armed nation was organized according to the existing structure of authority while drawing on the strongest developing elements of the British polity—gentry leadership, a unified propertied class, positive interaction between the government

---

[54] Cf. Harling and Mandler, 'From "Fiscal-Military" State', 50–2.

and the localities. Its more specific contribution can only be stated tentatively until we know more about what connected individuals to different kinds of public action and public service. First, national defence produced an impressive social mobilization under the authority and leadership of the propertied class, immensely satisfying to paternalistic ideals because of the opportunities it seemed to present. In particular, there seems to be a connection worth pursuing further between patriotic activity which collected and recruited from the lower orders and philanthropy which was inclining towards personal contact and supervision.[55] Secondly, national defence provided an enormous number of lesser men below the landed gentry with opportunities of public leadership and service. William Brackenbury, listed as a grocer in a directory of 1793, ended up as colonel of an Isle of Ely volunteer battalion and enough of a public figure to have his obituary in the county newspaper. Thomas Lloyd's memorial in Leeds parish church was erected by public subscription; his public career, likewise, was founded on his command of the local volunteers.[56] Perhaps here can be found the key feature of the late Hanoverian state, not just the end of whig exclusionist politics but a widening of participation in public affairs on the sort of scale that sooner or later could only make issues of representation unavoidable.

[55] The Victorian militia immediately became a vehicle for moral paternalism. Beckett, *Amateur Military Tradition*, 151.

[56] Cookson, 'Ely Volunteers', 168. For Lloyd see the obituary in *Gentleman's Magazine*, 143 (1828), 472–3; Arch, 'Mark of Esteem', 201–6.

Bibliography

PRIMARY SOURCES

Manuscripts

London

British Library

Add. MSS

33048, 33109, 33118–20 Pelham Papers
35669–70, 35675–6, 35702–5, 35719–22, 35768, 35773–5, 35919, 45031–2, 45036–7, 45040–1 Hardwicke Papers
37842, 37877, 37881, 37883–6, 37890–1, 37903–4 Windham Papers
38734–6, 38759 Huskisson Papers
38241–7, 38358–64, 38377–9 Liverpool Papers
40100–2, 43770 Melville Papers
40185, 40187, 40220, 40236, 40245, 40562 Peel Papers
49472–3, 49476, 49480, 49494, 49500–4, 49510, 49512A J. W. Gordon Papers
51468 Holland House Papers
58879, 58918, 59286–8, 59290, 59306 Dropmore Papers
Loan 57 Bathurst Papers, Correspondence, 5–7, 21.

National Army Museum

6807 Nugent Papers

Public Record Office

Home Office Records

HO30/1–3 Secretary of State for War
HO42/25–8, 107–8 Correspondence and Papers, Domestic and General
HO50/2–3, 6, 29–30, 62, 97, 453 Military
HO100/39–41, 47–50, 53–5, 60–1, 67–9, 73–4, 83–4, 90–2, 101–2, 108, 111 Ireland Military Correspondence
HO102/7–22, 63–4 Scotland Correspondence

War Office Records

WO1/407, 612, 617, 619–58, 766–76, 778, 902–4, 942, 946, 1119 In-letters
WO3/157, 579, 583–5 Out-letters, Commander-in-Chief
WO4/345 Out-letters Secretary at War, Chaplain-General 1810–15

WO6/131–3 Out-letters Secretary of State
WO7/60–1, 66–7 Out-letters Departmental, Chaplain-General
WO13/4207 Cambridgeshire Volunteer Pay Lists
WO17/2813 Monthly Returns
WO25/3224–5 Documents Relating to Establishments and Recruiting, 1809–15
WO27/76–7, 82, 90, 102, 121–3 Inspection Returns
WO30/58, 64–6, 68, 73, 76, 80 Papers Relating to Defence
WO133 Brownrigg Papers

PRO30/8/101–94, 240–5, 317, 323–31 Chatham Papers
PRO30/9 Colchester Papers
PRO30/11 Cornwallis Papers

Edinburgh

National Library of Scotland

5, 7, 21, 1048–9, 3834–5, 6524 Melville Papers
638 C. R. Cockerell Papers
872 Correspondence of Royal Edinburgh Volunteer Light Dragoons
1500–4 Delvine Papers (Perthshire fencibles, volunteers, local militia)
1754 A. Dirom, 'Memoir of the Military State of North Britain in 1803'
2732 Sederunt Book, Committee for Sir John Moore's Monument, Glasgow
2735 Sederunt Book, Committee for Lord Nelson's Monument, Glasgow
7099 Yester Papers, East Lothian Defence Letterbook 1794–8
10895–6, 10958–9 Airth Papers
11747 Minto Papers
14299 Miscellaneous (fos. 154–7 Angus Fencibles)
15973 Miscellaneous (fos. 12–13 printed circular, Committee for National Monument, 1822)
16197 Lynedoch Papers
17506 Saltoun Papers

Adv. 22. 2. 21 Minute Book, Royal Edinburgh Volunteer Light Dragoons 1797–1801
Adv. 46. 1. 6 Sir George Murray Papers

Scottish Record Office

GD26/9 Leven and Melville MSS
GD44/47, 49, 50 Gordon Castle MSS
GD46/6, 17 Seaforth MSS
GD50/18, 110 John MacGregor Collection
GD51/1, 5, 9, 16 Melville Castle MSS
GD80/938 Macpherson of Cluny MSS
GD112/52 Breadalbane MSS
GD132/831 Robertson of Lude MSS
GD136/441 Sinclair of Freswick MSS
GD224/30, 423–42, 628, 668, 682, 687, 689 Buccleuch MSS
GD225/1044 Leith Hall Muniments

GD237/192 Tods, Murray and Jamieson Collection
GD248/190, 213, 984, 2013–15, 2023, 3408, 3416 Seafield MSS
GD267/1 Home of Wedderburn MSS
GD302/40, 45 East Lothian Antiquarian and Field Naturalists' Society Papers
GD364/1 Hope of Lufness MSS

University of Edinburgh Library

Laing Collection, Robert Dundas Papers La. ii. 501
General Collection, Gen. 1995

Dublin

National Archives of Ireland

M. 464 Paymaster-General's Register
MS 3474, 3478 Longford Militia Letterbook

National Library of Ireland

54A–55 Melville Papers
58–75A Richmond Papers
131 Letterbook, Lt.-Col. S. Browne, Deputy Quarter-Master General (Ireland), 1810–26
177–8 Westmeath Militia Records
695 Memorandum Book, Sir W. H. Clinton, Quarter-Master General (Ireland), 1804–12
809 Transcripts of Documents Relating to French Invasion of Ireland, 1796
1002–6, 1228–30, 1330–4, 1349 Kilmainham (Commander of the Forces) Papers
5006 Morrison Papers
5073 Documents Relating to Fencible Regiments in Ireland
5194 Ordnance Office (Ireland) Letterbook 1813–15
8351 Statement of Troops in Ireland 1798–1800, Adjutant-General's Office, Jan. 1833
10214–17 Clinton Papers
14303 Letterbook of Col. F. Beckwith, Secretary to Commander of the Forces, 1802–3
15895–902, 15904, 15906 Bolton Papers
20311–12, 20330 O'Hara Papers
20845 *Nelson's Pillar*

Armagh Militia Records (microfilm P. 1014)
Sir Vere Hunt Papers (microfilm P. 5528)
Longford Militia Record of Service Book (microfilm P. 5556)

State Paper Office

Records of the Chief Secretary's Office
Official Papers: OP10–456
Letterbooks: VIIIA/1/3–4 (Private and Secret Correspondence, 1789–93, 1806–11); VIIIA/
 1/5 (Private Government Correspondence, 1811–23); VIIIA/1/13 (General Private
 Correspondence, 1804–14).
Westmorland Correspondence

Trinity College Library

T. 2541/IA2/6–10 Transcripts of Abercorn MSS

Belfast

Northern Ireland Public Record Office

D. 3030 Castlereagh Papers

Provinces

Bedford Record Office, Bedford

LCM 2 Lieutenancy, Militia Records
WI Whitbread Papers, Correspondence

Buckinghamshire Record Office, Aylesbury

D/MH/H/War Hobart Papers

Cambridge Record Office, Cambridge

Ely and South Witchford Subdivisional Records

Cambridge Record Office, Huntingdon

DDM 80 Manchester Papers

Devon Record Office, Exeter

152M/C1801–3 Sidmouth Papers

Dundee Archives and Record Centre, Dundee

ACC 10 Angus (Forfar) Lieutenancy Records

University of Durham Library

Grey Papers, 1st Earl (Sir Charles Grey)

Essex Record Office, Chelmsford

D/DHa Papers Relating to Tendring Volunteers
D/P 242/17–18 Debden Parish Returns
L/R 1, L/U 3/8 Essex Lieutenancy Papers
Library Folder (Military)

Hampshire Record Office, Winchester

38M49/1, 5 Wickham Papers

Hertford Record Office, Hertford

Hitchin Volunteers MSS

Lincoln Record Office, Lincoln

4BNL Brownlow MSS
2 Cragg 1/13 Memorandum Book of J. Cragg
Kesteven Quarter Sessions Records

Liverpool Record Office, Liverpool

920 Cur. 26 Currie Papers

North Yorkshire Record Office, Northallerton

7/2/119 Wyvill Papers

Perth and Kinross District Library, Perth

B59 Perth Burgh Records
CC1 Perthshire Lieutenancy Minute Book, 1801–3
PE66 Miscellaneous Papers Relating to Perthshire Militia and Volunteers

Sheffield Central Library, Sheffield

F5, 30 Fitzwilliam MSS

University of Southampton Library, Southampton

WP1/182–298 Wellington Papers (correspondence and papers, 1807–9)

Central Region (Scotland) Archives, Stirling

B66 Stirling Burgh Records
SC8 Loyal Stirling Volunteers Minute Book 1800–4; Militia Letterbook

Suffolk Record Office, Bury St Edmunds

HA 521 James Oakes Diary

Private Collections

Campbell of Ardchattan MSS, Ardchattan House, Argyllshire
Macpherson Grant of Ballindalloch MSS, Ballindalloch Castle, Banffshire

Newspapers and Periodicals

Annual Register
Baptist Magazine
Blackwood's Edinburgh Magazine
Caledonian Mercury
Cambridge Chronicle
Creswell and Burbage's Nottingham Journal
Dublin Evening Post
Edinburgh Advertiser
Edinburgh Evening Courant

Edinburgh Magazine
Edinburgh Review
Examiner
Faulkner's Dublin Journal
Freeman's Journal
Gentleman's Magazine
Independent Whig
Leeds Mercury
Nottingham Review
Quarterly Review
Scots Magazine
Stamford News
The Times
York Courant

Correspondence, Diaries, Memoirs

BATHURST, *HMC, Bathurst MSS* (London, 1923).
CASTLEREAGH, *Memoirs and Correspondence of Viscount Castlereagh*, ed. Marquess of Londonderry (12 vols., London, 1848–53).
COCKBURN, H., *Memorials of His Time*, ed. K. F. C. Miller (Chigago, 1974).
CORNWALLIS, *Correspondence of the 1st Marquis Cornwallis*, ed. C. Ross (3 vols., London, 1859).
GEORGE III, *Later Correspondence of George III*, ed. A. Aspinall (5 vols., Cambridge, 1962–70).
GEORGE IV, *Letters of King George IV 1812–30*, ed. A. Aspinall (3 vols., Cambridge, 1938).
GRAHAM, *HMC, Graham of Fintry MSS* (London, 1942).
GRENVILLE, *HMC, Dropmore MSS* (10 vols., London, 1894–1927).
LAING, *HMC, Laing MSS* (2 vols., London, 1914–25), vol. ii.
MOIRA, *HMC, Hastings MSS* (4 vols., London, 1928–), vol. iii.
MOORE, *Diary of Sir John Moore*, ed. J. F. Maurice (2 vols., London, 1904).
SPENCER, *Private Papers of George, 2nd Earl Spencer*, ed. J. S. Corbett (4 vols., London, 1913–24).
STANHOPE, Earl of, *Notes of Conversations with the Duke of Wellington, 1831–51* (London, 1938).
WELLINGTON, *Despatches During His Various Campaigns*, ed. Lt.-Col. Gurwood (12 vols., London, 1837–8).
——*Supplementary Despatches, Correspondence and Memoranda of the Duke of Wellington*, ed. Duke of Wellington (15 vols., London, 1858–72).
WINDHAM, *The Diary of William Windham*, ed. Mrs H. Baring (London, 1866).
——*Windham Papers*, ed. Earl of Rosebery (2 vols., London, 1913).

Other Contemporary Works

Army List 1795, 1801, 1806, 1813.
AUFRERE, A., *A Warning to Britons Against French Perfidy and Cruelty* (London, 1798).

BEAUFORT, D. A., *Memoir of a Map of Ireland; Illustrating the Topography of That Kingdom, and Containing a Short Account of Its Present State, Civil and Ecclesiastical* (Dublin, 1792).

BISHOP OF LINCOLN, *A Sermon Preached at the Cathedral Church of St Paul . . . December 19th 1797* (London, 1798).

BROWN, J., *The Rise, Progress and Military Improvement of the Bristol Volunteers* (Bristol, 1798).

CARTWRIGHT, J., *England's Aegis: or the Military Energies of the Constitution* (1806).

COBBETT, W. (ed.), *Parliamentary History of England . . . to 1803* (36 vols., London, 1806–20).

COLQUHOUN, P., *A Treatise on the Wealth, Power and Resources of the British Empire* (repr. New York, 1965).

CRICHTON, P., *Hints for the Economical and Internal Regulation of Volunteer Companies in Scotland* (Edinburgh, 1797).

[CURRIE, J.], *A Letter Commercial and Political Addressed to the Rt. Hon. William Pitt by Jasper Wilson* (Liverpool, 1793).

DIROM, A., *Plans for the Defence of Great Britain and Ireland* (Edinburgh, 1797).

FRASER, R.(?), *Hints to the Volunteers of the United Kingdom* (London, 1801).

Friendly Address to the Volunteers of Great Britain (Hitchin, 1803).

[GREGORY, W.], *The Picture of Dublin* (Dublin, 1811).

HIGHLAND SOCIETY, *Prize Essays and Transactions of the Highland Society of Scotland* (14 vols., Edinburgh, 1799–1843).

HOUSE OF COMMONS, *Sessional Papers of the Eighteenth Century*, ed. S. Lambert (19 vols., Wilmington, Del., 1975).

HOUSE OF COMMONS, *British Sessional Papers, 1801–1900*, ed. E. Erickson (microprint, 1964).

Journal of the House of Commons.

[KEATING, H.], *Thoughts on the Military Relations of Great Britain and Ireland* (Leominster, 1803).

Parliamentary Debates

Report of the Patriotic Fund (London, 1803).

[ROSCOE, W.], *Thoughts on the Causes of the Present Failures* (London, 1793).

Rules and Regulations to be Observed by the Bristol Volunteer Association (Bristol, 1797).

Selections from the Papers of the London Corresponding Society 1792–1799, ed. M. Thale (Cambridge, 1983).

SELKIRK, Earl of, *On the Necessity of a More Effectual System of National Defence and the Means of Establishing the Permanent Security of the Kingdom* (London, 1808).

SINCLAIR, Sir J., *The Statistical Account of Scotland 1791–1799*, ed. D. Withrington and I. Grant (repr., 20 vols., East Ardsley, 1977–83).

STEWART, D., *Sketches of the Character, Manners and Present State of the Highlanders of Scotland* (repr., 2 vols., Edinburgh, 1977).

STEWART, W., *Outlines of a Plan for the General Reform of the British Land Forces* (London, 1806).

TELFORD, W., *Transparencies Exhibited in Bristol and Its Vicinity on the Day of Proclaiming Peace* (Bristol, 1802).

WAKEFIELD, E., *An Account of Ireland, Statistical and Political* (2 vols., London, 1812).

WARBURTON, J., WHITELAW, J., and WALSH, R., *History of the City of Dublin* (2 vols., Dublin, 1818).

WILSON, Sir R., *History of the British Expedition to Egypt* (London, 1802).

SECONDARY SOURCES

Books

ANDERSON, J. E., *A Short Account of the Mortlake Company of the Royal Putney, Roehampton and Mortlake Volunteer Corps 1803–6* (Richmond, 1893).

ANDERSON, M. S., *War and Society in Europe of the Old Regime 1618–1789* (London, 1988).

ASHCROFT, M., *To Escape the Monster's Clutches: Notes and Documents Illustrating the Preparations in North Yorkshire to Repel Invasion* (Northallerton, 1977).

BARTLETT, T., *The Fall and Rise of the Irish Nation: The Catholic Question 1690–1830* (Savage, Md., 1992).

—— 'Indiscipline and Disaffection in the Armed Forces in Ireland in the 1790s', in P. Corish (ed.), *Radicals, Rebels and Establishments* (Belfast, 1985), 115–34.

—— 'Indiscipline and Disaffection in the French and Irish Armies during the Revolutionary Period', in H. Gough and D. Dickson (eds.), *Ireland and the French Revolution* (Dublin, 1990), 179–201.

—— '"A Weapon of War Yet Untried": Irish Catholics and the Armed Forces of the Crown 1760–1830', in T. G. Fraser and K. Jeffrey (eds.), *Men, Women and War* (Dublin, 1993), 66–85.

BECKETT, I. F. W., *The Amateur Military Tradition 1558–1945* (Manchester, 1991).

—— *The Buckinghamshire Posse Comitatus 1798* (Buckingham, 1985).

BERRY, R. P., *A History of the Formation and Development of the Volunteer Infantry* (London, 1903).

BEST, G., *War and Society in Revolutionary Europe 1770–1870* (London, 1982).

BLACK, J., *European Warfare 1660–1815* (London, 1994).

—— *Natural and Necessary Enemies: Anglo-French Relations in the Eighteenth Century* (London, 1986).

BLACKSTOCK, A., 'The Social and Political Implications of the Raising of the Yeomanry in Ulster, 1796–8', in D. Dickson, D. Keogh, and K. Whelan (eds.), *The United Irishmen: Republicanism, Radicalism and Rebellion* (Dublin, 1993).

BOHSTEDT, J., *Riots and Community Politics in England and Wales 1790–1810* (Cambridge, Mass., 1983).

BOND, G. C., *The Grand Expedition: The British Invasion of Holland in 1809* (Athens, Ga., 1979).

BORSAY, P., '"All the World's a Stage": Urban Ritual and Ceremony 1660–1800', in P. Clark (ed.), *The Transformation of English Provincial Towns* (London, 1984), 228–58.

BREWER, J., 'The Eighteenth-Century British State: Contexts and Issues', in L. Stone (ed.), *An Imperial State at War* (London, 1994), 52–71.

—— *The Sinews of War: War, Money and the English State 1688–1783* (London, 1989).

BRIGGS, A., *The Age of Improvement* (London, 1959).

BROEKER, G., *Rural Disorder and Police Reform in Ireland 1812–36* (London, 1970).

BULLOCH, J. M., *Territorial Soldiering in the North-East of Scotland During 1759–1814* (Aberdeen, 1914).

BUMSTEAD, J. M., *The People's Clearance: Highland Emigration to British North America 1770–1815* (Edinburgh, 1982).

CANNON, J., *Aristocratic Century: The Peerage of Eighteenth-Century England* (Cambridge, 1984).

CLARK, J. C. D., *English Society 1688–1832* (Cambridge, 1985).

COLLEY, L., *Britons: Forging the Nation 1707–1837* (New Haven, 1992).

—— 'Radical Patriotism in Eighteenth-Century England', in R. Samuel (ed.), *Patriotism: The Making and Unmaking of British National Identity* (3 vols., London, 1989), i. 169–87.

—— 'The Reach of the State, the Appeal of the Nation: Mass Arming and Political Culture in the Napoleonic Wars', in L. Stone (ed.), *An Imperial State at War* (London, 1994), 165–84.

COOKSON, J. E., *The Friends of Peace: Anti-War Liberalism in England 1793–1815* (Cambridge, 1982).

—— *Lord Liverpool's Administration 1815–22* (Edinburgh, 1975).

CORFIELD, P. J., *The Impact of English Towns 1700–1800* (Oxford, 1982).

CORVISIER, A., *Armies and Societies in Europe 1494–1789* (Bloomington, Ind., 1979).

COTTRELL, S., 'The Devil on Two Sticks: Franco-phobia in 1803', in R. Samuel (ed.), *Patriotism: The Making and Unmaking of British National Identity* (3 vols., London, 1989), i. 259–73.

CRIPPS, W. J., *The Royal North Gloucester* (London, 1875).

CULLEN, L. M., 'The Irish Diaspora of the 17th and 18th Centuries', in N. Canny (ed.), *Europeans on the Move: Studies in European Migration 1500–1800* (Oxford, 1994), 120–49.

—— 'Scotland and Ireland, 1600–1800: Their Role in the Evolution of British Society', in R. A. Houston and I. D. Whyte (eds.), *Scottish Society 1500–1800* (Cambridge, 1989), 226–44.

CUNLIFFE, M., *The Royal Irish Fusiliers 1793–1950* (London, 1952).

CUNNINGHAM, H., *The Volunteer Force: A Social and Political History 1859–1908* (London, 1975).

DANN, O., and DINWIDDY, J. R. (eds.), *Nationalism in the Age of the French Revolution* (London, 1988).

DARVALL, F. O., *Popular Disturbances and Public Order in Regency England* (London, 1934).

DEVINE, T. M., and MITCHISON, R. (eds.), *People and Society in Scotland: vol. 1, 1760–1830* (Edinburgh, 1988).

DICKINSON, H. T. (ed.), *Britain and the French Revolution 1789–1815* (Basingstoke, 1989).

—— 'Popular Loyalism in Britain in the 1790s', in E. Hellmuth (ed.), *The Transformation of Political Culture: England and Germany in the Late Eighteenth Century* (London, 1990), 503–33.

—— 'Radical Culture', in C. Fox (ed.), *London—World City 1800–40* (New Haven, 1992), 209–24.

DINWIDDY, J. R., 'England', in O. Dann and J. R. Dinwiddy (eds.), *Nationalism in the Age of the French Revolution* (London, 1988), 53–70.

DOZIER, R., *For King, Constitution and Country: The English Loyalists and the French Revolution* (Lexington, Ky., 1983).

DUFF, D., *Edward of Kent* (London, 1973).

DUFFY, M., *The Englishman and the Foreigner* (Cambridge, 1986).

—— 'Pitt, Grenville and the Control of British Foreign Policy in the 1790s', in J. Black (ed.), *Knights Errant and True Englishmen: British Foreign Policy 1660–1800* (Edinburgh, 1989), 151–77.

—— *Soldiers, Sugar and Seapower: The British Expeditions to the West Indies and the War Against Revolutionary France* (Oxford, 1987).

EASTWOOD, D., *Governing Rural England: Tradition and Transformation in Local Government 1780–1840* (Oxford, 1994).

——'Patriotism and the English State in the 1790s', in M. Philp (ed.), *The French Revolution and British Popular Politics* (Cambridge, 1991), 146–68.

EHRMAN, J., *The Younger Pitt: The Reluctant Transition* (London, 1983).

ELLIOTT, M., 'Ireland', in O. Dann and J. R. Dinwiddy (eds.), *Nationalism in the Age of the French Revolution* (London, 1988), 71–86.

——*Partners in Revolution: The United Irishmen and France* (New Haven, 1989).

EMSLEY, C., *British Society and the French Wars 1793–1815* (London, 1979).

——'The Impact of War and Military Participation on Britain and France 1792–1815', in C. Emsley and J. Walvin (eds.), *Artisans, Peasants and Proletarians 1760–1860* (London, 1985), 57–80.

——*Policing and its Context 1750–1870* (London, 1983).

EVANS, E. J., *The Forging of the Modern State: Early Industrial Britain 1783–1870* (London, 1983).

FINLAYSON, G., *Citizen, State and Social Welfare in Britain 1830–1990* (Oxford, 1994).

FISHER, W. G., *History of Somerset Yeomanry, Volunteer and Territorial Units* (Taunton, 1924).

FLINN, M. W., *Scottish Population History* (Cambridge, 1977).

FORTESCUE, J. W., *The County Lieutenancies and the Army 1803–14* (London, 1909).

——*History of the British Army* (13 vols., repr. New York, 1970).

FREDERICK, J. B. M., *Lineage Book of the British Army: Mounted Corps and Infantry 1660–1968* (Cornwallville, NY, 1969).

FRENCH, D., *The British Way in Warfare 1688–2000* (London, 1990).

FRY, M., *The Dundas Despotism* (Edinburgh, 1992).

——'The Whig Interpretation of Scottish History', in I. Donnachie and C. Whatley (eds.), *The Manufacture of Scottish History* (Edinburgh, 1992), 72–89.

GARDYNE, C. G., *The Life of a Regiment: The History of the Gordon Highlanders from its Formation in 1794 to 1816* (London, 1929).

GASH, N., *Lord Liverpool* (Cambridge, Mass., 1984).

——(ed.), *Wellington: Studies in the Military and Political Career of the 1st Duke of Wellington* (Manchester, 1990).

GLASS, D. V., *Numbering the People: The Eighteenth Century Population Controversy and the Development of Census and Vital Statistics in Britain* (Farnborough, 1973).

GLOVER, R., *Britain at Bay: Defence against Bonaparte 1803–1814* (London, 1973).

——*Peninsular Preparation: The Reform of the British Army 1795–1809* (Cambridge, 1963).

GOOCH, J., *Armies in Europe* (London, 1980).

GORDON, L. L., *British Battles and Medals* (London, 1979).

GOSDEN, P. H. J., *Self-Help: Voluntary Associations in 19th Century Great Britain* (London, 1973).

GRETTON, G., *The Campaigns and History of the Royal Irish Regiment from 1684 to 1902* (Edinburgh, 1911).

GUY, A. (ed.), *The Road to Waterloo: The British Army and the Struggle Against Revolutionary and Napoleonic France 1793–1815* (London, 1990).

HALL, C. D., *British Strategy in the Napoleonic War 1803–15* (Manchester, 1992).

HANHAM, H. J., 'Religion and Nationality in the Mid-Victorian Army', in M. R. D. Foot (ed.), *War and Society* (London, 1973), 159–81.

HARRISON, M., *Crowds and History: Mass Phenomena in English Towns 1790–1835* (Cambridge, 1988).

HART, C. J., *The History of the 1st Volunteer Battalion of the Royal Warwickshire Regiment and its Predecessors* (Birmingham, 1906).

HARVEY, A. D., *Collision of Empires: Britain in Three World Wars 1793–1945* (London, 1992).

——*English Literature and the Great War With France* (London, 1981).

HELLMUTH, E. (ed.), *The Transformation of Political Culture: England and Germany in the Late Eighteenth Century* (London, 1990).

HENDERSON, D. M., *Highland Soldier: A Social Study of the Highland Regiments 1820–1920* (Edinburgh, 1989).

HICHBERGER, J. W. M., *Images of the Army: The Military in British Art 1815–1914* (Manchester, 1988).

Historical Records of the Queen's Own Cameron Highlanders (7 vols., Edinburgh, 1909–61).

HOULDING, J. A., *Fit For Service: The Training of the British Army 1715–95* (Oxford, 1981).

HOUSTON, R. A., and WHYTE, I. D. (eds.), *Scottish Society 1500–1800* (Cambridge, 1989).

HOWARD, M., *War in European History* (London, 1976).

INNES, J., 'The Domestic Face of the Military-Fiscal State: Government and Society in Eighteenth-Century Britain', in L. Stone (ed.), *An Imperial State at War* (London, 1994), 96–127.

JAMES, F. G., *Ireland in the Empire 1688–1770* (Cambridge, Mass., 1973).

JAMES, W., *The Naval History of Great Britain* (6 vols., London, 1886).

JOHNSTON, S. H. F., *History of the Cameronians: vol. 1, 1689–1910* (Aldershot, 1957).

JOURDAIN, H. F. N., and Fraser, E., *The Connaught Rangers* (3 vols., London, 1924–8).

JUPP, P., *Lord Grenville* (Oxford, 1985).

KIDD, C., *Subverting Scotland's Past: Scottish Whig Historians and the Creation of an Anglo-British Identity 1689–c. 1830* (Cambridge, 1993).

KLINGBERG, F. J., and HUSTVEDT, S. B., *The Warning Drum: The British Home Front Faces Napoleon: Broadsides of 1803* (Berkeley, 1944).

KNOTT, J., *Popular Opposition to the 1834 Poor Law* (London, 1986).

LANGFORD, P., *Public Life and the Propertied Englishman 1689–1798* (Oxford, 1991).

LAQUEUR, W., *Guerilla: A Historical and Critical Study* (London, 1977).

LAURIE, G. B., *History of the Royal Irish Rifles* (London, 1914).

LENEMAN, L., 'A New Role for a Lost Cause: Lowland Romanticisation of the Jacobite Highlander', in L. Leneman (ed.), *Perspectives in Scottish Social History* (Aberdeen, 1988), 107–24.

LENMAN, B., *The Jacobite Clans of the Great Glen 1650–1784* (London, 1984).

LINKLATER, E. and A., *The Black Watch: The History of the Royal Highland Regiment* (London, 1977).

LOGUE, K., *Popular Disturbances in Scotland 1780–1815* (Edinburgh, 1979).

LONGMATE, N., *Island Fortress: The Defence of Great Britain 1603–1945* (London, 1991).

MCANALLY, H., *The Irish Militia 1793–1816* (Dublin, 1949).

MCCAHILL, M. W., *Order and Equipoise: The Peerage and the House of Lords 1783–1830* (London, 1978).

MCCORD, N., *British History 1815–1906* (Oxford, 1991).

MCDOWELL, R. B., *Ireland in the Age of Imperialism and Revolution 1760–1801* (Oxford, 1991).

MACKAY, J., *The Reay Fencibles* (Glasgow, 1890).

MACKESY, P., *Statesmen at War: The Strategy of Overthrow 1798–9* (London, 1974).

—— *The War For America 1775–83* (London, 1964).

—— *War Without Victory: The Downfall of Pitt 1799–1802* (Oxford, 1984).

—— 'What the British Army Learned', in R. Hoffman and P. J. Albert (eds.), *Arms and Independence: The Military Character of the American Revolution* (Charlottesville, Va., 1984), 191–215.

MACKINTOSH, H. B., *The Grant, Strathspey or 1st Highland Fencible Regiment 1793–9* (Elgin, 1934).

—— *The Inverness-shire Highlanders or 97th Regiment of Foot 1794–6* (Elgin, 1926).

MACLEAN, L., *The Raising of the 79th Highlanders* (Inverness, 1980).

McLYNN, F., *Invasion: From the Armada to Hitler 1588–1945* (London, 1987).

MARKHAM, C. A., *History of the Northamptonshire and Rutland Militia* (London, 1924).

MATHER, F. C., *Public Order in the Age of the Chartists* (Manchester, 1959).

MEIKLE, H. W., *Scotland and the French Revolution* (repr. London, 1969).

MILNE, S. N., *The Standards and Colours of the Army from the Restoration* (Leeds, 1893).

MITCHELL, B. R., *Abstract of British Historical Statistics* (Cambridge, 1962).

MITCHISON, R., 'Patriotism and National Identity in Eighteenth Century Scotland', in T. W. Moody (ed.), *Nationality and the Pursuit of National Independence* (Belfast, 1978), 73–95.

—— 'Scotland 1750–1850', in F. M. L. Thompson (ed.), *The Cambridge Social History of Britain 1750–1950* (3 vols., Cambridge, 1990), i. 155–208.

MOODY, T. W., MARTIN, F. X., and BYRNE, F. J. (eds.), *A New History of Ireland* (5 vols., pub. Oxford, 1976–).

MORRIS, R. J., *Class, Sect and Party: The Making of the British Middle Class, Leeds 1820–1850* (Manchester, 1990).

—— 'Clubs, Societies and Associations', in F. M. L. Thompson (ed.), *Cambridge Social History of Britain 1750–1850* (3 vols., Cambridge, 1990), iii. 395–443.

—— 'The Middle Class and British Towns and Cities of the Industrial Revolution, 1780–1870', in D. Fraser and A. Sutcliffe (eds.), *The Pursuit of Urban History* (London, 1983), 286–306.

MUENGER, E. A., *The British Military Dilemma in Ireland: Occupation Politics 1886–1914* (Lawrence, Kan., 1991).

NEWMAN, G., *The Rise of English Nationalism: A Cultural History 1740–1830* (London, 1987).

O'BRIEN, G., *Anglo-Irish Politics in the Age of Grattan and Pitt* (Dublin, 1987).

O'GRADA, C., *Ireland: A New Economic History 1780–1939* (Oxford, 1994).

OWEN, D., *English Philanthropy 1660–1960* (Cambridge, Mass., 1965).

PALMER, S. H., *Police and Protest in England and Ireland 1780–1850* (Cambridge, 1988).

PHILP, M. (ed.), *The French Revolution and British Popular Politics* (Cambridge, 1991).

PREBBLE, J., *The King's Jaunt: George IV in Scotland August 1822* (London, 1988).

—— *Mutiny: Highland Regiments in Revolt 1743–1804* (London, 1975).

PRESTON, T., *The Jubilee of George III* (London, 1887).

—— *Patriots in Arms: Addresses and Sermons . . . in Praise of the Volunteer Movement* (London, 1881).

PRY, K. B., *'Dread the Boist'rous Gale': Theatre in Wartime Britain 1793–1802* (Ann Arbor, n.d.).

RISK, J. C., *The History of the Order of the Bath* (London, 1972).

ROBERTSON, J., *The Scottish Enlightenment and the Militia Issue* (Edinburgh, 1985).

ROSEBERY, Lord, *Life of Pitt* (London, 1891).

Royal Inniskilling Fusiliers (London, 1934).

SACK, J. J., *From Jacobite to Conservative: Reaction and Orthodoxy in Britain c. 1760–1832* (Cambridge, 1983).

SAUNDERS, A., *Fortress Britain: Artillery Fortification in the British Isles and Ireland* (Liphook, Hants, 1989).

SCHROEDER, P. W., *The Transformation of European Politics 1763–1848* (Oxford, 1994).

SCULLY, D., *The Irish Catholic Petition of 1805: The Diary of Denys Scully*, ed. B. MacDermot (Dublin, 1992).

SEBAG-MONTEFIORE, C., *A History of the Volunteer Forces* (London, 1908).

SEED, J., 'Theologies of Power: Unitarianism and the Social Relations of Religious Discourse 1800–50', in R. J. Morris (ed.), *Class, Power and Social Structure in British Nineteenth-Century Towns* (Leicester, 1986), 108–56.

SENIOR, H., *Orangeism in Ireland and Britain 1795–1836* (London, 1966).

SHAW, W. A., *The Knights of England* (2 vols., London, 1906).

SMITH, E. A., *Whig Principles and Party Politics: Earl Fitzwilliam and the Whig Party 1748–1833* (Manchester, 1975).

SMOUT, T. C., 'Problems of Nationalism, Identity and Improvement in Later Eighteenth-Century Scotland', in T. M. Devine (ed.), *Improvement and Enlightenment* (Edinburgh, 1989), 1–21.

SPIERS, E. M., *The Army and Society 1815–1914* (London, 1980).

STANHOPE, Earl of, *Life of William Pitt* (4 vols., London, 1862).

STRACHAN, H., *Wellington's Legacy: The Reform of the British Army 1830–54* (Manchester, 1984).

SUNTER, R., *Patronage and Politics in Scotland 1707–1832* (Edinburgh, 1986).

Sussex Militia List, Pevensey Rape 1803: Northern Division (Eastbourne, 1988).

SYKES, J., *Local Records of Remarkable Events Which Have Occurred in Northumberland and Durham* (2 vols., repr. Stockton-on-Tees, 1973).

SYM, J., *Seaforth Highlanders* (Aldershot, 1962).

THORNE, R. G. (ed.), *The House of Commons 1790–1820* (5 vols., London, 1986).

THOYTS, E., *The Royal Berkshire Militia* (Reading, 1897).

TREVOR-ROPER, H., 'The Invention of Tradition: The Highland Tradition of Scotland', in E. Hobsbawm and T. Ranger (eds.), *The Invention of Tradition* (Cambridge, 1983), 15–41.

TWISS, H., *Life of Lord Eldon* (3 vols., London, 1844).

VAISEY, D. G., 'The Pledge of Patriotism: Staffordshire and the Voluntary Contribution 1798', in M. W. Greenslade (ed.), *Essays in Staffordshire History* (Stafford, 1970), 209–23.

VIDLER, L. A., *The Story of the Rye Volunteers* (Rye, 1954).

WELLS, R., *Insurrection: The British Experience 1795–1803* (Gloucester, 1986).

——'The Militia Mutinies of 1795', in J. Rule (ed.), *Outside the Law: Studies in Crime and Order 1650–1850* (Exeter, 1982), 35–64.

WESTERN, J. R., *The English Militia in the Eighteenth Century* (London, 1965).

WHATLEY, C., 'Royal Day, People's Day: The Monarch's Birthday in Scotland c. 1660–1860', in R. Mason and N. Macdougall (eds.), *People and Power in Scotland* (Edinburgh, 1992), 170–88.

WHEELER, H. F. B., and BROADLEY, A. M., *Napoleon and the Invasion of England* (2 vols., London, 1908).

WHETSTONE, A., *Scottish County Government in the 18th and 19th Centuries* (Edinburgh, 1981).

WILKINS, H. J., *History of the Loyal Westbury Volunteer Corps 1803–14* (Bristol, 1918).

WITHERS, C., 'The Historical Creation of the Scottish Highlands', in I. Donnachie and C. Whatley (eds.), *The Manufacture of Scottish History* (Edinburgh, 1992), 143–56.

WOMACK, P., *Improvement and Romance: Constructing the Myth of the Highlands* (Basingstoke, 1989).

YARRINGTON, A., *The Commemoration of the Hero 1800–64: Monuments to the British Victors of the Napoleonic Wars* (New York, 1988).

YOUNGSON, A. J., *After the Forty-Five: The Economic Impact on the Scottish Highlands* (Edinburgh, 1973).

—— *The Making of Classical Edinburgh 1750–1840* (Edinburgh, 1975).

ZIEGLER, P., *Addington* (London, 1965).

Periodical Literature

ALLEN, B., 'Rule Britannia? History Painting in 18th Century Britain', *Hist. Today*, 45/6 (June 1995), 12–18.

ANDERSON, O., 'The Growth of Christian Militarism in Mid-Victorian Britain', *Eng. Hist. Rev.* 86 (1971), 46–72.

ARCH, N. J., '"A Mark of Esteem for their Beloved Commander": Thomas Lloyd and the Leeds Volunteers', *J. Soc. for Army Hist. Res.* 59 (1981), 201–6.

ASKEW, R., 'Shropshire Patriotism in 1798', *Transactions of the Shropshire Archaeological and Natural History Society*, 1 (1878), 255–80.

BAMFORD, A. B., 'The Loyal Chelmsford Volunteers', *Essex Rev.* 36 (1927), 88–96.

BARTLETT, T., 'An End to Moral Economy: The Irish Militia Disturbances of 1793', *Past and Present*, 99 (1983), 41–64.

BECKETT, I. F. W., 'The Amateur Military Tradition', *War and Society*, 4 (1986), 1–16.

BURNS, R. E., 'Ireland and British Military Preparations for War in America in 1775', *Cithara*, 2 (1963), 42–61.

BUSBY, J. H., 'Local Military Forces in Hertfordshire 1793–1814', *J. Soc. for Army Hist. Res.* 31 (1953), 15–24.

CAMBRIDGE, Marquess of, 'The Volunteer Reviews in Hyde Park in 1799, 1800 and 1803', *J. Soc. for Army Hist. Res.* 40 (1962), 117–24.

CAMERON, N. E., 'The Loyal Chelmsford Volunteers 1803–9', *Essex Rev.* 58 (1949), 82–9.

CARDEW-RENDLE, H. C., 'Commissioned Officers of the Surrey Volunteers', *Notes & Queries*, 194 (1949), 543–4; 195 (1950), 59–60, 81–2, 99–103, 126, 146–8, 170, 210–14.

CHART, D. A., 'The Irish Levies During the Great French War', *Eng. Hist. Rev.* 32 (1917), 497–516.

CHENEVIX-TRENCH, R., 'Dorset Under Arms in 1803', *Proceedings of the Dorset Natural History and Archaeological Society*, 90 (1969), 303–12.

CLAEYS, G., 'The French Revolution Debate and British Political Thought', *History of Political Thought*, 11 (1990), 59–80.

CLARK, J. C. D., 'England's Ancien Regime as a Confessional State', *Albion*, 21 (1989), 450–74.

—— 'English History's Forgotten Context: Scotland, Ireland, Wales', *Hist. J.* 32 (1989), 211–28.

COLLEY, L., 'The Apotheosis of George III: Loyalty, Royalty and the British Nation 1760–1820', *Past and Present*, 102 (1984), 94–129.

COLLEY, L., 'Britishness and Otherness: An Argument', *J. Brit. Studies*, 31 (1992), 309–29.
——'Whose Nation? Class and National Consciousness in Britain 1750–1830', *Past and Present*, 113 (1986), 97–117.
COOKSON, J. E., 'British Society and the French Wars 1793–1815', *Australian Journal of Politics and History*, 31 (1985), 192–203.
——'The English Volunteer Movement of the French Wars 1793–1815: Some Contexts', *Hist. J.* 32 (1989), 867–91.
——'Patriotism and Social Structure: The Ely Volunteers, 1798–1808', *J. Soc. for Army Hist. Res.* 71 (1993), 160–79.
——'Political Arithmetic and War in Britain 1793–1815', *War and Society*, 1 (1983), 37–60.
——'The Rise and Fall of the Sutton Volunteers, 1803–4', *Hist. Research*, 64 (1991), 46–53.
CORFIELD, P. J., 'Class by Name and Number in Eighteenth-Century Britain', *History*, 72 (1987), 38–61.
CRAMNER-BYNG, J., 'Essex Prepares For Invasion', *Essex Rev.* 60 (1951), 127–34, 184–93; 61 (1952), 43–7, 57–74.
CUNNINGHAM, H., 'The Language of Patriotism 1750–1914', *Hist. Workshop J.* 12 (1981), 8–33.
DINWIDDY, J. R., '"The Patriotic Linen-Draper": Robert Waithman and the Revival of Radicalism in the City of London 1795–1818', *Bull. Inst. Hist. Res.* 46 (1973), 72–94.
DONOVAN, R. K., 'The Military Origins of the Roman Catholic Relief Programme of 1778', *Hist. J.* 28 (1985), 79–102.
DUFFY, M., '"The Noisie, Empty, Fluttring French": English Images of the French 1689–1815', *Hist. Today*, 32/9 (Sept. 1982), 21–6.
ELLIOTT, M., 'The "Despard Conspiracy" Reconsidered', *Past and Present*, 75 (1977), 46–61.
EMSLEY, C., 'The Military and Popular Disorder in England 1790–1801', *J. Soc. for Army Hist. Res.* 61 (1983), 10–21, 96–112.
——'Political Disaffection and the British Army in 1792', *Bull. Inst. Hist. Res.* 48 (1975), 230–45.
'Extracts from the *Leeds Intelligencer* 1791–6', *Thoresby Society Publications*, 44 (1956), 1–90.
FANE, W. K., 'The Orderly Book of Captain Daniel Hebb's Company in the Loveden Volunteers (Lincolnshire) 1803–8', *J. Soc. for Army Hist. Res.* 4 (1925), 149–61.
FERGUSON, K. P., 'The Volunteer Movement and the Government 1778–93', *Irish Sword*, 13 (1979), 208–16.
GINTER, D., 'The Loyalist Association Movement of 1792–3 and British Public Opinion', *Hist. J.* 9 (1966), 179–90.
GLOVER, R., 'The French Fleet: Britain's Problem, and Madison's Opportunity', *J. Mod. Hist.* 39 (1967), 233–52.
GOULD, E. H., 'To Strengthen the King's Hands: Dynastic Legitimacy, Militia Reform and Ideas of National Unity in England 1745–1760', *Hist. J.* 34 (1991), 329–48.
GRAY, D. S., '"A Gross Violation of the Publick Peace": The Tullamore Incident 1806', *Irish Sword*, 12 (1976), 298–301.
HALL, C. D., 'Addington at War: Unspectacular but not Unsuccessful', *Bull. Inst. Hist. Res.* 61 (1988), 306–16.
HARGRAVE, E., 'The Early Leeds Volunteers', *Thoresby Society Publications*, 28 (1923–7), 255–319.
HARLING, P., and MANDLER, P., 'From "Fiscal-Military" State to Laissez-Faire State, 1760–1850', *J. Brit. Studies*, 32 (1993), 44–70.

HAYES, J., 'Scottish Officers in the British Army 1714–63', *Scot. Hist. Rev.* 37 (1958), 23–33.

HAYTHORNTHWAITE, P., 'The Volunteer Force 1803–4', *J. Soc. for Army Hist. Res.* 64 (1986), 193–204.

HEBDITCH, M., 'Late Eighteenth and Early Nineteenth Century Papers Relating to Organisation of the Country Against a Possible Invasion', *Yorkshire Archaeological Journal*, 36 (1944–7), 109–11.

HILL, J. R., 'National Festivals, the State and "Protestant Ascendancy" in Ireland 1790–1829', *Irish Hist. Studies*, 24 (1984–5), 30–51.

HILTON, B., 'The Political Arts of Lord Liverpool', *Trans. Royal Hist. Soc.* 5th ser. 38 (1988), 147–70.

HODGE, W. B., 'On the Mortality Arising from Military Operations', *Journal of the Royal Statistical Society*, 19 (1856), 216–72.

HORN, P., 'The Mutiny of the Oxfordshire Militia in 1795', *Cake and Cockhorse*, 7 (1979), 232–41.

HUDSON, A., 'Volunteer Soldiers in Sussex During the Revolutionary and Napoleonic Wars 1793–1815', *Sussex Archaeological Collections*, 122 (1984), 165–81.

KARSTEN, P., 'Irish Soldiers in the British Army 1792–1922: Suborned or Subordinate?', *J. of Soc. Hist.* 17 (1983–4), 31–64.

KOPPERMAN, P. E., 'Religion and Religious Policy in the British Army c. 1700–1796', *Journal of Religious History* [Australia], 14 (1987), 390–405.

LEE, J. W., 'Devon on Guard 1759–1815', *Transactions of the Devonshire Association*, 40 (1908), 226–37.

MCCAHILL, M. W., 'Peerage Creations and the Changing Character of the British Nobility 1750–1830', *Eng. Hist. Rev.* 96 (1981), 259–84.

MCDOWELL, R. B., 'The Fitzwilliam Episode', *Irish Hist. Studies*, 15 (1966), 115–30.

MCGUFFIE, T. H., 'The Short Life and Sudden Death of an English Regiment of Foot: An Account of the Raising, Recruiting, Mutiny and Disbandment of the 113th Regiment . . . April 1794 to September 1795', *J. Soc. for Army Hist. Res.* 33 (1955), 16–25, 48–56.

—— 'The Significance of Military Rank in the British Army Between 1790 and 1820', *Bull. Inst. Hist. Res.* 30 (1957), 207–24.

MORRIS, R. J., 'Voluntary Societies and British Urban Elites 1780–1850: An Analysis', *Hist. J.* 26 (1983), 95–118.

MORTON, R. G., 'The Rise of the Yeomanry', *Irish Sword*, 8 (1967), 58–64.

PENDLETON, G. T., 'Towards a Bibliography of the *Reflections* and *Rights of Man* Controversy', *Bulletin of Research in the Humanities*, 85 (1982), 65–103.

PHILP, M., 'Vulgar Conservatism 1792–3', *Eng. Hist. Rev.* 110 (1995), 42–69.

RAZZELL, P. E., 'Social Origins of Officers in the Indian and British Home Army 1758–1962', *Brit. J. Sociology*, 14 (1963), 248–60.

ROWBOTHAM, W. B., 'The Flag Officer's and Captain's Gold Medal 1794–1815', *Mariner's Mirror*, 37 (1951), 260–81.

TEICHMAN, O., 'The Yeomanry as an Aid to Civil Power 1795–1867', *J. Soc. for Army Hist. Res.* 19 (1940), 75–91, 127–43.

THOMAS, C., 'Cornish Volunteers in the Early Nineteenth Century', *Devon and Cornwall Notes and Queries*, 28 (1959–61), 46–9, 77–82, 166–74.

—— 'Cornish Volunteers in the Eighteenth Century', *Devon and Cornwall Notes and Queries*, 27 (1956–8), 229–36, 326–31; 28 (1959–61), 10–16.

WESTERN, J. R., 'The Formation of the Scottish Militia in 1797', *Scot. Hist. Rev.* 34 (1955), 1–18.

WESTERN, J. R., 'Roman Catholics Holding Military Commissions in 1798', *Eng. Hist. Rev.* 70 (1955), 428–32.

——'The Volunteer Movement as an Anti-Revolutionary Force', *Eng. Hist. Rev.* 71 (1956), 603–14.

WHITE, A. S., and MARTIN, E. J., 'A Bibliography of Volunteering', *J. Soc. for Army Hist. Res.* 23 (1945), 2–29; 24 (1946), 88–91.

WHITING, J. R. S., 'The Frampton Volunteers', *J. Soc. for Army Hist. Res.* 48 (1970), 14–28.

WYATT, R. J., 'Suffolk Volunteers at Worlingworth 1798–1802', *J. Soc. for Army Hist. Res.* 61 (1983), 92–5.

Unpublished Dissertations

CARPENTER, S. D. M., 'Patterns of Recruitment of the Highland Regiments of the British Army 1756–1815', M.Litt. (St Andrews, 1977).

COTTRELL, S. M. N. G., 'English Views of France and the French 1789–1815', D.Phil. (Oxford, 1990).

FERGUSON, K. P., 'The Army in Ireland From the Restoration to the Act of Union', Ph.D. (Trinity Coll., Dublin, 1981).

HAIRE, D. N., 'The British Army in Ireland 1868–1890', M.Litt. (Trinity Coll., Dublin, 1973).

SMITH, S. C., 'Loyalty and Opposition in the Napoleonic Wars: The Impact of the Local Militia 1807–15', D.Phil. (Oxford, 1984).

WESTERN, J. R., 'The Recruitment of the Land Forces in Great Britain 1793–9', Ph.D. (Edinburgh, 1953).

WILKIE, R., 'The Set Scene: English Theatre and Public Opinion 1789–1799', BA Hons. (Canterbury, 1986).

Index

Abbot, Charles 200
Abercromby, Sir Ralph 46, 54 n., 55, 56, 150, 154, 161, 178
Aberdeen 140, 142
Aberdeenshire 136, 139, 141
Addington, Henry 36, 66–7, 75, 77, 82, 115, 166–7, 185–6, 194, 196, 198, 200–1, 206
  levée en masse (1803) 70, 80–1
Additional Force (1804–6) 7, 115–16, 121, 171, 178
American War 10, 19–20, 30–1, 106, 121, 131, 145, 153
Amherst, Lord 33, 147
ancien régime 2, 3, 7, 13, 94, 98, 209, 245
Angerstein, J. J. 218
Anstruther, Col. Robert 33
Anti-Jacobin Review 214
Antwerp 39
Argyll 141, 143
Argyll, Duke of 35, 134, 135
Arklow 171
armed nation 1–2, 12–13, 19–23, 28, 37, 59–65, 80, 93–4, 96, 125, 168, 182, 185, 188, 208, 248–50, 259, 262–3
armed peasantry 85, 193
armed population, fear of 182–3, 185–6, 195–6
army 55, 90
  medals 222
  national composition of 126–8, 146–7, 154
  officers 132, 142, 225–32, 256–7
  popular attitudes to 21–3, 28, 100, 111, 119–20, 234, 254–5
  recruitment 21, 28, 32, 81, 96, 100, 109–19, 121–2, 129–32, 135–7, 148, 154, 170, 260
  soldiers 110–11, 120, 124–5, 184, 190–1
  strength 5, 32, 41, 91, 95, 112, 224, 246–7
  see also artillery; infantry; regiments
Army of Reserve (1803–4) 82–3, 86, 98, 101, 103, 108, 114–16, 122, 124–5, 148, 171, 176, 178
artillery 194–5
Athlone 172, 199
Atholl, Duke of 135, 144

Austria 16, 32, 95, 96, 247
Ayr 139

Baillie, John, col. of fencibles 136
Banffshire 140
Bantry Bay 41, 52–3, 58, 68, 161
barracks 58, 124, 155–6, 184, 189, 204, 258
Bartlett, James, Banffshire volunteers 142
Bath 189
Bath, Order of the 222–3
Belfast 132, 196
Belgium 39, 247–8
Bell, Benjamin 96
Berkshire 7
Birmingham 25, 137, 238–40
Boer War 258
Brackenbury, William, Ely volunteers 263
Bradford 195
Breadalbane, Earl of 131–2, 134–5
Brest 52
Bristol 132
Britain:
  mobilization figures 95
  population 99–100
  special conditions for defence 91, 96
Brodie, Alexander 135–6
Bruce, Robert, King of Scotland 151, 256
Buccleuch, Duke of 139–40, 233
Buckingham, Marquis of 75
Burke, Edmund 19
Bury St Edmunds 241

Caithness 140, 143
Cambridge, peace festival (1814) 242
Cambridge, Duke of 254
Cambridgeshire 50, 234
Camden, Earl 160, 162
Cameron, Alan (79th regt.) 135, 147
Camperdown 215
Canada 155
Canning, George 202, 221
Canterbury 204
Caribbean 60, 69, 114
Carlyle, Alexander 19
Cartwright, Major John 217, 231, 251
Castlebar 61

Castlereagh, Lord 14, 33, 39, 52, 67, 82, 117,
  122, 166–7, 188, 197, 200–2, 221, 246
  home defence organization 85–9, 93
  opposition to armed peasantry 85, 87
  and Windham's plan 84
Catholics 11–12, 231, 257
  British military recruitment 153, 158, 175
  emancipation 62, 156, 161, 164–7, 181,
    201–3, 219, 250–1
  Irish militia 163–70, 172–5, 195–7, 198–200
Catholic Relief Acts (1792–3) 153–4, 156
cavalry, provisional 7, 28, 68, 70
census (1801) 96–100
Channel Islands 61, 200
Chatham 45, 204
Chelmsford 45, 74, 204, 216
Chichester 204, 228
Cobbett, William 188
Cockburn, Henry 150–1
Colchester 204
Colquhoun, Patrick 99, 224
conscription 70, 82, 88–9, 91, 93–4, 100,
  108–9, 260–1
Connaught 114, 176
Cookstown 173
Copenhagen 38, 53
Cork 53, 56–8, 60, 61, 63, 158, 173, 198, 199
Cornwall 79
Cornwallis, Lord 33–4, 53 n., 55, 62, 69, 81,
  85, 166, 197, 199–200
  as lord-lieutenant (1798–1801) 45, 57
  attitudes to Prussian army 31
  in America (1780–1) 19
  national mobilization 29–30
Corsica 147
counties:
  defence 27, 48, 93, 138
  lieutenancies 6, 49–50, 94, 133, 228
  regiments 121–2, 138–9, 171–2
  subscriptions 49, 50 n., 139, 216–17
  volunteering 26–7, 66–70, 72–3, 91–2
Craig, Gen. Sir James 120
Crichton, Patrick (Edinburgh) 229–30
Crimean War 119, 255, 259
Cromarty 143

Dartmouth, Earl of 238
Defence of the Realm Acts (1798 and 1803)
  48–9, 71, 99, 212, 216
Defenders (Ireland) 157, 161–2, 176
Denmark 133
  Danish fleet 53
Despard conspiracy (1802) 184

Devon 21, 79, 189
Dillon, Col. Henry Augustus 114
Dirom, Col. Alexander 144
Donaghadee 60
Dorset 7
Dover 204
Dublin 52, 53, 56–7, 62, 171, 180, 196
Dundas, Gen. Sir David 28, 29–31, 32–3, 42,
  44, 46, 47, 53, 57, 77, 94
Dundas, Henry (Lord Melville) 2, 11, 12, 29,
  47, 49, 62–4, 69, 71–3, 75, 77, 79, 81, 93,
  105–6, 137–8, 147–8, 156, 186, 193, 200,
  206–7, 262
  and armed nation 33–7, 64, 71
  conscription 68, 70
  Irish policy 156–62, 164–6, 180
  military patronage 133–5
  national defence 45, 66–8, 81–2, 85, 212, 214

East India Company 18, 135, 137, 245, 257
East Lothian 139
Edinburgh 39, 102, 107, 130, 144, 149, 150,
  195, 229, 233
  National Monument 150
Eglintoun, Earl of 134–5
Egypt 34, 46, 63–5, 149, 178, 197
Eldon, Lord 78, 166
Ely 233
  volunteers 192, 235–6, 263
Emmet's rising (1803) 169–70, 202
England, volunteering in 79, 140, 144
Enlightenment, Scottish 19
Essex 39, 40, 44, 45, 48, 60, 141

Fawcett, Sir William 31
fencibles 17, 28, 59, 64, 68, 106, 127, 129,
  131–7, 144–5, 159, 190
Ferguson, Adam 19
Fife, Earl of 159
Fingall, Lord 202
First Coalition 96
Fitzwilliam, Earl 157, 160–2, 198
Flanders, military defeat (1794) 149
Flushing 39
Forfarshire 136
Fort William 142
Fox, Charles James 202
France 30, 38, 47, 64, 95–7, 99, 236
  expenditure on armed forces 247
  levée en masse of 1793 20
  Franco-Russian *rapprochement* (1807) 38
  Franco-Spanish alliances 53
  resistance to conscription 100–1, 106, 111–12

Francophobia 1, 9, 23–4, 91, 193, 207, 210, 243
Fraser, Gen. Simon 137
French revolution 2, 16, 37, 95, 109, 182, 209, 213
Fyvie (Aberdeen) 233

Galway 53, 54, 58, 114, 171, 173
George III 22, 25, 81–2, 84, 159, 202, 211, 218–20, 240, 254
George IV 202, 254
Germany 20, 34, 236
Gibraltar 137, 155
Glasgow 108, 140, 241
    weavers' protest (1812) 185, 187
Gloucester 27
Gloucester, Duke of 254
Gordon, Duke of 35, 49, 131, 134–5, 139
Gordon, Lord Adam 38, 145
Grant, Sir James 131, 132, 134–5, 143, 148
Grattan, Henry 175–6
Grenville, Lord 36, 165–6, 215
Grey, Sir Charles (later Earl) 31
Graham, Col. Thomas 56, 137
Guadeloupe 246

Haldane, Lord 260
Hanover 158
Hanson, Joseph 238
Hardwicke, Earl of 166–7, 169, 198, 200, 202
Hatfield 75, 219
Havelock, Sir Henry 255
Highlands 35, 113, 128, 143
    clan chiefs 131, 138, 166
    emigration 128, 131, 149
    recruiting area 11, 137
    regiments 129–31, 135, 146, 149
    Scottish identity 12, 129
Hobart, Lord 75–9, 186–7, 193, 196
Holland 20, 40, 64, 142, 149, 247–8
    Dutch fleet 32, 39
    Dutch revolt (1813) 38, 39
Hope, Col. Alexander 53, 55–6, 62, 74
Hope, Sir John 164, 204
Hopetoun, Earl of 134
Howe, Gen. Sir William 31
Humbert, Gen. 164
Hutchinson, Gen. 61, 164

India 63, 72, 106, 111, 133, 135, 147, 244
    Indian Mutiny 255
infantry, light 31, 116, 194
Insurrection Act, Irish (1796) 195

invasion:
    defence plans 27, 29–30, 40, 42–6, 47–8, 69, 72–4, 214, 261
    defence organization 41–2, 48–9, 51–2, 59, 91
    fortifications 45–6, 57–8
    Ireland 33, 40–1, 45, 52–3, 68, 161–2, 168, 200, 258
    Scotland 40, 141, 144
    threats 23, 72–3, 186, 210–11, 233, 236, 248
    volunteers 49
    see also Bantry Bay; Castlebar; Killala Bay; Martello towers
Inverness 132, 142, 143
Ionian Islands 246
Ireland 10–13, 100–1, 115, 118, 126, 155, 176
    British army in 153, 257–8
    constabulary (1822) 164, 206–7
    Dublin Castle 156–7, 160, 162, 168
    military tradition 12, 170–1, 179–80
    national identity 11, 14, 170–80
    rebellion (1798) 45, 61, 63, 154–5, 161–4, 199, 219
    recruiting 113–14
    regionalism in 171
    see also militia, Ireland; yeomanry, Ireland
Irish brigade 114, 159–60
Irwin, Col. John 174

Jacobins 26, 196, 207
Java 246

Kenmare, Lord 158
Kent 40, 41, 42, 44–5, 60, 63
Kerry 158
Kilbeggan 54
Killala Bay 61, 199
Killarney 173
King, Gregory 99

Lanarkshire 139
Lancashire 27
    weavers' strike (1808) 191
League of Armed Neutrality (1801) 38
Lee, Charles, American gen. 20
Leeds 27, 235, 238, 241, 243, 263
Legion of Honour 222
Leicester 137
    fencibles 199
    militia 102
Leinster 176
Leith, James 136

Louth 204
Lincolnshire 139, 141
Liverpool 60, 62, 217, 239
Liverpool, Lord (also Lord Hawkesbury) 53, 85, 95, 156, 166–7, 202, 206, 247
Lloyd, Thomas (Leeds) 263
Loch Ryan 61
London 30, 36, 40, 42, 44, 72, 132, 137, 150, 184, 218–21, 241
   Burdett disorders (1810) 191
Longford 172
L'Orient 52
Lough Foyle 58
Lough Swilly 58
Low Countries 114, 190
loyalism 15, 24–7, 37, 169, 210–14, 219–20, 228, 241, 252–3
Luddites 182, 191, 194, 204

Macdonald, Lord 131
Mackenzie, F. H. of Seaforth 131–3, 135
Maida, battle of (1806) 222
Manchester 137, 238, 244
Manners, Lord 197
Marengo 73
Martello towers 45–6, 53, 56, 58
Martinique 246
Maule, William 136
Mauritius 246
Mayo 114, 177
Mediterranean 60, 64, 72, 247
militia 3, 7, 21, 67, 260
   army recruitment from 113, 116–18, 155
   ballot 30, 33, 36–7, 76, 84–8, 93, 101–9, 115–16, 234, 246, 250
   colonels 7, 67, 87, 89–90, 117–19, 203
   county quotas 98–9
   disturbances 100, 106–7, 145, 171–3, 188–9, 207
   interchange 60, 62, 64, 90, 155–6, 165–6, 168, 196, 198–204
   popular attitudes to 89, 103–4
Militia Act 91, 98
militia, Irish 62, 85, 101, 104–5, 155, 159–61, 163–9, 171–5, 177, 180, 196–8, 201, 204
   Carlow 204
   Donegal 173
   Kings 200
   Limerick 172
   Longford 173
   Louth 204
   Mayo 171–2
   Roscommon 174

   Sligo 174
   Tyrone 173
   Waterford 174
   Wexford 177, 200
   Wicklow 177
militia, local 6, 7, 52, 64, 67, 86–90, 93–4, 110, 187–8, 191, 204, 226
militia, Scottish 13, 28, 35, 70, 98, 101–2, 105–8, 127–8
militia, supplementary 28–9, 33, 68, 70, 85, 93, 98, 127, 185
Moir, Alexander (Aberdeen) 140
Moira, Lord 178
monarchy 219–20
Montrose, Duke of 29
Moore, Sir John 121, 150, 241
Mulgrave, Lord 44
mutinies, of 1794–5 189
   of 1797 183
   of 1809–10 191

Napoleon 39, 40, 41, 42, 53, 56, 59, 63, 71, 73, 96, 210, 213, 218
Napoleon III 248
Naval and Military Order of Merit (1804) 222
navy 32, 38, 45, 47, 52–3
   medals 221–2
   'naval pillar' proposed 216–17
   naval thanksgiving (1797) 72, 215
Nelson, Lord 217, 218, 224, 239
Newhaven, occupation of (1795) 189
North, Lord 11, 156, 166
Nottingham 137

O'Connell, Daniel 251
Ostend 72

Patriotic Fund 212, 217–18, 220–1
patriotism 4, 9–10, 24–6, 228, 230–1
   lower orders 9, 187–8, 213, 233–44
   national defence 7–8, 15, 37, 187, 207–8, 211–12, 214–16, 236–45, 252–3
   see also loyalism
Peel, Robert 164
peerage 223
Pelham, Lord 75, 78, 80, 85, 186, 196
Peninsular War 84, 120, 178, 184, 232
Perceval, Spencer 156
Perthshire 35, 130, 139, 141, 143
Peterloo massacre (1819) 207, 244
Pevensey (Sussex) 141
philanthropy 240–3, 254–5, 263

Pitt, William 2, 6, 14, 28, 44, 71–2, 75, 77, 135, 211
  Additional Force scheme (1804) 115–16, 121
  Irish policy 12, 62–3, 156–62, 164–6, 180, 196, 200
  mass arming 36–7, 67–8, 79–81, 185–8, 193, 207
  voluntary contribution (1798) 214–17, 220
Plymouth 204
Portland, Duke of 36, 63, 166, 196
Portpatrick 60
Portsmouth 60, 61, 204
Portugal 34, 158
Protestants, Irish 12, 62, 154, 157, 162–4, 169–71, 175
  Ascendancy 11, 154, 164–5, 167, 170, 173, 179–81, 197–8, 257
  see also militia, Irish; yeomanry, Irish
Prussia 16, 17, 20, 30–1, 78, 95, 204

Quota Acts (1795–6) 28, 33, 114

Radnor, Lord 6
Redesdale, Lord 202, 258
Reeves, John 212, 228
Reform Act (1832) 250, 251, 253
regiments:
  18th (Royal Irish) 171, 177, 178
  21st (Royal North British Fusiliers) 148
  23rd 177
  26th 148
  27th (Inniskillings) 171, 177, 178
  42nd (Black Watch) 130, 146, 148–9
  54th 177
  64th 177
  68th 177
  71st 130, 148
  72nd 130, 148
  74th 130, 147
  75th 130, 147
  78th 113, 135, 146
  79th (Cameron Highlanders) 113, 130, 135, 146, 147–8, 149
  83rd 165, 171, 197
  85th 177
  87th (Prince of Wales Irish) 165, 171, 177, 178–9
  88th (Connaught Rangers) 165, 171, 177, 178, 197
  89th 165, 197
  90th 130, 137
  91st 130
  92nd 146, 147, 148, 149–50, 190

93rd 146
94th 130
97th 148
105th 190
113th 190
Clan Alpine 129
King's German Legion 188
Loyal Macleods 137
Prince of Wales' Own 137
Regiment of the Isles 129
Renfrewshire 48, 141, 243
Ribbonmen 176
Richmond, Duke of 172, 200, 202, 228
Rickman, John 96–8
Robertson of Lude 132
Roscoe, William 239
Ross 133, 143
Russia 41, 95–6, 202, 259
Rutland 7
Ryder, Richard 156, 202

St Patrick's Day 178–9
Scheldt 38
Scotland 6, 10–12, 32–3, 35, 44, 79, 180–1
  Lowlands 129, 138, 141, 143
  military recruitment 128–9
  militia disturbances (1797) 100, 106–7
  national identity 14, 142, 146, 149–52, 179–80, 256
  population 97
  soldiers in British army 126–7
  strategic union 60–1
  see also Highlands; militia, Scotland; volunteers, Scottish
Scott, Sir Walter 151
Second Coalition 73, 96, 219
Selkirk 139
Senegal 246
Seven Years War (1756–63) 35, 144, 153, 156, 166
Shannon River 54, 56
Shrewsbury 137
Sicily 246
Simcoe, Gen. 31
Sinclair, Sir John 97
slave trade, abolition of 244
Smith, Adam 34
Somerset 27, 139
Spain 16, 32, 34, 52, 56, 120, 184, 209, 236
Staffordshire 216
Stewart, Col. David 146
Sussex 21, 40, 41, 42, 228
Sussex, Duke of 254

Sutherland 143, 144
Sutherland, Countess of 35, 131, 134
Sweden 34
Switzerland 20

Telford, Thomas 61
Tipperary 56, 113
Tone, Wolfe 11
towns 5, 10, 238–45, 253
Trafalgar 39, 41, 222
Training Act (1806) 52, 78, 81, 83–4
training, general military 29, 34, 66, 96, 188,
    193, 204, 207
Trimleston, Lord 158
Tuam 173
Tullamore incident (1806) 171 n.
Twiss, Col. William 57

Ulster 56, 167–8, 171, 176, 177
United Irishmen 11, 154, 157, 161–2, 183, 194

Volunteer Act (1802) 187
volunteer corps, Aberdeen 140
    Banff 142
    Birmingham 25, 238
    Bradford 195
    Chichester 228
    Edinburgh 140, 195, 233
    Ely 192, 233, 235–6, 263
    Fyvie (Aberdeen) 233
    Halifax 195
    Hitchin 74–5, 232
    Iver (Bucks) 234
    Leeds 27, 235, 238–9
    Leith 140
    Lewes 228
    Liverpool 239
    Manchester 238
    Moidart (Inverness) 143
    Monquitter (Aberdeen) 234
    Mortlake (Surrey) 187, 233
    Royston 25
    Stirling 186
    Whitby 233
volunteers 6, 8–9, 24–8, 37, 42, 59, 191–4,
    225–38, 249, 252, 255
    disbandment 75–7, 89, 92–3, 192
    expansion 68, 72–3
    inefficiency of 67, 77, 192, 204
    Irish (of American War) 18, 75, 162, 168,
        170, 180, 195–6

localism 7, 71, 91–2, 110, 144, 163
militia exemption of 74, 77
officers 73, 82–3, 87, 91
Scottish 14, 28, 67, 69, 79, 128, 138, 140–4,
    211, 233–4
strength 73, 79, 80
terms of enlistment 83
urban 10, 74, 109–10, 240
    see also yeomanry
Vienna, Treaty of 248

Wakefield, Edward 171, 176, 181, 198
Walcheren expedition (1809) 39
Wales 26, 44, 79, 177
Wallace, William 151, 256
Washington, George 19
Waterford 58, 61, 63, 173
Waterloo, battle of 146, 150, 235
    Fund 217
    Medal 222
Webster, Alexander 99
Wellington, Duke of (Sir Arthur Wellesley)
    52, 53–5, 119, 150, 167, 180, 200, 223,
    257
West Indies 106, 111, 147, 160, 190
Westmorland, Earl of 70–1, 75, 166, 180, 186,
    196
Wexford 58, 63, 173, 177
Wicklow 171
Wilberforce, William 79
William IV 254
Windham, William 2, 14, 33, 52, 67, 78, 81–4,
    85, 93, 122–4, 188, 196
Windsor Castle 219
World War I 260
Wyvill, Rev. Christopher 231

yeomanry 26, 27–8, 34, 68, 70, 73, 191, 205–7,
    250
yeomanry, Irish 55, 156, 160–4, 167–70, 180,
    197, 206
York, Duke of 31, 32, 38, 42, 44–6, 81, 87, 94,
    106, 113, 115, 136, 154, 159, 193–4, 202,
    223, 259
    military plan (1807) 83–4, 147–8
    short service enlistment 122–4
Yorke, Charles 75, 78, 80, 186, 192, 202
Yorkshire 27, 182

Zuider Zee 38

2-1-00

ROCK VALLEY COLLEGE

DEMCO